A Millennium of Fame of East Lothian

200 Lives of Achievement

David Dick

Foreword by

Sir Hew Hamilton-Dalrymple Bt, KCVO

Lord Lieutenant of East Lothian

Published by:
Clerkington Publishing Co., Ltd.,
West Lodge Clerkington,
Haddington,
East Lothian EH41 4NJ

Tel. 01620 825341

ISBN 0 9530274 3 0

Printed by: Kelso Graphics, The Knowes, Kelso TD5 7BH

The photographs are by the author except where otherwise acknowledged.

Front Cover photographs:
Top row:
John Knox, Samuel Smiles*, John Rennie*, Francis Balfour, Jane Welsh Carlyle*
Bottom row:
Andrew Fletcher* (the 'Patriot'), Archibald Skirving*, Alexander Muirhead**, William Wood+, Eleanora Jenkinson
Rear Cover :
Leuchie, Hailes Castle, Bankton House, Tantallan Castle, Cadell House, Dirleton Castle

* Courtesy Scottish National Portrait Gallery
** Courtesy Oxford University Museum of Natural History
\+ Courtesy of Mrs D Nicholson

For my wife, Muriel,
with love and gratitude;
her encouragement, unceasing interest and humour
were my inspiration

CONTENTS

CONTENTS BY TOWN AND VILLAGE

Dick, Derek, Fish (1958-)
Ferguson, Sir Robert of Raith (1767-1840)
Gillies, Sir William George (1898-1973)
Goodchild MBE, Doris (1906-)
Grant, Sir Alastair (1937-)
Grant JP, William Laird (1928-)
Hamilton, 14th &15th Dukes of
Harley, Professor George (1829-1896)
Knox, John (c1505-1572)
McLaren, Lennox-Milne OBE (1909-1980)
McLean, William Farquharson Dr (1888-1951)
MacVie, Prof. John Gordon (1945 -)
Maitlands of Lethington; 1st-17th Earls of Lauderdale
Porteous, Alexander (1896-1981) and Norman (1898-)
Rae, William (1833-1911)
Robarts, Henry (1879-1951), Frederick (1913-88), James (1916-)
Smiles, Samuel (1812-1904)
Spowage MBE, JP, Alexander Fraser (1924 -)
Vert, John (1852-1934)
Vetch, James (1789-1869)
Wemyss, Andrew (Jock) (1893- 1974)
Wemyss, Lady Catherine (Kitty) Charteris (c.1725-86)
William I (the Lion) (1143-1214)

Hailes Castle - Bothwell, Earls of
Harperdean - Jenkinson, Mrs Eleonora
Humbie - Nicol, William (c.1771-1851)
Musselburgh - Dalrymple, Sir David of Hailes (1726-92)
Moir, David Macbeth (1798- 1851)
Newbyth - Baird, Sir David (1757-1829)
North Berwick - Anderson, William (c.1750-1778)
Dalrymple: 1st -10th Baronets of North Berwick
Douglas, Gavin of Tantallon (1474-1522)
Douglas, George, 4th Earl of Angus of Tantallon (1412-1462)
Sayers, 'Old'Ben (1857-1924), 'Young' Ben (1884-1961)
Syme, Ebeneezer (1826-59), David (1827-1908)
Oldhamstocks/ Cockburnspath -
Broadwood, John (1732-1812)
Imrie CBE, Dr John (1923-1996)
Somerville, Alexander (1811-1855)

Ormiston -	Cockburn, Adam (1656-1735) and John (1679-1758)
	Moffat, Robert (1795-1883)
Phantassie -	Rennie, George (1749-1828), John (1761-1821), George (1791-1866), Sir John (1794-1874)
Port Seton -	Bellany, John CBE (1942-)
	Seton, Lords, Earls of
Prestonpans -	Abercrombie, John (1726-1806)
	Alexander, Thomas CB (1812-60)
	Fergusson, Sir William (1808-77)
	Gardiner, Col. James (1687-1745)
Sandersdean -	Laurie, Sir Peter (1778-1861)
Saltoun -	Fletcher, Andrew '(The Patriot') (1655-1716)
	Fletcher, Andrew, Lord Milton (1692-1766)
	Meikle, James, Andrew and George
	Muirhead, Alexander (1848-1920)
	Thomson, Sir John Arthur (1861-1933)
Spott -	Waterson, William (1729-1780)
Stenton -	Hamilton John, 2nd Lord Belhaven (1656-1708)
Tranent -	Brown, Peter Hume (1849-1918)
Traprain Law -	Loth, King (c.517-?)
Tyninghame -	Haddington, Earls of (1st to 12th)
Wallyford -	Oliphant, Mrs Margaret nee Wilson (1828-97)
Whittinghame -	Balfour, Arthur James, 1st Earl (1848-1930)
	Balfour, Francis Maitland (1851-1882)
Yester -	Gifford, Sir Hugh de (c1190- 1267)
	Tweeddale, 8th Marquis, George Hay (1787-1876)

Foreword

by **Sir Hew Hamilton-Dalrymple Bt, KCVO**
Lord Lieutenant of East Lothian

It is a rare pleasure to be asked to write a *Foreword* to this fascinating book written by David Dick to mark the millennium.

His erudition and sense of history has produced a rare treat for each of us who live in East Lothian and who love this part of Scotland. It can now be said that East Lothian has its own equivalent of the *Dictionary of National Biography*.

A brief glance at the *Contents* page indicates the breadth of David Dick's research into the lives of so many people who have made a contribution over the years to the history of Scotland - both local and national. On reading these pages we should surely be proud of both East Lothian's heritage and of its sons and daughters.

As David Dick comments in his *Introduction,* this book is a splendid antidote to the present day tendency to denigrate achievement and success. There are plenty of both in these pages. It must be a good thing, as we enter the new millennium, to look back on the lives of our East Lothian forebears and vow to build on the splendid foundation that they have laid down for us.

Hew Hamilton-Dalrymple

Introduction

The description of East Lothian as 'The Garden of Scotland' usually refers to its lush woodland, wonderful soil, its well maintained farms and its superb scenery but this volume covering about two hundred lives, past and present, is a tribute not simply to its agricultural produce and scenery but to the fame of some of its sons and daughters. Potted biographies of many, by no means all, of those eminent people who were born in the county are given with a few outsiders who have been adopted by East Lothian. Their long residency and considerable contribution to the county and to their country give them a well-merited place in these pages.

The philosophy and perhaps the unwitting testimony behind these short biographies is concerned firstly with human endeavour and achievement and secondly to provide a balance to that human failing which seems to have a compulsion to denigrate, to find fault and to revel in the misfortune of others. That is not to say that I write about good fortune or luck, nor am I uncritical, I write about success and try to give an inkling of the means towards it. In this respect certain deductions are made from the outcomes and actions of historical figures and observations are made of the motives of living figures who have been kind enough to grant me one to one interviews.

This volume digs into the distant past as well as the present and attempts to illustrate the importance of the contribution of my choice of East Lothian lives in the development and the history of Scotland over the past one thousand years. The scholarship of great men and women of religion, philosophy, law, literature, science, medicine, engineering and the arts, those who influenced the church and both national and local political affairs, those who distinguished themselves in the fields of battle and exploration and those whose forte was sport and entertainment make splendid and interesting stories.

Finally, an apology to all, and there must be many, who do not appear in these pages. This was not intended to neglect them but is simply due to my ignorance of their contribution to East Lothian.

David Dick

Acknowledgements:

I owe debts of gratitude to many people in East Lothian for help in so many ways - help from the staff of the Central Library in Edinburgh and the local Library of Haddington, loans of books from friends, papers and family photographs with dozens of interviews coupled with kind hospitality from many of the subjects of this volume

Special thanks must firstly be given to **Mrs Pauline Jaffray**, editor of *East Lothian Life*, who published many of my East Lothian biographies and who kindly allowed me to reproduce them as part of this volume. Her unfailing encouragement and courtesy are greatly appreciated.

Mrs Margaret Ainslie, Private Secretary of the Dowager Duchess of Hamilton, for her kindness in adding to and checking the stories of the Dukes of Hamilton, the Duchess of Hamilton and that of Lennox Milne McLaren for whom Mrs Ainslie obtained for me a copy of her obituary and helped me to gain permission to publish her photograph by Darling and Douglas-Hamilton Photography.

Mr George Anderson, custodian of the Mansell Collection, London, for the engraving of Francis Balfour

George Angus, past-secretary of Haddington's History Society and the well-known photographer and author of *Haddington Then and Now,* whose knowledge of Haddington is so helpful to visitors and was especially helpful to me.

William Baillie, son of Richard Baillie, who kindly granted me several interviews at his home in Elgin. His recollections of the life and times of his father, Richard Baillie of Haddington, are greatly appreciated. I am also grateful to him for the loan of several family photographs and an oil painting of his father by David Alison RSA.

Mrs Mary Barlee, the daughter of Dr McLean of Hilton Lodge, Haddington for her kind hospitality and help with the story of her father as well as that of Sir William Fergusson.

Gordon Bathgate, secretary of Haddington Rugby Club, for lending me a photograph, a letter of Jock Wemyss and a copy of The History of Haddington Rugby Football Club.

Mrs Elizabeth Beattie of Longniddry for her help with the lives of her father Dr Henry H Robarts and her brothers Mr Frederick and Dr James Robarts.

John Bellany CBE, RA for his help with his life story and for permission to publish his photograph.

The **British Boadcasting Corporation** for permission to quote from the BBC Radio 4 broadcast: Making Radio Waves, 15th May 2000 for the biography of Alexander Muirhead.

The British Museum for permission to reproduce the photograph of Dr Henry Moyes and William Nicol (page 302)

Sir Hew Hamilton-Dalrymple Bt, KCVO of Leuchie for his kindess not only in lending me irreplaceable family papers and publications (70,76,77) but also for checking my version of his family story and for his hospitality during our interesting discussions at Leuchie about each of the baronets of Leuchie. I am especially grateful to him for consenting to write a most excellent foreword for this publication.

Derek Dick, *Fish* for his kind hospitality and patience during interviews, for lending me biographical material and helping me to unravel the strange (to me) world of a singer-song-writer and actor.

Anne Donnely the librarian of the Royal Sick Children's Hospital Edinburgh for her help with the life of FH Robarts.

Mrs. Isabel Easton of Barnhill, Dundee, a niece of Jock Wemyss who generously gave of her time in answering my questions about her uncle and his family

Nessie Gell of Haddington's History Society for her interest, and her help in researching the life of 'Black Agnes', the Countess of Dunbar.

Sir Alistair Grant *q.v.*, who in spite of illness and with such indomitable spirit, visited me at my home to help me with his life story. I am also grateful to him for lending me a photograph.

Eric Groome whose knowledge of people and places in East Lothian is encyclopaedic. I was very fortunate and grateful to have been allowed access to his enormous collection of files, books, papers and photographs. He kindly provided me with many photographs, out-of-print texts and various published articles for reference.

His Grace, the 15th Duke of Hamilton for his kindness in granting me an interview and help with the life story of his father, the 14th Duke, the life of his mother, the Dowager Duchess of Hamilton and his own life. I am specially grateful for the trouble he took to read and amend with suggestions for improvements the story of his family.

Juliet Hay of the Oxford University Museum of Natural History for the photograph of Salton born Dr Alexander Muirhead.

Nick Hobley of East of Scotland Water at Hopes Filter Station for his help with Hopes Reservoir in lending me newspaper cuttings and an article published in the Journal of the Stephenson Locomotive Society Vol XLVII 1971 relating to the life of Richard Baillie.

Mrs Valerie Imrie of Edinburgh for her help in correcting and providing additional information about the life of her late husband Dr John Imrie of Oldhamstocks and for lending me his photograph.

Eleonora Jenkinson *q.v.* of Harperdean Farm for her kind hospitality in granting me several interviews about her life and for her suggestions of eminent women of East Lothian. She is not only a wonderful example to the young but an inspiration to me. Her enthusiasm and encouragement is greatly appreciated.

Sir David Kinloch of Gilmerton for his kindness and help with many biographical details of his predecessors and for lending me irreplaceable family papers and books from his library; it is always good to write from primary sources. I am grateful to him for checking my version of his family's story.

The Earl of Lauderdale *qv* for his kindness and hospitality at the New Club of Edinburgh and in granting me several interviews about his own life and about the history of his illustrious Maitland family.

Professor John Gordon McVie *qv* for his help in checking his own life story and for supplying a photograph.

John McVie, former Town Clerk of Haddington and father of Professor John Gordon McVie, for his help in checking and adding to the story of his son, lending me his son's enormous cv, and many newspaper cuttings.

Patrick Muirhead of BBC London, the great-great nephew of Dr Alexander Muirhead *qv*, for his help in correcting and providing information about this co-inventor of radio from Saltoun.

Kenny Munro, local artist, for information about Forerunner II the replica of the small craft built by Francis Cadell the original being used to explore the navigation of the Murray River, Australia in 1850.

Joy Pitman the Assistant Librarian/Archivist of the Royal College of surgeons for useful material relating to the life of FH Robarts.

Professor Norman Porteous *qv*, his daughter **Lesley Porteous** and his son **Malcolm Porteous** who allowed me the privilege of several interviews as well as the kind hospitality of their home in Edinburgh. Professor Porteous was 100 years of age at the time of our meetings and his memories of Haddington during the early part of this century form an interesting and valuable contribution to this publication. The story of his life and that of his brother Professor Alexander Porteous are classic examples of a dedicated theologian and philosopher and brilliant scholarship.

Mr Colin Porteous of Aughton near Ormskirk in Lancashire, the surgeon son of Professor Alexander Porteous *qv*, (the elder brother of Professor Norman Porteous) who added much to the story of his father. I am most grateful for the kindness and generosity of Mr and Mrs Porteous shown me during my visit to their home at Ormskirk.

Margaret Pringle, a past committee member of Haddington's History Society, was a source of encouragement and great help especially in her suggestions of Haddington born subjects. I am grateful to her for the material and the photograph of William Rae *q.v.* taken in New Zealand about 1900

The late **Mrs Dorothy C. Rennie** for her help with the life of her brother Frederick H Robarts, Senior Paediatric Surgeon of the Royal Sick Children's Hospital, Edinburgh.

Dr James and **Mrs Robarts** for their kind hospitality and help in writing the story of their family of Haddington.

Rev. Ray Sawyer for his kindness in lending me several historical volumes and Books of the Old Edinburgh Club from which I gleaned the story of William Nicol of Humbie.

Dr Mark Shipway of the University Archive of the University of Leeds who kindly sent me details of the life and work of Sir James Black Baillie *qv* published in The Journal of the University of Leeds - The Gryphon of May 1938, Sir James's Obituary which appeared in the Yorkshire Post and Leeds Mercury of 10th June 1940 and an extract from the Introduction to Sir James Baillie, Reflections on Life and Religion published by George Allen and Unwin, 1952.

Alexander Fraser Spowage MBE, JP *qv*, an ex-Provost of Haddington, who, almost from the day I arrived in Haddington, gave generously and continuously of his time and help with information about several East Lothian lives. I am grateful too for his many suggestions of famous people, for his kindness, his hospitality and his unfailing interest, encouragement and most of all his belief in the need for such a book.

Mrs Doreen Sayers Stephenson and her grandson, Douglas Sterphenson of North Berwick, for permission to quote liberally from her publication: *100 Years of Golf in North Berwick, 1857 to 1962, BEN SAYERS*, 1994 on which the Ben Sayers story is based.

The late **Nigel Tranter OBE** *qv*, Scotland's most prolific author of historical novels and Scottish fortalices; he was kindness itself not only giving generously of his valuable time at his home in Aberlady but in his many helpful suggestions. He is, of course, one of my favourite famous lives; it was indeed a privilege and a pleasure to have known him.

Mr Jack Tully-Jackson, a past committee member of Haddington's History Society, for lending me several documents and the scrap book with newspaper cuttings pertaining to the life of Mrs Catherine Blair *qv*.

Mrs Eunice Walker of Victoria Australia for her help with the story of her great uncle, William Rae *qv* of Haddington.

Veronica Wallace of Haddington's Library Service gave me such willing and courteous assistance with so many biographies that I marvel at her patience.

The Earl and Countess of Wemyss for their kindness in lending me a handwritten Wemyss family tree and for amending and checking my version of the history of the earldom; its accuracy is due to the painstaking care of the Earl himself.

Kenneth Whitson, Chief Executive of D&J Croall Ltd for his help with the life of Miss Evelyne Croall and for his permission to publish the Courier photograph of Sir Hew Dalrymple and Princess Royal.

William Walker Wood MBE, the Haddington born world champion bowler, for granting me several enjoyable interviews, for compiling the long list of his championship victories and for his permission to publish his action photograph.

To many members of **Haddington's History Society** and the Haddington Remembered Group I owe a debt of gratitude for many small contributions during informal chats and formal talks by various speakers.

To my daughters **Mrs Pamela Armstrong MSc, DipM, MCIM, Dr Moira Hughes B.Sc(Hons), Ph.D,** and **Sandra Millar Grad.IPM** and to **Alan Hughes** (Moira's husband) for their interest, their suggestions and their care in proof reading.

Lastly, to my wife **Muriel** for her humour, patience, constant interest and encouragement throughout the preparation of this book. She designed the cover, read and re-read the manuscript, searched out photographs and gravestones, made many suggestions, asked relevant questions, the answers to which added much to the content, and lastly, made sure that I finished it - glad that I did so, so that a social life may be resumed!

JOHN ABERCROMBIE

The famous gardener of Prestonpans

It is perhaps not surprising that the first comprehensive book on practical gardening was written by a son of East Lothian over 200 years ago. He was John Abercrombie of Prestonpans who, in 1767, published his *Every man his own Gardener*. It was so popular it ran to seven editions and was reprinted in 1879, seventy-three years after his death.

John Abercrombie was born in 1726 and was brought up in a family which earned its livelihood from gardening. His father was a market gardener of great experience and his enthusiasm and love of plants rubbed off on young John who, showing an early interest in gardening, was apprenticed to his father.

He left Prestonpans shortly after the brief Battle of Prestonpans in 1745 when Prince Charles Edward Stuart defeated Cope's army. He arrived in London and obtained employment at Kew Gardens. His reputation for hard work and his unusual breadth of knowledge impressed several noble families who asked him to design and to lay out their gardens, one of which was at Leicester House in London. When he had earned sufficient money he set himself up in business as a market gardener at Hackney.

There were very few publications on gardening at that time and of the few that existed none were comprehensive and none dealt with the practical aspects of gardening. Abercrombie filled that need. His *Man his own Gardener*, when it was first produced, had as its author Mr J Maw who was well-established and well-known as the gardener to the Duke of Leeds. The newcomer, Abercrombie, realising that because he was unknown, paid £20 for the privilege of using Maw's name. Maw never even troubled to read a line of Abercrombie's book. Abercrombie's next publication, in 1779, filled yet another gap and dealt with fruit production. It was *The British Fruit Gardener and the Art of Pruning* - an immediate success and this time its authorship was correct.

He moved his business to Tottenham and spent most of his time in writing. He had reached a crossroad - whether or not to spent more time on writing or on planting. Fortunately for the gardeners of the world writing won and he produced a formidable list of useful publications:

Gardener's Pocket Journal and Daily Assistant - reached 35 editions by 1857.

Complete Gardener's Pocket Journal and Daily Forcing Gardener, 1781
Complete Wall-Tree Pruner, 1783
Propagation and Botanical Management of Plants and Trees, 1784
Hot House Gardener, 1789 - German translation, 1792
The Practical Gardener, published posthumously.

He died in his eightieth year in London in 1806.

COUNTESS ADA DE WARENNE

daughter-in-law of David I

The 'Abbey' or Cistercian Nunnery of St Mary, which was situated about one mile east of Haddington near the present Abbey Bridge over the Tyne and of which nothing remains, was founded by Countess Ada de Varenne, daughter of the 2nd Earl of Surrey, between 1153 and 1178.

Her father was the Earl of Varenne and Surrey and she spent most of her youth at Tours in France. In 1139 she married Prince Henry, the Earl of Northumbria and only son and heir of David I (r.1124-1153). When her father-in-law, the king, gave her the Royal Burgh of Haddington, the Nungate and other land surrounding Haddington as a wedding present, she decided to found the Cistercian Nunnery of St Mary.

She had three sons the first of whom, Malcolm, was born in 1141, two years later William was born to be followed by David, but her husband, Prince Henry, died in 1152 after 13 years of marriage. This was a tragedy not only for Princess Ada but for his doting father, King David, who had high hopes for his only son as he had shown great promise to become a good king. Princess Ada's eldest son succeeded his grandfather as Malcolm IV in 1153 at the age of twelve. He died aged 25 and his brother William the Lyon succeeded him in 1165.

Little is recorded of Princess Ada's life except of course that she had three sons: Malcolm (1141-1165), William (1143-1214) and David (who became Earl of Huntingdon) but it is known that after the death of her husband she spent the rest of her life in seclusion and in religious devotion. It was about that time she founded the Cistercian Abbey of Haddington dedicated to the Virgin Mary having received a gift of some land from the Sheriff of Haddington, Alexander de Martin, in a deed of conveyance of 1153-1178 (50 p.83). The chantry chapel of St Martin, the oldest ecclesiastic structure in Haddington, still exists in a ruinous state in the Nungate and was possibly named by Princess Ada to commemorate St Martin of Tours where she spent her childhood.

She grieved over the premature death of her eldest son, Malcolm IV, who died at the age of twenty-five in 1165. Her second son, William, succeeded the throne and was known as Guillaume de Varenne from his mother's French background. In fact, Donaldson (10) in his *Scottish Kings* notes that kings of Scots considered themselves to be more French than Scots in language and culture at that time. William 'the Lion', as he came to be known from the single lion he used for his emblem, reigned for 49 years, the longest in the history of Scotland until James VI in 1567. His mother, Princess Ada, died during the 13th year of his warlike reign in 1178.

ALEXANDER II

A Royal Anniversary for Haddington in 1998

Haddingtonians rightly boast of a Royal birth in the Royal Burgh. The year was **1198** when King William the Lion and Queen Ermengarde had almost given up hope of having a son to succeed to the Scottish throne. Greatly relieved, their baby, a healthy boy, Alexander was born in the King's Palace which stood on the site of the County Buildings in Court Street. A plaque commemorates the event and is inscribed:

This is the site of
THE ROYAL PALACE,
occupied by KING WILLIAM I,
styled WILLIAM the LION,
and here his son,
ALEXANDER II of SCOTLAND,
was born, 24th August, 1198.

Alexander spent his boyhood in Haddington and he was three years old when a General Council of Nobles confirmed him as Heir Designate at Musselburgh. One can imagine that this royal prince played on the meadow behind the palace. The few remaining ruins of the palace were finally removed and replaced by the County Buildings in 1833. The name given to the Primary School on that meadow is appropriately **King's Meadow Primary School**. The old name for Court Street was **King's Street**, commemorating the royal birth but such was the euphoria at the laying of the foundation stone of the new County Buildings by Sir Gordon Sinclair Stevenson on 27th May 1833 that the Council decided to rename the street. The plaque and the name of the school are therefore our only reminders of the birth of a king in Haddington.

Alexander succeeded to the Scottish throne on 5th December 1214. His coronation took place at the centre of Scottish monarchy at Scone. An early preoccupation of King Alexander was the protection he gave to English nobles who requested it against King John of England. Not a little irked by this King John invaded Dunbar and Haddington which he wantonly burned down in 1216. In retaliation Alexander assembled his army at the Esk and King John retreated to Berwick which he sacked without mercy. King Alexander followed him as far as Richmond in North Yorkshire. His Highlanders burned and pillaged as they went, equalling King John's ferocity. King John was understandably very aggrieved and complained to the Pope who promptly excommunicated Alexander from the Church of Rome.

Alexander was a good and wise ruler and when Henry III acceded to the English throne he signed a peace treaty in 1217 and a year later a Papal Bull of Honorius III, which liberated the Scottish Church from subjection to any archbishop, was reissued to 'his dearest son in Christ, Alexander, illustrious king of Scots, and his successors forever' (60 p.30).

Alexander was anxious to achieve unity in Scotland and in 1221 he set out to subdue his rebellious and disobedient subjects of Argyll. However, his fleet, which had sailed late in the year from the Firth of Clyde, was stormbound and partly wrecked. He repeated the invasion early the following year and found no opposition from the lords and chiefs of Argyll; he subdivided the land and gave it to those lords whom he could trust.

During the winter of 1221 Alexander married Henry's eldest sister, Princess Joan, thus ensuring peace for the next seventeen years. However, King Henry, ambitious for more power, tried through the Papacy to secure the unreserved homage of Alexander. This would have seriously offended the Highlanders and Alexander would have none of it. However, in 1237, with the signing of the Treaty of York, Alexander surrendered to Henry the earldoms of Northumberland, Cumberland and Westmoreland but he retained land within these earldoms - 'and the said king of Scots has done homage for these lands to the said king of England, and has sworn fealty to him' (60 p.34).

King Alexander's marriage was childless and the Princess died in 1238. His choice of a second wife was Mary a daughter of Baron Couci, a French noble, who was said to be even richer than the Dauphin of France himself. Their son Alexander was born in 1241, twenty-seven years after he had become king, but this marriage annoyed King Henry who considered that a threat from France was now a distinct possibility and Henry's army marched on Scotland in 1244 to demand Alexander's homage. The Earl of Gloucester, with the help of the Earl of Dunbar, captured Edinburgh Castle and took Alexander and his wife Mary to Roxburgh. They were released a few years later and Alexander now sought to gain the Hebrides from Norway.

The Hebrides had been held by the kings of Norway since 1098 and Alexander firstly tried to persuade King Haakon to return the islands to Scotland. This was refused. He then offered to buy them but again he was refused. Alexander now decided to take the islands by force and he amassed a great fleet. On his journey north he became ill and was forced to return to the bay at Oban to be put ashore on the island of Kerrera where he died in 1249.

His son succeeded him at the age of eight as Alexander III and, determined to succeed where his father had failed, he regained control of the Western Isles in 1263. Then three years later following a bargain with King Magnus of Norway the islands were finally purchased for 400 marks plus 100 marks each year afterwards (61 p. 60).

THOMAS ALEXANDER CB

of Prestonpans 'The Soldiers' Friend'

On the landward side of the main street of Prestonpans there is a beautifully kept stepped garden above which is the graveyard of Prestongrange Parish Church. In this garden stands the statue of Thomas Alexander of Prestonpans. It was sculpted by William Brodie (1815-81) and was erected in 1862, two years after his death. Its plinth is inscribed:

Front:

In memory of THOMAS ALEXANDER CB Director General of the Medical Department of the British Army. Born at Prestonpans 6th May 1812. Died 1st February 1860.

East Side:

Throughout a long military career he laboured incessantly to elevate the condition of the soldier and during the Crimean War his indefatigable efforts as Principal Medical Officer of the Light Division to alleviate the suffering of the troops were of inestimable value in stimulating others to follow his example.

West Side:

The improved sanitary conditions of the British Army as well as the elevation in rank and consideration of its medical officers are mainly due to his exertions. His high professional attainments and his great administrative powers were wholly devoted to the service of his country and the cause of humanity.

North Side:

West Indies, North America, Gaffraria, Alma, Inkerman, Sebastopol

Thomas Alexander was born at Prestonpans on 6th May 1812. His father, William Alexander (1786-1865) was a prosperous merchant and his mother was Helen Kemp (1783-1865). Thomas was educated at the University of Edinburgh where he studied medicine. Shortly after he qualified he entered the army (on 10th October 1834) and was almost immediately sent to the West Indies. He was a member of the peace-keeping force where, only a year before, the slaves had been freed. Absentee landlords complained about the negro wage-labourers and inadequate money compensation. The landlords and their often cruel overseers defied Imperial government, detested missionaries and oppressed their workers. The British army had the unenviable task of containing the rebels. This was Alexander's first experience of the dreadful neglect of the British soldier who was regarded as mere cannon fodder and whose suffering from tropical diseases was the main cause of hundreds of deaths. He pleaded for medical supplies and facilities but to little avail; most of the soldiers died untreated as expendable and easily replaceable.

His next posting was to Nova Scotia which was a separate colony and not yet a province of Canada. The British army was sent to protect the American loyalists from Maryland rebels. Again, conditions were primitive. Freezing cold was the problem for the foot soldier, woefully ill-equipped for the dramatic change in climate. Alexander again pleaded for clothing and blankets as well as medical supplies and facilities in which to treat these dying men. Amputations and operations had to be carried out without anaesthetic; it would be another ten years before James Young Simpson discovered the effects of chloroform.

During his service in Canada the army was called upon to quell a spate of rebellions in 1837. In 'Lower Canada' the French detested the fact that the Governor and his officials were all British but from a military point of view the rebellions were easily put down. However, the Elgin riots of 1847 were more serious when the Parliament buildings in Montreal were burned down.

In 1845 Alexander returned home to Prestonpans and in December he purchased land and a house on the site of the garden where his statue now stands. He was now posted to the Cape of Good Hope - the Boers had become resentful of the British inability to deal with Kaffirs and had begun their Great Trek northwards across the Orange River. Another Kaffir War in 1850 required the presence of British troops and Alexander's experience in dealing with the tropical ailments of the West Indies was now invaluable but still medical supplies were inadequate and many young men were buried in the African bush.

Next, Alexander was posted to the Crimea; this was to prove the most horrendous of his medical experience. In Turkey the Russians had annihilated a Turkish flotilla at Sinope and Britain clamoured for war. The fleet was despatched to prevent Russian ships from leaving Sebastopol and war began in March 1854. Alexander almost worked himself to death in battling against the incompetence of the British Government in its neglect of the most basic needs of the soldiers of the Crimean War. Their conditions were indescribable, their suffering unbearable, their loss of life through sickness and injury unnecessary, their supplies of clothing non-existent; transport, fuel, medical supplies were all inadequate and even food shortages led to suffering on a monumental scale of despair and death. This was the scene at Crimea early in 1855 which confronted Thomas Alexander, as Principal Medical Officer of the Light Division. The only relief arrived at Scutari when the heroic Florence Nightingale and her dedicated nurses, rejected at first, provided desperately needed medical care.

The aftermath of Sebastopol had left an ill-prepared army in an appalling state and Dr Alexander worked non-stop in desperation to alleviate the plight of the rank and file soldier. Cholera had broken out even before the attack on Sebastopol and injuries which had been left untreated were now gangrenous. The stench of death was all-pervasive. To make matters worse, equipment and clothing was simply not available for the forthcoming winter campaign. This campaign could have been avoided if only General Raglan's intention to advance quickly after his victory over the Russians at Alma had not been delayed. The French, under General St Arnaud, chose to wait and the initiative which could have ended the war was lost. Lord Raglan's despatch describes Alexander 'as deserving to be the most honourably mentioned.' In July 1856 Alexander's dedicated work was recognised when he was given the local rank of Inspector-General.

After the war Thomas Alexander's great achievements were again recognised in his award of the honour of Companion of the Bath (CB) on 4th February 1856. He was now appointed Director-General of the Army Medical Department and he founded the Army Medical School at Fort Pitt, the Royal Victoria Hospital at Netley and the Herbert Hospital at Woolwich. Such was his enormous reputation, he was appointed honorary surgeon to Queen Victoria on 16th August 1859.

The announcement of his death at 26 Norfolk Square, London, only four years after the war and at the age of only 49 years on 1st February 1860, was received with shock and sorrow in Prestonpans. His body was brought from London to the town of his birth and the burial service was held on 6th February. All shops and businesses closed that day as a mark of respect to this famous son of Prestonpans. The funeral cortege exceeded the length of the town. He was buried beside his parents in the garden where his statue stands. He was survived by his wife Mary Alice, sister of T Heath Haviland, Lieutenant-Governor of Prince Edward Island. She died on 12 April 1881.

WILLIAM ANDERSON of North Berwick

The Ship's Doctor who sailed with Captain Cook

There is a small island in the Bering Sea called Anderson's Island; it was named by Captain Cook on the day that his well-respected ship's doctor and botanist William Anderson of North Berwick died aboard the *Resolution*.

His father was the schoolmaster of North Berwick Grammar School (now demolished and replaced by Victoria House) where young William received his early education. He qualified as a surgeon at the University of Edinburgh when the great teacher of clinical medicine, William Cullen, was his professor and instigator of the importance of the nervous system in health and disease.

In 1772 Anderson joined Captain Cook aboard H.M. Sloop *Resolution* as surgeon's mate doubling as the naturalist on Cook's second voyage of discovery. He had read stirring accounts of James Cook's voyage of 1768-71 and after long discussions with his father he decided to apply for a place on Cook's next voyage. Of special interest to Anderson were the great variety of new ferns and flowers found at Botany Bay by the English botanist Joseph Banks who had been a demanding passenger aboard the *Endeavour*. Banks had made rather a fool of himself in his insistence in having an extra deck for seventeen additional members of his party. This was refused and the sulking Banks refused to go (79 p.391). Anderson was given his place.

Cook had been promoted to the rank of Commander after charting New Zealand and exploring the east coast of Australia and the Torres Strait. He was preparing for his next voyage of discovery in command of two ships, the 462-ton *Resolution* and the 330-ton *Adventure*. On 13th July 1772 William Anderson, filled with excitement to be aboard the Commander's ship, sailed from Plymouth. William Anderson had been selected not only for his congeniality and medical training but for his deep interest in botany; this was a great adventure for the young man from North Berwick.

They sailed firstly to the Cape of Good Hope and then to the Antarctic Circle to find a southern continent. After a fruitless search for the non-existent continent they made their way through the dangers of floating ice, reef-strewn seas and fog. They became separated from the *Adventure* and spent several weeks in search of her. At Queen Charlotte's Sound, British Columbia they found each other and went ashore to be greeted by armed savages who had never before seen white men.

They charted the exact positions of the Marquesas and the Friendly Islands, rediscovering the New Hebrides and making new discoveries of New Caledonia, Norfolk Island and the Isle of Pines.

Although he attended to the medical needs of the crew, it was in the field of botany and oceanic life that the young surgeon, William Anderson, excelled. He recorded new plants, poisonous fish and found the Kerguelen cabbage which he named *Pringlea antiscorbutica.* This was an important find because of the curative effects in ridding the crew of the dreaded scurvy and Anderson's papers on poisonous fish and a detached rock near Cape Town were published in the *Philosophical Transactions* of London.

They returned to New Zealand and explored the South Pacific from South Australia to Tierra del Fuego and on the way home they rediscovered South Georgia. They crossed the South Atlantic to the Cape and reached Plymouth on 25th July 1775 - a journey of 60,000 miles. Anderson was highly praised by Captain Cook for his valuable and devoted work. During this three-year voyage William Anderson had learned and contributed a great deal. Only one man had died during the long voyage which was extraordinary during a time when it was not uncommon to lose almost half the crew from the scourge of scurvy. The good health of the crew was due to Cook's insistence on a diet which included his 'portable broth' made from a concoction of vegetables, syrup of lemon, sauerkraut and scurvy grass. This eliminated the dreaded killer, scurvy and, with Anderson's help and insistence on hygiene, the health of the crew was maintained. Cook's paper to the Royal Society on the subject of diet and hygiene during long voyages astounded medical opinion of the day and Cook was awarded the Copley Medal. He owed much to the success of his voyage to a previous Copley Medal recipient, the famous John Harrison whose chronometer had enabled him to find longitude with much greater accuracy than the lunar distance method. In his journal he wrote, 'that indeed our error [in Longitude] can never be great, so long as we have so good a guide as [the] watch' (80 p.139)

William Anderson was so pleased with the results of his botanical and marine discoveries he was determined to accompany Cook's third and last voyage in 1776. Cook had been promoted Post-Captain and made Captain of Greenwich Hospital and with the *Resolution* and the *Discovery* they left on 25th June to sail for the Cape of Good Hope. After landing at Tasmania they sailed for New Zealand, the Tonga Islands and Tahiti, then northwards to rediscover the Hawaiian Islands. On their way to the west coast of America, William Anderson's health deteriorated. He had contracted the dreaded consumption (tuberculosis) and he died on board ship on 3rd August 1778 in the Bering Sea. Captain Cook and the whole crew felt the loss of this fine young man and on that sad day, when his body was 'committed to the deep' and the service had been read, Captain Cook decided to honour his young friend by naming a newly discovered island after him; it was given the name *Anderson's Island.*

Cook's narrative of the voyage describes Anderson in glowing terms and many years later Robert Brown (1773-1858), the great Scottish botanist who accompanied Captain Flinders in his explorations off the Australian coasts, named the genus *Andersonia* after William Anderson of North Berwick.

A few months after the death of Anderson, Captain Cook returned to the warmth of the Pacific and was murdered at Karakakoa Bay in Hawaii in January 1779.

SIR JAMES BLACK BAILLIE
of Haddington

Philosopher and Academic

James Black Baillie, was born in Haddington on 24th October 1872, the son of a nurseryman, William Baillie. His brilliant academic career culminated in his appointment from his professorship in Moral Philosophy at Aberdeen to the Vice Chancellorship of Leeds University in 1924. He received the Freedom of the City of London, and was knighted in 1931 for his important public service.

His early education took place at the Burgh School of Haddington and at the newly opened (1879) Knox Institute under the Rectorship of J.C. Graham MA, previously classics master of Merchiston. At the University of Edinburgh he graduated with first class honours in Philosophy having studied under Professors Campbell Fraser and S S Laurie. It now seemed clear that Baillie was destined for a brilliant academic career. He continued his studies at the University of Halle in Germany and at the Sorbonne in Paris. He won several scholarships and fellowships and studied divinity and modern history. After his studies at Strasbourg he entered Trinity College, Cambridge where he took his BA degree to be followed by his doctorate (D.Phil.) from the University of Edinburgh.

His first teaching post, in 1899, was at the University of St Andrews where he was appointed assistant to Professor Ritchie, the Professor of Logic and Metaphysics. A year later he became a Lecturer in Philosophy at University College Dundee and, in 1901, he published his masterly *Hegel's Logic*. He had spent several years in studying the work of this, the greatest of the German idealist philosophers, Georg Hegel (1770-1831). Such was Baillie's high reputation in 1902, at the age of thirty, he was offered and accepted the Chair of Moral Philosophy at Aberdeen University where he was to remain for the next twenty-two eventful years.

In 1906 he married Helena May James a niece of Lord James of Hereford. That year he published his *The Idealistic Construction of Experience* to be followed by his translation of Hegel's *Phenomenology of Mind* in 1910 (written by Hegel over one hundred years before). Baillie's introduction and notes which accompanied the translation created great interest and attention by scholars of his day.

In 1914, at the start of World War I, Professor Baillie's work and high reputation led him to give important public service to the Intelligence Division of the Admiralty and the Ministry of Labour for which he settled over 300 cases under the Munitions of War and the Industrial Court Acts. He was Chairman of the Panel of Arbitration Courts of the Court of Inquiry into the trawling industry at Hull. He chaired committees on wages and conditions in the motor transport industry and an arbitration tribunal to settle disputes in the oilfields of Trinidad and Tobago. He was a member of the Royal Commission on the Civil Service.

After the 1914-18 War he returned to academic work at Aberdeen and in 1921 he published his *Studies in Human Nature*. This was his last book; he became more practical in his outlook and more critical of academic philosophy and of the Heglian school. The service he had given to the Admiralty and for the Ministry of Labour had undoubtedly diverted and broadened his outlook towards matters practical. He was now in great demand as a Chairman of Trade Boards.

In 1924 he was appointed Vice Chancellor of the University of Leeds in which office he remained until his retiral in 1938. During his 14-year tenure of office the university benefited materially as well as academically from his successes in gaining the support of business leaders in West Yorkshire. Almost immediately, he launched a building development appeal for £500,000 which was attended and encouraged by the Duke of York (later George VI). £700,000 was raised and new buildings were erected for Mining, Physics, Chemistry, Dentistry, Physiology, Pathology and other subjects. Five new Chairs were instituted in Experimental Pathology and Cancer Research, Electrical Engineering, Theology, Industrial Relations and Dentistry. He raised £130,000 for the university's general fund and £50,000 in special endowments for scholarships. His work for student amenities was remarkable: the playing fields were reconditioned with the addition of a new pavilion, a new Students' Union building, two women's hostels were enlarged and the Devonshire Hall was built as a men's hostel. A monument to his zealous attention to detail and hard work was the Brotherton Library. In the midst of hectic money-raising Sir James Baillie took enormous care in the advancement of learning and research.

As a philosopher of international distinction (he was awarded the Cavaliere Ufficiale of the Order of the Crown of Italy for his services to Italian culture) he took a long and broad view of the world of academia. His charm, kindliness and brilliant conversation endeared him to all who met him and it was no coincidence that he was so successful in fostering the aims of the university.

He was knighted in 1931 and given an honorary Doctorate of Laws of Aberdeen University. In addition he was made a Freeman of the City of London, an Honorary Freeman of the Company of Clothmakers and a Knight Commander of the Crown of Italy. This distinguished and honoured academic died suddenly of a heart attack on 9th June 1940, aged 68 years at his home at Weybridge, Surrey.

RICHARD BAILLIE

The Genius Builder and Artist of the Nungate of Haddington

Richard Baillie, a son of Haddington, was in the words of Professor Norman Porteous (1898-) *q.v.*, "the one man in Haddington who showed true genius, a brilliant artist, full of stories; he could recite poetry endlessly - he could have been Prime Minister!"

Richard Baillie was a building contractor who combined his talent for business with painting in oils; he was an untutored and exceptionally gifted artist. He was the second of a family of five children and after the death of his father his mother maintained the family from her little general store on the edge of the Tyne near the Nungate Bridge.

Richard Baillie is reputed to have started his building business in the Nungate with nothing more than a barrow, a few tools and a huge heart. He was born in the Nungate on 12th November 1884 and following a rudimentary education at the Knox Institute he left to take up an apprenticeship as a mason under James Moncrieff (grandfather of the present James Moncrieff, Builders in Haddington).

Richard Baillie from a painting by David Alison RSA (Courtesy of William Baillie of Elgin)

Baillie was a skilled mason and became foreman mason with a building firm in Linlithgow. Early every Monday morning, after a short weekend at home, he cycled to his work from Haddington to Linlithgow, a distance of 40 miles, and after about three years, in 1902, he decided to start his own business in Pencaitland. He was a fit young man who kept in trim by sparring with Harold Fergus, a plumber of Haddington, who became the Scottish lightweight boxing champion in 1904.

He started with small building jobs until the hospital at Hermandflat invited tenders for the building of two new wings and Richard Baillie decided to apply. He needed a sponsor and, having given reliable service in transporting coal from the Reid coal pit at Woodhall to Haddington, Mr Reid of Tyneholme in Pencaitland readily agreed to stand as his guarantor. This was an act of great faith which would be repaid handsomely. After the successful completion of the new wings at Herdmanflat Hospital other work followed and gradually he built up a huge building contracting business single-handedly.

In 1910 he married the only love of his life, Margaret Somerville of Haddington, daughter of John Somerville, a millwright at Stevenson's Agricultural Machinery business in Pencaitland Road opposite the site of the old Gas Works. The Somerville family lived in Station Road and were neighbours of the Porteous family.

Richard and Margaret Baillie had five sons four of whom joined their father to help run his business; the second son became an architect.

In 1923 Richard Baillie took another brave step by purchasing the great but ruined mansion house of the Earls of Wemyss at Amisfield. This beautiful house, the finest example of Palladian building in Scotland, was in a deplorable state having been used in successive wars by the army. Richard Baillie bought it for its red sandstone which he used to build the Vert Hospital (now Vert Court), the new Secondary School at Prestonpans and several houses in Longniddry.

After the General Strike of 1926 he took on a huge contract to build the gravity earth dam of Hopes Reservoir in the Lammermuir Hills. His first task was to lay a 3-foot gauge single railway line from the present filter house through the valley passed West Hopes Farm to the site of the dam. The dam was completed in 1934 its reservoir supplying 1.5 million gallons (6.8 million litres) per day for the western part of East Lothian. Some of the stone for the dam came from the demolished Calton Jail in Edinburgh, Scotland's largest prison in its day. The bridge over the spillway of the dam was that over which prisoners, who had been sentenced to death, took their last walk on their way to the hangman's noose. The inscription in stone on the parapet reads:

The arch of this bridge and the walls of the water course which it spans were brought from the Calton Jail, Edinburgh upon its demolition in 1930-31.

That year Richard Baillie was given the contract for the extension of the County Buildings in Court Street, Haddington. Following its successful completion he gained the major contract for the biggest earth dam in Britain - the Lady Bower Reservoir which would provide 54 million gallons (245 million litres) of water per day for the cities of Sheffield, Nottingham, Leicester and Derby. During the construction of the dam work had to be stopped on many occasions when the wartime 'Dambusters' flew over the Howden Reservoir nearby to test their dummy bouncing bombs. His building company had to shift over a million tons of earth, 100,000 tons of clay and pour 100,000 tons of concrete for the completion of the dam in 1945. Richard Baillie was a proud man on being presented to King George VI and Queen Elizabeth who performed the opening ceremony.

Richard Baillie was an entrepreneur *par excellence* whose interests extended to farming and his gift shop in Market Street was a great attraction to local children; he donated the toys for 'Santa Claus' at the annual Christmas party in the Corn Exchange. Sadly, his shop was destroyed when a German bomb was dropped on it during the 1939-45 war. His talents were not confined to the building industry; this exceptionally active man became an unusually gifted artist. He discovered this talent almost by accident when he, admiring a painting in the Porteous household in Haddington, made the astounding statement, "I am sure I could paint that picture." He picked up the lid of an old hat box and produced a magnificent copy. He simply could not rest and during family holidays he occupied himself with painting in oils. During one such holiday in the north of Scotland he, with one of his twin sons, William who was to become a Major in the Royal Engineers during the 1939/45 War, visited a cattle auction at Helmsdale and Richard Baillie was talked into bidding for one hundred lambs. The seller was an old drover who had walked his lambs over 50 miles from Bettyhill and the auctioneer tried to open the bidding at five shillings (25p) per lamb. However, there was a price ring in operation; no-one would bid and Richard Baillie opened the bidding at 1/6d; his final bid of 2/6d won the lambs. On receiving his bill he insisted on paying the old drover the going rate of five shillings per lamb. His next problem was to transport the lambs to his farm at Jerusalem on the Haddington/Pencaitland Road where he was a tenant farmer on the Winton Estate. The hungry lambs were met at the station in Haddington and trotted along West Road where they stripped the gardens of almost all of their flowers. The residents were furious but he had made an old drover a happy man on his long trek home. It cost Richard Baillie over £100 to replace the lost blooms in West Road.

He became totally captivated by colour and every spare moment was spent at his easel. Even on fishing trips at Loch Awe, he would ask his sons to row him into the side of the loch where he set up his easel and happily painted the scene before him, rarely spending more than an hour on each painting - even in art he was in a hurry and the results were astounding. He painted landscapes, seascapes, woodland scenes, and flowers. He had no training but he had a photographic memory and was able to paint his interpretation of a scene entirely from memory; there were no preliminary sketches, no second visits and certainly no photographs; his painting was spontaneous.

His reputation grew to such an extent that a deputation of artists from Edinburgh called upon him at his house in Pencaitland to see his work for themselves. He was reputed to be able to copy an old master in about half-an-hour. They arrived to test this extraordinary feat. They were given the usual courtesy of coffee while Richard Baillie absented himself to return within the allotted time complete with an astoundingly accurate copy of an old master. He was quite unaffected by his talent and seemed almost surprised when his works were exhibited at the Royal Scottish Academy in Edinburgh, the Royal Academy of London and at the Southport Art Gallery.

He lived at Deanwood in Pencaitland where he sponsored the local football team of the same name; his five sons were keen footballers.

He died on 9th November 1952 at Pencaitland. Sadly death duties meant the winding up of his excellent building company. His sons had no option but to declare insolvency. He left many of his paintings to East Lothian County Council and several Haddingtonians are the proud possessors of one or more of Dick Baillie's wonderful oil paintings.

SIR DAVID BAIRD of Newbyth

The hero of Seringapatam

Although he is best known as **Sir David Baird of Seringapatam** of India where he suffered imprisonment in chains for three and a half years and where he gained ultimate victory, this heroic son of East Lothian distinguished himself in many battlefields throughout the world: 1780-84 the 2nd Mysore War, 1801 Aboukir Bay in Egypt, 1805 South Africa, 1807 Siege of Copenhagen, 1808 Corunna, Peninsular War.

Courtesy of the management of Crieff Hydro Hotel. Photograph by Pamela Armstrong

He was a big, robust, fearless Scot, a natural soldier and a thorough gentleman who tore into battle and yet showed sorrow and pity on hearing of the injury, illness or death of any of his compatriots.

The small hamlet of Newbyth in East Lothian is the seat of the Bairds of Newbyth. It was here that David Baird was born on 6th December 1757, the fifth son of William Baird. However, Grant in his *Old and New Edinburgh* and Chambers in his *Traditions of Edinburgh* make the claim that he was born and educated in the Gordon mansion at Baird's Close in Castlehill, Edinburgh, formerly the residence of the 1st Duke of Gordon (1643-1716) purchased by Sir Robert Baird and disponed to his son William in 1694. David Baird spent some of his boyhood at both Castlehill and at Newbyth.

He was destined for a military career of great distinction and through his mother's influence he enlisted as an ensign (sub-lieutenant) in the

2nd Regiment in 1772. He served at Gibraltar in 1776 and after promotion in 1778 he was selected by Lord Mcleod (his mother's neighbour) as a Captain of the Grenadier Company. In 1779 he sailed to India where war threatened.

The 2nd Mysore War (1780-4) followed the first Anglo-Mysore war which had ended in a draw in 1769. In 1772 the ruler of Mysore, Haidar Ali, had been defeated by the Mahrattas. He was refused British support and, with his son Tippoo Sahib, he took his revenge by joining with the French to drive the British out of the Carnatic. He despoiled the country to within 40 miles of Madras. It was in this war that David Baird found himself and within a few months of his arrival he was in the thick of fierce fighting. Hyder Ali's troops inflicted a severe defeat on the 3800 British force as they attempted to reach Sir Hector Munro's army. Baird was badly injured and captured at the battle of Polilur (1780). He was taken to Seringapatam and, with other prisoners, he was forced to present his barbarous captor with the heads of their comrades. He was kept in irons in the fortress capital of the Sultan of Mysore. A cave-like cell was to be his disgusting abode for the next three and a half years. It almost killed him. His mother, on hearing that he was chained to a brother officer, was reputed to have remarked, "Lord pity the chiel that's tied to oor Davie!"

After his release he made a remarkable recovery and was soon leading sieges and attacks with a vigour which seemed to be compensating for his lost years. A spell at home completed his recovery and he married Miss Campbell-Preston, the heiress of Ferntower near Crieff. Before her marriage Miss Campbell-Preston had long managed her estates and Sir David had to give in to her supremacy and, although very happily married, he was heard to express the view that he "could command ten thousand men better than one woman!" (83 p.86)

He returned to India in 1799 as a Major-General. Tippoo had lost half of his empire after the 3rd Anglo-Mysore War and again, allying himself with the French, he attacked the British. On 4th May 1799 Major-General David Baird volunteered to lead the attack on Tippoo's fort at Seringapatam in command of 4000 men. Colonel Arthur Wellesley (later the Duke of Wellington) took charge of the reserve (81 p.75). Within six minutes of his stirring shout to his men, the British flag was planted at the summit. Tippoo's men fled and ten French officers surrendered; Tippoo was killed and the town was destroyed. At home there were ecstatic rejoicings. Baird was presented with the state sword of Tippoo Saib by General Harris in the name of the army; he also received Tippoo's gold saddle and other spoils of war.

The British now ruled over India. Baird was the hero of the day but it was marred for him when young Wellesley (he was twelve years younger than Baird) approached him at breakfast with his order from General Harris giving him command of Seringapatam. Baird seethed in silent anger and wrote a vitriolic letter of complaint to Harris. Wellesley was an 'inferior officer' but his brother was the Governor-General (81 p.77). After protesting to Lord Wellesley, Baird gained command at Batavia (Java), but in the event Batvia was cancelled and instead Baird was sent to Egypt with Colonel Wellesley as subordinate.

In 1801 Napoleon had invaded Egypt as a stepping-stone to India and General Sir Ralph Abercrombie landed at Aboukir Bay where he was killed by a stray musket-ball after he had beaten off the French and the opportune arrival of David Baird completed the capture of 20,000 Frenchmen. For this victory Baird was knighted (Knight Commander of the Most Honourable of the Bath) by George III.

Now General Sir David Baird, he gained his next victory at the Cape of Good Hope against the Dutch who had had the Cape returned to them after the signing of the Peace of Amiens in 1802. However Napoleon had taken control of Batavia from the Dutch and the new Dutch Governor of the Cape, General Janssens, began preparations for an invasion by the British. Baird was in command when the awesome British Armada arrived on 4th January 1806. Janssens put up a good defence but his motley army fled and Janssens joined the French contigent. The British had formed two parallel columns; the right was commanded by General Baird's brother, Lieutenant-Colonel Baird, and the left by yet another Scot, Brigadier-General Fergusson. Baird's advance was impeded with some tough fighting and lack of water in the burning sun, but the superior training of the seasoned British soldiers was obvious to Janssens. Baird and he exchanged polite letters to avoid further bloodshed and arranged the signing of the capitulation of Cape Town. The National Anthem was played but Baird stopped it out respect of his gallant enemy. But there is an unfortunate postscript to Baird's victory and wise rule of the Cape: he had been advised by the daredevil Sir Home Popham, who professed to have the ear of Lord Melville and Mr Pitt, of an attack on Spanish America. Baird sanctioned troops for this expedition. Buenos Aires was taken but the small British force was attacked by an overwhelming force and had to give up. The Whig government, which would have happily accepted profit in victory now berated Home Popham and Baird was recalled in disgrace.

At the Siege of Copenhagen, in 1807 under the supreme command of Lord Cathcart, the irrepressible Baird landed at Zealand with 18,000 British and Hanoverian troops. He surrounded Copenhagen which capitulated after heavy bombardment from land and sea. Sir David Baird had commanded a division whilst Sir Arthur Wellesley commanded a brigade. The capture of the Danish fleet foiled Napoleon's efforts to take it.

In October 1808 the great Glasgow born general, Sir John Moore, having tactically retreated with 29,000 men over 250 miles of snow-covered mountains was joined by Sir David Baird with 10,000 men at Corunna. The Spanish army had disintegrated and the British, heavily outnumbered, fought a successful rearguard action against Napoleon's 300,000 men. Moore's right wing was commanded by Sir David Baird and his left wing by Sir John Hope (commemorated by the Hopetoun Monument standing high in the Garleton Hills near Haddington). At the hour of victory Moore, who was at the centre of the battle, was killed. The victory cost Baird dearly; he was so severely injured that it was thought he would surely die but after the amputation of his left arm his sturdiness and determination pulled him through. Hope took over command and organised the successful embarkation of the British troops.

This was Sir David Baird's last battle. He received the thanks of Parliament for the fourth time and was created a baronet by George III. He retired from active service and was raised to the rank of General in 1814. He was appointed Governor of Kinsale in Ireland in 1819 and of Fort George in 1827. He returned home to Ferntower, near Crieff, the inheritance of his wife, and died there on 18th August 1829. Lady Baird commissioned the erection of a granite obelisk, 82 feet 4 inches in height on the summit of Tomashastile at a cost of £15,000 to his memory (83 p.86). The obelisk is inscribed on each side of its square plinth:

In honour and to the memory of
GENERAL SIR DAVID BAIRD Bart. GCB & KC
This column was erected
AD 1832
To the indomitable courage in the field he united wisdom and prudence in the Council.
A brave but generous enemy his victories were ever tempered by mercy and with his ardent love of glory was blended the tenderest care for his gallant and devoted followers.
The details of his public services are recorded in the annals of his country. His private virtues are embalmed in the hearts of his friends.
Honour and duty were the guiding stars of his destiny, piety and charity, the leading characteristics of his mind. He felt no jealousies. He harboured no resentments. He knew no guile in the land of his fathers.

He at last found repose and happiness in domestic life forgetting the cares and turmoils of his eventful and brilliant career and in the exercise of every social and Christian virtue.
He died beloved and lamented as he had lived honoured and renowned.

Seringapatam taken by
storm 4th May 1799

To commemorate the march
of the Anglo-Indian army
across the great desert
from Kossier to
Alexanxdria 1801

Cape of Good Hope
captured January 8th 180
Coruna January 16th 1809

ARTHUR JAMES BALFOUR
of Whittingehame

1st Earl Balfour - Prime Minister from 1902-06 - philosopher and statesman of distinction

---

Arthur James Balfour was the eldest son of an illustrious family: his sister, Eleanor, became Principal of Newnham College in 1892, his brother, Francis, was a brilliant researcher and could be regarded as the father of embryology and his youngest brother, Gerald, who became the 2nd Earl, was a Fellow of Trinity College Cambridge and a statesman of distinction.

Arthur Balfour was born to wealth. He was one of the fortunates to be able to see 'a great deal of life from afar' - to quote Ramsay MacDonald. He inherited his magnificent Whittingehame home in East Lothian in 1856 on the death of his father, James Maitland Balfour, who acquired the estate in 1817 when he built Whittingehame House (designed by Sir Robert Smirke and altered by his pupil William Burn ten years later). James Balfour rebuilt the Parish Church and established the new village of Whittingehame. His monument, an obelisk which stands on the hillside about 2 km west of the village, is a testimony to his popularity and is inscribed:

Erected to the Memory of
James Maitland Balfour Esq. of Whittingehame
Major Commandant of the East Lothian Cavalry
by the Officers, non commissioned Officers
and Privates of that Corps
In testimony of their great respect and esteem
for him as a commanding officer
of their affectionate regard for him
as an amiable and able country gentleman
and of their deep and lasting regret
for his premature removal from among them.
MDCCCLVIII

Arthur Balfour's inheritance was not simply property. His self discipline and his Covenanting self restraint he gained from his father and his courtesan aloofness from his mother. She was Lady Blanche, sister of Lord Robert Cecil. His mother's dedicated interest and powerful influence undoubtedly shaped the intellectual development of each of her children in philosophy and science. Arthur James Balfour was eight years old when his father died.

His political life spanned twenty-seven years in Cabinet which was longer even than Pitt (1759-1806) or Palmerston (1784-1865) or Gladstone (1809-98) before him, and Churchill (1874-1965) after him. Balfour was Prime Minister from 1902 to 1906.

His education followed the path of the ruling classes - Eton and Trinity College, Cambridge. School holidays were always spent at Whittingehame and during one summer vacation, that of 1860, he accompanied his mother to the Whittingehame Games. She presented the prizes and the twelve year-old Arthur 'returned thanks for his mother and himself in a most manly manner' - so reported *The Haddingtonshire Courier*. In 1869 he delivered a lecture in Haddington; his subject was Sir Walter Scott and he was accompanied musically by his sisters. He loved East Lothian which he considered to be "the paradise of golfers, and Whittingehame lies at its centre."

1st Earl Balfour by James Guthrie (Courtesy of the Scottish National Portrait Gallery)

Aged twenty-six he entered Parliament as Conservative Member for Hertford. His connections were impeccable and soon he was private secretary to his uncle, Lord Salisbury (Prime Minister in 1885). It was during this two-year period that his intellectual strength shone through in his publication: *Defence of Philosophic Doubt* (1879). This was a serious young man, above mere party politics, he was to bring intellect and philosophy into politics. He never married. His icy, self-assured exterior was unsuited to the opposite sex and yet on social occasions his company was always sought. Whittingehame was a centre of social prestige and superb hospitality; Balfour's coterie became known as the 'Souls'. In January 1880 he opened the newly-built Knox Institute (now Knox Court) in Haddington.

In 1885 he was elected MP for East Manchester and was given a rapid succession of appointments:

1885-6 President of the Local Government Board,
1886 Secretary for Scotland,
1887 Chief Secretary for Ireland,
1892-93 First Lord of the Treasury,
1892-1902 Leader in the Commons,
1902-06 Prime Minister,
1916-19 Foreign Secretary (under Lloyd George)

His preparation and attention to detail was that of an academic and he was equal to any as a philosopher. There was no question which could trap him. Whilst he was known to sleep late, sometimes until noon, and he rarely read newspapers - two matters for which he was mistakenly criticised - one for self indulgence and the other for being out of touch. Both were unfounded because he would often work on papers or a speech until dawn. His knowledge of his subject was unchallengeable. Churchill in his *Great Contemporaries* gave a superb description of his reaction to an outburst against him in the House of Commons. The Irish member lost his temper and during the debate, he roared and shook his fist, - 'but' as Churchill wrote, ' Arthur Balfour, Leader of the House, regarded the frantic figure with no more and no less than the interest of a biologist examining through a microscope the contortions of a rare and provoked insect' (62 p.240). The cause of the outburst against 'Bloody Balfour', as he was known, was his suppression of the riots and the prosecution of William O'Brien, the founder of 'United Ireland' who sat in Parliament as a Nationalist. He was prosecuted nine times and imprisoned for two years. But Ireland benefited from Balfour's extension of land purchase, the reduction of judicial rents, the creation of the Congested District Board and the provision of subsidies for fishermen and crofters.

Balfour as Prime Minister was pre-eminently intellectual and what he lacked in public appeal and conviction he more than compensated for by gathering around him the best brains in politics including his brother Gerald, Herbert Henry Asquith (1852-1928) who would become Premier in 1908 and the 1st Viscount Haldane, Richard Burdon (1856-1928) *q.v.*, a future Lord Chancellor (1912-15) and Minister of Labour (1924) who, like Balfour, would be awarded the Order of Merit (1915) and would give the Gifford Lectures at St Andrews (1902-04). Enormous credit is due to Balfour for his Education Act of 1902 which took the bold step of abolishing the School Boards, and replacing them with special *ad hoc* bodies with a single authority. County Education Committees could at last make secondary education, previously available only to the wealthy, within reach of all.

Balfour tackled the neglect and incompetence of the military from lessons learned in Boer War - in 1903 he appointed the powerful Esher Committee which abolished the office of commander-in-chief and set up an Army Council on similar lines to the Board of the Admiralty. Balfour appointed two strong First Lords of the Admiralty, Selbourne and Cawdor, who diverted the main force from the Mediterranean to the Atlantic and created Rosyth as a northern battle-base (1902). He created the Committee of Imperial Defence, a non-party council of experts chaired by the Prime Minister. In foreign policy he departed from Queen Victoria's preference for a German friendship by encouraging the *Entente Cordiale* with France in 1904 and he renewed the Anglo-Japanese agreement in 1905. However, the bitter feud in the party with Chamberlain's offensive and the growth of the Labour party, forced Balfour's resignation. He lost his seat in the January 1906 election but two months later he was elected MP for the City of London to become leader of the opposition. He resigned in 1911 because of the constitutional crisis over Lloyd George's 'war budget' - war against poverty. Balfour now delivered the Gifford Lectures on *Theism and Humanism* and in the same year, 1915, he, as Foreign Secretary, was responsible for the Balfour Declaration of 1917 promising the Zionists a homeland in Palestine.

After the war he was elected Chancellor of Cambridge University and in 1921, as Lord President of the Council, his cancellation of the Allied war debts to America was controversial. He was chairman of the Department of Scientific and Industrial Research and chairman of the Medical Research Council giving stimulation and inspiration to transform the Lord Presidency into a Ministry of Research. He resigned in 1922 and was created 1st Earl Balfour. In 1925 he served again as Lord President until 1929.

He was honoured by almost every university in the land but the honour he valued above all was that of the Order of Merit (1916). He was a man of huge intellect, a polymath whose quest for truth was in religion, philosophy, history, science, art and music.

East Lothian beckoned him home from a busy schedule many times. A favourite relaxation was golf at North Berwick where he partnered Edward VII and was tutored by the inimitable Ben Sayers *qv*. He unveiled the war memorials at Whittingehame and East Linton and during his last visit he opened the new school at Prestonpans which had been built from the red sandstone of Amisfield House. The East Lothian Antiquarian and Field Naturalists' Society elected him its first Honorary President, a title he was pleased to retain until his death on 19th March 1930.

His memorial plaque at Whittingehame Parish Church is inscribed:

To the Glory of God and in Remembrance of
ARTHUR JAMES
First Earl of Balfour KG OM
Who by his great gifts of heart and mind
both as a statesman and philosopher enriched
the realms of thought and advanced truth,
righteousness and peace in the world.
The Beloved Laird of Whittingehame.
A Loyal son of the Church of Scotland
born July 25 1848, died March 19 1930

FRANCIS MAITLAND BALFOUR of Whittingehame

The father of the science of embryology

The father of the science of embryology was a son of East Lothian - Francis Maitland Balfour. Could he have imagined in 1878 that this obscure branch of science would become the subject of sensational media speculation? The establishment of an 'Human Fertilisation and Embryonic Authority' to study the ethics of creating human embryos from immature eggs from foetuses would have been unimaginable to him. It was this chain of scientific discovery which was set in motion by this brilliant scientist from Whittingehame.

His two-volume magnum opus, *A Treatise on Comparative Embryology*, was the masterly authority of its day. It was published in 1880-1 and was received with great approbation by the highest academic opinion in the land. He was elected to the Fellowship of the Royal Society and awarded a 'Royal Medal' for his remarkable discoveries. This was a man whose observations were not only rapid but exact; he gave the lead to all future biologists.

Courtesy of Mr George Anderson, custodian of the Mansell Collection, London

Francis Balfour was born on 10th November 1851 while his parents were temporarily in residence in Edinburgh. He was the second son of James Maitland Balfour of Whittingehame who died when Francis was eight years old. His mother, Lady Blanche, daughter of the 2nd Marquis of Salisbury, gave enormous encouragement to the development of the intellectual strengths and aspirations of her sons and her daughter. The eldest of whom, Arthur James Balfour (1848-1930) *qv*, was the greatest intellect of his day in British politics. He was a philosopher and statesman and became Prime Minister in 1902-06, and a recipient of the Order of Merit to be created 1st Earl Balfour. The third son, Gerald (1853-1945), also a leading statesman, became President of the Board of Trade and of the Local Government Board, he succeeded his brother as 2nd Earl in 1930. The daughter, Eleanor (1845-1936), a distinguished academic, became Principal of Newnham College in 1892.

Their father, James Balfour, was the highly respected laird of Whittingehame who acquired the estate in 1817. He built 'a splendid mansion of Grecian architecture' (30 p.469), rebuilt the Parish Church and established the new village. Francis's boyhood was spent in this idyllic setting and his interest in nature was carefully nurtured and encouraged. His childhood collections of local fossils and birds were remarkable for his age. His early education at preparatory school in Hoddesdon in Hertfordshire preceded his entry to Harrow where he showed little promise in the day-to-day work but in geology and the natural sciences his attention to detail and sustained concentration made it obvious that this boy would make his mark. In his first year at Trinity College, Cambridge he became the natural science scholar of the college and was soon researching the development of the chick with almost obsessed enthusiasm. He decided that the study of animal morphology was best tackled from the study of embryology and his early work was published in the *Quarterly Journal of Microscopical Science* in July 1873. This was an auspicious start for a twenty-one year-old undergraduate.

Almost immediately after gaining his BA degree in December 1873, he set out for Naples. Dr Anton Dohrn had founded a new laboratory there and Balfour studied the embryonic history of sharks, rays and many other fish. His results produced new facts relating to kidney development, the origin of spinal nerves, initial changes in the ovum and the early stages of the embryo. He was soon appointed to a Chair at the University of Naples at the Statzione Zoologica. His work was recognised immediately at home with a fellowship of his old college; it was evident among research biologists that a new force had entered the international scene. Working between Cambridge and Italy he published a monograph in 1878. He was now a lecturer on animal morphology of the university and his students benefited from his enthusiasm and his original research. There is no greater gift to a student than to be taught by a gifted researcher especially one who can inculcate an anxiety to go beyond mere facts and explore the unknown. Such was Balfour's reputation and love of his subject, students attended his lectures in droves from all parts of the world.

Balfour now started his major work - a complete treatise on embryology. It contained the results of many of his investigations and of those of his students. It was a masterly work 'full of new light from beginning to end' (25 p.51). With the hallmark of a true master, he acknowledged and praised the work of the young morphologists thus giving encouragement to a new generation of researchers.

In 1878 he was elected a Fellow of the Royal Society, the highest academic accolade in the land and in 1881 he was awarded the 'Royal Medal' for his numerous discoveries. He was now in great demand: Oxford was anxious that he should succeed the late Professor George Rolleston (1829-81), the famous anatomist and physiologist and Edinburgh offered him their Chair of Natural History several times, but Balfour, loyal to his 'alma mater', remained at Cambridge to be given a personal Professorship of Animal Morphology in recognition of his valued work.

Professor Francis Balfour was now in his prime as a distinguished researcher. His future would undoubtedly produce even greater discoveries. Everything he did seemed to be possessed of masterly wisdom which was only a part of his character - as a friend he was generous, courteous and steadfast. He was a brilliant conversationalist - a moment in his company was uplifting, he won the hearts of all who were privileged to know him. He was awarded an honorary LL.D. of Glasgow, elected a Fellow of Trinity College, a Fellow of the Royal Society and President of the Cambridge Philosophical Society.

Suddenly, he was gone. He had visited Switzerland in the hope of building up his lost strength from an attack of typhoid fever. On 18th July 1882 he set out with his guide, Johann Petrus of Stalden, to climb the Aiguille Blanche de Peuteret near Martigny-Ville. They fell to their deaths on the 19th and were found on rocks a few days later by a climbing party. His body was brought back to Scotland to be buried at his beloved Whittingehame where his wonderful researches began as a boy. He was mourned by his family, his friends and by scientists world wide.

JOHN BELLANY CBE, RA of Port Seton

East Lothian's internationally acclaimed artist

This is a man of East Lothian who simply lives for art - he eats sleeps and dreams of colour and beauty. Some talk of life, some write of it, others take photographs, John Bellany paints it in all its enigmatic glory; he is an internationally acclaimed artist.

In 1988 he astounded the art world with a series of self portraits while recovering from a liver transplant at Addenbrookes Hospital in Cambridge. As soon as he got out of intensive care, in fact, as soon as he opened his eyes, he asked for paper and paint and was heard to explain that in order to check whether or not he was still alive he simply had to see colour on paper for himself - his compulsion to paint was almost a reflex action.

He was born in Port Seton of fisherman stock on 18th June 1942 at 18 Gosford Road; his father and two grandfathers were fishermen. His early boyhood during World War II was spent with his mother at Eyemouth while his father was on active service in the navy. It was about this time that he started drawing boats and instinctively he began to recognise them from not only their rigging but from the horizon line.

Courtesy of East Lothian Council Library Service

In 1947, having returned home to Port Seton, he attended Cockenzie Primary School on weekdays and Chalmers Memorial Church three times every Sunday. His first fishing trip, at the age of thirteen was aboard the *Bethel.* At that impressionable age everything was new; the wingspan of the floating seagulls seemed gigantic and suddenly in total contrast the boat seemed like a matchbox being tossed around in rough seas. These early experiences of a Scottish fishing port and hard

Presbyterian preaching produced a man of character of argument and of sensibility and pictures often puzzling and challengingly difficult to interpret with their wide ranging images and metaphors.

At Preston Lodge School he gained his 'highers' for entry to Edinburgh College of Art in 1960 - the first boy to do so from Port Seton. This was during the Principalship of another great East Lothian artist, Sir William Gillies CBE, RA *q.v.* At the college Bellany had the good fortune to study under Robin Philipson and the competence to win the Andrew Grant Scholarship which took him to Paris in 1962. But at Art College he was something of a rebel. The 'establishment' irked him to such an extent that he and fellow student Sandy Moffat decided one summer's day to mount their own outdoor exhibitions; they hung their paintings on the railings by the National Gallery at The Mound in Edinburgh in the full knowledge that all visitors to this august centre of art would have to pass by their exhibits.

Soon after his marriage to Helen Percy in 1964 he won a post-graduate travelling scholarship to Holland and Belgium. Not long after his return home to Scotland his first child was born; a son, Jonathon. It was about this time that he received his first large commission - a series of murals for Chesser House in Edinburgh for the Department of Agriculture and Fisheries.

In 1965 he gained another scholarship, the Burston Award, which enabled him to attend the Royal College of Art in London where he studied under Carel Weight and Peter de Francia. Two years later, in 1967, he was invited to take part in a cultural visit to East Germany with Alan Bold and Alexander Moffat. As well as visiting Dresden, Halle, Weimar and East Berlin he visited the Nazi concentration camp of Buchenwald. This experience of the Holocaust left a deep impression which manifested itself in his paintings which represented a dark side of Europe in comparison to the self-congratulatory flower power of the hippy '60s.

After the birth of his second son, Paul, in 1968 he was appointed to a lecturership in painting at the Brighton College of Art and in 1969 he was appointed to a lectureship in Fine Art at Winchester College of Art. He was now a family man and had to earn a steady living, fortunately he loved teaching and because of this his students were the benificiaries. His daughter Anya was born in 1970 and such was his reputation he was appointed Head of the Faculty of Painting at Croydon College of Art in 1973, a post he held for the next five years.During this time he was a visiting lecturer at the Royal College of Art in London and to add to his already heavy workload, he lectured at Goldsmiths' College from 1978 to 1984 and won the John Moore Prize in 1980. Without realising it he was working himself to death and possibly in order to maintain this agonising pace he sought help from drugs. Inevitably, his body rebelled and by 1988 his liver had given up; he was standing at the open door of death aged only forty-six.

He was fortunate to be living within the area where there was a hospital with vast experience and developed skill in the science of liver transplants - Addenbrookes at Cambridge. The operation was a success and as soon as he came out of the intensive care unit he asked for paper and paint. The result over his weeks of convalescence was not only a remarkable recovery but an astonishing series of self-portraits and portraits of the hospital staff and of his family which portrayed almost every aspect of his slow recovery - the frailty, the agony, the ecstasy, his gratitude and his verve for the future. Some forty of these paintings were exhibited at The Scottish National Gallery of Modern Art in Edinburgh as *John Bellany A Renaissance*. Such was the public interest, BBC 1 broadcast a 35-minute television programme made by broadcaster Joan Bakewell in her *The Heart of the Matter* programme on Easter Sunday of 1989. Overnight the name John Bellany was nationally known.

His one-man exhibitions through Arts Council touring shows in New York, Melbourne, Birmingham, Liverpool, Sydney, London and Amsterdam were among his successes. His retrospective exhibitions held in Edinburgh, London, Hamburg, Dortmund, New York, Berlin and Cambridge achieved even greater success and acclaim and in 1985 he won, jointly, the first prize of the Athena International Award. In 1987 he was honoured by the Royal Scottish Academy in his election as academician. In 1992 he was given a 50th birthday tribute by the Kelvingrove Museum and Art Gallery and one year afterwards he won the Korn/Ferry Picture of the Year award of the Royal Academy in London. In 1994 he was made a Commander of the British Empire (CBE) for his services to Modern Art. In 1998 Heriot-Watt University, Edinburgh honoured him with an honorary doctorate and he generously reciprocated with a gift of a self portrait to the university.

John Bellany has never forgotton his roots and he never tires of returning to Port Seton, to visit family and friends and to admire the view of River Forth across to Fife. Such is the affection for him in Port Seton, even the local day centre bears his name: the John Bellany Day Centre. His latest sojourn to the town of his birth took place in April 2000 to open a mini-retrospective exhibition at Port Seton Library from 28th April to 9th June in which a mass of paintings, photographs and memorabilia were loaned by John, members of his family and friends.

'BLACK AGNES', Countess of Dunbar and March

The heroine of the seige of Dunbar Castle

This was a true Scottish heroine, a lady of great charisma, a dark beauty whose brave confidence astounded her attackers, the English, into giving up their siege of Dunbar Castle in the year1337. She was Agnes Dunbar, the Countess of Dunbar and March who came to be known as "Black Agnes" not simply from her dark hair but from the defiance towards and the fear she instilled in her English attackers who besieged her in Dunbar Castle.

It was perhaps not surprising that she was so heroic in her defence of the castle when she successfully held off the baffled English invader - she was the eldest daughter of Sir Thomas Randolph and Isabel, daughter of Sir John Stewart of Bonkill. Sir Thomas was created the Earl of Moray by her great uncle, King Robert the Bruce - her ancestry was thus impeccable; deeds of daring and bravery were in her blood. She was two years old in 1314 when her father, with thirty men, scaled the castle rock of Edinburgh, just before the Battle of Bannockburn, and he successfully expelled the English intruder. He was one of King Robert's most loyal supporters. As a girl young Agnes was weaned on the brave deeds of heroism of her ancestors.

Dunbar had a fortalice in the 9th century. Holingshed's Scotland gives the derivation of the name:

> *...during the reign of Kenneth, King of Scotland, the strongest castle in the whole country, Kenneth bestowed upon that valiant captene, named 'Bar', whose counsel and forward service stood the Scots, in no small stead, in the English wars - that fortress ever after called by the name Dunbar, that is to say, the castle of 'Bar'.*

'Black Agnes', as she came to be called, married Patrick Dunbar, the 8th Earl of March or Dunbar, a cousin of King Robert and twenty-seven years her senior. This was his second marriage which took place in September 1320. But the Earl of Dunbar had given shelter in his castle of Dunbar to Edward II after the Battle of Bannockburn on 24th June 1314 and he ensured his safe return to England. However, soon afterwards, no doubt realising his mistake and that Bruce was a now a powerful force in Scotland, he wisely decided to support his cousin and became a member of the Scottish Parliament at Ayr on 27th April 1315 which settled the succession to the Scottish crown in favour of Robert the Bruce (60 p.52).

Agnes's father, the Earl of Moray and Guardian of Scotland, died suddenly in 1332 and his successor as Guardian, the 12th Earl of Mar, was weak. His army, commanded by Patrick Dunbar, was surprised and defeated by John Balliol at Dupplin. After the ignominy of a second defeat at the Battle of Halidon Hill in 1333 Patrick Dunbar had little option but to place himself under the protection of King Edward and he attended Edward Baliol at the Scottish Parliament in Edinburgh. He supported Agnes's father in the capture of Berwick and he signed the letter to the Pope asserting Scotland's independence. As Governor of Berwick Castle he defended it against English attack but he surrendered it to Edward III and joined the English for a second time. Had he failed to swear fealty to the English king he would have been put to death. However, this allegiance was short-lived he deserted the English side and fought a few skirmishes against them. At the end of 1334 Dunbar renounced his allegiance to Edward III and from henceforward he remained a strong supporter of the cause for the maintenance of Scotland's independence.

It was during her husband's second defection from the English side that Black Agnes found herself alone and in charge of the castle, the Earl having left to fight the English invaders of Scotland. Dunbar Castle was an important fortress which stood guard over a valuable port - Dunbar, and so far the English had been frustrated in every attempt to capture it. In the freezing cold of January 1337 the English, led by William (de Montagu) the Earl of Salisbury and Arundel, laid siege to the castle. Now 'Black Agnes' showed her true spirit: the besiegers advanced towards the castle walls under cover of a huge wheeled shelter which was called *the Sow* (a testudo not unlike that used by the Romans) and the Countess scorned them shouting:

"Beware Montagow, for farrow shall thy sow"

She then ordered that a huge rock be rolled down on them crushing their 'Sow' and scattering the attackers 'like a litter of pigs' (11 vol IV, p. 505). Not only did she direct the defence but she taunted the attackers by walking along the high battlements of the castle to jeer the enemy. After another particularly vicious assault she, with her beautifully dressed maids, calmly walked outside the castle to clean off the marks on the walls made by the stone and lead balls of English cannons. The attackers were not only puzzled but astonished. They imagined that she must have reinforcements. There must be some hidden army. However, disaster almost befell her when one of her porters was bribed to leave open a gate. Fortunately, this was discovered in time and again her attackers were repelled. There is no record of what happened to the porter.

The English now changed tactics. The castle seemed impregnable and they decided to block the harbour entrance in an attempt to starve out the occupants. Sir Alexander Ramsay of Dalhousie Castle had heard of Black Agnes's brave stand and, knowing that she had slender resources, he came to her rescue with forty men from the Bass Rock. His surprise attack upon the unsuspecting English brought much needed supplies to the castle, but the siege continued for another four months when the English at last gave up and returned home. Agnes and her maids were overjoyed, they had saved the great castle for her husband and for Scotland.

Black Agnes's two brothers, Thomas and John, were killed in battle, one at Dupplin in 1332 and the other at Durham in 1346. She, therefore, became heir to her father's Earldom of Moray with extensive lands including the Isle of Man, the lordship of Annandale and several baronies.

In 1368 Agnes's husband, aged eighty three, decided to resign his earldom to the Crown who granted it to his great-nephew George Dunbar and his heirs. The beautiful daughter of the old Earl, Countess Agnes, also Agnes, had caught the eye of David II and became his mistress which led to his divorce. She married Sir James Douglas of Dalkeith and their daughter, Elizabeth, married Sir John Maitland of Lethington. It was from her that John Maitland, the Duke of Lauderdale (1616-82) *qv*, was descended.

The heroic lady, 'Black Agnes', the Countess of Dunbar, aged fifty-seven, died shortly after the death of her husband, the Earl of Dunbar, now Sir Patrick, in 1368.

Two hundred and thirty years after the siege of Dunbar Castle, the castle was almost completely destroyed in the year 1567 on the orders of the Scottish Parliament following the abdication of Mary Queen of Scots.

CATHERINE BLAIR
of Hoprig Mains Farm, Gladsmuir

The suffragette who used the pen rather than the sword

In 1847, Sir James Young Simpson discovered the use of chloroform as an anaesthetic for women in childbirth and some frosty old ministers of the Church of Scotland were heard to say: "It will take away the curse from women." On learning of that reaction some forty years later Catherine Blair of Hoprig Mains Farm at Gladsmuir knew that she had to do something to help the plight of women.

In today's world it seems incredible that any male, far less a minister of the Scottish Kirk could express such a view. This was enough for Catherine Blair. From that moment she became a staunch supporter of the Suffragette Movement. She was not one of those who chained themselves to railings or had herself imprisoned; her contribution was through her pen as an instrument "mightier than the sword." She showered letters upon the Scottish Press in support of the Women's Social and Political Union; her press cuttings book contains over 600 letters.

She expressed often that which she perceived to be her own insufficiency in comparison to those who suffered scorn, imprisonment and sometimes torture, but she was assured that her pen and her provision of a safe haven of respite at Hoprig Mains for those women who had suffered imprisonment was of inestimable value to the cause of women. Many a sufferer of the penal system of the day convalesced and received the kindly care of Mrs Blair.

This courageous, highly articulate lady, with the determined and loving support of her farmer husband, was to become the founder of the Women's Rural Institute in Scotland. But it was her father, James Shields, to whom she owed her sense of fair play, democracy and equality for women. He had brought her up on a diet of Tom Paine's* *Rights of Man* and the *Freewill of Man against the Doctrine of Predestination.*

*Thomas Paine (1737-1809) political radical, author of many revolutionary pamphlets, supporter of the French and American Revolutions. He was outlawed and tried for treason *in absentia* and for some seditious sentences in his *Rights of Man* and his *Age of Reason* he was denounced as an atheist. He was made an honorary citizen of France in 1792. He died in poverty in America.

A little card found amongst her press cuttings, written in her own hand and composed by Robert Burns expresses a little of her motivation:

While quacks of State must each produce his plan,
And even children lisp 'The Rights of Man',
Amid this mighty fuss, just let me mention,
The Rights of Woman merit some attention.

James Shields was the supporter, the defender and the champion of tenant farmers. He was an exemplary employer who took pride in the long service of his workers, eight of whom were to be proud to carry his coffin to his last resting place in East Lothian. His death was a dreadful loss to his admiring and loving family.

Catherine Shields was the eldest daughter of Susan and James Shields. The third of six children, she was born on 8th January 1872 at Byres Farm in Bathgate. With her two older brothers, two younger sisters and her younger brother her childhood was idyllic. Catherine was five years old when her mother died having given birth to her sixth child in 1877 at the age of thirty-four. For the sensitive five year-old this was a devastating loss but her aunt Elisabeth, her mother's sister, took over the family and performed the miracle of giving love and happiness and stability to this large family. She loved her nephews and nieces all the more for their loss. As the years rolled on the hard-working, good-living James Shields discovered that his gratitude and admiration for his sister-in-law had turned to love. The law of the land would not permit them to marry. Young Catherine was eighteen years old when her father and her aunt decided to bypass Scottish law; they travelled to Norway to be married. The family were delighted and young Catherine had had her first lesson in the fallibility of man-made laws.

At school, Bathgate Academy, she was a bright pupil which was not surprising - both father and step-mother inculcated in the young minds of the children the importance of learning and of education in the old Scottish tradition.

As a farmer's daughter she considered that she had the best life possible but she was acutely aware that the life of a farmer's wife was one of very hard work and many cares. She resolved never to marry a farmer but this resolve melted when she met Thomas Blair, a farmer eleven years her senior. They married in July 1894 at Tranent and set up home at Hoprig Mains farm in Gladsmuir as tenant farmers of Lord and Lady Lamington, 'the most appreciative of lairds.' They had four children: Thomas born in June 1895, Bertram in February 1897, Jean Chisholm in November 1900 and James Sheilds in April 1906. Despite her busy life, that of the farmer's wife she had promised to avoid, she revelled in it.

She read avidly the reports of the struggles and privations of the Suffragettes. By 1903 Emily Pankhusrt and her daughters were leading the cause for women and Catherine Blair longed to be part of the struggle. She became a prominent figure in the Women's Social and Political Union (WSPU), she wrote letters and articles by the score and welcomed Suffragettes on their release from prison where they had suffered the humiliations of force-feeding and sometimes torture. She recalled with glee the press reports of the escape of a Suffragette to France who was sunning herself on a hammock in the garden of Hoprig Mains.

Her concern for the women of the community grew from her work for the Suffragette movement; she organised meetings for the exchange of ideas, for learning new crafts and for the improvement of the quality of life for women. In December 1916 she addressed the Glasgow and West of Scotland Discussion Society and strongly advocated the formation of Women's Institutes particularly with reference to the untapped abilities of women in "The Farm House in relation to Food Supply and Labour". Her later report to the Board of Agriculture was received with approbation by the Council and Sir Robert Wright, the Board's Chairman, then presided over a meeting in Edinburgh which was organised by Mrs Blair. It was agreed to establish women's rural institutes in Scotland as already existed in Canada and Belgium.

From this beginning the Scottish Women's Rural Institute was born. Catherine Blair could not wait for the slow grind of officialdom; she arranged the first meeting of the first branch in the schoolroom at Macmerry in June 1917 but an outbreak of measles meant that this inaugural meeting was held in Longniddry on 26th June 1917. Mrs Catherine Blair had founded the first branch in Scotland. Two years later she founded the *Mak'Merry Pottery Studio* in her garden shed and guided through to fruition the *Hame Arts Guild* in 1921; its members producing home made arts and crafts and pottery painting which were sold at exhibitions, fairs and Highland shows.

The aims and achievements of the Institute became known throughout Scotland and by 1931 there were almost 850 Institutes with 42,000 members. By its twenty-first birthday party, in 1938, membership had reached 55,000. Mrs Blair was presented with the Institute badge in gold and given the honour of cutting the largest of the four birthday cakes. To great applause she encouraged her audience to "plan for more than you can do, then do it."

Her husband, Thomas Blair, had died in 1936 after fifty-two years of farming at Hoprig and thirty-eight years as a member of the East Lothian County Council. Four years before his death Catherine and he gave up their tenancy at Hoprig Mains and moved to North Berwick. From this new base Catherine continued energetically to foster the aims and objectives of the WRI movement, intensifying her interests in the study and development of arts and crafts. In 1940 she published her book, outlining the history, the work and the achievements of the Institute, *Bread and Roses*. Copies of it were accepted by Her Majesty the Queen and Queen Mary. At the next celebration, the Institute's 25th anniversary in 1942, she was presented to the Queen at Gosford House, the home of the 12th Earl of Wemyss who had graciously hosted the occasion.

Catherine Blair died at her home, Glen House, North Berwick, on Monday 18th November 1946. She was mourned by her two sons and two daughters as well as by the whole of Scotland's Womens' Rural Institute.

EARLS OF BOTHWELL

The family name of the Earls of Bothwell is Hepburn descended from Northumbrian nobility. One of their knights, Adam de Hepburne, was captured in East Lothian in 1271 by Lord Dunbar, the Earl of March. Soon afterwards Hepburn saved Lord Dunbar's life by diverting the charge of a wild horse which would have killed him. For this act of bravery he was given the privilege of becoming a vassal to Dunbar and given charge of Hailes Castle which included the lands of 'Merkill' nearby.

By the early 1400s the Hepburns became powerful Lothian lairds and owned extensive lands and property in East Lothian including Markle Castle north of East Linton, Hailes Castle south west of East Linton, Waughton Castle, a town house in Haddington, St Martins and Nunraw Tower. (E.L. Life Issue 22 p.28).

Markle Castle, of which little remains, was built by the Hepburns during the latter part of the 14th century. Hailes Castle was probably built by Hugo de Gourlay (or Graydon) of Northumberland towards the end of the 13th century but the lands of Edward de Gourlay were forfeited by Robert the Bruce for his support of the English during the War of Independence against Edwards I, II and III and the barony passed to Sir Adam de Hepburn of Northumberland.

Markle, Hailes and Traprain were on the English invasion route and were looted and burned with monotonous regularity. In 1402 young Patrick Hepburn, son of Hepburn of Hailes and Markle, was taken prisoner and executed after the Battle of Nisbet which was led by George Dunbar and the fiery tempered 'Hotspur' Percy.

In 1434 Adam Hepburn of Hailes and William Douglas of Tantallon took Dunbar Castle, the Dunbars fleeing to England but returning with reinforcements to be beaten back by Hepburn and Douglas at the Battle of Piperdean near Cockburnspath. Eight years later in 1443 Archibald Dunbar took his revenge when he stormed Hailes Castle and burned out the occupants (E.L. Life issue 22 p.29). [Markle Castle was finally razed to the ground in 1544 at the start of the 'Rough Wooing' which was the result of breaking the marriage treaty between the infant Mary Queen of Scots and Prince Edward, the son of Henry VIII.]

The Hepburns were therefore the Lords of Hailes and **Patrick Hepburn, the 3rd Lord Hailes** became My *Lord* Provost of Edinburgh on 8th August 1483. He was the first to have the title Lord Provost probably because he had inherited his lordship that year. He was the eldest son of Adam, 2nd Lord Hailes and Helen, eldest daughter of the

1st Lord Home. He was knighted in 1480 and was appointed Governor of Berwick Castle in 1482. James III, a weak king, considered himself an absolute ruler and many of the nobles of Scotland including Hepburn vehemently opposed absolutism* and in 1488 at Sauchieburn the army of the nobles led by the king's son met that of the king who was killed. The fifteen -year old James IV rewarded Hepburn with the forfieted lands of Bothwell and created him **1st Earl of Bothwell** on 17th October 1488 (11 p.237-8). In addition his grateful monarch gave him many titles and offices including Keeper of Edinburgh Castle, Master of the Household, High Admiral of Scotland and several others. He married Janet a daughter of the 1st Earl of Morton and after her death in 1490 he married Margaret, daughter of the Earl of Huntly. The 1st Earl of Bothwell died in 1508.

The **2nd Earl** was Adam Hepburn the son and heir of the 1st Earl and his second wife. He was born c1492 and succeeded to his father's large estates and titles on 7th November 1508. At the Battle of Flodden, a daring young officer aged twenty-one, he almost captured the English Standard but he was among the nine earls and 10,000 Scots who succumbed to the English halberds with their king, James IV, on 9th September 1513 after which all Scotland mourned.

Hailes Castle where Mary Queen of Scots stayed on 5th May 1567 on her journey to Edinburgh with the 4th Earl of Bothwell

The **3rd Earl**, Patrick Hepburn, was born c1511 and was barely two years old when he succeeded to the Earldom. He fled to England in 1531 having plotted against James V. On his return to Scotland he was imprisoned in Edinburgh Castle and lost his Lordship of Liddesdale in 1538 but he recovered it in 1543 after the death of the king. In his desperation to marry Mary of Guise, the Queen Regent he divorced his wife, Agnes Sinclair. Lady Agnes was given the lands of Morham in compensation and she took up residence with her children at the castle at Mainshill as the Lady of Morham. At the parliament of 1543 he opposed the marriage treaty between the infant Mary Queen of Scots and the son of Henry

*(*absolutism - government without restriction, accountable to none except God, a term used by historians after the French Revolution 1789)*

VIII, Prince Edward. However, having failed in his marriage bid and having lost much of his fortune, he supported the English side against James Hamilton, 2nd Earl of Arran, who was governor of Scotland, and was imprisoned in 1545. In 1547 Bothwell was forced to surrender Hailes Castle to the Scottish government. On 3rd September 1549 Edward VI proclaimed Bothwell to be 'under our protection'. He died in Dumfries in 1556.

James Hepburn, 4th Earl of Bothwell (Courtesy the Scottish National Portrait Gallery)

The **4th Earl** of Bothwell, James Hepburn, was born c1535 and succeeded his father on 3rd November 1556 as 4th Earl and Lord High Admiral of Scotland. He inherited in addition the titles of Lord of Hailes, Crichton and Liddesdale, the Sheriffdom of Berwickshire, East and Mid Lothian and Baillie of Lauderdale. As keeper of Dunbar Castle from 1565 his position in East Lothian was strong. He was a 'glorious, rash and hazardous young man' (11 p.239), the most prominent troublemaker of the Hepburns in the history of Scotland as the third husband of Mary Queen of Scots. He was one of several nobles accused of the murder of her second husband, Lord Darnley. In Bothwell's rigged trial in his absence on 12th April 1567 he was found guiltless. He abducted Mary Queen of Scots twelve days later at the Bridges of Almond and took her to Dunbar Castle.

She seems to have been a willing victim. They travelled to Edinburgh via Hailes Castle and married at the Palace of Holyroodhouse in a Protestant ceremony. This was insisted upon by Adam Bothwell, the Bishop of Orkney who conducted the service, Bothwell having obtained a hasty divorce from his young wife. In June of 1567 the Confederate Lords confronted the Royal pair at Carberry. Bothwell promptly exiled himself in Denmark where he died insane in prison in 1578. Mary was taken through jeering mobs to Edinburgh and forced to abdicate in her island prison on Loch Leven.

The **5th Earl of Bothwell**, Francis Stewart, the Commendator of Kelso, was born 1563. He was the son and heir of John Stewart Prior of Coldingham who was an illegitimate son of James V by Jean Hepburn a daughter of the 4th Earl of Bothwell. Because of this royal descent he was created 5th Earl of Bothwell and Lord Hailes on 16th June 1581.

Francis Stewart was appointed Lord Admiral of Scotland in 1583 and Commissioner to negotiate with the English for joint government in 1589. He was a kinsman of the 'Bonnie Earl of Moray' who was murdered in February 1592 by the Earl of Huntly and his men at his House of Donibristle in Fife.

King James VI, found it impossible to maintain peace between the nobles many of whom were still Catholics. Bothwell, a Protestant, was arrested with a coven of witches on a charge of witchcraft at North Berwick on 2nd June 1591 in creating a storm at sea in an alleged attempt to drown the king on his voyage to Norway for his marriage to Anne of Denmark. James VI blamed 96 witches (51 p. 741) whose defence claimed that Francis Stewart, 5th Earl of Bothwell had appeared to them from the pulpit of the Parish church and had instructed them to kill the king.

Bothwell escaped three weeks later and he made James's Government look foolish in its repeated attempts to capture him. On 27th December Bothwell almost succeeded in his attempt to kidnap the king at Holyrood. For this he was finally attainted losing his titles and honours. His final attempt to seize the king took place at Falkland Palace on 12th July 1592 but again he failed and he fled to England then to France, Spain and Italy. In Naples he lived in near poverty and eked out a living by giving horoscopes and performing magic. He died in Naples in 1612.

This ended the Earldom of Bothwell the 5th Earl's sons being excluded from their inheritance because of the attainder of their father.

JOHN BROADWOOD

the celebrated piano-maker of Cockburnspath

The bell-tower of Oldhamstocks Church is the commemoration of a famous piano-maker, John Broadwood. His two sons James and Thomas decided, near the end of their lives, to meet the cost of rebuilding this bell-tower in 1851 in memory of their famous father.

Oldhamstocks Parish Church Bell Tower gifted by James and Thomas Broadwood in 1851.

They had inherited the highly successful piano-making company which their father had built up in London. From the equally important legacy of thorough training by their father they had, in their own right, developed their inheritance into a world-renowned and successful business.

Cockburnspath was the birthplace of John Broadwood, but his father and grandfather were born in Oldhamstocks. John became an internationally renowned piano-maker having developed the 'English action'. His company supplied pianos to Clementi, Haydn, Beethoven, Chopin, Mendelssohn, Elgar, the Royal family and to customers world wide.

His ancestors were Northumbrian and in the 16th century they owned land near Hexham. The Broadwood family moved to Scotland during the 18th century when grandfather John Broadwood married Katherine Boan, a distant relative of the great Haddington-born Reformer John Knox. Their youngest son, James, married Margaret Pewes and their eldest of three sons, John, was born on 6th October 1732 and became the famous piano maker in London.

He was baptised at St Helen's Church at Cockburnspath and he attended the parish school where he received a sound grounding in the 'three Rs', reading writing and arithmetic, with an elementary study of Latin. Knowledge of the catechism was examined by the church elders.

He proved his dexterity and skill under the tutelage of his father becoming an apprentice wright or cabinet-maker.

Times were hard in East Lothian; there were few new contracts and insufficient work for the three sons in their father's workshop at Oldhamstocks. The Brodie* family in Edinburgh seemed to have a monopoly on all cabinet-making and locksmith work and the twenty-nine year-old John Broadwood decided to find work in London.

In 1761 he set off for London on foot with half-a-crown in his pocket. He may have walked part of journey but it is unlikely that he walked the whole way. His family in Cockburnspath were fairly well to-do and his arrival in London with a letter of introduction from Sir John Hall, 3rd Baronet of Dunglass and Magdalen, to a Swiss harpsichord maker, Burkhardt Tschudi, was undoubtedly planned ahead.

The Hall family took a special interest in John Broadwood who never forgot the laird's kindness. He gave a gold snuff box to John Broadwood in 1801 who, in 1802, presented a magnificent grand piano (No.2231) to Lady Helen Hall, wife of Sir James Hall with the Hall crest and the initials 'HH' on the nameboard (65 p.15).

John Broadwood started his apprenticeship with Burkat Shudi (he abbreviated his name) in Great Pulteney Street in September 1761. Shudi was a friend of Handel and his clientele in 1740 included not only the aristocracy but Frederick, the Prince of Wales, and, with another harpsichord maker, Jacob Kirkman, he shared the London harpsichord trade.

John was given fairly simple tasks at first such as rough joinery work and the gluing of baseboards together. He shared his attic room with another Scot, Andrew Clark, also from East Lothian. Within three years John Broadwood had become one of Shudi's most trusted craftsmen and worked on the most prestigious harpsichords. In fact, the nine year-old prodigy Wolfgang Amadeus Mozart played on one of his instruments before its export to Potsdam to Frederick the Great.

John Broadwood now equalled the skill of his master and by 1767 he had become part of the Shudi family. Shudi was pleased to observe Broadwood's growing fondness for his twenty year-old daughter Barbara. The couple married on 2nd January 1769 and from then the new harpschords were inscribed *Burkat Shudi et Johannes Broadwood*. He became a partner in the firm, now called *Tschudi and Broadwood*.

For several years before his marriage John Broadwood had become interested in the work of one of his fellow craftsmen, Johannes Zumpe, who had achieved considerable success with sales of his 'square pianos' the first of which appeared in England in 1768 from Germany (65 p.41).

* *Francis Brodie, Deacon of Wrights, Lawnmarket, Edinburgh father of Deacon William Brodie, a respectable member of the Edinburgh bourgeoisie by day and an infamous reprobate robber by night; he was hanged in 1788.*

From about this time Broadwood with his apprentice, Robert Stodart, assisted a piano maker called Americus Backers in the evenings in the development of the 'English Grand Action' in his Jermyn Street workshop. Stodart was a private in the Royal Horse Guards (having paid £100 for the privilege of admission to the ranks of the corps) and he had embarked upon a three-year apprenticeship under the tutelage of Broadwood. The three men perfected their new piano action. Stodart eventually patented the action and was the first to use the word 'grand' in describing a piano.

On 7th March 1771 Shudi, with complete confidence that his son-in-law was entirely capable of running his business, signed over the legal indentures of the business to him. In addition he leased the premises of Great Pulteney Street and Bridle Lane at £50 per year to him but he reserved for himself some royalties from the sales of harpsichords.

By now John Broadwood was running four businesses - making harpsichords for markets at home and abroad, hiring harpsichords, tuning harpsichords and selling a variety of other instruments. As he prospered he and his young wife and daughter moved house from Great Pulteney Street to Charlotte Street off Tottenham Court Road.

Shudi died on 19th August 1773 and John Broadwood inherited the rights of Shudi's patented 'Venetian swell'. Broadwood started to make harpsichords for stock rather than to order but he insisted on making the whole instrument himself. He supplied parts and allowed other makers to use Shudi's Venetian swell. His reputation was now internationally renowned and orders arrived from Denmark, France, Italy, Portugal, Russia, the West Indies and his agents in America.

On 8th July 1776 his beloved wife Barbara died giving birth to their fourth child, a son who was named John after his father. She was twenty-seven years old and John Broadwood was left to bring up three young children: Catherine aged five, James aged three and the baby John (a baby daughter had died in childbirth some years before). John Broadwood was heart-broken. The challenge of business and his inventiveness diminished. He could not bring himself to do any work for a week after his bereavement and during the second week he went for long treks into the countryside ostensibly to tune the harpschords of distant customers. For the next five years he produced no new innovations in the development of the piano and he was content to leave the marketing of grand piano to his friend and previous employee Robert Stodart.

In 1871 he met Mary Kitson who seemed to bring him to life again and a few days before Christmas they were married; they had six children between 1782 and 1793. Broadwood now concentrated on the development of the square piano which he remodelled and added a second sound board in 1780. He patented these improvements on 17th July 1783 describing it as *a new constructed pianoforte, which is superior to any instrument of the kind heretofore constructed.* It ranked him among the great German masters of piano-making who had emigrated to London some years before. The piano now overtook the harpsichord, although Broadwood's production of the latter was almost double that of Shudi in his best year. As the demand for pianos grew he employed more craftsmen (preferably skilled Scots) and his son James who had been in France to learn the language was happy to join the firm as ordering clerk to deal with the new demand.

John Broadwood was a deeply religious man and every Sunday it seemed that not only his family but the families of his Scottish craftsmen had to accompany him to the Scottish Chapel in Wells Street.

The firm of Shudi & Broadwood was so inundated with orders that space was urgently required and in 1787 an additional workshop was built on the roof of Great Pulteney Street and twenty-one year leases were taken on two houses at Nos. 14 and 15 Kensington Gore for a total of £35 per year. John Broadwood and his family moved into the larger house at No. 14 with its view over the park to Kensington Palace (in 1851 the whole row of houses was demolished to make way for the Centre of Arts and Sciences, the site of no.14 being used for the Royal College of Art).

Having concentrated on the square piano Broadwood now turned his complete attention to the grand piano. He consulted two scientists, Tiberius Cavallo FRS, an expert in acoustics, and Dr Edward Whitaker Gray of the British Museum. They discovered that a striking point at about one ninth of the vibrating length of a piano string gave the best tone and John Broadwood made this possible by introducing a separate bass bridge. From that day all pianos adopted this improvement and sales increased yet again.

At the start of the French Revolution in 1789 refugees from France flocked to England bringing many highly skilled craftsmen and with them the pianist Jan Ladislav Duseck, a favourite of Marie Antoinette. He suggested to Broadwood he should add a further half-octave to the conventional five. The piano purchased by Duseck was lent to Franz Joseph Haydn (1732-1809), the most famous composer of his day and teacher of Beethoven. On his first visit to London in 1791, Haydn lodged at Shudi & Broadwood's pianoforte shop in Great Pulteney Street with his impresario and he used a room there for composing.

The Royal family were regular customers and orders for grand pianos exceeded supply. Business expanded and by 1794 over 500 grands and 1000 squares had been sold during the previous decade. James Shudi Broadwood had revised the firm's recording procedures and had devised new accounting methods. He had become an indispensable and valuable member of the firm and in 1795 he was given a half share of the business which was renamed Broadwood & Son.

Ownership of a Broadwood square piano became a social necessity of the new middle classes and orders at home and abroad increased and, in spite of fears of French invasion (the French Republic had declared war on Britain in 1793), Broadwood became very rich indeed. He entered the banking business making loans and mortgages on property and investing in other businesses. He bought a country estate of 534 acres and Reeves Hall in Essex (65 p.95). His family had increased, his second wife having had seven children.

In 1808 John Broadwood's eldest surviving grandson Thomas, now twenty-three years old, was company accountant and his father, James, gave him a quarter share in the business retaining a quarter for himself. The company was now John Broadwood & Sons. Old John paid himself £5000 per annum, whilst his son James received about £3500; a craftsman at that time earned £100 per year.

John Broadwood the man had that rare mixture of friendliness, charm and culture with the capacity for exceedingly hard work, inventiveness and sound business acumen. He decided to retire on 4th April 1811 and gave his quarter share of the business to his son Thomas so that his two sons now had an equal share. He had the enormous satisfaction of having transformed the business from a modest harpsichord maker to become the world's leading piano-making company employing one hundred craftsmen from the original three.

He died aged 80 years on 17th July 1812 at Great Pulteney Street where he suffered a stroke while dining with his son Thomas. He was buried beside his first wife Barbara and their two children who had died in infancy in the cemetery of the Methodist Chapel in Tottenham Court Road, London (it was destroyed by the last bomb which fell on London during the 1939-45 war). Excluding the business he left £106,364 plus £20,000 owed to him, a considerable fortune for one who left East Lothian to look for work in London fifty-one years before with half-a-crown in his pocket.

His grandson, Henry Fowler Broadwood, (1811-93) followed in his grandfather's footsteps becoming a great improver of the piano.

Almost 240 years have passed since John Broadwood set out from East Lothian to become a piano maker and today the firm of John Broadwood & Sons Limited still thrives in London.

THE REV JOHN BROWN DD
of Haddington

"That old man speaks as if Christ stood at his elbow" - David Hume

There is a tiny Court tucked away at the south side of Market Street in Haddington. It is called **John Brown Court** where the manse of the Old Burgher Church (now converted into flats) on the site of which was the old church in which the Reverend John Brown preached for almost forty years.

It was here that he wrote his famous "Self-Interpreting Bible". There are still a few households in Haddington which treasure this Bible - a mammoth piece of dedicated work which was written especially for family reading on the Sabbath Day - a custom long since neglected, forgotten and replaced by activities unheard of in the 1700s. The present building, the Burgher Church as it was called, was built in 1806, almost twenty years after the death of John Brown; it replaced his old meeting house and has been tastefully converted into sheltered housing. The plaque on the manse wall nearby reminds visitors and Haddingtonians alike of this dedicated, tolerant and talented minister.

The story of John Brown is one of a 'lad o' pairts', so greatly admired in Scotland. John Brown was a humble herd boy in the Parish of Abernethy where he attended the local school for a mere two years in the first half of the eighteenth century. He was born in the small village of Carpow in 1722 and his father, a poor weaver, insisted that his son be sent to school - he learned the basics of reading, writing and arithmetic. After his meagre schooling he became a shepherd boy. There was no thought that the boy should enter the ministry, not for the want of Christian sincerity but from the economic impossibility of such an apparently unattainable ambition. However, young John Brown, unknown to his father, studied Latin, philosophy and divinity under the supervision of the local minister, the Rev. Ebeneezer Erskine.

During his long treks in the hills he put his mind to the further study of Latin and Greek always returning to the minister for help with a difficult passage. Such studies by a country lad were so unusual as to arouse the suspicions of the superstitious local community who remembered the days of witch burning and devil worship. John Brown's learning and sparkling intelligence frightened them and, as was so often the case, their fear turned into threats of violence. His exceptional learning was attributed to Satan and he was forced to undergo an inquisition. It is a remarkable coincidence that many years later, his malicious inquisitor was excommunicated on the day that John Brown was licensed to preach the Gospel (1). John Brown had to clear out; there was no sense in alienating the villagers because of something they did not understand. He became a wandering packman.

He had been orphaned by the age of eleven years, but to quote his eighth son, Samuel Brown: "he used to aver in his hyperbolic way that he never missed his parents, for when his father and mother had forsaken him the Lord had taken him up." (2)

In 1745, the year of the Jacobite Rebellion, we find him in Edinburgh during the month of Bonnie Prince Charlie's occupation of Edinburgh, and John Brown, disgusted by the barbarity of the Jacobite Highlanders and fearing a return to Catholicism, joined the garrison forces in Edinburgh Castle.

Soon after Culloden he returned to his wanderings as a packman, but he was not content; the acquisition of wealth held no interest for him. He became a teacher and started his own school in 1747 near Kinross. Its success was due not only to his sincerity but to the fact that being self-taught he, more than most, understood the learning difficulties of his pupils; eight of them entered the ministry. His own studies were remarkable: in one evening after school he memorised fifteen chapters of the book of Genesis. He rarely required more than four hours sleep and his work schedule was prodigious. In addition to his studies of Latin, Greek and Hebrew he learned several oriental languages and during school vacations he attended classes in philosophy and divinity under the Rev. Ebenezzer Erskine and James Fisher. He easily satisfied the Presbytery of Edinburgh and gained his licence to preach the Gospel.

In 1751, on completion of his probationary period, he was offered two calls - one from Haddington and the other from Stow. He chose the Burgher Church of Haddington partly because this congregation had already received several disappointments but also because this congregation was the smallest and would allow him more time to continue his studies. He remained there for the rest of his life but in compensation for Stow's disappointment he preached there for several Sundays until a new minister arrived.

The 'Breach' of 1747 had brought about the 'Burghers' and 'Anti-Burghers'. The latter considered it unlawful to take the Burgess' oath swearing allegiance to King George and renouncing the 'Old Pretender'. The Anti-Burghers however, were more concerned that by swearing the oath they would be committing themselves to acceptance 'to their life's end' of a 'mutilated form, a corrupted shadow' of the reformed religion (1). As far as the lawfulness or otherwise of the oath was concerned John Brown had his doubts; he believed that the dispute merely split the Church unnecessarily and he preached forbearance but he remained with the Burgher Synod.

When John Brown arrived in Haddington to take up his new charge one member of the congregation expressed his opposition. John Martine in his *Reminiscences* relates the conversation (4):

"Why do you think of leaving us?" mildly inquired Mr Brown.

"Because I don't think you a good preacher," said the sturdy oppositionist.

"That is quite my own opinion," admitted the minister, "but the great majority of the congregation think the reverse, and it would not do for you and me to set up our opinions against theirs. I have given in, you see, and I would suggest you might do so too."

"Weel, weel," said the grumbler, quite reconciled by Mr Brown's frank confession, "I think I'll just follow your example, sir."'

John Brown was Professor of Divinity to the Associate Burgher Synod for over twenty-five years. This was a labour of love. In this unpaid post he taught students in a five-year course of study for entry to the ministry of the Secession and during his ministry he took four services each Sunday. He regularly visited members of his poor congregation and still found time to write his famous Self-Interpreting Bible, the two volumes of which were published in 1778 for family worship after church. A copy of his Bible is displayed on his original pulpit in St Mary's Parish Church in Haddington. During his ministry his stipend was £50 per year and his publications earned him very little money but were a testimony to his great scholarship. His other works were equally scholarly and included his *Dictionary of the Holy Bible, A General History of the Christian Church from the birth of our Saviour to the present time,* 2 Volumes, *A History of the Churches of Scotland and England, from the earliest period*, 2 Volumes, and many others.

He was well-known for his preaching of tolerance and forbearance. His influence reached the young poet, Robert Fergusson (1750-74) so admired by Robert Burns, who was said to have burned several of his unpublished works and took to a study of the Bible after meeting the wise and dedicated minister (3). John Brown was also respected for his work in natural sciences and for his knowledge of Oriental and European languages including Arabic, Syriac, Persian, Ethiopic, French, Spanish, Italian, Dutch, and German. A man of great intellect, his preaching was both powerful and scholarly and yet his message was clearly understood by the humblest of his congregation. A strong voice in support of religious freedom, he raised questions about the alliance of the church with the state. A staunch Calvinist, he corresponded with and befriended the Countess of Huntingdon in her stand against Arminianism (the Arminians were against rigid Calvinism and were suspected of trying to re-introduce Catholicism).

His first wife was Janet Thomson, daughter of a Musselburgh merchant; after eighteen years of happy marriage she died suddenly. They had several children but only two boys, John and Ebeneezer, survived. Both entered the Secession ministry. In 1773, two years after the death of his first wife he married Violet Croumbie of Stenton; they had nine children.

John Brown never retired, he dedicated his life to the church and to his adoring congregation. Early in 1787 the effects of his punishing work load had taken their toll; he was exhausted. He preached his last sermon on 25th January. His weakened state was obvious to his congregation and as he preached his farewell message they knew that they would not see him again. They cried openly. After thirty-seven years as minister he died on 19th June 1787 and he was buried in St Mary's Churchyard, Haddington. Many from far off places and the whole population of Haddington attended. His tombstone is inscribed:

To the Memory of
MR. JOHN BROWN
Thirty-six years Minister of the Gospel
at Haddington
and Twenty-five Years PROFESSOR OF DIVINITY
under the Associate Synod
After maintaining an eminent Character for
PIETY, CHARITY, LEARNING, AND DILIGENCE,
HE DIED
Rejoicing in the hope of the glory of GOD,
And admiring the riches of Divine Grace to him as a sinner,
The 19th June, A.D. 1787,
AGED 65 YEARS

Four of his sons entered the ministry: Rev. John Brown of Longridge, Rev. Ebeneezer Brown of Inverkeithing, Rev. Dr. Thomas Brown of Dalkieth and the Rev. George Brown of North Berwick. His eighth son, Samuel Brown, was the last Provost of Haddington under the old self-perpetuating Councils with its trade bailies and councillors and he was elected the first Provost under the Reformed system in 1833. He founded the Haddington School of Art and started the first of the 'Itinerating libraries' of East Lothian (2).

A final tribute to this great minister is a recollection of the famous Scottish philosopher and historian David Hume (1711-76), who on hearing one of John Brown's sermons, was heard to remark, "That old man speaks as if Christ stood at his elbow." (3)

PETER HUME BROWN of Tranent

The Historiographer Royal for Scotland

Arguably the most easily read history of Scotland was written by a lad from Tranent who became Professor of Ancient (Scottish) History and Palaeography of the University of Edinburgh and Historiographer Royal for Scotland. He was Peter Hume Brown, born on 17th December 1850 at Tranent. He was orphaned as a youth having lost his father at the age of two and his mother at the age of sixteen. He became a critically scrupulous historian whose *A Short History of Scotland*, written for senior school pupils, was, and still is, the most readable and informative of its kind. It was first published in 1908, reprinted many times and revised and enlarged after his death in 1918.

His early education was at the Free Church School in Prestonpans from the age of eight. He became a pupil teacher and left the school at the age of twenty. His home was a poor one, his mother struggled to bring up her young family and she died of overwork in 1866 when Peter was sixteen. His early life was therefore sad but Peter found solace in study. In 1872, the year of the great Education (Scotland) Act when pupil teacherships came to an end and responsibility for schools was transferred from the Church to local authorities, Peter entered the University of Edinburgh. His first intention was to train for the ministry but he was attracted by the teaching of Professor David Masson (Scots history and literature) and Professor Alexander Campbell Fraser (Chair of Logic and Metaphysics) and he gave up his studies in theology to concentrate on Scottish history. During these student days he befriended Richard Haldane (later Viscount Haldane *qv*, the Liberal MP who ousted Lord Elcho from his safe Conservative seat in East Lothian). It was from this friendship that Hume Brown gained his interest in French and German literature; so absorbed did he become that he wrote the *Life of Goethe*.

Following his graduation as Master of Arts in 1875 he started a private school in Edinburgh but, preferring to concentrate on his historical studies, he gave up the school after seven years and instead took a few private pupils. In 1890 he published *George Buchanan, Humanist and Reformer*, a year later he published his *Early Travellers in Scotland*, in 1893 his *Scotland Before 1700 from Contemporary Documents* and in 1895 his biography of *John Knox* in two volumes; this was a scholarly examination of Knox's political, rather than his theological career.

Hume Brown's scholarly reputation was now well-known and he was asked to succeed his old professor, David Masson, as editor of the Register of the Privy Council of Scotland and three years later, in 1901, he was appointed Fraser Professor of Ancient (Scottish) History and Palaeography, a Chair endowed by his other old professor, Alexander Campbell Fraser. He devoted these years to a carefully researched study in three volumes of the *History of Scotland*. His Rhind Lectures of 1904 were published as *Scotland in the Time of Queen Mary* and his Ford Lectures were published in 1914 as *The Legislative Union of England and Scotland.* After his death his *Surveys of Scottish History* was edited by his student friend, Lord Haldane.

This unassuming, scholarly man died on 30th November 1918. His name lives in the minds of many Scots with his *A Short History of Scotland*; its conversational style brought Scottish history in the form of beautifully written stories to generations of Scottish school pupils, their parents and grandparents - he had bridged the gap between the man in the street and the academic in his ivory tower.

The CADELLS of Cockenzie House

(1) Robert Cadell, (1788-1849), *Publisher and friend of Sir Walter Scott*
(2) Francis Cadell,(1822-1879), *Ship's Captain and Explorer*
(3) Col. Thomas Cadell, VC (1835-1919), *A hero of the Siege of Delhi*

The occupants of Cockenzie House in Prestonpans must have had a magnificient view of the Battle of Prestonpans in 1745 when the Jacobite Highlanders quickly despatched the Royalist troops under General John Cope. It was during that battle, which only lasted for about ten minutes, that Colonel James Gardiner *qv* of Bankton House nearby was killed having sustained two gunshots wounds and six sabre cuts on his head. 'Bonnie Prince Charlie' was entertained in Cockenzie House shortly after the battle. He left about two hundred Lochaber axes which were subsequently found during exvcavations for alterations at the back of the house.

The house was built by the Winton estate in the late 17th century possibly as a residence for the manager of the harbour and salt pan. However, in 1715 because the Seton family were attainted for their support of the Jacobite cause, Cockenzie House was forfeited and taken over by the York Building Company (30 p.139).

The so-called Hanseatic Barn or the 'Great Custom' was named presumably because it was a custom post and was used as a store for goods to be exported to and imported from the low countries of the continent in the thriving import/export business of the Cadell family. It was built about the middle of the 18th century and John Cadell (1740-1814) bought the property in 1779. He also bought the lands of Tranent and replaced the old wooden tramway with an iron one. His sons **William** (1774 -1840) and **Hugh Francis** (1774-1873) were coal owners. His third son **Robert** (1788- 1849) *qv* became a successful publisher in Edinburgh. William and Hugh Francis took over the lease of the Tranent coalfields and sunk an additional shaft, extending the work face by two miles during which many lives were lost. The Cadell brothers were in dispute with the villagers of Tranent over the loss of their water supply. The cause was the sinking of a mine shaft through the Great Sand Bed and resulted in diversion of water down the shaft. After three years of dispute with a committee of feuars the Cadells reluctantly agreed to pay for 'iron tubbing'. The water supply was duly restored to a greater flow than before and the disease and epidemic in the village gradually abated; many lives had been lost. However, in 1837 another shaft was driven through the sand bed and again the water supply diminished to nothing. 'The same old battle with laird and lessee had again to be fought... and the state of misery to which the village was reduced for a long term of years thereafter is almost beyond description' (75p.45). After the death of Hugh Francis Cadell on 27th April 1873 the Tranent coal works were leased by one James Snowdon (75 p.24).

The Cadell brothers, William, Robert and Hugh Francis, spent £6000 on the reconstruction of the harbour at the west end of Cockenzie. The foundation stone of the new harbour was laid on 19th July 1833, the harbour having been designed by the eminent Civil engineer Robert Stevenson (after whom Stevenson College in Edinburgh is named). The old harbour at Port Seton had been destroyed by severe storms in 1810 and the new harbour was a blessing to the fishermen as well as to the Cadells whose vessels for the export of salt from the pans at Cockenzie sheltered there; '....so long as this port remained in the hands of the Cadell family no dues whatever were at any time extracted from the fishermen' (75 p.196).

ROBERT CADELL *Publisher and friend of Sir Walter Scott*

Robert Cadell of Cockenzie made a name for himself in the world of publishing during the era of Sir Walter Scott who had cause to be grateful to Cadell and upon whose wise advice and friendship Scott was to depend.

Robert Cadell was born on 16th December 1788, the youngest son of John Cadell (1740-1814), a prosperous merchant of Cockenzie who could well afford to send him to the High School in Edinburgh. He started work in a bookseller's shop and at the age of nineteen (1807) he obtained employment in Archibald Constable's publishing house in Craig's Close in the High Street of Edinburgh from which the *Edinburgh Review* and *The Edinburgh Medical and Surgical Journal* were produced. Walter Scott's *The Lay of the Last Minstrel* was the start of a long association with this new author - 'The Great Unknown'.

Cadell was a hard-working and conscientious young man and after about five years Constable made him a partner in the firm. He fell in love with Constable's daughter and they married in 1827. She died after only a year of marriage and in their grief Cadell and Constable rather than sympathise with each other they became quarrelsome and argued over the running of the company. Constable was the entrepreneur and in Cadell's opinion he was lavish to the point of rashness. Cadell, on the other hand, was cautious to the point of frugality, but quite unlike himself, he offered Walter Scott £1000 for his *Halidon Hill* even before it was written. This offer, however, was made in Constable's absence and was about the only matter on which they both agreed - the value to the firm of Walter Scott.

The stock market crash of 1825-6 in London brought massive debts to several publishers and their agents. Constable was badly affected and Scott was brought to the verge of bankruptcy, in debt to the extent of £120,000. He refused bankruptcy with the words, "I will involve no friend, rich or poor, my own right hand shall do it."

But, of course, arrangements had to be made and Cadell, having split from Constable, advised Scott to reject Constable's proposal to save the firm. Scott would have become more heavily in debt and the firm would not have been saved in any case. Scott's diary entry of 15th December 1825 makes reference to Cadell's kindness and personal feeling in spite of having previously thought of Cadell as 'a mere counting-house'. After Cadell's visit to inform him that their London agent, Hurst and Robinson, 'had stood the storm without the need to borrow from the banks, Scott felt much relieved.

When Constable and Cadell finally split, Scott was to write in his diary, 'Constable without Cadell is like getting the clock without the pendulum, the one having the ingenuity, the other the caution of business.' But recriminations followed, the Bank of Scotland called in £1900 withdrawn by Cadell on the day before the accounts were frozen. On 4th February 1826, Cadell took refuge in the Sanctuary, (an ancient court near Holyrood where debtors could avoid arrest) but he emerged on 7th February, being assured that no action against him would be pursued.

Cadell became Scott's sole publisher and they decided to purchase the copyrights of *Waverley* and *Quentin Durward* with the majority of the shares in Scott's poetical works. Cadell bought the copyrights of the *Waverley Novels* for £8500 and the *Author's Edition* of 1827 with prefaces and notes by Scott was very successful.

Scott had involved himself in the political scene some years before when he published his *Malachi Malagrowther* against parliamentary reform. But times had changed, there was now a growing climate of reform and Cadell sensed that Scott's opinions, if they became too obvious, could affect the sales of his new edition of the novels. He managed to convince Scott not to publish his fourth edition of the letters. Cadell had now become a truly trusted friend and he was entrusted with the keeping of Scott's Will at his house in Edinburgh where the Will was originally made.

Cadell accompanied Scott from London to Edinburgh aboard the steamship *James Watt* when Scott became so seriously ill that the captain gave up his cabin for the comfort of the great man. Scott died on 21st September 1832 at his beloved Abbotsford shortly after this journey. His greatly reduced debts, through his partnership with Ballantyne's, amounted to £30,000 and in 1833 Cadell offered to settle with Scott's creditors. In recompense he would receive the profits from Scott's copyrights. There was no profit to Cadell and his offer was accepted immediately.

Cadell now retricted his business entirely to Scott's works and issued the Abbotsford edition of the *Waverley Novels* (48 volumes) between 1830 and 1834. In 1842 this success was followed by an elaborately illustrated 12-volume edition on which he was reputed to have spent £40,000. By 1847 there was still a considerable sum owed to Cadell and to other creditors. Scott had borrowed on the house and lands of Abbotsford and Cadell now generously agreed to relieve the guardians of Scott's grand-daughter from the sums owed to himself and to mortgagees of Abbotsford. For this he received the remaining rights of Scott's works plus future profits from the famous biography, *Life of Scott* by his accomplished son-in-law, John Gibson Lockhart (1794-1854). In addition Lockhart agreed to write an abridged version of the biography in gratitude for Cadell's 'conduct in the whole business.'

Cadell, the man, was entirely dependable, fastidious and conscientious in every respect. By his careful attention to business he had become fairly wealthy and he purchased an estate at Ratho. Such was his punctuality, anyone living on his route from Ratho House to his office at No.41 St Andrew Square could set their clocks by what came to be called the 'Ratho Coach'. On the 20th January 1849 no clocks were set; the Ratho Coach did not arrive; Robert Cadell died that day in his sixty-first year.

FRANCIS CADELL, born on 9th February 1822, eldest son of Hugh Francis Cadell an officer in the Royal Navy, was to become a well-respected and honoured explorer in Australia. After many heroic exploits in China, he arrived in Australia in 1848 and two years later he explored its south-eastern rivers. He is especially known as the first to navigate the Murray River, the Darling and other tributaries but this trusting and intrepid explorer who contributed greatly to the development and resources of Australia met a tragic and murderous end in the South China Sea.

His father, Hugh Francis Cadell, was a mineowner and shipbuilder whose mansion was Cockenzie House. Young Francis had a secure and happy upbringing in relatively opulent surroundings. After a brief education in Edinburgh and Germany, Francis Cadell signed up as a Midshipman at the age of fourteen aboard the *Minerva*, a vessel of the East India Company. His ship was chartered by the government as a transport vessel and he found himself in the thick of the fighting at the start of the first Chinese war in 1840 - the so-called 'Opium War'. He took part in the siege of Canton and the capture of Amoy, Niagpo and other Chinese towns. He won several honours and prize money for the capture of alien vessels.

His bravery and initiative was soon to be recognised when, at the age of twenty-two, he was given his first full command. The Treaty of Nanking (29th August 1842) gave the cession of Hong Kong to Britain as well as the opening of five ports for trade as reparation in 1842. Trading in China was thus opened up and Cadell sailed the South China Sea for the next few years.

During his rest periods between voyages Cadell was not one to spend his free time relaxing in the hostelries of seaports, instead he used the time to study the practicalities of shipbuilding at the shipyards of Tyneside and the Clyde. In the workshops of Robert Napier & Sons he learned the operational details of marine steam-engines - a new innovation in the 1840s. This was the age of the clipper ships and he had the *Queen of Sheba* built to his specification.

In 1848 he visited Australia for the first time and found great interest in the steam-navigation of the Murray River which rises in the Australian Alps in New South Wales and on the banks of which several townships had been established. His agent and partner, William Younghusband, a member of the Legislative Council, negotiated with the Governor of

South Australia, Sir Henry Young, to offer a reward of £4000 to the first to navigate this river from Lake Alexandrina at Goolwa to the junction of the Darling River at Swan Hill, a distance of 1,300 miles. The journey had to be undertaken by two 'iron steamers, of not less than 40 horse-power and of not more than 2 feet draught of water when loaded.' (25 vol. II p.177)

Cadell returned home but this challenge remained with him and he returned to Australia in 1850 - the year of the gold rush. The river had not yet been navigated and there was a growing need to transport stores to the outback and return with wool and wheat. He decided to study the great river and to do so he started out over land from Melbourne with pack-horses to carry his supplies and a boat made of beer barrel staves and canvas. He reached Swan Hill in the upper reaches of the Murray River and launched his small craft, *Forerunner*, downstream [a 21-foot scale replica of which was launched at the Childrens' Gala Day at Port Seton on 3rd June 2000]. Accompanied by four gold-diggers he examined the river for several hundred miles and decided that its navigation by steamer was a feasible proposition.

Cadell now formed his own steamship company. He purchased a two-funnel paddle-steamer at Sydney and sailed it south to Lake Alexandrina. There, he began the fitting out in preparation for the 1,300-mile journey on which the Governor and his wife, Lady Augusta, had expressed the wish to make the trip. He renamed the vessel *Lady Augusta* in her honour and in August 1853 Captain Cadell commenced his journey upstream with his auspicious party accompanied by the barge *Eureka*. He anticipated a leisurely, serenely peaceful and beautiful journey but this notion was brought to an abrupt end when he discovered that Captain Randell in the *Mary Ann* was ahead of him. The race was on. Neither Captain had realised that the other was on the river. In fact Randell had started out ahead and had stopped for a rest when he heard the unexpected noise of a steam engine. He was nonplussed when the *Lady Augusta* sailed leisurely by. Randall's log reads:

We were now within three days' journey of Swan Hill, and after having moored the boat at the bank of the river, and gone to rest, we were awakened by an unusual noise upon the water, and when we turned out to ascertain the cause of the commotion we beheld the Lady Augusta, steaming up the river at the rate of three or four knots. It was then near eleven o' clock at night, and although our sleep had been disturbed, we followed in a few hours, and passed her again the next morning.

Captain Cadell, never a man to be beaten, especially by a smaller craft, now stoked his boilers, raised maximum steam pressure and opened his throttle to 'full steam ahead'. They passed and re-passed each other when they stopped to chop wood for fuel, but on the last long bend the *Lady Augusta* steamed ahead and reached Swan Hill on 17th September 1853. The celebrations and congratulations were ecstatic, toasts were drunk and the arrival of the *Mary Ann* shortly after was greeted with equal enthusiasm.

The families of the outback had not seen a supply wagon for over two years and they had been reduced to boiling weeds for vegetables, their flour was musty and their boots and saddles had long since worn out. Their wool stores were overloaded from two years of waiting for transport. Now, at last, they could trade. The journey from Adelaide was now only a few weeks away. From now on their flour would be fresh from the mills at Adelaide, boxes of sugar loaf, cases of brandy, sperm candles and many other supplies would now arrive in spick and span condition. The river boats would transform their lives; civilisation had arrived - thanks to Captain Francis Cadell the hero of the Murray River.

Cadell received his £4000 prize money and a gold medal. The Australian Government awarded Captain Randell £300 which was supplemented by another £700 from a public subscription. Sir Henry Young was given a magnificent banquet in his honour and Cadell was presented with a gold Candelabra valued at almost £1000. (68 vol. 3)

Cadell and Randell acquired more steamers and increased their trading by extending their journeys. Cadell decided to undertake the 1740-mile journey to *Albury*, a newly created township in the upper Murray. He named his latest steamboat Albury and reached this remote place in 1855. In 1856 he explored the Edward River, a branch of the Murray which rejoined it after 600 miles. His next challenge was over 2000 miles inland from the sea. He named this steamer *Gundagai* and, having explored the Murrumbidgee River, he reached the township of the same name in 1858. His next exploration was that of the Darling River to Mount Murchison also in 1858. Again he had opened the way for trade and had given a new civilisation to the families of the outback, but for himself there was little profit. Monetary grants hardly met his expenses but his love of exploration and adventure led to the neglect of his business; the grants he received rarely covered his expenses.

He dissolved the Murray Steamship Company to retire into the bush and to settle on a farm near Mount Murchison on the Darling River. But exploring was in his blood: early in 1867 the South Australian Government appointed him to explore the Northern Territories and to choose a site for its capital. In November 1867 he discovered the mouth of the River Roper and navigated it to Port Darwin, Anson Bay and the Victoria River. He found a tract of fine pastoral land but his recommendations were ignored.

In 1870 while whaling in New Zealand he was reported to have tried unsuccessfully to trade with Maoris. He then traded between Fiji and other islands. A combination of dry seasons and bad luck led him, in 1879, to accept a trading voyage across the South China Sea, the Java Sea to the Spice Islands (Mulocca). He had fitted out his schooner, the *Gem*, with an auxiliary engine but his crew were a discontented and untrustworthy lot whose tempers were not improved with the sweltering heat of a long and boring journey from Amboyna Island to the Kei Islands. They mutinied and callously murdered their captain. On reaching land they sunk the vessel with Cadell's body on board in an attempt to hide their crime which took place in June 1879. Thus ended the career of an enterprising discoverer, navigator and honourable man. His name is commemorated by **Cadell Strait** in the Northern Territory.

COLONEL THOMAS CADELL VC (1835-1919)

Thomas Cadell, the third and youngest son of Hugh F Cadell, was born on 5th September 1835 at Cockenzie House, renamed Cadell House. After his early education at Edinburgh Academy he was sent to the Grange School in Sunderland. He was seven years old when his brother Francis was appointed a ship's captain sailing the South China Seas. This was a family with a strong sense of adventure and Thomas enlisted for the army soon after leaving school at the age of eighteen.

He served firstly with the 2nd European Bengal Fusiliers (which became the Royal Munster Fusiliers) at the siege of Delhi in 1857 during the Indian Mutiny on 10th May when sepoys mutinied and captured the prison at Meerut. They marched on Delhi and the twenty-two year old Cadell in command of a platoon showed exceptional heroism in saving the lives of two of his men in separate battles. The first, under heavy fire, was a wounded bugler whom he saved from certain death by the rebels. He rescued the second on the same day when the Fusiliers

were ordered to retire. He discovered that one of his men had been left behind severely wounded and unable to move; Lieutenant Cadell, with three men, returned towards the enemy and, again under the heavy fire of the advancing enemy, he brought the wounded soldier to safety. He was astonished five years after these rescues to be gazetted for the award of the foremost distinction for very exceptional gallantry, the Victoria Cross (which was introduced the year before at the end of the Crimean War).
Date of Gazette 29th April 1862
Account of Deed:

> "On 12th June 1857 at Delhi, India during the siege Lt. Cadell brought in a wounded bugler of his own regiment under severe fire. Later on the same day, when the fusiliers were retiring, the officer went back of his own accord and, accompanied by three men, brought in a severely wounded man under heavy fire from the advancing enemy."

[Source: The Register of the Victoria Cross by 'This England Books', Cheltenham.]

He was promoted to the 3rd Bengal Cavalry during the subsequent operations of the Oudh campaign and was 'mentioned in despatches' before proceeding to take command of a 'flying column' in Bundelkh to receive the gratitude of the Governor-General in Council and was made a Companion of the Most Honourable Order of the Bath (CB) for his service during the Indian Mutiny.

His career now changed direction when he became an administrator and was appointed to a variety of political appointments in central India and Rajputana. In 1879, the year of his brother Francis's murder, he was appointed Governor of the Andaman and Nicobar Islands in the Bay of Bengal.

He returned home on a three-year furlough to Cadell House in 1882. He was elected chairman of the Tranent School Board and spent some of his time in remodelling and extending the garden of his house. He had acquired a huge and sacred marble bull which had been captured by the Somerset Regiment from Nana Sahib during the Indian Mutiny and to house it he decided to build a temple for it in his garden. There was some religious objection to the use of local stone for this purpose and the colonel overcame the objection by using some of the ship's ballast of Iclandic lava from the volcano *Hecla* which had been used during the Cadell trading era with Iceland. The final structure, of about 20 feet in height, had the name of the volcano in raised letters above the Gothic arch entrance which had been formed using giant whale bones.

The acquisition of the bull was brought about when Colonel Cadell offered to supply the means of its transport from India by making use of his father's shipping connections and although he was not the original finder, the law of loot in those days allowed that he who brought it back to Britain should become the owner. Today there is no sign of the marble bull but the temple, which is listed in the the book of 'Folly Fellowship', still stands in the garden.

Colonel Cadell died at Cadell house on 6th April 1919.

JIM and FINLAY CALDER

Scottish Rugby Internationalists of Haddington

The Calder brothers had rugby in their blood and as small boys they practised every move and learned the skill of the game from their father, Robin Calder, whom they followed into the Haddington Rugby Club. On their arrival at Daniel Stewart's and Melville College in Edinburgh their first choice of sport was of course rugby. They played for their school every Saturday morning and occasionally in 'friendlies' for Haddington. Soon they were selected for the school's first team and later for the Former Pupils' team - brilliant careers were launched.

Jim and Finlay Calder are twins born on 20th August 1957. Jim achieved his boyhood ambition at the age of twenty-three when he was selected to play for Scotland against France in Paris. He was 'capped' no fewer than 27 times and in 1983 he toured with the British Lions. But his never-to-be-forgotten great day was his match-winning try to win the 'Grand Slam' for Scotland against the French in 1984. That day he was the hero of all Scotland - the 'Grand Slam' meant defeat at the hands of the Scots for every competing team - the English, the Welsh, the Irish and the French and Jim Calder of Haddington had done it.

Strangely, the brothers were never selected for Scotland at the same time; Finlay Calder's international career seemed to start when his twin brother Jim's ended. Finlay was first selected as a Scottish internationalist in 1986. Again, this was cause for great celebration in the Calder household and at Haddington Rugby Club where, 46 years before, the club produced its very first international in the famous Andrew 'Jock' Wemyss (1893-1974) *qv*, one of the founders of the club. This was a goal for which Finlay had striven all his young life. He was to be capped for Scotland no fewer than 34 times and ultimately to captain Scotland's team in 1989 in which year he was chosen captain of the British Lions.

The year 1990 was the most dramatic of all. Scotland versus England for the 'Grand Slam', the Championship, the triple crown and the Calcutta Cup to be decided on 17th March. It was the talk of all Scotland and England and no doubt every ex-patriot Scot abroad. England seemed invincible; there were no discernible weaknesses; England was the favourite. This was to be Scotland's greatest ever triumph and Finlay Calder had the privilege of contributing his best on that momentous day.

Finlay Calder is a grain exporter in Leith and describes his recreation as "work". He lives in the Borders with wife Elizabeth and their family, David and Hazel. He was made an Officer of the Order of the British

Empire (OBE) for his services to rugby in 1990. He was recalled to play in the World Cup in 1991.

In Haddington, the Royal Bank of Scotland paid an unusual tribute to the Calder brothers in January 1991 when the bank commissioned two paintings commemorating their triumphs in Scotland's 'Grand Slams' of 1984 and 1990. The first was entitled "The Turning Point" and the other "Underdog Rampant". Matching prints were presented to the Calder family and were proudly displayed at Dale House in Calder's Lawn - rightly named after the Calder family.

JANE WELSH CALRLYLE

Thomas Carlyle was captivated by her mercurial intelligence, her love of life, fun and charm

Haddingtonians are proud of the bright and beautiful only daughter of Dr and Mrs Welsh of Lodge Street, Jane Welsh, who married the great literary genius Thomas Carlyle. The house in Lodge Street where she was born and lived in a happy and prosperous family life has been preserved almost as it might have been in her day; it is now the Jane Welsh Carlyle Museum.

Jane Welsh was born on 14th July 1801, the only daughter of Dr John Welsh who arrived in Haddington with his wife, Grace Welsh, in 1800. Jane was a bright child and at St Anne's School she excelled to become dux of the school. Her childhood days were full of fun and challenge. She refused to be beaten by the boys and having been dared to walk the parapet of the Nungate Bridge she prepared herself in secret. Alone and at night she crawled across it, slowly at first. Then she walked falteringly and finally she ran across almost skipping gleefully above the rushing waters of the Tyne below. Again, to equal if not to excel the boys she, with the help of her friend William Dods (who was to become Provost of Haddington and a well-known seedsman), learned to decline a Latin verb and recited it to her father. She pleaded with him to teach her Latin, saying:

Jane Baillie Welsh Carlyle by Kenneth MacLeay (Courtesy of the Scottish National Portrait Gallery)

"I want to learn Latin, please let me be a boy." Her father readily agreed but her mother was doubtful.

When Jane attended the Mathematical School, almost next door to her house, her first teacher was the youthful Edward Irving. He was a charismatic teacher who had the ability to attract and motivate the children to enjoy the experience of learning. In Jane Welsh he found mercurial intelligence, a love of life, fun and charm. That she became the 'Flower of Haddington' to be wooed by several aspiring suitors was not surprising; that she turned them away disappointed, tongue-tied and embarrassed seemed almost to be expected.

In 1818, aged seventeen, she was sent to Miss Hall's finishing school in Leith. Edward Irving had left Haddington to take up a teaching post in Kirkcaldy and on meeting Jane again he remembered her early infatuation of him and promptly fell in love with this polished, incredibly beautiful and intelligent young lady. However, when he introduced her to his friend, Thomas Carlyle, he lost her. For Carlyle it was love at first sight. Jane's beauty was matched by scholarly intellect and she recognised instantly a kindred spirit, a free and enquiring mind, a scholar of talent - at last she was impressed. This was the start of their five-year courtship.

They married in 1826 and took up residence at Comely Bank in Edinburgh. After eighteen months they moved to Craigenputtock, near the Solway Firth, a house owned by Jane's mother. Carlyle wrote most of his best works during the next six years in the peace of this idyllic place. In a letter to her cousin, Eliza Stodart of George Square, Edinburgh, she wrote:

> "The solitude is not so irksome as one might think. If we are cut off from good society, we are also delivered from bad; the roads are less pleasant to walk on than the pavement of Princes Street, but we have horses to ride, and, instead of shopping and making calls, I have bread to bake and chickens to hatch. I read and work, and talk with my husband and never weary. Letters from Germany and all parts of the earth reach us here as before. It is strange to see 'Craigenputtock' written in Goethe's hand."

The Carlyles left their idyllic life in Dumfriesshire in 1834. Thomas Carlyle had published some of his best works and he was in great demand by the literati not only of London but of Europe. They moved to Cheyne Row in Chelsea. This was a complete change for Jane; she was bored. Her husband had taken on a monumental work load. His neglect of her led to nervous hypochondria alleviated occasionally by visits from literary friends: Leigh Hunt, the essayist and poet who lived a few doors away, Charles Dickens, Lord Tennyson, William Makepeace Thackeray and many other admirers were welcomed by Jane who seemed to light up on their arrival.

Thomas Carlyle was by now hailed as a literary genius and in 1866 he was elected Rector of the University of Edinburgh. He and Jane worked themselves into a frenetic state of nervousness over his forthcoming rectorial address to the students. He detested public speaking and travelled to Edinburgh three weeks before the event to be feted and admired, but his anxiety only worsened. He need not have worried; he held the students spellbound for ninety minutes. Reassured by the spontaneous applause he telegraphed Jane with the words: "A perfect triumph." Jane was overjoyed and two days before he was due to return to her she took her pet dog for a ride in her carriage. She stopped to allow the dog to walk and no sooner had it touched the ground than it was struck by a passing carriage. Fortunately, the dog was only slightly injured but Jane was so shocked she took a heart attack and died in her carriage. Her coachman returned the pet dog to the carriage and continued the journey to Cheyne Row. He was shocked to find that he been transporting her dead body.

Thomas Carlyle was in Dumfries when he received the numbing news. Heartbroken he hurried to London. His grief was almost beyond endurance when he read her memoirs. He had no idea of her loneliness and boredom. The beauty and perfection of her writing astounded him; he had not known of her exceptional talent, now lost forever.

Jane had expressed the wish to be buried beside her father in St Mary's Parish Church at Haddington. Accordingly, Thomas Carlyle had her body brought north to be met by William Dods, Jane's childhood friend who readily agreed to have the coffin brought to his spacious house at No. 32 Court Street (now the Royal Bank of Scotland). That night the dejected figure of the great man walked slowly through the streets of Haddington until he came to the entrance of Dr Welsh's house in Lodge Street. Entering the garden he gazed longingly and tearfully at the window of the room in which he had first met Jane, and he wrote late of this visit: "1821 on a summer evening after sunset - five and forty years ago. The beautifullest young creature I had ever beheld."

Next day, 26th April 1866, Jane's funeral was attended by a few friends. She was buried beside her father. Thomas Carlyle composed the inscription for her gravestone:

Here likewise now rests Jane Welsh Carlyle, spouse of Thomas Carlyle, Chelsea, London. She was born at Haddington. 14th July 1801; only child of the above John Welsh, and of Grace Welsh, Caplegill, Dumfriesshire, his wife. In her bright existence she had more sorrows than are common; but also a soft invincibility, a clearness of discernment, a noble loyalty of heart, which are rare. For forty years she was the true and everloving helpmate of her husband; and by act and word, unweariedly forwarded him, as none else could, in all of worthy that he did or attempted. She died at London, 21st April 1866; suddenly snatched away from him, and the light of his life has gone out.

JAMES CARMICHAEL

Scholar and Perpetual Moderator of the Presbytery of Haddington

James Carmichael was a well-known name in 16th century Scotland. In Haddington, he was minister, schoolmaster, author and ultimately perpetual moderator of the Presbytery of Haddington. He was chosen as one of the most scholarly ministers of his day by the Privy Council of Scotland to revise the famous Second Book of Discipline and to correct the translation of Skene's *Regiam Majestatem* and such was his high reputation the Privy Council requested the Presbytery of Haddington to allow him leave of absence to complete this translation from Latin of the old Scots laws.

In his boyhood Carmichael was a devotee of John Knox who had been released from imprisonment by the French in 1549 when Carmichael was fifteen years of age. The English had arrived to take possession of Haddington in 1548 and the youthful Carmichael was doubtless critical of the French presence encouraged by Mary of Guise, mother of Queen of Scots when she climbed the narrow steps of St Mary's Church tower to observe the English troops who were besieged in the town during the siege of Haddington (1548-9).

James Carmichael was born in the year 1533 but of his early life little is known. He was undoubtedly scholarly, evidence of which comes later with his appointment as schoolmaster of the Burgh in April 1572 and his publication of his Latin Grammar, *Grammaticae Latinae, de Etymologia, liber secundus* written in 1587.

After the Reformation of 1560 the Priory of St Martin's in the Nungate of Haddington was taken over by the Town Council for use by the Presbyterians and ten years later, on 2nd November 1571, James Carmichael was presented there as minister. Within six months he was appointed schoolmaster of the Burgh.

At this time Regent Morton, wishing to reduce the number of ministers in the Church, had decreed that Presbyterian ministers should have charge of several churches simultaneously and in 1574 Carmichael was given charge of Athelstaneford and Bolton in addition to Haddington. This additional responsibility required his occasional absences from the Burgh School of Haddington and in 1576 he was relieved of his responsibility as schoolmaster. He worked quietly and assiduously for his congregations for the next eight years until, in 1584, he refused to recognise the position of the bishop as superior. This imposition of bishops was against the new democracy of the Presbyterians as contained in the Second Book of Discipline. Carmichael was forced to resign his ministry.

Some historical background is necessary here to paint the picture of turmoil between Catholic supporters of Mary Queen of Scots and Protestant leaders of the King's party. Her son, James VI, born in 1566, was a child when he became king and there had been several enforced changes of Regent. Regent Moray, the 'Good Regent' was murdered in 1570. His successor, the Earl of Lennox, was shot within a year and was replaced by the Earl of Mar in 1571 who was said to have died of a broken-heart because he could not achieve peace. In 1572 the Earl of Morton became Regent on the day after John Knox's death and he continued to hold Scotland in his firm grip, having been Lord General of the Kingdom during Mar's Regency. The Reformers were in ferment and in England there was pressure for Mary's execution. Morton supported Elizabeth I's policies but his tendency towards Episcopalianism antagonised the General Assembly of the Church of Scotland. He insisted that Church monies be collected by the government and he reduced the number of ministers by assigning one minister to several churches

The real trouble in Scotland was the impression made upon the youthful King James by his newly arrived French relative, Esme Stewart, Lord Aubigny, a Catholic who pretended Protestantism and in whom James had placed his trust which verged on hero worship. James created him an Earl, then Duke of Lennox and he conspired to have Morton accused of complicity in the murder of Mary's odious husband, Lord Darnley. The murder had taken place fifteen years before and Morton, although not involved, was beheaded in 1581.

During these precarious times James Carmichael bravely stood against the imposition of bishops. Having been relieved of his ministry he had to flee to England under the protection of Elizabeth I's Protestant rule. He was the leading exile of several other exiled Scottish ministers; several of the nobility fled with them including the Earls of Angus and Mar. During his exile in England, Carmichael had meetings with English politicians and he met Sir Francis Walsingham, Elizabeth's trusted secretary and spy who revealed the Babington Plot which implicated Mary Queen of Scots in a treasonable plot. Scottish ambassadors to England did their best to denigrate the exiles but Carmichael cleverly thwarted their devious aims. Several of the Scottish ministers returned to Scotland after about eighteen months but Carmichael remained in England for a further two years during which he wrote his *Grammaticae Latinae* with a dedication to James VI. This was a masterly piece of scholarship dated 1587 and written in Cambridge. It undoubtedly eased his path back to Scotland. In Haddington he resumed his ministry with an allowance from the Town Council of 22 merks annually for house rent.

Carmichael's reputation as a scholar had been established especially after his work in providing an abridged version of the Acts of the General Assembly; he had served on the committee which had drawn up these Acts between 1592 and 1595. In addition he helped to revise the Second Book of Discipline which averred that no bishops should be allowed in the Church and that the Church of Scotland should be ruled by its General Assembly and not by the king or Parliament. [This principle was embodied in the Act of Union in 1707 and today the Supreme Governor of the Church of Scotland is Jesus Christ, not the monarch as is the case in the Church of England.]

Carmichael had worked with the learned Andrew Melville (1545-c1622), Knox's successor, who advocated that all ministers should be equal and was totally against the introduction of bishops in the Church, in drawing up the Second Book of Discipline.

In recognition of his theological scholarship Carmichael was appointed at the age of seventy-three to perpetual moderatorship of the Presbytery of Haddington and in 1607 the Privy Council of Scotland requested him to correct Sir John Skene's *Regiam Majestatum*. This was a collection of old laws translated from Latin into Scots and the Privy Council had requested the Presbytery of Haddington to allow Carmichael two months leave of absence to complete the task.

Andrew Melville, the eminent Scottish theologian and Principal of Glasgow and St Mary's College, St Andrews and several times Moderator of the General Assembly, held the highest opinions of Carmichael's scholarship. The two men had travelled and worked together and, building on the foundation of the work of John Knox, they produced the revised edition of the Second Book of Discipline which expounded the philosophy and governance of the Church of Scotland.

James Carmichael, East Lothian's theologian, scholar and architect of Scottish Presbyterianism, died in his eighty-fifth year in 1628.

COLONEL FRANCIS CHARTERIS
of Amisfield in Haddington
notorious criminal, cardsharp, scoundrel and thief

Francis Charteris spent most of his life in East Lothian where he left his mark of darkness. He was variously described as a notorious criminal, a cardsharp, a scoundrel and a thief; the superstitious thought that he was in league with the devil. It was he who brought the name Amisfield to Haddington having purchased the lands of Newmills and changed the name to that of his grandfather's seat in Dumfriesshire - Amisfield.

Born in 1675, he was the son of James Charteris, Writer to the Signet, and Mary Kinloch, third daughter of Sir Francis Kinloch, 1st baronet of Gilmerton *qv*, Athelstaneford and grandson of Sir John Charteris of Amisfield in Dumfriesshire (94 p.123). On the death of his uncle (his father's elder brother) he became the male representative of the family but because of the disgrace he had brought to the family name the Amisfield estate in Dumfriesshire was inherited by his cousin Elizabeth, the sole heiress of his uncle. He was doubtless irked if not angry at the loss of this inheritance and decided to have his own Amisfield elsewhere - he chose Haddington.

His reprobate ways started early. Still in his teens, Francis Charteris entered the army as an ensign but he was drummed out of his regiment for cheating at cards. He simply could not resist cheating and stealing: having served in a Dutch Regiment of Foot he was now expelled for stealing beef at Bruges in Belgium. He returned to Scotland and his father, no doubt to be rid of him, purchased another commission for him in the 3rd Regiment of Foot Guards under the command of Major-General Ramsay. His brother officers, knowing of his reputation, refused to enrol him. However, he gained entry to the 1st Regiment of Foot Guards and a few years later, while in command of a company, he enlisted several criminals, ostensibly to save them from prison, but, he had taken sums of money from each of them and in 1711 he was charged and found guilty by a committee of the House of Commons where, being made to kneel before the Speaker, he was given a severe reprimand.

A career in the army was now out of question; he had no option but to resign his commission and gambling became his way of life. He had learned the skills and trickery of successful cheating. He was conscienceless. It is remarkable that anyone would agree to play with him, but play they did, and Charteris seemed able to pick the richest of stupid victims. He cheated and tricked them out of large fortunes and became exceedingly rich from his ill-gotten gains. His effrontery knew no bounds; he used his fortune to lend money to his victims at exorbitant rates of interest. When they proved unable to meet their payments he gleefully took their lands in payment of their debts. In a relatively short time his annual income exceeded £7000 a year and his capital was valued at about £100,000 (in today's terms that is about £1.5 million a year income and £20 million in capital). At one sitting at cards he cheated the Duchess of Queensberry out of the vast sum of £3000, allegedly by the use of mirrors. The Duke was so furious that he tried, without success, to have a Bill passed in Parliament to limit the amount which could be gambled in games of chance.

Charteris's vices were not by any means confined to cheating at cards. He womanised shamelessly and had not the slightest concern for either his reputation or his victims. His behaviour inevitably led to challenges to duels. Some he refused, careless of accusations of cowardice, others he accepted and killed without mercy; always with an evil smile. He was an expert swordsman.

Francis Charteris became the epitome of evil for several writers of his day: Alexander Pope (1688-1744), the poet and satirist, often used his name: for example in his *Moral Essays* he refers to 'Charteris and the devil'. William Hogarth (1697-1764), the English painter and engraver, made his first plate of his *Rakes Progress* of the infamous Charteris.

Eventually the law caught up with him. He had raped his maid servant, Anne Bond, and was convicted at the Old Bailey to be sentenced to imprisonment in Newgate but he was pardoned by George II after a few confiscations of land.

He married Helen, daughter of Lord Mornington of the College of Justice. They had one daughter, Janet who married James, 5th Earl of Wemyss in secret. She was thoroughly spoilt and an incorrigible spendthrift. They separated in 1732 after her father's death. Colonel Francis Charteris left £1000 to his daughter, the countess, and £10,000 to his favourite, their second son, Francis, with the provision that he adopted the name Charteris. The young man adopted the title de jure 7th Earl of Wemyss on the death of his attainted brother, the de jure 6th Earl in 1787 (they had been attainted for their support of Prince Charles Edward Stuart during the '45 Rising). Janet's gravestone is in St Mary's Churchyard in Haddington and is engraved:

> 'To the memory of the Wemyss family. Janet, Countess of
> Wemyss daughter and heiress of Colonel Charteris of Amisfield
> is buried at Hitcham Bucks.'

The Colonel's death was a reflection of his notorious life. When he knew that he was dying he promised £30,000 to anyone who could prove that hell did not exist whilst making it known that if there was a heaven he cared nothing for it. However, he must have had some doubts - he stopped swearing and gave orders that his just debts should be paid. On his deathbed he was attended by a minister, Mr Cumming, and when he asked his daughter how much money he should give the minister for his services, she replied that 'it was unusual to give anything on such occasions.' Charteris almost sitting up in bed, was heard to say: "Well then, let us have another flourish from him!"

On the night he died at Stoneyhill near Musselburgh in February 1732 there was a terrifying storm which was considered locally to be a token of divine vengeance. But worse was to come: at his funeral, at the cemetery at Dalkeith, a riot broke out and spectators almost tore his body from its coffin. When eventually the coffin was lowered into the grave, dead dogs and offal were thrown on top of it. And so East Lothian was rid of an evil genius, the most feared and notoriously cruel man of his day. He was cursed into his grave.

Today the name Charteris survives but with great distinction: the 12th Earl of Wemyss and March is Francis David Charteris who with his forebears have more than compensated for the misdeeds of the notorious 'Colonel Charteris' in exemplary service to his Sovereign, the country, the church and the community.

ADAM and JOHN COCKBURN

the 'Improving Lairds' of Ormiston

A man far in advance of his time in matters agricultural and fruit growing and in his concern for the welfare of his tenants in East Lothian was **John Cockburn** of Ormiston. He followed in his father's footsteps in his enthusiasm to regenerate trade and industry at a time of dire poverty in Scotland following the Act of Union of 1707. But his innovative ideas for improvement met with local opposition and were to put him into huge debt.

Commissioner for the Union in 1689 and Lord Justice Clerk in 1692. As a Privy Councillor he was a member of the Royal Commission on the Inquiry into the Massacre of Glencoe (1692). He was, and could well afford to be, a fine gentleman but intolerant of any who were not Presbyterian. His devotion to his monarch, William III, was of fawning adoration. (14)

The Commission described the massacre of Glencoe as 'murder under trust' and laid the blame squarely on the shoulders of the Master of Stair, Sir John Dalrymple. Adam Cockburn concurred with this opinion absolutely and this incurred the displeasure, verging on the enmity, of the Marquis of Argyle who successfully blocked Cockburn's elevation as a Lord of Session. He was instead, appointed Treasurer Depute. He lost this post when Queen Anne was crowned in 1702 but he regained the Lord Justice Clerkship and was appointed a Lord of Session in 1705. His Whig politics lost him these appointments again and he was replaced by James Erskine of Grange. When George I, 'the Wee German Lairdie', came to the British throne, Cockburn was once again reinstated, this time for life.

Adam Cockburn's first wife was Lady Susan, daughter of the 4th Earl of Haddington. She had three sons of whom the eldest, John, was born in 1679. John followed in father's footsteps in the development of agriculture in East Lothian with the aim of improving not only methodology but prosperity for the impoverished Scots. He took his father's improvements to greater heights. As an MP he lived in London but travelled extensively, observing carefully the English methods of farming. John Walker, also of East Lothian, was the first in Scotland to practise 'fallowing' - in 1690 he ploughed land which had hitherto been fit only for sparse grazing, he then left it before sowing and was thus able to grow a good crop. One of Adam Cockburn's early improvements in Scotland was the introduction of ploughing in the autumn and the sowing of winter wheat. Ploughing before Candlemas (2nd February) had been unheard of in Scotland.

Adam Cockburn was the first to enclose fields in Scotland and his son John went even further by planting hedgerows of bramble, rose, honeysuckle, elder and privet. Another innovation of his father was in the extension of tenancies. He tried to abolish the short-lease system (a legacy of the medieval system of land tenure) by giving one of his tenants an eleven-year lease. John offered thirty-eight-year leases and even longer leases to old tenant families with the words:

"I hate tyranny in every shape, and shall always have greater pleasure in seeing my tenants making something under me which they can call their own than in getting a little more myself by squeezing a hundred poor families till their necessities make them my slaves!"

However, John Cockburn was the exception rather than the rule in Scotland, he was one of very few enlightened landlords. The vast majority of Scottish peasants lived in miserable hardship, but paradoxically the changes introduced by John Cockburn were not always welcome. The peasants were suspicious of change. The filth of their houses seemed not to aggravate them except when disease struck them down; the old adage, "the clartier the cosier" comforted them.

John Cockburn was a Member of Parliament from 1707 until 1741 and a Lord of the Admiralty. While in England he was impressed by the methods of farming, the layout of farms and their produce. The idea of market gardening had not reached Scotland and he conceived a picture of Ormiston as productive and prosperous from distant London. His first step was to search for an experienced manager and in Charles Bell he found a Scot who had lived in England and had gained sound experience in gardening, forestry and farming. He was the ideal man to carry out Cockburn's schemes.

In 1730 Bell started work for John Cockburn but it was to be farming by correspondence. He took his orders from long letters the delivery time of which often took several weeks between 1727 to 1747. From London Cockburn sent seeds and saplings and spent lavishly on his estate. He opened his market gardens and fruit-growing schemes, he planted trees around his house and near those of his tenants so that they would in future have a supply of firewood, he improved the village of Ormiston and founded the farmers' club. But this management from a distance was impracticable. There were times when Bell was at a loss to understand his master's instructions, mistakes were made and put right. The cost was high and to pay for it all he mortgaged his land and property to the Earl of Hopetoun. When his debts reached £10,000 (approximately £1.5 million today) he was forced to give up. He was bankrupted and the only buyer for what was left was the Earl of Hopetoun who paid £12,000, a bargain price, for the remaining land, the mines, the distillery, the brewery and the mill. It was a tragedy for Cockburn. His dream dissipated into nothing but he had left a great gift to East Lothian.

In 1747 he left East Lothian for good to live with his son in London where he died in 1758.

SIR THOMAS CRAIG

the judge who presided over the trials of those accused of the murder of Rizzio, the secretary to Mary Queen of Scots

Sir Thomas Craig was the learned Scottish feudalist who presided over the trials of those accused of the murder of Rizzio in 1566, the talented but hated Italian secretary of Mary Queen of Scots.

Craig's connection with East Lothian was his ownership of the village of St Laurence on the west side of the Royal Burgh of Haddington (4). He had the properties of St Laurence legally transferred to him on 23rd March 1587 (or 1588) by his relative Sir Lewis Bellenden of Auchenoule (50 p.26). A second East Lothian connection was through his marriage to Helen Heriot daughter of the Laird of Trabroun whose mother was a relative of George Buchanan, tutor to Mary Queen of Scots and James VI.

Sir Thomas Craig was born in 1538 in Edinburgh and educated at St Leonard's College in St Andrews where he studied Latin, logic, rhetoric, ethics and physics. In 1555 he attended the University of Paris and when he returned home in 1561 he was tutored by John Craig, the Assistant Minister of John Knox at St Giles Cathedral in Edinburgh. This young minister had escaped from Rome where he had been condemned to be burned at the stake for heresy against the Catholic Church; his epic journey in disguise through Europe was the thrilling story of his day.

Thomas Craig was admitted an Advocate in February 1563 and the following year he was appointed Justice-Depute representing the Justice-General, a hereditary office of the 5th Duke of Argyll. After the murder of David Rizzio, Craig presided over the trials (1st April 1566) of Thomas Scott, the depute-sheriff of Perth, and Henry Yaire, a priest, both of whom he condemned to death for this crime which had been perpetrated by the hated Lord Darnley (Mary's husband) and the Protestant Lords including the Earls of Moray, Morton, Argyle, Glencairn and others. Darnley suffered the same fate as his victim and again Craig conducted the trials of Stephen Dalgleish, Hay and Powrie for their complicity in Darnley's murder. It was common knowledge that James, Earl of Bothwell *qv* was the instigator of this crime but Craig was saved from the ignominy of presiding over his farcical trial (at which Bothwell was not present); it was taken by the Duke of Argyll himself and vindicated Bothwell.

Thomas Craig was a fastidious student of the law; he kept strictly to the precepts of the legal system; his correctitude kept him free from the intrigues and corruption of the age. He was something of a poet and his *Genethliacon* was a collection of verses written as a compliment to the birth of James VI. He was best known, however for his highly respected legal treatises; *Jus Feudale*, written in Latin, was published in 1603 and was translated and republished in Leipzig in 1716 and again in 1732; it was the clearest statement of feudal law in existence which showed that feudal law in Scotland had a common origin with that of England.

Such was the respect in which he was held, he was appointed Counsel for the king, James VI, in 1592 who was then twenty-five years of age. Craig's *Treatise on the right of James VI to the Succession to the English Crown* and his *Treatise on the Union* were masterly dissertations but proved unnecessary, the process leading to James VI's accession as James I of England being surprisingly peaceful. To prove that the Scots had never paid homage to the English crown he wrote *De Homino* and in 1603 he accompanied James VI to London to be present at his coronation. He was offered a knighthood but declined it, however, the king insisted and he was knighted without the formal ceremony. James VI appreciated the intellectual support of Craig and appointed him as a Commissioner to examine a closer union between Scotland and England and to this end he wrote his *De Unione Regnorum Brittaniae* in 1605. However James's aspirations for unity were thwarted by vitriolic prejudice against all things Scottish, especially that of Lady Ann Clifford's diary comments. (82 p.121)

When he returned to Scotland he was nominated to the Inner House of Advocates - a privileged position for the trusted few. He was appointed Advocate for the Church and in 1606 he defended six ministers accused of treason for holding a general assembly in Aberdeen. In 1607 he was appointed by the Scottish Parliament as a member of a Commission which was responsible for agreeing a Latin Grammar for schools. This was his last scholarly service, he died on 26th February 1608 aged seventy. He was a courtly, tolerant and scholarly man who sought neither riches nor fame.

EVELYNE M CROAL

Editor of the Haddingtonshire Courier

Miss Evelyne Croal was the daughter of the illustrious family of newspaper editors who founded East Lothian's first successful newspaper - *The Haddingtonshire Courier*. She took over the editorship and managership when her father died in 1924. It is probable that she was the only lady editor in the country. As one of very few women with a 1914-15 Star for service during the 'Great War' she was undoubtedly a lady of substance and great character who simply refused to recognise the usual conventions of a male dominated profession.

During World War I this tall, rather formidable and indefatigable lady was a volunteer ambulance driver in France when men were being killed in their thousands at the front. Twenty years later, during World War II she served as an Air Raid Warden and worked assiduously for the Red Cross as well as for the welfare of Polish troops in East Lothian.

The Haddingtonshire Courier was founded in 1859 as a weekly newspaper by her grandfather, James Croal (1829-1883), and her great uncle, David Croal JP (1819-1904). It was a brave venture; indeed, some thought of it as foolhardy. East Lothian had been declared a journalist's desert but these two men had a solid background and sound training in the newspaper business.

Evelyne Croal was born in Haddington in 1893. Her father, James Gibson Croal (1860-1924), took over the management of the *Courier* in 1904 at the age of twenty-two when his father died. Evelyne was educated firstly at the Knox Institute in Haddington, later at St George's School for Girls in Edinburgh and finally at Brussels where she studied French and German. On her return home to Haddington she took a lively interest in voluntary work, drama, the Red Cross and the work of the family business D & J Croal Printers and Publishers.

In 1914, shortly after her 21st birthday, she was one of the first to join the Volunteer Aid Detachment (VAD) and became an ambulance driver in France during the whole of World War I when Dr Elsie Inglis set up her field hospitals at the front.

She was a family friend of Dr William MacLean MC (*qv*) and his wife Edith of Hilton Lodge; they had much in common both having experienced the horrors of the Great War. The Misses Alice and Mary Burnet and the Mills family who were her neighbours in Park Lane, Haddington were also close friends. Together they enjoyed the social life of the sports of motoring and golf. A natural leader and a fine golfer, Evelyne Croal became Ladies' Captain of Haddington Golf Club.

During World War II she was again active, this time as an Air Raid Warden, and in giving generously of her plenteous energies for the welfare of Polish troops in East Lothian. For the latter she was presented with an illuminated address from the Polish Army. Through her work in the Red Cross she organised parcels of food and clothing for Haddingtonians who were prisoners of war in Germany and as the commandant of the Haddington VAD she was an active helper at Haddington's First Aid Post.

She died aged 59 years on 17th June 1952 at Roodlands Hospital, and her mother, who died nine years after her daughter on 24th January 1961 aged 90, became the only surviving partner in the firm of D & J Croal.

THE DALRYMPLE FAMILY,

Baronets of North Berwick

"There never was trouble brewing in Scotland but that a Dalrymple or a Campbell was at the bottom of it", so said Charles II. This was the recollection of William III in 1691 when the untamed Highlands seemed to him to consist of psalm singers and savages.

The Christian name Hew has been used in the Dalrymple family for many generations and is attributed to a heraldic myth in which a brave Dalrymple in defence of his king threw rocks at his attackers from the top of the Bass Rock. The king encouraged him by shouting, "Hew, Dalrymple, Hew", until the attackers fled under a hail of rocks. The king ordered that he should be known as 'Hew' from that day! [There is no record to which Dalrymple or to which king this story refers.]

The Dalrymple family celebrated their tercentenary in North Berwick in 1994. The first member of this illustrious family arrived in North Berwick in December 1694 when **Sir Hew Dalrymple, 1st Baronet of North Berwick (1652-1737)** took over the heritable debts of the confiscated estate of North Berwick.

Today, a Dalrymple, Sir Hew Hamilton-Dalrymple, Bt., KCVO, the 10th baronet, still lives at Leuchie. The name Dalrymple is therefore well-known in North Berwick - the **Dalrymple Arms Hotel, Lord President Road** commemorating Sir Hew Dalrymple, 1st Baronet of North Berwick (1652-1737), **South Hamilton Road** and **Hamilton Road** after his wife Marion, **Sainthill Court** after Margaret, wife of the 2nd Baronet, **Duff Court** after Janet, wife of the 3rd Baronet, **Duncan Court** after Lady Jane Duncan, wife of the 4th Baronet, **Warrender Court** after Charlotte, wife of the 5th Baronet, **Arkwright Court**, after Francis Elizabeth, wife of the 6th Baronet, **Pattle Court** after Sophia, wife of the 7th Baronet, **Clifford Road** after Alice Mary, wife of the 8th Baronet, **Thorne Court** after Ann, wife of the 9th Baronet, **Keppel Road** after Lady Ann-Louise, wife of the present 10th Baronet whose family home is also commemorated in **Quidenham Court**.

Sir Hew Dalrymple, the 1st Baronet, born in 1652, was the third son of the great jurist James Dalrymple, the 1st Viscount Stair (1619-95) and Margaret, the eldest daughter of James Ross of Balniel, Wigtonshire. Sir Hew's eldest brother was Sir John Dalrymple (1648-1707), the Master of Stair (a courtesy title), 2nd Viscount and 1st Earl of Stair; it was he who gave the order for the extermination of the clan MacDonald of Glencoe (1692).

Sir Hew Dalrymple 1st Bt. (Courtesy of the Scottish National Portrait Gallery)

After legal training in the family tradition Hew Dalrymple was admitted to the Faculty of Advocates on 23rd February 1677. There are many stories of his court room battles, for example, in 1684 while representing the Earl of Monteith in his divorce action he suffered a series of badgering interruptions by his opposing advocate, Mr A MacFerson, during the questioning of witnesses. The exchanges became so heated between the two advocates, they challenged each other to physical combat and were ordered to apologise to the judge, but such was the bitterness between them they had to be imprisoned until they cooled off!

In August 1690 Hew Dalrymple was elected to the Scottish Parliament for New Galloway and acted as substitute for his brother, Sir James Dalrymple, as 'their Majesties' Advocate' (their Majesties being William III and Mary). On 11th January 1695 he was chosen as Dean of the Faculty of Advocates succeeding Sir James Stewart, the Lord Advocate. In 1702 he was elected as the Member of the last Scottish Parliament for North Berwick (1702-1707).

Hew Dalrymple was appointed judge of the Commissary Court, on the resignation of his brother, Sir John Dalrymple, the Master of Stair. During the enquiry into the Massacre of Glencoe Hew Dalrymple wrote and circulated a pamphlet in defence of his brother. For this 'false and calumnious impertinence' he was called to the bar of the House of Parliament and censured. He was ordered to 'ask his Grace and Parliament pardon'. This he did, but explained that 'what was offensive in that paper had happened through mistake.' (25 p.407)

On 17th March 1698 Sir Hew Dalrymple was nominated Lord President of the Court of Session by William III but a commission had already appointed Sir William Hamilton. The problem was solved by revoking Hamilton's appointment and the Lords of Session decided to delay Dalrymple's appointment until June and that he should 'sit in the outer house' for a probationary period of three days before his swearing in on 7th June 1698. He had been created a Baronet of Nova Scotia in 1697 ('Nova Scotia' was a piece of land on which the esplanade of Edinburgh Castle now stands, so mandated by Charles I for the purpose of granting baronetcies to those who invested in the new Canadian colony of New Scotland (13 Vol. I p.86). Robert Chambers, in his *Traditions of Edinburgh*, exclaimed that he was not beyond using his power to favour an accused by arranging a court hearing at a time most convenient to the favoured one by ensuring that those judges against him were otherwise engaged! (16 p.123)

Having acquired the lands of North Berwick in 1694, Sir Hew purchased Tantallon Castle in 1699 from the Douglas family (ref. George Douglas, 4th Earl of Angus *q.v.*) In 1701 he bought the lands of Leuchie from the Marjoribanks family and in 1706 he bought the Bass Rock from the Crown.

He was appointed a Commissioner to draw up the articles of Union of the Scottish and English Parliaments of which he was a strong supporter, much to the disgust of another son of East Lothian - Andrew Fletcher of Saltoun (1655-1716) *qv* , "The Patriot." The commission was dominated by Dalrymples: Sir John, (the Master of Stair), Sir Hew and Sir David (as Solicitor-General for Scotland) met in Whitehall to be "bought and sold for English gold" - so sang the Jacobites who detested the Dalrymples as 'evil incarnate'. Sir Hew signed the Act of Union on 16th January 1707 in which 16 Peers and 45 MPs represented Scotland but his brother, the Master of Stair, had died of overwork only nine days before. His memorial, no doubt, was the Union, his relatives preferring to forget the Massacre of Glencoe. In North Berwick the Union was celebrated by planting many trees on the east side of the Law but others in Scotland deplored the Union with the "The Curses", the last verse of which gives an indication of the depth of feeling:

Curs'd be the Parliament that day,
Who gave their confirmation;
And cursed be every whining Whig,
For they have damned the nation!

A thorn in the flesh of Sir Hew Dalrymple was the Lord Chancellor, the 1st Earl of Seafield, who, although he had signed the Act of Union, proposed that it be dissolved in 1713. He persisted in presiding over Dalrymple's court. This was intolerable to Dalrymple who absented himself from the Sessions to form a party against Seafield. However, in 1726 he petitioned the king, George I, to be allowed to resign with a pension equal to his salary. The king's reply seems to have indicated his satisfaction with Dalrymple and that he should continue in office. Sir Hew Dalrymple remained Lord President until his death in his eighty-fifth year on 1st February 1737; he was buried at North Berwick.

Sir Hew married Marion, daughter of Sir Robert Hamilton on 12th March 1682. Their large family consisted of seven sons and five daughters. His second wife was Elizabeth Hamilton and they had two daughters. Tragically, all seven of his sons predeceased him and he was succeeded by his grandson.

The 2nd Baronet, Sir Hew Dalrymple (1712-1790) succeeded his grandfather in 1737, his father, **Sir Robert Dalrymple of Castleton**, having died on 21st August 1734. The grandson inherited the old house at Leuchie at the age of 25 years. He was born on 12th March 1712 and was appointed King's Remembrancer (an officer of the exchequer) in 1768. He became MP for Haddington Burghs from 1741 to 1747 and for the County of Haddington from 1747 to 1761. He spent about £700 repairing and trying to restore the old house at Leuchie but it was money wasted; he pulled it down and designed and built a new mansion house on the foundations of the old one in 1779. It took over six years to complete the building work and the finished result was 'an eclectic house both within and without, and unusually innocent of the urge to be consistently fashionable.' (30 p.282). The English painter Joseph Farington RA (1747-1821), during a visit to East Lothian in 1788, recorded in his diary: 'It is an excellent house, very plain on the outside, but highly and elegantly furnished within, and was wholly designed by Mr Dalrymple' (77). Sir Hew was 'known to all for his love of agriculture' and greatly improved the estate by draining the land and providing hedges (74 p.189).

He married Margaret, daughter of Peter Sainthill Esq., a prosperous surgeon in the City of London on 7th July 1743. Sir Hew and Margaret were deeply in love and, as is evident from their many loving letters (76), they hated to be parted from each other. As MP for the Haddington Burghs and as the laird of the estates of North Berwick he had to leave his wife and baby son in London while he attended to his affairs in East Lothian.

They had three sons: Robert Stair, a Captain in the 11th regiment of Dragoons who died in 1768, Peter, born in 1746, who died young and Hew born on 26th October 1746. Margaret died on 31 December 1747 a few weeks after the birth of her third son. Sir Hew was broken-hearted and mourned for many years. He remarried on 17th August 1756 Martha, daughter of Charles Edwin a barrister; they had no family. She died in 1782 in London.

The 2nd Baronet had only five years to enjoy his new home at Leuchie where he died on 30th November 1790 and was succeeded by his third and only surviving son.

Hew Dalrymple, 3rd Baronet, (1746-1800) was born on 26th October 1746 and became MP for Haddingtonshire from 1780 to 1786. He married in 1770 Janet Duff, daughter of William Duff of Crombie. They had a large family of eight sons and four daughters. His eldest son Hew died young and his second son, also Hew, born in 1774, succeeded him. The 3rd Baronet died at Bargany in Ayrshire on 13th February 1800. (70 p.14)

Hew Dalrymple, 4th Baronet, (1774-1834), the second son of the 3rd Baronet (his elder brother, also Hew, having died young), was born at North Berwick on 3rd January 1774. He joined the army to serve with the Grenadier Guards. He was a Lieutenant-Colonel in the Ayrshire Militia in 1803. As MP for Haddingtonshire between 1795 and 1800, Ayrshire 1803 to 1806 and for Haddington Burghs from 1820 to 1826 he was a strong supporter of Henry Dundas, Viscount Melville, during the Pitt-Dundas era when Dundas held despotic power over almost the whole of Scotland.

Sir Hew married Jane, the eldest daughter of Admiral 1st Viscount Duncan of Camperdown. They had one daughter, Henrietta Dundas Dalrymple. The 4th Baronet died on 23rd February 1834 at Bargany and the Baronetcy was inherited by his young brother, John, the fifth and next surviving son of the 3rd Baronet.

John Dalrymple, 5th Baronet (1780-1835), the second son of Sir Hew Hamilton-Dalrymple 3rd baronet and great-grandson of Sir Robert Dalrymple of Castleton, was born on 5th December 1780 at North Berwick. He spent part of his youth in the Cape; a keen horseman and an excellent shot, he joined the army firstly as a Cornet in 28th Light Dragoons. A conscientious and competent officer he attained the rank of Major-General, serving for a time in Mauritius, the island having been gained from France following the abdication of Napoleon in April 1814. He was MP for Haddingtonshire in 1805-06. Shortly after his arrival in India in 1831 he was devastated to learn of the sad news that ten of his servants at Leuchie had drowned when their boat, *The Czar*, had sunk off the rocks below Seacliff House. These loyal people had journeyed to London to bid farewell to the Major-General on his departure to India (59 p.235).

He succeeded his brother in 1834 and died at Bruntsfield House in Edinburgh a year later, on 26th May 1835. He was buried at North Berwick. In 1806 he married Charlotte, daughter of Sir Peter Warrender Bart., of Lochend and had two sons, Hew (1814-1887) and John Warrender (1824-1888) and five daughters: Helen Jane (1807-1882), Georgina Hacking (1810-1872), Charlotte Sophia (1816-1864), Janet Jemima (1818-1883), Patricia (1826-?).

Sir Hew Dalrymple, 6th Baronet (1814-1887) was born in Mauritius on 26th November 1814. Following his father, he entered the army and served with the 71st Highlanders attaining the rank of Lieutenant-Colonel having served in the East Indies. He was present at the annexation of Coorg when the administration of Mysore was taken over by the Whig Governor-General William Bentinck (1828-35). He succeeded his father as 6th Baronet in 1835 and he retired from active service in 1852.

Having been appointed Deputy Lieutenant of the County of Haddington in 1846 he arrived home to Leuchie and was elected Convenor of the County in 1861. He soon became immersed in the public life of East Lothian becoming Chairman of the County Road Board, Justice of the Peace, Chairman of the Parochial Board and, after the passing of the Education (Scotland) Act of 1872, he was appointed Chairman of the School Board in North Berwick. He was described in his obituary as 'abrupt and somewhat brusque....[he] concealed his real goodness of heart, for Sir Hew was one of the kindest of men....As a landlord he was scrupulously just.'

On 27th July 1852 he married Francis Elizabeth, daughter of Robert Arkwright of Sutton Scarsdale. They had no family and Sir Hew died 27th April 1887 at Leuchie and was buried at North Berwick. His young brother, Sir John Warrender Dalrymple succeeded to the title and estates.

John Warrender, 7th Baronet (1824-1888) was born on 28th May 1824. He joined the Bengal Civil Service during the memorable and efficient term of office of the 1st Marquis of Dalhousie, a Peelite Governor-General. Sir John was appointed the Civil and Session judge at Hooghly, south of Calcutta, in 1858 and 1860. He succeeded his brother in 1887 and lived less than two years as 7th Baronet; he died 28th December 1888 and was buried at North Berwick, being succeeded by his only surviving son Walter.

On 7th June 1847 he married Sophia, youngest daughter of James Pattle. She was exceptionally beautiful, graceful and charming and was painted by George Frederick Watts OM, RA (1817-1904) who, on a visit to Sophia's sister Sarah Prinsep, 'came to stay for three days and stayed thirty years'. They had two sons and one daughter: Hew (1848-1869), Walter (1854-1920) and Virginea Julian (1850-?).

Walter H Dalrymple 8th Baronet (1854-1920) was born on 6th January 1854. An immensely clever student at Slade he became a talented sculptor and pianist. He planned and developed North Berwick to the west of St Baldred's Church and his layouts, executed before the advent of town planning approval, were praised by future planners. He was a keen golfer and played with the 1st Earl Balfour, Arthur James Balfour of Whittinghame *qv*, (Prime Minister from 1902-06, a philosopher and statesman of distinction) and Edward VII during his visits to the links in North Berwick. In fact, Sir Walter designed the east links ('Burgh Links') and laid out the nine seaside holes of the golf course. Such was his enthusiasm for the game he invented a set of combination golf clubs in 1899 and had them patented. He was director of the Edinburgh United Breweries Ltd. He died in Italy in 1920.

He married Alice Mary, daughter of Major-General Hon. Sir Henry Hugh Clifford KCMG,CB,VC on 7th November 1882. They had five children: Hew Clifford (1888-1959); John (1889-1915, killed in Flanders); Agnes Mary (1884-1945); Marjorie (1885-1939); Sybil (1887-?)

Hew Clifford Dalrymple 9th Baronet of North Berwick was born on 11th August 1888 at The Lodge, North Berwick. Although extremely deaf from the age of eight, he was an adept lip-reader and missed little in conversation. He was educated at Christchurch, Oxford after which he worked for the Canadian Pacific Railway as an accountant. At the outbreak of World War I in 1914 he rushed home determined to enlist in the army, but, because of his deafness, he failed the medical examination on no fewer than ten occasions. He almost succeeded in one medical examination when his lip-reading completely deceived his examiners until he was called back when leaving the room with his back to his examiners; it was only then that his deafness was discovered. He remained in London to become chief accountant of the Sheffield Simplex Company.

Shortly after the war, in 1919, he married Ann, daughter of Augustus Thorne DL, JP; they had two sons and two daughters: Hew (1926-); John (1928-1985); Elsie (1922-); Jean (1923-1947). He returned to North Berwick on the death of his father in 1920 to find his newly inherited estate at North Berwick in rather precarious circumstances. He devoted the rest of his life to his estates but he was unable, because of his deafness, to participate in public life as he would have wished. However, he was a keen golfer and he commanded the Leuchie platoon of the Home Guard during the 1939-45 war becoming second in command of the Home Guard in East Lothian. He died at Leuchie in 1959.

Sir Hew Hamilton-Dalrymple and the Princess Royal (Courtesy of East Lothian Courier)

The present **Baronet, the 10th, is Sir Hew (Fleetwood) Hamilton Dalrymple** who was born on 9th April 1926 at The Lodge, North Berwick. His early education at Ampleforth was followed by military training from which he was commissioned, in November 1944, into the Grenadier Guards. He sailed to British mandated Palestine in 1945 and for the next two years he was heavily involved in the containment of the resistance fighters under Menachem Begin, Commander-in-Chief of the Irgun Zvia Resistance Group. In India he was ADC to General

Sir Frank Messervy in the Northern Command during which he saw the end of the Raj and the birth of Pakistan.

After service in Germany, Egypt and Cyprus he returned to the Staff College, Camberly in 1958 and was then appointed Deputy (Assistant) Adjutant-General of the 3rd Division. His final military appointment from 1960 was Regimental Adjutant, Grenadier Guards

Back home in East Lothian he found the mansion at Leuchie too large for his needs and he built a single-storey house within the garden walls of Leuchie. He had it designed so that the old paintings of his ancestors could be properly displayed. The mansion house was leased for a peppercorn rent to the Servite Convent as a Richard Cave Multiple Sclerosis Holiday Home.

He was appointed a director of Scottish and Newcastle Breweries in 1967, becoming vice chairman in 1983. He was also a director and later Chairman of the Scottish American Investment Company plc. On the retiral of Lord Wemyss in 1987 Sir Hew was appointed Lord Lieutenant of East Lothian.

In 1950 he was appointed a Lieutenant of the Queen's Bodyguard for Scotland (The Royal Company of Archers) and became Adjutant in 1964 until 1985 and President of the Council of Archers in 1988 to 1996. On the tenth anniversary of his Adjutancy he was appointed a Commander of the Royal Victorian Order (1974). In 1996 he was appointed Captain-General and Gold Stick for Scotland and was created a Knight Commander of the Royal Victorian Order (KCVO). He was present at the historic ceremony of the opening of the Scottish Parliament by HM Queen Elizabeth II on 1st July 1999.

He married Lady Ann-Louise Mary Keppel, daughter of the 9th Earl of Albemarle, in 1954. They have four sons, the eldest, Hew Richard his heir who lives at Blackdykes, North Berwick with his wife, Jane (nee Morris), their son Hew and three daughters.

THE DALRYMPLES of North Berwick - family tree

James Dalrymple, Laird of Stair, of Drummurchie, Ayrshire (d.1625
married 1617 Janet Kennedy daughter of Fergus Kennedy of Knockdaw

son: James Dalrymple, 1st Viscount Stair (1619-1695)
married 1643, Margaret Ross, widow of Fergus Kennedy of Knockdaw

sons: (1) John Dalrymple, Master of Stair , 1st Earl of Stair (1648-1707)
(2) Sir James Dalrymple of Borthwick (1650-171
(3) **Sir Hew Dalrymple of North Berwick, 1st Baronet (1652-1737)**

(4) Thomas Dalrymple MD (1663-1725) dsp
(5) Sir David Dalrymple of Hailes (1665-1721)

married (i) 1682, Marion, daughter of Sir Robert Hamilton of Pressmannen

sons: (1) James Dalrymple (1684 dsp)
(2) Sir Robert Dalrymple of Castleton (d.1734)
(3) Hew Dalrymple of Drummore, East Lothian (c.1690-1755)
(4) John Dalrymple (1692-1753)
(5) William Dalrymple (1693-?)
(6) Alexander Dalrymple (1690-?)
(7) James Dalrymple of Nunraw (1698-1766)
daughters: (1) Margaret (1683-1737)
(2) Marion (1686-?)
(3) Anne (1687-1736)
(4) Elizabeth (1695-1739)
(5) Eleanor (c.1700)

married (ii) 1711, Elizabeth, heiress of John Hamilton of Bangour

daughters: (6) Marion (1712-1735
(7) Johanna (1714-?)

married (i): 1707, Johanna Hamilton of Bargany

sons: (1) **Sir Hew Dalrymple 2nd Baronet (1712-1790)**
(2) John Hamilton Dalrymple (1715-1796)
(3) Robert Dalrymple (1716-1745 in Rome)
(4) James Dalrymple (1717-died young) dsp
daughters: (1) Marion (1708-1740)
(2) Jean (1709-1712)
(3) Elizabeth (1717-1781)

married (ii) 1725, Anne Cunningham of Caprington

sons: (1) William Dalrymple (d. 1782)
(2) James Dalrymple (1731-?)
(3) Charles Dalrymple (d.1799)
(4) Stair Dalrymple (d.1756 in East Indies)
daughters: (1) Janet (1726-died young)
(2) Anne (1727-?)

married (i) 1743: Margaret, daughter of Peter Sainthill Esq.

sons: (1) Robert Stair Dalrymple (1744-1768)
(2) Peter Dalrymple (died young)
(3) **Sir Hew Dalrymple, 3rd Baronet (1746-1800)**

married (ii) 1756, Martha, daughter of Charles Edwin dsp

married: 1770 Janet, daughter of William Duff of Crombie

sons: (1) Hew Dalrymple (1772-died young)
(2) **Sir Hew Dalrymple, 4th Baronet (1774-1834)**
(3) Robert Dalrymple (1775-?)
(4) William Dalrymple (1778-?)
(5) **Sir John Dalrymple, 5th Baronet (1780-1835)**
(6) James Dalrymple (1782-?)
(7) Peter Dalrymple (1786-?)
(8) Robert Stair Dalrymple (1788-?)
daughters: (1) Elizabeth (1776-?)
(2) Margaret (1778-?)
(3) Janet (1783-?)
(4) Anne (1784-?)

married 1779, Lady Jane Duncan, eldest daughter of 1st Viscount Duncan of Camperdown

daughter: Henrietta Dundas Dalrymple Hamilton (1801-1869)

married: Charlotte, daughter of Sir Peter Warrender Bt. of Lochend

sons: (1) **Sir Hew Dalrymple, 6th Baronet (1814-1887dsp)**
married: Francis Elizabeth, only daughter of Robert Arkwright of Sutton Scarsdale
(2) **Sir John Warrender Dalrymple, 7th Baronet (1824-1888)**
daughters: (1) Helen Jane (1807-1882)
(2) Georgina Hacking (1810-
(3) Charlotte Sophia (1816-1864)
(4) Janet Jemima (1818-1883)
(5) Patricia (1826-?)

married 1847 Sophia, younger daughter of James Pattle

sons: (1) Hew Dalrymple (1848-1868 dsp)
(2) **Sir Walter H Dalrymple, 8th Baronet (1854-1920)**
daughter: Virginea Julia (1850-?)

married1882, Alice Mary Clifford, daughter of Major-General Sir Henry Clifford KCMG, CB, VC

sons: (1) **Sir Hew Dalrymple, 9th Baronet (1888-1959)**
(2) John Dalrymple (1889-1915)
daughters: (1) Agnes (1884-1945)
(2) Marjery (1885-1939)
(3) Sybil (1888-?)

married: Anne Thorne, daughter of Augustus Thorne DL, JP

sons: (1) **Sir Hew (Fleetwood) Hamilton Dalrymple, 10th Baronet (1926 -)**
(2) John Dalrymple (1928 -1985)
daughters: (1) Elsie (1922-)
(2) Jean (1923-1947)

married: 1954, Lady Anne-Louise Mary Keppel, daughter of the 9th Earl of Albemarle,

sons: (1) Hew Dalrymple (1955-
(2) John Dalrymple (1957-
(3) Robert Dalrymple (1959-
(4) William Dalrymple (1965-

SIR DAVID DALRYMPLE of Hailes

Sir David Dalrymple, Lord Hailes, lived most of his life at Newhailes House near Musselburgh and was a distinguished member of the 'literati' of Edinburgh's 'Golden Age' of intellectual geniuses. His learned and accurate *Annals of Scotland 1057-1371* (1776-79) was the most exhaustive and scholarly work of its day and such was his reputation, Europe's greatest philosopher and historian, David Hume, asked him to revise his *Enquiry into the Human Mind* in 1753 - even before Dalrymple had published anything of note.

He was born on 26th October 1726 in Edinburgh, the eldest of sixteen children of Sir James Dalrymple of Hailes of Haddingtonshire. His grandfather, Sir David Dalrymple, was MP for the Haddington Burghs and solicitor-general to Queen Anne and his great-grandfather was Sir James Dalrymple, the 1st Viscount Stair, President of the Court of Session and author of the famous *Institutes of the Law of Scotland*. But possibly his most illustrious relation was his great-uncle the Master of Stair, Sir John Dalrymple (1648-1707), 2nd Viscount of Stair and 1st Earl of Stair who, as Secretary of State for Scotland, gave the order for the extermination of the clan Macdonald in the 'Massacre of Glencoe' on 13th February 1692.

Sir David Dalrymple was educated at Eton and studied civil law at Utrecht. He returned to Scotland just after the Battle of Culloden and was admitted to the bar in 1748. His father died when he was 24 years old and he inherited a tidy fortune; he was therefore able to follow his literary interests and to amass a great library of some 7000 books at Newhailes House which was built in 1686 and had been bought by his grandfather in 1707 - even the normally critical Dr Samuel Johnson of *Dictionary* fame referred to the library as "the foremost room of learning in Europe".

Today Newhailes House remains almost exactly as it was during the Scottish Enlightenment and will be restored to its former glory by the National Trust for Scotland by the year 2000. The mansion was designed by the architect, James Smith, who was the first to borrow from the ideas of Andrea Palladio (1508-80) and Smith therefore can be credited as the founder of the Palladian movement in Britain with his design of Newhailes House which he named Whitehill. Smith lived in the house until 1702 when John, 3rd Lord Bellenden of Broughton and Auchnoule bought it. A coal mining venture bankrupted him in 1707 and in that momentous year of the Union Sir David Dalrymple bought the property which remained in the hands of the Dalrymple family for the next 290 years. Sir David carried out several alterations between 1718 and 1742 when he added two wings and had the front entrance put to the back of the house.

Although not a particularly strong orator in court David Dalrymple proved himself to be a punctiliously accurate lawyer which won him many cases through his written pleadings such as the cause of the Countess of Sutherland in her claim for her title through the female line. He was raised to the bench of the Court of Session in 1766 and took the title Lord Hailes. In 1776 he became a judge of the criminal court distinguishing himself for his humane sentencing in comparison to many disgraceful judgements of the day. He was unsurpassed in his knowledge of the history of law.

He was a member of the Select Society in Edinburgh but he distanced himself from fellow members David Hume, Adam Smith and Principal Robertson through his devotion to study at Newhailes and instead he preferred to correspond with English scholars such as Samuel Johnson (1709-84), Edmund Burke (1729-97), William Warburton (1698-1779), Bishop Richard Hurd (1720-1808) and others.

The list of his published work is prodigious and learned; he was critical and completely free of prejudice and covered a wide range of subjects - legal, religious, philosophical, political, linguistic and historical - each with equal thoroughness and accuracy.

His first wife, Anne Brown, was a daughter of the Scottish judge, Lord Coalston. She died giving birth to twins. His second wife, Helen, was the daughter of Sir James Fergusson, Lord Kilkerran, another judge.

He died on 29th November 1792 and was survived by two daughters, one from each marriage.

SIR DAVID DAVIDSON of Haddington

the strength behind the Rifle Volunteer Movement

Known in Haddington as Colonel Davidson, David Davidson was the strength behind the Rifle Volunteer Movement from 1860. It was he who planted the oak tree overlooking the Tyne to commemorate the birthplace of John Knox at Giffordgate; this was at the instigation of no less a literary giant than Thomas Carlyle.

David Davidson was born at Haddington in 1811, the son of Henry M. Davidson, the Sheriff Clerk of the county. Henry Davidson's signature appears with that of William Pringle, a deacon, on the final record of the Guild of Skinners dated 1801, a craft which had existed in Haddington since 1545. (Skinners' Knowe behind the Episcopal Church in Haddington is reminiscent of this ancient craft).

David Davidson was a pupil of the Old Burgh School until he was sixteen years of age. During his schooldays he befriended Jane Welsh *qv* and became a staunch friend of both Jane and her future husband, the illustrious literary figure, Thomas Carlyle. At the age of sixteen Davidson left Haddington for India as a new recruit in the Bengal Native Infantry. The Governor-General was Lord William Bentinck whose first act was to abolish the Hindu practice of 'Suttee', the burning of young, childless widows, and to get rid of the murderous members of the religious fraternity of 'Thugees'. English language and thought were introduced in India at that time and after the British victory of the first Sikh War in 1846 and the second Sikh War in 1849, the Governor-General Lord Dalhousie, on his own responsibility, annexed the vast area of the Punjab. Steam navigation between India and Suez meant that British wives could join their husbands and Davidson's young wife, Margaret, was reunited with her husband; they were married in 1849.

Davidson was no ordinary soldier, he displayed an inventive bent and sent his plans for his invention of the rifled canon with his design of the elongated bullet to Sir Arthur Wellesley (later the Duke of Wellington); it was eventually used by the British Army. Davidson played his part in helping to quell the Indian Mutiny of 1857 when Dalhousie's successor, Charles Canning, was given the nick-name 'Clemency Canning'. At the end of the mutiny, after over thirty years of distinguished service in India and having reached the rank of Lieutenant-Colonel, David Davidson returned home to East Lothian in 1860.

At home the energetic Colonel Davidson gave strong support to the Earl of Wemyss in the formation of the Rifle Volunteer movement which had been started as far back as 1803 as the *Haddington Volunteers* (50 p.66) in response to the threat of invasion by the French. Davidson commanded the East Lothian Regiment which took part in the Royal Scottish Volunteer Review on the dull wet day of 25th August 1881 before Queen Victoria, Prince Albert, the ageing Duchess of Kent, and the royal children at Holyrood Park in Edinburgh. Davidson commanded the Queen's Brigade of Edinburgh and became its Honorary Colonel.

He spent his later years at south Edinburgh where he built a large mansion on 5 acres purchased from the East Morningside Estate in 1858 - Woodcroft, above the doorway of which he had the inscription *Meliora semper cogita* (always improve thought) carved at the suggestion of Haddington born Jane Welsh Carlyle (the same motto appeared above the doorway of a house, long since demolished, in the Hardgate, Haddington). His magnificent mansion was built from pink sandstone which was quarried in his grounds. During the construction Davidson lived at St Margaret's Cottage in the Greenhill district (near Bruntsfield) of Edinburgh where he was visited by Jane Welsh Carlyle and enjoyed many memories of happy youthful days in Haddington. He visited the Carlyles at their home in Cheyne Row in Chelsea where he met several literary figures including Alfred Tennyson. Sadly, Woodcroft was demolished in 1962 and replaced by Woodcroft Telephone Exchange (21).

Shortly after the death of Thomas Carlyle in February 1881 the *Haddington Advertiser* reported the last conversation between the two old friends:

> 'After a touching allusion to the grave of his loyal wife, Thomas Carlyle had said he had a request to make, namely that he would like a tree planted to mark the site of the house where Knox was born so that it might be seen from the Church Yard ... "a tree will not last long" (Colonel Davidson)... "an oak will last a long time" (Carlyle) ... "perhaps as long as the world which seems to be getting into its death throes" (Col. Davidson)... "the world will last a long time yet" (Carlyle)'.

The tree was planted on 29th March 1881; the commemorative stone adjacent reads:

> *Near this spot stood the house in which was born JOHN KNOX AD 1505 in commemoration an oak tree was here planted 29th March 1881 after the wish of the late Thomas Carlyle.*

In 1890 Davidson published his *Memorials of a Long Life*. For his long service to the Rifle Volunteer movement he was created a Knight of the Most Honourable Order of the Bath (KCB) by Queen Victoria in

1897. He died at Woodcroft three years afterwards, on 18th May 1900, six months after the death of his beloved wife of fifty years marriage, and was buried beside his ancestors in St Mary's Parish Churchyard, Haddington. His family gravestone reads:

In Memory of
SIR DAVID DAVIDSON KCB
Bombay Army and Colonel of the
the Queen's Edinburgh Volunteer Brigade
second son of Henry Davidson
Born at Haddington 18th August 1811
died 18th May 1900

Saved by Grace
and of his beloved wife
MARGARET
for fifty years his devoted helpmate
born 22nd April 1829
died 18th November 1899

blessed are the pure in heart.

DERREK DICK - *FISH*

East Lothian's International Star Singer-Songwriter, Actor

Derek William Dick, an internationally known singer-songwriter and actor, is best known by his professional name in the world of pop music - *Fish*. It is often the case that 'stars' remain almost hidden in their local communities; many are hardly seen at all. Not so with *Fish*. In East Lothian he has endeared himself to his doting fans through his music and by giving several local concerts ('gigs'), often at the end of long and strenuous world tours.

Courtesy of Derek Dick

Whilst the story of his life is not necessarily a formula for success as a singer-song-writer it never-the-less tells us of the frustrations and elations which can lead to success in the music business.

He was born at the Simpson Memorial Hospital in Edinburgh on 25th April 1958 and his boyhood home was in Dalkeith where his father, Robert Dick owned a garage and his mother Isa Dick (nee Paterson) was born in the village of Dewarton. Derek's Primary School days at King's Park were happy as was his secondary education at the High School in Dalkeith where his favourite subjects were history, music and English.

He had a boyhood ambition to become an archaeologist. However, his admiration for the singing of Ray Davies and the music of *Genesis, Yes* and *Pink Floyd* and others sparked a love of the idea of setting words to music to tell a story. Whilst his eventual choice to become a singer-songwriter and actor suited his coruscating temperament he had not yet found his career path. Instead, being a big lad of over six feet five inches in height, eighteen years old and unable to decide on his future, he took the unlikely step of applying for entry to Sandhurst Military College. However, during his second interview and after an argument he decided against proceeding further.

In total contrast he decided to seek the country life and to study forestry. After a few months at Bush House estate in Midlothian he worked with the Forestry Commission at Speymouth and afterwards, in 1979/80, he studied for his National Diploma in Forestry at Newtonrigg at Penrith. This led to his appointment in 1980 as a trainee forester at Bowhill in Selkirk on the estate of the Duke of Buccleuch - all rather a far cry from the world of the screaming fans of rock music which would greet him in later years.

It was at this time, in May 1980, that he met the members of a five-piece band named *Blewitt* in Galashiels. He joined the band as a singer on trial and he continued with *Blewitt* for another fifteen gigs throughout the Borders.

In November 1980 he decided to follow his dream of becoming a singer/songwriter. He met a bass player, Diz Minnitt, in Retford. They rented a cottage in Ettrick Bridge and started a band which toured the whole country. Having built up a large following he then joined *Marillion* which was to become famous after signing their world wide contract with EMI Records in September 1982. Derek's first single was *Market Square Heroes*, released in October 1982; it sold over 40,000 copies. During the Falklands War in 1982 his song *Forgotten Sons* from his first album *Script for a Jester's Tear* which was written with the band *Marillion*, was requested by the British troops and broadcast many times on Falkland Radio.

Success had been achieved but would he grasp it to reach greater heights? The answer was an unequivocal 'yes' and the year 1985 was a major turning point. His second album was *Fugazi* and his single *Kayleigh* was an immediate success at no. 2 in the charts; its album, *Misplaced Childhood* entered the UK charts at no.1. However, this was one half of the turning point: it was on the video set of Kayleigh that his life changed completely - he met and fell in love with a beautiful German girl, Tamara, who would become his wife.

The next six years were mind-blowingly hectic. He completed *Clutching at Straws* in 1987 and two massive world tours. He had certainly grasped success but not without cost: he described it as:

> *that entire era was a blur of travelling, performing and endless interviews combined with the excesses of a touring rock band with their first worldwide hit. I was wasted physically and spiritually at the end of that road.*

Tamara and Derek decided to be married in St Mary's Parish Church, Haddington. They took their vows before Rev. Alastair MacDonnell on 25th July 1987 and left almost immediately for Los Angeles for a press tour after which they returned to their house at Gerrards Cross near London.

Roadwork was now over and he resigned rather dramatically from *Marillion* and from EMI Records in October 1988 to embark on his solo career. He needed a co-writer, rehearsal rooms, storage space, finance and artistic help. Tamara and he decided to sell the house in London, pay off the mortgage and return to Scotland.

Derek's parents, who were keen to see their only son settled near at hand in East Lothian, searched out a new base for the young couple. They found the ideal spot at Spittalrig near Haddington. The place was somewhat run down but it was here that he would commence the building of his own recording studio (in a shed which had been occupied by Italian prisoners of war) and his third career was launched.

Jon Cavanagh, an ex-EMI executive, a good friend and manager, arrived to help transform Derek into a solo artist and create the band which would 'tour the album'. The result was the album *Vigil in a Wilderness of Mirrors*. They left for London to record it at Townhouse Studios.

These were halcyon days in 1989: singing live with full orchestra on the album, *A Gentleman's Excuse Me* at Abbey Road Studio 2 and using a horn section for the first time on *Big Wedge*. It was a proud moment for Derek when he delivered the finished album to EMI in the late summer of 1989, hopefully for release in October with a 'world shattering promotion campaign' but a delay was imposed to avoid a clash with *Marillion's* new release. It was released by EMI in January 1990.

However, dark clouds gathered: the single, *State of Mind*, released in 1989 died after its release in the UK Top 40 charts and a Highlands and Islands tour proved prohibitively expensive but received excellent reviews. *Big Wedge* reached the UK Top 20 but thereafter dropped into oblivion. However, in the summer of 1990 his gig at the Albert Hall was a sellout.

Derek was now unhappy with his EMI contract and attempts to renegotiate it failed. A High Court injunction forbade him from releasing his own recordings. Legal costs and the expense of building his new studio meant that he had to give up the dispute with EMI. But there was a shining light of happiness: Tammy was pregnant and the birth of their daughter, Tara, on 1st January 1991 gave them boundless joy in spite of seemingly insoluble financial pressures.

Such was his reputation a saviour arrived, Polydor Records Ltd offered him sufficient funds in advances to stabilize his financial position. This, with the backing of investors, enabled him to build his new studio, 'Funny Farm', at Spittalrig (later renamed 'Millennium Studios'). The result was a single, *Internal Exile* which was taken from the album of the same name and was released in September 1991. This was a mix of styles, however, his producer, Chris Kimsey was uncomfortable working in an unfinished studio with his 56-channel equipment under test. Problems seemed to multiply and even the engineer, Thomas Stiehler began to think that the studio must be haunted. He consulted a German medium who told him to smoke out the rooms with burning Italian sage. It worked! Suddenly, there were no more gremlins. The new album was completed in time and delivered to an enthusiastic Polydor Records. A tour was now necessary to get back into the public eye and Brian Lane the *ex-Yes* manager took over.

Derek and Tamara with their daughter Tara decided to have their first holiday to Kenya; they badly needed a break. During their absence misfortune struck again: his good friend and production manager, Andy Field, died, his principal co-writer, Mickey Simmonds, resigned and his tour promoter became bankrupt. Derek released two cover-version albums: *Internal Exile* and *Songs from the Mirror*, but Polydor wanted no more cover-version albums. A lesser man would have simply given up, instead Derek Dick decided to form his own recording company.

This decision was prompted by his belief in the spirit world through which his deceased grandfather, the founder of the garage *Dick Bros* in Dalkeith, advised him to manufacture and sell his own products. He asked permission of his father to use the name *Dick Bros* for his proposed recording company. His father was more than delighted to agree; there was much emotional encouragement between father and son that day and especially on the day of his first release, *Sushi* a double live cd in March 1994.

By now Derek was gaining in confidence in his song writing especially after James Cassidy, the producer of Polydor's *Songs from the Mirror*, had joined the writing team. The fact that he owned his studio gave him new and relatively inexpensive freedom to create and to record his future albums. The success of this financed the promotion and marketing of the *Suits* album, his first major release from Dick Bros. This was followed by the video *Lady Let it Lie* in May 1994, the single of which reached no.1 in the UK independent charts in April. *Acoustic Session* was released for fanclub members only and his single *Fortunes of War* was released in September and also reached the charts. At this juncture a new career opened up for him: he was invited to play a major film role in *Chasing the Deer* which had its screen debut in the 1994 Edinburgh Film Festival.

Early in 1995 he concentrated on two anthology albums, *Yin* and *Yang*, the record of which contained twenty-six tracks with 150 minutes of quality music. It was now essential to begin touring again - 'a great album means nothing if no-one hears it'. His *Yin and Yang* world tour of 1996 was a hectic dash through 24 countries throughout Europe to

South Africa and South America. He then answered a special request of the peace-keeping troops of the United Nations in war-torn Bosnia and Crotia by giving eleven concerts during his two-week concert tour in August 1996 - an unforgettable experience. However, 1996 was the year in which he experienced the dream of a lifetime: he was asked by UEFA Euro '96 to sing the Scottish 'national anthem' *Flower of Scotland* at the England v Scotland match at Wembley on 15th June.

In October he hosted his own three-hour night-time radio show, *Fish Head Curry*, on *Radio Forth FM*. This spicy concoction of music tripled his ratings within three months. He was now desperate to begin writing again. Steve Wilson and Mickey Simmonds were his inspiration and his musical education in the production of *Sunsets on Empire* which was released in May 1997 with excellent reviews. This was his finest achievement to date, but lack of funds for advertising and marketing meant that it did not receive the 'airplay' it deserved. The only answer was to tour again. He gave a total of 115 concerts in 22 countries, the final one being in the Corn Exchange of Haddington. His fans in East Lothian were delighted. Although the fans world wide loved the music the tour incurred considerable debts and a new strategy was now not only necessary but urgent.

His new material was first rate and he decided to concentrate on writing rather than business and after a few weeks at Miles Copland's writing retreat in France he returned home to Scotland with six new songs, five of which would suit his new project - a collection of songs on one album which would represent his output over the past ten years - a compilation of styles - *Vigil in a Wilderness of Mirrors* was released in December 1997 and was followed by *Fortunes of War* in May 1998, *Tales from the Big Bus* in July and *Kettle of Fish* in November forming part of his solo catalogue.

His film and television appearances are evidence of his versatility - with his clear Scottish brogue and 6 foot five (1.56m) height he is ideal for 'hard man' parts having already played a tough record producer in the television play *Guide to becoming a Rock Star*, a hardened ex-convict in *Taggart* and a drug-dealing night club owner in ITV's *Rebus*. However, his aspirations for film and television parts have not eclipsed his love for music: he released *Raingods with Zippos* in 1999 and he is working on a new album to be called *Fellini Day* (commemorating the great Italian film director, Fellini) bringing his total to twenty-five albums. In October 2000 he will appear in the film *Nine Dead Gay Guys* and he has been given a part in the new film *Clarinda*. He is planning another world tour and several concerts for British troops in Bosnia and Kosova later in the year 2000.

GAVIN DOUGLAS

the Poet-Bishop of Tantallon

This son of the nobility, Gavin Douglas, was the third son of Archibald, 5th Earl of Angus, known as 'The Great Earl' or 'Bell-the-Cat'. He was born in the Douglas stronghold of Tantallon Castle c.1474. Little is known of his childhood except that as a boy in East Lothian it was evident that he was destined for the Church. He was serious and studious and befriended a local boy who, although a few years his junior, displayed exceptional intellect. The boy was John Major *qv* of Gleghornie who was to achieve distinction throughout Europe as a theologian and historian. Gavin Douglas became his patron and earned for himself distinction as a poet-bishop. It is to Gavin Douglas that we owe the first translation of Virgil's *Aenid* into 'Middle Scots', the literary language of Scottish poets in medieval times.

Tantallon Castle,stronghold of the Douglases

Gavin Douglas was educated for the priesthood at St Andrews from 1489 to 1494 and afterwards he studied at the University of Paris. After his ordination in 1496 he was presented at Monymusk in Aberdeenshire and then at the parish of Prestonkirk (called Lynton in the 12th century) in East Lothian. In 1501 James IV appointed him dean of St Giles Church in Edinburgh where he was chosen as a burgess in 1513. The St Giles appointment was said to have been the result of his poetical address to James IV at the end of his earliest work, the *Palice of Honour*. It was his translation of *Virgil* which was the first metrical version of a classical poem by a Scot to be seen in Scotland or England and his prologues depicting wild scenery were a new form of literature.

After the disastrous defeat of the Scots at Flodden in 1513 the widow of James IV, Queen Margaret, daughter of Henry VII and sister of Henry VIII, married Gavin Douglas's handsome nephew, Archibald Douglas, the 6th Earl of Angus in 1514. She was Queen Regent, her only surviving seventeen-month old son having been crowned two weeks after the death, at Flodden, of James IV. It was as a result of her Regency that Gavin Douglas's expectations rose; he expected and received some preferment. However, her position in relation to her son was now weak and an unseemly quarrel arose when the Duke of Albany, as Governor, demanded possession of the child.

The Queen Dowager made it known that she wished Gavin Douglas to become Archbishop of St Andrews. He travelled to St Andrews and took up residence at the Castle, but Hepburn, the prior of St Andrews, had himself voted as Archbishop. Soon afterwards Hepburn was ejected and James Beaton, the Archbishop of Glasgow, became Archbishop of St Andrews in 1522.

In January 1515 Gavin Douglas was given the Bishopric of Dunkeld, but opposition from the Earl of Atholl in favour of his brother, prevented his appointment. The Queen now appealed to Pope Leo X, as did her brother, Henry VIII, on behalf of Douglas but, with the return of the Duke of Albany from France, Gavin Douglas was arrested and imprisoned on an old statute - that of receiving Papal bulls. He was released after about a year and, following a severe reprimand to Albany from the Pope, Douglas was consecrated as Bishop of Dunkeld in 1516 but not without firstly making an apology to Albany - such were the niceties of the church.

Gavin Douglas's literary work included *King Hart* which was printed for the first time in 1786, 264 years after his death. He had become a member of the Scottish Chaucerians and was known and respected for his two allegorical poems and his translation of *Aeneid* in 1513 - the first translation of a classic from Latin into English. As a poet he was of the highest level and exceptional learning. The enduring quality of his work was such that four volumes of his poems and literature were edited by Dr John Small in 1874, but much of Douglas's work was lost in the mists of antiquity.

His nephew's marriage ended with prolonged acrimony in public. Margaret Tudor was almost as notoriously free with her affections as her brother Henry VIII, but her main concern was over her son, the heir to the throne. There was quarrelling amongst the nobles, some of whom wanted Margaret as Regent but friends of the Duke of Albany who were desperate that he (Albany) should become Regent, imprisoned the Queen. Albany, a close friend of the King of France, was certainly not the choice of Henry VIII as Albany would inevitably be an enemy of England.

Gavin Douglas, as Bishop of Dunkeld, much preferred the quiet life as bishop among his people to whom he simply wished to attend to their social and spiritual welfare. However, when Albany left Scotland he was accompanied by Gavin Douglas to assist him in the negotiations leading to the Treaty of Rouen (1517) which 'renewed and strengthened the traditional alliance between Scotland and France' (60 p.98). During

Albany's absence the 'young witless fool', the Earl of Angus, became bored with the co-operation which Albany had demanded with the earls of Arran, Huntly and Argyll and had taken control of Edinburgh. The two powerful families, the Hamiltons and the Douglases, vied with each other for ascendancy. In 1520, when Parliament was due to meet in Edinburgh, Gavin Douglas, having returned from France, learned that the Hamiltons were preparing to kill off every Douglas they could find. He warned his nephew who took immediate steps to barricade off all closes in which the Hamiltons lived. When the fighting started the Hamiltons were at a great disadvantage especially when 800 horsemen arrived in support of the Douglas cause. This fight became known in Scottish history as *Cleanse the Causeway*; the Hamiltons were cleared out of Edinburgh.

Angus's wife, the queen, returned from England and decided to divorce her husband. Albany returned and Angus fled. Gavin Douglas sought refuge at the court of Henry VIII and was deprived of his bishopric; even the Archbishop of Glasgow vilified him (25 vol.3 p.293). When England declared war on Scotland Gavin Douglas found himself in the heart of enemy territory. He had no option but to remain in England.

He became a firm friend of Polidoro Vergilio (c1470-1555) the Italian diplomat and historian whose *Anglica Historia* (1534) was in part influenced by Gavin Douglas who provided him with the correct view of events in Scotland.

Gavin Douglas was infected with the bubonic plague and died at the home of his great friend Lord D'Acre in London in September 1522. He was buried in the Hospital Church of the Savoy next to Thomas Halsey, Bishop of Leighlin.

GEORGE DOUGLAS, 4th Earl of Angus

a 'Red Douglas' who took the side of James II against the 'Black Douglases'

This was the Earl of Angus who was granted Tantallon Castle near North Berwick by Royal Charter from James II in 1452. His brother, the 3rd Earl, had died that year and, having no family, George Douglas inherited the titles and estates.

Tantallon Castle stands majestically on the cliff edge facing the River Forth, 3 km from North Berwick. The Castle dates from about 1370 and was built by William, the 1st Earl of Douglas to whom had passed the lands of Fife and North Berwick from the Earl of Fife. The Douglases maintained their hold on Tantallon for the next eighty-two years but their defiance of the king, James II, lost them their estates - the Douglas loss was an Angus gain. Tantallon remained in the hands of the Earldom of Angus for the next seventy-seven years, until in 1529 when James V, who had been a virtual prisoner under the harsh guardianship of Angus, took his revenge and destroyed the Castle.

George Douglas was born c.1412, the younger son of William the 2nd Earl of Angus and Margaret Hay, daughter of Sir William Hay of Yester. He was a 'Red Douglas' who took the side of James II against the 'Black Douglases'. The background was a trial of strength over several years between the powerful 8th Earl of Douglas and the king who murdered him at Stirling Castle in 1452. His brother, the 9th Earl of Douglas, now 'put the king to the horn'. This was an open declaration naming the king as a murderer and an outlaw. This was a brave but foolhardy act and the Douglases were finally defeated at Arkinholm (Langholm) on 1st May 1455 when the Earl of Angus commanded the Royal Army. The Earl of Douglas fled to England and had his lands and titles forfeited.

In 1458 the Earl of Douglas and the Earl of Northumberland suffered final defeat at the hands of the Earl of Angus who was now rewarded with the lordship of Douglas. In 1460 the king besieged Roxburgh Castle, then held by the English, and the Earl of Angus was present when one of his cannons burst when fired and killed the king; the spot is marked in the grounds of Floors Castle in Kelso.

In England the Wars of the Roses with House of Lancaster against the House of York drove Henry VI from his throne and with his wife, Queen Margaret, they took refuge in Scotland. They made a pact with the Earl of Angus in which he would receive the lands between the Trent and the Humber with a dukedom for his help in restoring them to the English throne. However, the banished traitor, the Earl of Douglas with his old allies, the Earl of Ross and Donald Balloch, made a treaty with the Yorkist King, Edward IV, in which Douglas would have his lands restored and Edward IV would become Lord of Scotland with Douglas and Ross as his vassals. The plan was for Ross to raise a rebellion in the north while Douglas would invade Scotland from the south. The Earl of Angus thwarted this invasion when he relieved a French garrison at Alnwick which was besieged by Edward IV and Douglas was defeated by the Scottish army. The Lord of the Isles lost his title, Earl of Ross, but he continued to cause trouble for many years.

After the death of James II the question of the Regency arose - James III was only eight years of age when his succession was announced on 10th August 1460 at Kelso Abbey. The contenders were the Earl of Angus and the dowager Queen. She compromised by naming two lords from each side. Angus's name did not appear on the Council of Regency and he is presumed to have died towards the end of 1462. He had married Isabel, daughter of Sir John Sibbald of Balgony in Fife, and was succeeded by their son Archibald who became the celebrated 'Bell-the-Cat' and founded his earldom as a border chief.

THE EARLDOM OF DUNBAR

The Earldom of Dunbar is thought to have been created through a grant of land, *The Merse* or March in Berwickshire in 1072 by Malcolm III to **Earl Gospatrick de Dunbar**. However, the first record is a signature on the Charter of Scone of 1115 by Gospatric de Dunbar, son of the above, who is considered to be the **1st Earl** and was probably 'the leader of the men of Lothian' who was killed at the Battle of Standard (22nd August 1138) when David I invaded England to regain Northumberland. The brutality of the Scots inspired the English defenders to consider themselves as taking part in a 'holy war' which was organised by Archbishop Thurstan of York who met the Scots at Cowton Moor near Northallerton; it was there that the 1st Earl of Dunbar was killed.

The **2nd Earl of Dunbar, Gospatric de Dunbar**, son of the 1st earl inherited the earldom in 1138 and as if to compensate for the savagery of the Scots at the Battle of the Standard he lived a peaceable and religious life and founded Cistercian Nunneries in Northumberland. He died in 1166.

The **3rd Earl, Walthe de Dunbar**, continued the peaceable ways of his father in granting a charter to the monks of Durham when he inherited the earldom in 1166. He was a hostage of the English to obtain the release of William the Lion. William had been captured at Alnwick in 1174 during one of his attacks on England to regain counties lost to Henry II during the reign of Malcolm IV. The 3rd Earl of Dunbar died in 1182.

The **4th Earl of Dunbar, Partrick de Dunbar** was born in 1152 and became the Justiciary Keeper of Lothian and Keeper of Berwick. He was the first earl to assume his title from Dunbar Castle. He attended William the Lion to Lincoln in 1200 and Alexander II *qv* to York in 1221 when the king married Henry III's sister, Princess Joan. The earl founded the Monastery of the Red Friars at Dunbar in 1218 and such was his religious fervour he became a monk shortly before his death in 1232 aged 80 years.

The **5th Earl of Dunbar, Patrick de Dunbar**, married Eupheme, daughter of Walter Fitzalan, the Lord High Steward of Scotland c1213. He commanded an army to subdue the 'bastard of Galloway' in 1235 and was a guarantor at the Treaty of York in 1237 when Alexander II surrendered the earldoms of Northumberland, Cumberland and Westmoreland to Henry III but Alexander retained land within these earldoms. Again in 1244 the Earl of Dunbar was guarantor in ensuring peace between England and Scotland. In November 1247 he started out to join the Crusade to the Holy Land under Louis IX, King of France, but between May and December 1248 he died at Marseilles. His widow lived at Whittinghame and died there c.1267.

The **6th Earl of Dunbar, Patrick de Dunbar** was 35 years of age when he succeeded to the earldom in 1248. In 1255 the fourteen-year-old Alexander III had been kidnapped by the Comyn family and the 6th Earl of Dunbar joined a pro-English faction of the Scottish nobility to rescue him. He was nominated Regent and Guardian of King Alexander and Queen Margaret (daughter of Henry III of England who married in 1251 when he was 10 and she was 11 years of age). When King Haakon of Norway invaded Scotland in 1263 the Earl of Dunbar held a command against the invaders at Largs and he was a signatory to the Treaty of Perth in 1266 for the cession of the Hebrides and the Isle of Man to Scotland. The earl also signed the Treaty of Marriage of Margaret of Scotland to Eric of Norway in 1281 and to the succession of the 'Maid of Norway' to the throne of Scotland. He died at Whittinghame on 24th August 1289 aged 76 and was buried at Dunbar.

The **7th Earl of Dunbar, Patrick de Dunbar**, was the first to be called the Earl of March (of the Scottish Marches or border lands) and he inherited his titles in 1289 at the age of 47. On 3rd August 1291 he lodged his petition as a competitor to the Crown of Scotland claiming that his great-grandmother was Princess Ada (mother of Malcolm IV and William the Lion). He withdrew this claim and with most of the nobility of Scotland he swore fealty to Edward I (the 'Hammer of the Scots') on 25th March 1296. He joined the English against the Scots and was appointed King's Lieutenant for Scotland. In 1300 he fought with his son Patrick at the Siege of Carlaverlock.

He married Marjory, daughter of Alexander Comyn, Earl of Buchan. Going against her husband she held the Castle of Dunbar against the English army of Edward I until she was forced to surrender in on 29th April 1296. The 7th Earl died on 10th October 1308.

The **8th Earl of March or Dunbar**, Patrick de Dunbar was born about 1285 and was 15 years old when he fought with the English alongside his father at Carlaverlock and after the defeat of Edward II at Bannockburn he gave him shelter at Dunbar Castle enabling him to escape by sea to England. Scotland was now a free country and the Earl now changed sides to support the Scots. He was in attendance at the Parliament of Scotland for the Settlement of Succession on 27th April 1315 recognising Edward , the brother of Robert the Bruce, as his heir in preference to Marjory, Bruce's daughter. In 1318 the Earl of Dunbar as Sheriff of Lothian was at the capture of Berwick. He was one of the signatories of the Letter of Barons of Scotland to Pope John XXII of 6th April 1320 - 'The Declaration of Arbroath' asserting the independence of Scotland.

After Bruce died in 1329 his son David II, aged five, was anointed and crowned king and John Balliol decided to try to regain the throne. The Earl of Dunbar fought against Balliol at Dupplin Moor near Perth in 1332 where the new Guardian, the Earl of Mar, was defeated and killed. Balliol was crowned at Scone but he had to flee to Carlisle. On 19th July 1333 at Halidon Hill, Balliol, openly supported by Edward III, defeated the Scots and took the fort of Berwick of which the Earl of Dunbar was Governor. Dunbar promptly joined the English side for the second time but in 1334 during small skirmishes against the English Dunbar switched sides yet again. Meantime, his countess 'Black Agnes' *qv*, eldest daughter of Thomas Randolph, Earl of Moray, bravely held the Castle of Dunbar for nineteen weeks against the English attackers.

Shortly before his death aged 83 years on 11th November 1368 the Earl of March or Dunbar resigned his Earldom to the Crown and on 25th July 1368 it was granted to his great-nephew George Dunbar and his heirs. The 8th Earl had held his earldom for 60 years.

Dunbar Castle was the seat of the Earls of March or Dunbar until forfeiture of titles and estates to James I in 1434 when he increased his income threefold from the forfeiture of five earldoms in Scotland. (18. p.145). In 1567 Dunbar Castle and lands were granted to the 4th Earl of Bothwell confirming his innocence in the murder of Lord Darnley. Bothwell took Mary Queen of Scots on 23rd April 1567 to Dunbar Castle ostensibly to protect her from angry crowds in Edinburgh. The castle was almost completely destroyed on the orders of the Scottish Parliament following the abdication of Mary Queen of Scots.

WILLIAM DUNBAR

The 'Rhymer of Scotland; the Chaucer of Scotland'

Almost three hundred years before the birth of Robert Burns, East Lothian born William Dunbar was described in the Privy Purse Accounts of Henry VII as the 'Rhymer of Scotland.' He was considered to be the Chaucer of Scotland whose technical mastery was and is unequalled.

He was born in East Lothian c1465 and there is a strong probability that he was the grandson of Sir Patrick Dunbar of Beill in East Lothian. History does not record the town or village of his birth. He entered St Andrews University at the age of about ten in 1475 and graduated Master of Arts in 1479 (the university at that time was equal in standard to a rather advanced secondary school for the sons of well to do families.)

He joined the order of the Franciscan Friars but "he found himself wholly unfitted for the exacting functions of a begging friar." (25 Vol.3 p.154) During this time he claimed to have "made good cheer in every flourishing town betwixt Berwick and Calais;.... I ascended the pulpit at Dernton and Canterbury; and crossed the sea at Dover, and instructed the inhabitants of Picardy." (25 Vol.3 p.154) However, he had little sympathy with beggars but his short life as a Franciscan Friar undoubtedly provided him with material for the satires he would write in later years.

Near the end of the 15th century he became attached to the court of James IV and visited several countries in Europe initially attending the 1st Earl of Bothwell during a visit to Paris in 1491 and shortly after which he continued alone beyond the Alps in the service of the king.

The Privy Seal Register of 15th August 1500 recorded a decree of £10 a year for the poet Dunbar for life or '*untill he be promoted by our sovereign lord to a benefice of the value of forty pounds or more yearly*' (25 Vol.3 p.154) but he had to complain often that he had received no payment. However, as a salaried court poet he was later to receive increases of £20 in 1507 and £80 in 1510; he was therefore financially comfortable in his old age. (10 p.133)

In 1503 he accompanied the ambassadors who were sent to the court of Henry VII to negotiate the marriage of James IV and Margaret Tudor. This visit inspired his poem *In Honour of the City of London.* At long last there might now be peace between England and Scotland and William Dunbar seems to have so pleased his royal audience that he received a sum of money as the 'rhymer of Scotland.' The forthcoming event of the royal marriage prompted Dunbar to write his first great poem *The Thrissill and the Rois* on '9th May 1503, three months before Margaret, the English rose arrived as consort of Scotland's thistle, James IV.' James and Margaret were married on 8th August 1503 at Holyrood and Scotland was at peace for the next ten years. It was during this period that Dunbar wrote his best poems - *The Golden Targe*, the *Flyting* (co-written with Walter Kennedy) and *The Lament for Makaris* all of which were printed when Walter Chepman, the first Scottish printer, issued them after 1507. His humorous satires, such as *The Twa Marritt Wemen and the Wedo* and the *Dance of the Sevin Deidly Synnis* prove his originality and keen observation.

He was a privileged and special favourite of the queen and accompanied her on her visit to the north of Scotland when he wrote *The Quenis Progress at Aberdeen*. This was written from his observations during the journey and is a valuable descriptive poem. Another was his *Orisone* which is a lament on public degeneracy and written in 1517 when the Duke of Albany went to France.

Towards the end of his life his works were mainly of a moral and religious nature probably because he had been given a Church preferment from the widowed queen, King James having been killed at Flodden in 1513. The year of his death is usually given as 1530 but it may have preceded that of Gavin Douglas *qv* the contemporary poet-bishop, who died in 1522.

ROBERT FERGUSON OF RAITH

Memorial in Haddington

The imposing figure of Sir Robert Ferguson, standing on a 45 ft (13.7 m) high pillar at the corner of Knox Place and Station Road in Haddington, is a splendid memorial to a much loved and well-respected radical Member of Parliament for East Lothian. The site chosen was originally occupied by the West Port tollhouse and the Ferguson Memorial is a smaller version of that to Lord Melville which stands in the centre of St Andrew Square in Edinburgh - the Haddington one being designed by the same sculptor, Robert Forrest (1791-1852) at a cost of £650.

The base of the memorial is inscribed as follows:

> *In Memory of Robert Ferguson of Raith M.P. Lord Lieutenant of Fife FRSD, FRSE &c &c. A kind landlord and liberal dispenser of wealth. A generous patron of literature, science and art. An enlightened supporter of his country. This monument is erected by the tenantry of East Lothian and many friends of all classes who united in admiring his public virtues and to whom he was endeared by every quality which flows from the goodness of heart. AD MDCCCXLIII.*

However, not everyone in East Lothian agreed that such an imposing monument was deserved. One dissenter writing to the editor of the Haddingtonshire Courier and referring to "this meaningless monument" commented:

> "He was not a Haddington man; his connection with the county was brief and sketchy; his public contribution called for no undying commemoration. It is rather silly, come to think of it, that in the county town of Knox, Rennie, Meikle, Jane

Welsh, Balfour, and other famous men and women with some claim to our remembrance, the most eye-catching memorial (and the finest site) should be reserved for a nobody."

Robert Ferguson of Raith in Kirkcaldy was born in 1767. He was the eldest son of William Ferguson of Raith in Fifeshire and Jane, daughter of Ronald Craufurd of Restalrig (sister of Margaret, Countess of Dumfries). He was educated in Edinburgh and trained for the law to be admitted to the Faculty of Advocates in 1791. He then went on his 'grand tour' of Europe, an activity which occupied the time of many young aristocrats of his day to broaden their minds through travel. It seems that Ferguson took his tour very seriously and became a member of the Institute of France. The events in France, the Revolution, appealed to Ferguson, indeed the ferment was considered by many including Charles James Fox (1749-1806 'the greatest debater the world ever saw') to be 'the greatest and best event that has happened in the world' - he was referring to the fall of the Bastille in 1789 followed by the sweeping powers adopted by the National Assembly in ridding the country of feudal rights, disestablishing the Church and taking power in the name of democracy and the rights of man.

These were exciting and risk-taking times for young radicals such as Ferguson. Arrests of any who expressed sympathy with the French cause were common. This was the era of 'Pitt's reign of terror' supported in Scotland by the Dundas family and Judge Braxfield, 'Scotland's hanging judge'. However, Ferguson's interests were wide as was evident from his membership of the Geological Society of London, his Fellowship of the Royal Society of Edinburgh and his presidency of several scientific societies. He married the divorced Mary Nisbet formerly Countess of Elgin whose ex-husband, the 7th Earl, saved (or gained) the Elgin marbles from the Parthenon in Athens. She was the heiress of William Hamilton Nisbet of Dirleton.

Following the passing of the 1832 Reform Act which gave the vote to the middle classes Robert Ferguson of Raith was the first to be elected in 1835 for the burgh of Haddington under the new law. The Whigs who supported the abolition of slavery, Roman Catholic Emancipation and who championed Parliamentary Reform were anxious to win the parliamentary seat of East Lothian against the Tories. Ferguson's majority of 34 over the Tory, John Thomas Hope, younger of Luffness, was a slender one but the electorate of 188 was small and the celebration dinner for 300 guests which followed was held on 6th February 1835 at the Assembly Room in Haddington. Ferguson had been MP for Kirkcaldy Burghs and was one of the supporters of the Reform Bill through its difficult passage through Parliament. This was a period of rapturous and nation-wide celebration; Prime Minister Earl Grey had, after three attempts, steered the Reform Bill through Parliament and his arrival in September 1835 in Haddington was greeted with the ringing of the town bells and a display of banners of various trades. Robert Ferguson was among the first to give a hearty welcome to Earl Grey. [This Reform Bill merely increased the franchise from 4.3% of the population in 1722 to 4.7 % in 1832 (96 p.349)]

In 1837 Ferguson, now aged seventy, lost in his bid for a second term as MP for East Lothian to Lord Ramsay (later Marquess of Dalhousie). George Hope of Fentonbarns commented that the Tories went to great lengths to prevent the re-election of Sir Robert Ferguson - they kidnapped some of his supporters - one was taken firstly to Garvald and then abandoned at Traprain Law, another was dumped as far away as possible in the Pentland Hills.

Sir Robert Ferguson died, aged seventy-three, on 3rd December 1840 in London and three years afterwards the Whigs of East Lothian organised the subscription for his monument which was unveiled on 2nd June 1843.

The Ferguson name continued in Parliament through his only son, Colonel Robert Ferguson, who was MP for Kirkcaldy in 1841 until 1862.

SIR WILLIAM FERGUSSON of Prestonpans

President of the Royal College of Surgeons in 1870, and Sergeant Surgeon to Queen Victoria

Prestonpans was the birth place of two eminent medical men, Sir William Fergusson who became Professor of Surgery at King's College, London, President of the Royal College of Surgeons in 1870,and Sergeant Surgeon to Queen Victoria and Thomas Alexander (1812-60) *qv* who became Director General of the Medical Department of the British Army.

A medical contemporary from East Lothian was Haddington born George Harley (1829-96) *qv*. These three dedicated doctors completed their medical training at the University of Edinburgh, the acknowledged centre of excellence in the country, if not in Europe.

William Fergusson was born at Prestonpans on 20th March 1808 and his first job was in an Edinburgh law office but he became bored with the work and, following his father's advice, he attended the University of Edinburgh to study medicine. He became a student of the celebrated Dr Robert Knox who thought so highly of him that he gave him the post as his demonstrator.

(Courtesy of the Scottish National Portrait Gallery)

William Fergusson must have been appalled to discover that his eminent teacher had been involved, knowingly or unknowingly, in the purchase of dead bodies from the infamous pair of criminals, Burke and Hare. That Knox was a brilliant anatomist and teacher there was no dispute, but what must have chilled the youthful William Fergusson, who was nineteen years old at the time of the trial of Burke and Hare which opened on Christmas eve, 1828, was Knox's cold indifference to the seventeen murders which had been committed to supply corpses for dissection. Knox was eventually hounded out of Edinburgh to die in obscurity in London in 1862. Burke was hanged after Hare turned King's Evidence and he died a blind beggar in London.

Such an experience might have dissuaded many another medical student from continuing his studies but young William Fergusson was determined to become a surgeon. He knew that Knox had been the best teacher and the acknowledged expert in anatomy and surgery. Fergusson had been thoroughly trained having spent twelve to sixteen hours per day in Knox's dissecting room.

He qualified as a surgeon and was admitted as a Fellow of the Edinburgh College of Surgeons to become surgeon to the Edinburgh Royal Infirmary in 1836. He became the finest surgeon in Edinburgh and, with Dr James Syme, he had the largest practice in Scotland. His reputation had become known nationally and he was invited to become Professor of Surgery at King's College, London in 1840. It was during this period that he invented many surgical instruments and improved dozens of others. In 1842 he published his *System of Practical Surgery*; this was to become the standard text and by 1870 would run to five editions.

William Fergusson was a tall, handsome man and although he gave the appearance of seriousness he was not without a dry dense of humour. He played the violin and was known as an excellent fly fisher during his visits to Scotland. In 1833 he married Helen Hamilton Ranken, the heiress of William Ranken of Spitalhaugh in Peeblesshire. Their home in London was welcoming and hospitable. Anyone in need received his medical advice without charge.

He was appointed Surgeon-Sergeant to Queen Victoria and was created a baronet in 1866 (the same year that James Young Simpson was knighted for his discovery of the use of chloroform as an anaesthetic, used for the first time by her majesty at the birth of Prince Leopold in 1853). Fergusson's popularity with his students was evident from their presentation to him of a magnificent silver dessert service.

In 1870 Fergusson was elected President of the Royal College of Surgeons and was certainly present when his Haddington born contemporary, Professor George Harley (1829-96) *qv*, was awarded the triennial prize by the Royal College of Surgeons for his brilliant medical research.

William Fergusson died at his house in London on 10th February 1877. He was buried beside his wife in the churchyard of The Parish Church of West Linton in which two stained-glass windows on the right and left of the pulpit are associated with the Fergusson family. In addition, a street Fergusson View bears the family name. The gravestone of Sir William is inscribed:

To the Memory of
SIR WILLIAM FERGUSSON
Sergeant Surgeon to the Queen
1st Baronet of Spitalhaugh
born 20th March 1808, died 10th February 1877
also of
HELEN HAMILTON RANKEN
his wife
born 12th March 1806, died 1st April 1861
and of
WILLIAM RANKEN FERGUSSON
their second son
born 24th February 1837, died 1st April 1864
their remains are interred below
"For as Adam all die, even so in Christ shall all be made alive"

The Fergusson family consisted of six children, each of whom were buried beside their parents:
Sir James Ranken Fergusson, 2nd Baronet (1835-1924),
William Ranken Fergusson (1837-1864),
Jane Porteous Fergusson (1838-1900),
Katherine Hamilton Fergusson (1840-1932),
Helen Seymour Fergusson (1844-1938),
Charles Hamilton Fergusson (Major Seaforth Highlanders 1849-1913).

FLETCHER OF SALTOUN - 'The Patriot'

"she [Scotland] was only fit for the slaves who sold her"

"They (the English) must not think that we have so far degenerated from the courage and honour of our ancestors as tamely to submit to become their vassals, when for two thousand years we have maintained our freedom, and therefore it is not in their interest to oppress us too much. If they consult their histories they will find that we always broke their yoke at the long run." (27 p.179-180)

The proposal to unite the Parliaments of England and Scotland was anathema to Andrew Fletcher of Saltoun. He wrote these words in December 1698 with vehemence against and disdain of all who supported the Union and earned for himself the accolade "The Patriot".

Andrew Fletcher of Saltoun (Courtesy of the Scottish National Portrait Gallery)

As a strong republican, 'he stood fearlessly in the interests of his country' but to stand against the all-powerful Duke of Lauderdale and to defy the Duke of York (later James II) was brave to the point of suicide; enemies of these men usually found themselves declared extinct.

Fletcher was viciously vociferous in his opposition to the Union of Parliaments of England and Scotland in 1707. His detestation of this event was born of a background of deep suspicion of the Stuart monarchy, antipathy of English domination, despair over the dire poverty of 20 per cent of the population of Scotland in which two out of three children died of malnutrition and disease, and of his bitterness over the disastrous Darien expedition of 1698.

Andrew Fletcher was one of the first to support the Darien Scheme of William Paterson, the Scottish founder of the Bank of England, who talked the whole of Scotland into his scheme. It was to have been the economic panacea for the nation which was in the midst of an economic crisis. The Scottish Parliament had passed an Act giving itself powers to trade in the Darien, as it was called. It was Panama. There was no canal to link the Atlantic with the Pacific but the prospect of trading was attractive, the access to the two great oceans was irresistible. The English Parliament was alarmed; the loss of trade by the East India Company would become Scotland's gain and everything was done to thwart the scheme. But the Scottish Parliament was a mass of contradiction, many feared the loss of favour of William III and others had invested heavily in Paterson's scheme. William was anxious not to offend Spain fearing they might be tempted to join France in a war against England. Fletcher was to say,

> *Let no man say that it cannot be proved that the English court has ever bestowed any bribe in this country. For they bestow all offices and pensions; they bribe us, and are masters of us at our own cost.* (27. p. 178)

Andrew Fletcher was born in 1655 at Saltoun. His father was Sir Robert Fletcher, a country gentleman of substance who was Parish minister of Salton at the time of Andrew's birth. But Scotland was under the rigid ruthless rule of Oliver Cromwell and was a divided nation. English soldiers were firmly encamped in all major towns and Andrew's early years were undoubtedly influenced by this unwanted presence. He was ten years old when his father died and before his death Sir Robert had secured a promise from Gilbert Burnet (1643-1715), who was to become Bishop of Salisbury, that he would supervise the boy's education. For the next five years, until he left Saltoun to become Professor of Divinity at Glasgow, Burnet undertook this task and was to describe Andrew Fletcher as "a Scotch gentleman of great parts and many virtues, but a most violent republican, and extremely passionate." But Andrew gave the credit for his early education to his mother, Katherine Bruce, whose encouragement of the joy of learning took precedence over Burnet's strict methodology.

As was the custom for young men of means, the 'grand tour' of Europe was prescribed - their education had to be broadened with the study of languages and other cultures. Andrew Fletcher toured Europe and on his return to Scotland his ideas for the future of his country had become firmly fixed. He represented Haddington in 1678 on the Convention of Estates and was quickly outspoken in his opposition to the Duke of Lauderdale's harsh treatment towards the Covenanters; for this he was a marked man. He, with the Duke of Hamilton, had dared to vote against the all-powerful Lauderdale; but Fletcher was not to be intimidated. In July 1680 he was rebuked and punished by the Privy Council for his obstruction in preventing militiamen being drafted into the standing army. His punishment was to have soldiers encamped on his estate to keep an eye on him and to 'overawe Presbyterian malcontents'. Naturally, Fletcher complained that this intrusion was 'contrare to law'.

After the Battle of Bothwell Bridge (2nd July 1679) and the callous treatment of the 1200 Covenanter prisoners held at Greyfriars Churchyard in Edinburgh, Lauderdale had to give up his Commissionership. He was replaced by the dreaded Duke of York (who became James II after the death of his elder brother, Charles II, in 1685). Fletcher, as a commissioner for East Lothian in the Scotch Parliament, had opposed the Duke of York's appointment by sending several anonymous letters to members of parliament urging their opposition. Anonymity was essential because the Duke of York could easily have had Fletcher arrested on the flimsiest of pretexts. James, Duke of York was a Catholic convert and it was feared that he would impose his religion upon Scotland.

Again, in April 1682, Fletcher was charged by the Privy Council - this time he had failed to levy local taxes to feed the soldiery. He was as thorny as a thistle to the establishment and he had to leave Scotland with the 'Scotch malcontents'.

Meanwhile, Archibald, 9th Earl of Argyll, who had supported the anti-royalists, had reluctantly signed the Test Act* of 1681and his doubts about its conflicting clauses led to his imprisonment in Edinburgh Castle.

However, much to the delight of Fletcher, he escaped dressed as a page boy, but the tentacles of the Duke of York reached out for Fletcher in Brussels; he had asked the Spanish Governor to have Fletcher arrested. Forewarned, Fletcher returned home in secret and joined the Duke of Monmouth, Lord William Russell and Algernon Sidney in the Rye House Plot (April 1683) which was no more than talk of a change in the system of government. After their exposure Russell was executed and Sidney was sent to the Tower. Monmouth fled to Holland and

**Test Act 1681 required that all state and municipal officials accept royal supremacy in Church and state and swear to uphold the 1560 Confession of Faith.*

Fletcher to Paris where Lord Preston, Charles II's envoy extraordinary, wrote of him:

> 'Here is one Fletcher... he is an ingenious but a violent fanatic and doubtless hath some commission, for I hear he is very busy and very virulent.'

Fletcher was not in favour of Monmouth's Rebellion (1685) against the Duke of York and, though he counselled against it, he never-the-less sailed with him to England as his secretary and paymaster, but when Monmouth proclaimed himself king at Taunton Fletcher left in disgust. An additional reason for his departure was that he had shot Alderman Dale, Monmouth's treasurer, who had accused Fletcher of stealing his best horse and had struck Fletcher across the face to challenge him.

He fled to Bilbao in Spain where, due to the Duke of York's influence, he was arrested and extradited. However, he escaped disguised as a peasant and wandered throughout the country learning about the people and their customs. His travels took him to Hungary where he fought under the Duke of Lorraine as a volunteer against the Turks.

At home Andrew Fletcher had been sentenced to death and his lands and Barony were forfeited on 4th June 1686 for treasonable complicity in Monmouth's rebellion. However, James II proclaimed an amnesty which Fletcher wisely ignored. Instead, he joined William of Orange at the Hague and returned to Scotland with the invasion of 1688. James II, having lost all support, fled from London; he was captured but was allowed to escape to France. However, he managed to raise a Catholic army in Ireland but was finally beaten at the Battle of the Boyne on 1st July 1690.

William, James II's son-in-law, and Mary, his daughter, were now firmly set upon the throne and Andrew Fletcher had his estates restored to him, but he continued his quest 'to diminish the power of the crown in Scotland'. He did not feel gratitude at all; as far as he was concerned, a wrong had been put right. He querulously questioned why it had taken so long and proceeded to create a 'Young Scotland and Scotch Home Rule Party'.

In 1695 he saw a brilliant opportunity to free Scotland of English domination when William Paterson proposed 'The Company of Scotland trading with Africa and the Indies' - the Darien Scheme. During Paterson's visit to East Lothian Fletcher introduced him to his neighbour, the Marquis of Tweeddale, to persuade him of the benefits of the scheme and Fletcher himself invested £1000 in it. But the scheme, in creating a Scottish colony in Panama, was doomed to failure. The English traders were alarmed and when the Spaniards attacked the Scots colonists King

William refused any assistance. Many Scots lost fortunes and had good reason to oppose the Union. Almost two thousand lives and over £200,000 had been lost and to make matters worse there was famine at home.

Fletcher's *A Discourse Concerning Militias and Standing Armies with relation to the past and present Governments of Europe and of England in particular* written in 1697 argued that governments which kept standing mercenary forces 'are changed from monarchies to tyrannies'. He averred that 'all governments are tyrannical, which have not in their constitution a sufficient security against the arbitrary power of the prince' (96 pps.229-9). In addition he considered that the money spent on a force of regulars would be better spent in promoting industry. In his social reforms he suggested that the 100,000 or so beggars and vagrants (almost 10 per cent of the population) should be taken into service, not as slaves but with the rights and protection of the law as for ordinary servants. Those who were known criminals, he averred, should be deported as galley slaves to fight against the Turks.

As a Commissioner in the Scotch Parliament he drafted an Act of Security giving home rule to Scotland after the death of Queen Anne. He proposed a Scotch Executive to be chosen by the Scotch Parliament and not by the Sovereign, the formation of a Scotch National Militia and that the Sovereign be deprived of power to declare war and make peace. However, in 1703 his Act was excluded by the Queen's Commissioner and Fletcher, incensed with anger, rose to his feet, to declare:

> 'After the decease of her Majesty we will separate our crown from that of England.'

The reverberation in England of this defiance resulted in the resurrection of the proposal of legislative union of Parliaments and the English Parliament retaliated with the Aliens Act of 1705, which empowered the Queen to appoint Union Commissioners, to treat Scots as aliens and effectively to cut off trade between the two countries. Fletcher, more irritable than before, worked unceasingly in Parliament but to less and less effect. He even proposed that the King of Prussia should become king of Scotland. The majority wanted the Union and Fletcher became so obsessed that he challenged the Duke of Hamilton, Lord Stair and others to duels but the Assembly interfered to prevent him. He was suspected of complicity leading to a French invasion of Scotland and was arrested. After his discharge he took no further part in public life. His friend and co-MP, George Lockhart of Carnwath (1673-1731) was to say of him;

'He was so steadfast to what he thought right that no hazard nor advantage, no, not the universal empire, nor the gold of America, could tempt him to yield or desert it.'

He stormed out of the Scotch Parliament at its last meeting on 3rd October 1706 with the often quoted words: 'It (Scotland) is fit only for the slaves who sold it.'

Fletcher now turned his energies to the land. During his visit to Holland he had been impressed by the machinery used to remove the husk of barley and its conversion into 'pot' barley. He employed a local millwright of Saltoun to go to Amsterdam to study the machinery. This was James Meikle *qv*, the father of the Andrew Meikle who gained fame through his invention of the thrashing machine. On his return, James Meikle set about building a barley mill at Saltoun which was the only one in Britain, Ireland and America for the next forty years. He was said to have used a drawing made from memory by architect William Adam. *Salton Barley* was soon to appear on every signboard of every retailer.

Andrew Fletcher 'The Patriot' died in London in September 1716 on his way home to his beloved Saltoun. He was buried in the family vault at Saltoun Church.

A bronze plaque on the church wall has the inscription:

In Memory of
ANDREW FLETCHER of SALTOUN
1655-1716
Commissioner in the last Scottish Parliament

A PATRIOT WHO STOOD FEARLESSLY FOR
THE INTERESTS OF HIS COUNTRY
Placed here by the Saltoun Society 1955

A stone tablet on the church spire is inscribed:

DEO. O.M. ET M. SACRUM
LORD INNERPEFFER, ANDREW FLETCHER ESQ. THE PATRIOT
LORD MILTON
THIS SPIRE WAS ERECTED BY GEN. FLETCHER CAMPBELL,
AS A MONUMENT TO THE VIRTUE OF HIS ANCESTORS AND
AN EXAMPLE FOR THEIR POSTERITY TO IMITATE, SALTON 1805

COLONEL JAMES GARDINER
of Bankton House, Prestonpans

He prayed on his knees every day for two hours and would not permit his men to swear.

Although this brave soldier, aide-de-camp and Master of the Horse was born in West Lothian, James Gardiner's association with East Lothian was through his mother, Mary Hodge, who was born at Gladsmuir and of course through his residence at Bankton House near Prestonpans.

He was born on 11th January 1687 at Carriden in West Lothian and he was educated at the Grammar School of Linlithgow. His father was a soldier, Captain Patrick Gardiner of Torwoodhead. James, his eldest son, was about ten years of age when his father was killed in battle and his widowed mother would be more than a little apprehensive when her son was enrolled as a cadet soon after the death of her husband.

James Gardiner became an ensign in a Scotch Regiment at the early age of fourteen. He served firstly in Holland and in 1702 he transferred into the service of Queen Anne. He was fifteen years old, an age when he sought the excitement of adventure and battle which he found in no small measure under the great Duke of Marlborough during the War of the Spanish Succession (1702-1713) in Europe.

He was a mere nineteen year-old when, during the battle of Ramillies (23rd May 1706), he was sent on what was considered to be an almost impossible mission to remove the French from their stronghold in a churchyard. This he did in spite of heavy odds against him. He captured the French colours but he was shot in the mouth. According to Doddrige (45) he was able to cough up blood clots and because of the freezing cold his wound sealed itself. The musket ball had passed through the side of his face. He was able to talk with great difficulty and he passed himself off as a nephew of the governor of a neutral town. He was taken to a convent nearby where he was nursed back to health and eventually exchanged to return to his regiment. He fought in several campaigns under the command of John Dalrymple, the 2nd Earl of Stair (1673-1768), including the battles of Oudenarde (11th July 1708) and Malplaquet (11th September 1709).

His fearless leadership was soon recognised and within the next three years he was promoted three times - January 1714, lieutenant in Colonel Kerr's Dragoons; July 1714, captain in Colonel Stanhope's dragoons; January 1717, major. He was not only a very brave soldier but an extraordinarily fine horseman. His exceptional skill attracted the attention of the 2nd Earl of Stair who, as a fellow Scot, made him his aide-de-camp and when Stair was appointed Ambassador to the French Court of Louis XV in 1719 it was Gardiner, as Master of the Horse, who made all the arrangements for Stair's extravagant and grand triumphal entry into Paris.

This was a time of sensual pleasure-seeking and Gardiner enjoyed the fruits of this ostentatious living becoming known for his dissolute ways in drinking and womanising. He was a tall, handsome young man, over six feet in height with a strong and confident voice, intrepid in battle and said to be the finest horseman in the army but he was gentle and kindly towards the ladies and he became known as the 'Happy Rake'.

When the Earl of Stair was Colonel of the 6th Dragoons (Stair's Grey Horse which became the Scots Greys) he made Gardiner a Major in his regiment (July 1724) and in January 1729 Gardiner was promoted to the rank of lieutenant-colonel of the Inniskillings.

It was about this time during one of his romantic assignations and while waiting for his lady that he happened to pick up a copy of Watson's *Christian Soldier*. He became completely absorbed by it and its effect upon him was accompanied by a shaft of light which played upon the book as he read it. At that moment he saw the figure of Christ who seemed to say to him that he had suffered on the cross for the frivolity and self indulgence of Gardiner's past. This had a profound effect on him and from that moment he became a converted Christian. He was a changed man; there is no record of whether or not he kept his assignation - one can only assume that the lady was disappointed that night. From that day he became a powerful advocate of the religious way of life. He prayed on his knees every day for two hours and would not permit his men to swear. He levied fines if they did so and the money was given to the families of soldiers killed in battle. He visited wounded soldiers regularly and this change in him amazed his fellow officers who were made keenly aware of his dismay of their gaiety in Edinburgh.

In July 1726 he married Lady Francis Erskine, a daughter of the 4th Earl of Buchan and they had thirteen children of whom only five survived. His religious fervour remained with him and there were many occasions when Gardiner was heard to moan in ecstatic reverie during his prayers.

In April 1743 Gardiner returned home to East Lothian to be given command of the Light Dragoons. He was appalled at the lack of defences and the nonchalance and frivolity of social life in Edinburgh. He had purchased the newly-built Bankton House (now restored and converted into apartments) some ten years before. But his homecoming was not to be peaceful, there were fears of a Jacobite rebellion and General John Cope decided that Gardiner's and Hamilton's Dragoons should defend the lowlands while Cope would defend the Highlands. When the Young Pretender's troops were reported to be advancing towards Perth, Gardiner marched four troops of his dragoons northwards. He concentrated his troops at Stirling and requested reinforcements to be sure of giving the Highlanders 'a warm reception'. His request for reinforcements was refused and the Highlanders crossed the River Forth a few miles west of Gardiner's position. Heavily outnumbered, Gardiner decided to return to Edinburgh where many of his men, now tired and dispirited with tales of the exploits of the ferocious enemy, panicked and fled eastwards to Prestonpans. The battle there was lost before it was fought. Gardiner slept in his own house on the eve of the battle and as he explained to Alexander Carlyle,

> 'It was a foul flight and they have not yet recovered from their panic; and I'll tell you, in confidence, that I have not above ten men in my regiment whom I am certain will follow me. But we must give them battle now, and God's will be done.' (2)

Cope's men had disembarked at Dunbar and marched to Prestonpans. The two armies sighted each other near Bankton House on 20th September. Cope took up his position for the night with the high walls of the house behind him.

Next day Gardiner's dragoons stationed themselves on Cope's right wing and were ordered to charge the enemy. Only a few obeyed the command but Gardiner stubbornly and bravely held his ground refusing to leave the infantry in their desperate plight. Almost immediately

Gardiner was wounded taking a bullet in the right side of his chest and the officer in charge of the foot soldiers was killed. Gardiner dismounted and took over his command. Again he was shot, this time in the shoulder. Yet again he was struck down, taking a slash with a broad sword on his left arm and finally he was struck viciously from behind with the Lochaber axe of a Highlander who stripped him of his valuables.

The Battle of Prestonpans lasted for only about ten minutes. Cope's army was beaten and the cheering Jacobites pillaged and looted and left soon afterwards.

The dying Colonel Gardiner was gently carried away from the field of battle to the manse at Tranent where he died next morning, 22nd September 1745. He was buried in the north west corner of the Churchyard. His monument at Bankton House is inscribed:

To
Col. Gardiner
who fell in the Battle of Prestonpans
Sept.1745

A Faithful man
and feared God above many

HUGH de GIFFARD (or Gifford) of Yester

Mystery and magic are attributed to him, the founder of the Goblin Hall'

The village of Gifford and Giffordgate in Haddington take their names from Hugh de Giffard [original spelling] who owned the lands of Yester in the 13th century. Many tales of mystery and magic are attributed to him and he was thought to have been endowed with magical powers, but his was an age of mysticism, sorcery and superstition.

The barony of Yester belonged to the Norman family of Gifford who built Yester Castle in which Goblin Hall was said to have been built by magical powers in one night. Hugh de Gifford had returned from the Crusades in the 13th century with several Moorish servants or slaves and he built the underground hall, possibly in secret. It is said to be endowed with some mysterious force and to this day some visitors experience the feeling of a presence. Dogs, when taken there, refuse to enter.

The lands of Giffordgate in Haddington belonged to Hugh de Giffard of Norman origin an ancestor of whom was Count de Longueville. The Count was a kinsman of William the Conqueror (1027-87); his aunt was the great-grandmother of the king, and Hugh de Giffard was the first to settle in Scotland having been given grants of land in East Lothian from David I (1124-53).

His son, also Hugh, was rich and powerful during the reign of William the Lyon (1143-1214). He was one of fifteen Regents following the 'safe-keeping' of Haddington-born Alexander II (1198-1249) and his Queen in 1244.

Hugh de Giffard (original spelling) owned the old barony of Yester and built Yester Castle as well as its mysterious vaulted cavern which came to be called Goblin Hall. Sir Walter Scott added to the romance in his Marmion in which there is reference to "Hobgoblin Hall.":

A Clerk could tell what years have flown
Since Alexander fill'd our throne,
(Third monarch of that warlike name,)
And eke the time when ere he came
To seek Sir Hugo, then our lord;
A braver never drew a sword;
A wiser never, at the hour
Of midnight, spoke the word of power:
The same, whom ancient records call
The founder of the Goblin Hall.

Sir Walter Scott

'A vaulted hall under the ancient castle of Gifford or Yester (for it bears either name indifferently,) the construction of which has from a very remote period been ascribed to magic.'

The Statistical Account of the Parish of Garvald and Baro gives the following account of the present state of this castle and apartment:-

'Upon a peninsula, formed by the water of Hopes on the east, and a large rivulet on the west, stands the ancient castle of Yester.'

Sir David Dalrymple *qv*, in his *Annals*, relates that 'Hugh Gifford de Yester died in 1267; that in his castle there was a capricious cavern, formed by magical art, and called in the country Bo-Hall, i.e. Hobgoblin Hall.'

Hugh de Giffard's son, William de Gifford, was one of the guardians of Alexander III (1241-86) and a Regent who was appointed through the Treaty of Roxburgh in 1255. He died in 1267 and was succeeded by his son, also William, who was to become a powerful force for the independence of Scotland. When Stirling Castle was captured by the 'Hammer of the Scots,' Edward I, in 1304, William de Gifford was captured and held prisoner for the next six years in Corfe Castle in England.

His son, Sir John Gifford, became owner of the lands of Morham through his marriage to the heiress of Sir Thomas de Morham. Their son Sir Hugh de Gifford was the last of the Gifford line. He died in 1409 and his lands were inherited by his four daughters the eldest of whom, Jean, married Sir William Hay the Sheriff of Peebles, an ancestor of the Marquis of Tweeddale, who thus acquired the barony of Yester.

Hugh Gifford of Yester owned the land from Giffordgate in Haddington to Yester including Lethington estate (now Lennoxlove). He disposed of Lethington to the Maitland family in 1345 - David II confirmed the grant of land on 15th October 1345.

In 1350, Hugh Gifford of Yester gave land in the village of Giffordgate (which explains the derivation of the name) for the upkeep of the Nungate Bridge (1 p.145). In 1418 Yester Castle was transferred to the Hay family through their marriage to Jean Gifford. Yester Castle became the ancient residence of the ancestors of the Marquess of Tweeddale.

SIR WILLIAM GEORGE GILLIES

He became Principal of the college in which he was a student

There can be few people who become Principal of the college in which they were students. This was one of the many attainments of Haddington born William Gillies. He studied at the Edinburgh College of Art in 1917 and became its Principal in 1959. This unpretentious, almost self-effacing man, became an internationally famous artist and teacher. His landscapes of the Scottish scene, mostly in water-colour, are well known in public and private collections and are exhibited at the Tate Gallery, London.

He was born in the house above his father's tobacconist shop at No.5 High Street, Haddington on 21st September 1898. His father, John Gillies was a tailor and tobacconist (his shop is now the Carlyle Cafe). His mother was Emma Smith, the fourth daughter of William Smith a hotelier in Kirriemuir. The family consisted of three children of which William was second eldest and only son.

Young William Gillies, or 'blondie' sometimes known as 'wee Willie Gillies' was a bright pupil of Knox Academy in Haddington where he took the Dux medal in 1916. His interest in painting seems to have developed from his schooldays. He was fortunate in the encouragement he was given by his maternal uncle in Dundee who was the art teacher of Grove Academy. Locally, the newspaper editor of the *Haddingtonshire Courier* (now *East Lothian Courier*), RA Dakers and a watchmaker of Haddington, Alexander Wright, each helped him, the latter by introducing him to the 'Scottish Impressionists'.

It was quite natural that this son of Haddington should become a student at the Edinburgh College of Art - little did his parents realise that one day he would become its inspiring Principal, the President of the Royal Scottish Society of Painters in Water-colour and be knighted for his services to art.

During his first year at Art College he was conscripted into the army. The first World War had been an unmitigated disaster, so many men had been killed that volunteers in sufficient numbers were no longer available. William Gillies found himself in the Scottish Rifles for the next two years. He was lucky to survive unscathed from the horrors of trench warfare at the front in what he succinctly described as, 'a waste of time'.

After the war in 1918 he returned to the college to continue his studies and to graduate in 1922. After a post-graduate year he spent a scholarship year in Paris under Andre Lhote. This was a disappointment to him; Lhote was a hopeless teacher and as far as he (Lhote) was concerned there was only one way to paint - his way. His methodology was pedantic and rigid and allowed no fluidity or experimentation. Gillies felt stifled and immediately afterwards he spent some time in Italy - this was refreshing.

He returned to Edinburgh and after two years he took a teaching post as art master of Inverness Academy, but he returned again to Edinburgh taking up an assistantship in the School of Drawing and Painting. It was about this time (1928) that the Gillies family moved from Haddington to Edinburgh. His father had died shortly after the war and William Gillies lived with his mother and two sisters. He gave all his time and energy to art; he never married.

In 1938 he was elected to membership of the 'Society of Eight' in which such eminent artists as Sir James Guthrie (1859-1930), the portrait-painter of politicians, and Sir John Lavery (1856-1941) whose portraits of JM Barrie and James Maxton hang in the Scottish National Portrait Gallery, were among its distinguished members.

Artists are people with highly developed and heightened senses of colour which to them is emotional. Gillies was no exception, but the influence of Lhote was ever present in him; somehow he had to be rid of it and when William MacTaggart (1903-1981), with whom Gillies shared a studio, exhibited the works of the Norwegian painter, Edvard Munch (1863-1944), this was the emotional trigger which produced newly-inspired paintings in still life and landscape from Gillies.

His sister's early death in 1936 affected him greatly and he moved from Edinburgh to live with his mother and elder sister in the idyllic village of Temple. Using this as a base he was often seen on his motor-bike travelling deep into the countryside; the results were genius-inspired landscapes. His students were the lucky ones - the greatest gift to students is to be taught by an inspired and eminent teacher. Gillies was a small man with sharp eyes. He could be likened to the hoopoe bird, always busily darting about from student to student giving advice here and criticism there, never at rest and difficult to please.

In 1940 his election as an Associate of the Royal Scottish Academy at age forty-two was something of a novelty for the Academy. In the first place, he was too young and in the second his art was new. The art establishment perhaps felt that they were taking a risk, but his election was popular with contemporary artists and within a few years he was honoured with full membership of the Academy and of the Royal Scottish Society of Painters in Water-colour; he was to become president of the latter in 1963

He was appointed head of the Edinburgh School of Drawing and Painting in 1946. His reputation, already well established, gave the

School a welcome impetus; it became a force to be reckoned with, not just locally but internationally. But fame to Gillies was simply not a dimension worthy of consideration, he was totally absorbed in the visual scene. For his great service to art he was made a Commander of the British Empire (CBE) in 1957 and two years later he was appointed Principal of his beloved college, the Edinburgh College of Art. On his retiral in 1966 the University of Edinburgh awarded him an honorary Doctorate of Laws and in 1970 he was awarded a knighthood of the Most Excellent Order of the British Empire. In 1971 Sir William Gillies was elected to the highest rank of the art world, that of Royal Academician (RA).

His mother and sister who had lived with him at Temple had both died (his mother in her 100th year) soon after his retirement and he lived alone for the remainder of his life. His artistic output was prodigious during his college days and continued to flow until his sudden death at his home in Temple on 15th April 1973. The Royal Scottish Academy were the main beneficiaries of his estate.

DORIS ANN GOODCHILD MBE

Author, writer, diarist, illustrator, artist, teacher

To say that Doris Ann Goodchild was singularly devoted to art is an understatement. It was difficult, well nigh impossible, to get her to describe herself. The words: author, writer, diarist, illustrator, artist, teacher - none seemed acceptable. She was all of these and much more. She preferred simply to say, "I am a lover of beauty."

Perhaps once in a lifetime one is privileged to meet and to talk with a person of purity of spirit. Such a one was Doris Goodchild. At ninety-three years of age she was constantly busy - painting, writing, illustrating, researching and communicating. Some of her memories give some clues about her life.

Although not strictly a daughter of East Lothian (she is a Londoner), she has lived and made her mark in Haddington for the past thirty odd years having written about and sketched almost every landmark from a welcome new perspective. She fell in love with East Lothian and certainly knew more about this 'Garden of Scotland' than most natives.

She settled in East Lothian after her retirement in 1965, but more of that later. Let us firstly look at Doris's early life.

She was one of life's fortunates who had the gift of changing adversity into advantage. Her books are numerous; she has published twelve of them, the first at the age of seventy-two, all in her own hand and superbly illustrated with such titles as:

The Spoils of Time - Some Aspects of Living in this 20th Century.

Diary Days in the 86th Year of Great Aunt Tit-Bit.

History of the Royal Mile.

Pen Portraits of Edinburgh

Glimpses of Cities

Travels in Scotland

Diary - How I spent my Ninetieth Birthday Weekend (March 1996)

But her interests have stretched furth of East Lothian into Edinburgh and beyond. The Capital City fascinated her and for her writing and drawings of Old Edinburgh she was awarded an Honorary Fellowship of the Royal Incorporation of Architects in Scotland.

Doris Goodchild was born the fourth of seven children on 11th March 1906 at Anerley, a penny tram fare away from Crystal Palace, in London, where her paternal grandfather had two shops. They were left to his brothers but were managed and eventually owned by Doris's father, Frederick Goodchild. He was an avid reader, a wonderful fireside philosopher and, according to Doris Goodchild, he should have been a don, not a shopkeeper. This was to be her happy home until she was thirty years of age. The Goodchilds suffered the devastation of German bombing during the war when her father was killed by a flying bomb in 1944. Her mother, Edith Ella Sanders, always there for them all, died in 1960 and her family photographs taken in the 1920s show a close-knit family, her mother at the piano and each child performing his or her 'party piece' to be followed by dancing in the dining room.

Schooldays from 1911 were a mixture of rigid discipline and achievement. These were the days of the squeaky slate, the inkwell and the twisted pen nib, reading aloud, multiplication tables, school uniform and more discipline. Her Victorian copperplate handwriting received full marks but being a 'scholarship girl', aged ten, she was to suffer from a vitriolic governess who taught through fear. Simple pleasures seemed heightened by contrast with visits to uncles and aunts in the countryside, to the zoo, rides on the back of brother Arthur's bike, her half-crown scooter, her wooden hoop - all the fun of childhood, to be saddened by the devastation and death of the first World War (1914-18).

Beckenham County School for Girls, a new one built in 1914 and used at first as a hospital, took its first intake of pupils in 1919. Doris, in her new school uniform (made at home), was one of those to be welcomed by new teachers who actually smiled! There was a feeling of trail-blazing and the setting of high standards for those to come afterwards.

At home, there was no privilege to count upon, each member of the family had to make their own success in life and their independence gave them strength. In 1923 she had gained six passes in the London Matriculation Examinations and with some trepidation she returned to her Elementary School as a Pupil Teacher. Nothing had changed but even so, she received a praiseworthy testimonial from the otherwise stern governess. The year passed quickly and then off to Goldsmiths' College, attendance at which was conditional upon three years teaching service in Kent. She chose art for her 'Advanced' subject and her special study was lettering and book illustration - the results of which are amply evident today. Two years of teaching practice from 1925 was at Lewisham and Deptford which required a daily nine-mile cycle journey in the absence of public transport during the General Strike of 1926.

Training complete and armed with a 'high above average' 1st Class Teaching Certificate, all that was available was a job as supply teacher to a nightmarish class of fifty ten year-old unruly boys; their eyes glinted with mischief and their one aim was to reduce this new young teacher to tears. College theory had to be put on hold and discipline imposed.

Her first permanent appointment, against formidable opposition, was at Bromley. These were the days when marriage meant dismissal, but this was a wonderful Church of England School for Girls where, after inspection, she received the endorsement of her Teacher's Certificate.

During one of her Saturday outings with her class (weekday outings were not permitted) and a fortuitous meeting with her old Head Mistress, she was encouraged to apply for a forthcoming vacancy. Childeric School in 1929 at New Cross, Deptford proved to be her happiest five years of teaching. The 'three Rs' were taught with kindness, encouragement and individual interest.

A new challenge in 1934 was her appointment at the internationally respected Froebel Training College in Bedford; this was a time of busy experimentation and new ideas in an idyllic rural setting to be rudely smashed by war. Gas masks, rationing, Anderson shelters, blackouts and evacuees were all part of the horror of German bombing. She arrived at bomb blasted Bristol in 1942 to find her new school roofless and wrecked. Teaching art and craft to juniors and seniors and at the same time tutoring teachers for the Froebel Diploma required the utmost ingenuity - old paper bags, newspaper and other waste material were used instead of proper art materials. On top of a hectic schedule of work she swotted for her degree finals, practised the piano and dug an allotment 'for victory'.

It was June 1944, amid the rush of courses and lectures, when the fateful telegram arrived: 'Dad killed by a buzz bomb.' On the day after his funeral she sat her Art Diploma final examinations - a test of her ability as well as her grit and determination to fulfil her father's wish.

The war over and tragedies past, she visited Paris and resisted the temptation to take a sabbatical in favour of a new post at Hockerill College in Essex, her mother's county, where she settled happily for the next twenty years. Hockerill was a Teacher Training College in which all students attended her art classes. She made many good friends, one of whom, Margaret McQueen Burnett, a Scot, became a lifelong companion. Margaret was a mathematics/physics lecturer who longed to return to her native Haddington. They got on so well that they decided to retire in Scotland and in 1965 Bishop Stortford's loss was East Lothian's gain.

The decision to come to Haddington was partly due to the fact that Margaret Burnett's cousins, Alice and Mary Burnett, lived there (their father, Alex Burnett MA, JP, was Headmaster of the Haddington Public School for 35 years). They placed an advert in the local press for a piece of land on which to build their new home and, receiving only one reply, they purchased one third of an acre in West Road. It was perfect;

the view over the Lammermuirs was breathtaking. With great enthusiasm Doris and Margaret paid many visits to the Building Centre at Holborn in London and set about the design of their ideal bungalow. Doris completed the drawings which were detailed by their architect and they followed its progress during weekend visits. This was to be home at last. They arrived in Haddington in 1966.

Doris had had seventeen different addresses, it was time for pure self-indulgence which in her case translated to a formidable schedule of new discovery, travel, writing and sketching of almost every landmark in Haddington and Edinburgh. With her friend and companion, Margaret Burnett, she toured Scotland to rediscover islands, castles, houses, churches and other quaint places - sketching and writing every detail. But her travels were not confined to Scotland. She recorded details, in her inimitable way, of journeys to Thailand, Australia (to visit her old and well-loved West Road neighbours, Dr and Mrs Sutherland in Sydney), Sicily and many other places throughout Europe. Those fortunate enough to have obtained copies of her books, published privately, have special records through the eyes of one who delights in design, architecture and beauty.

Her publication, *On becoming 90 Years of Age, My Birthday Weekend Dairy* contains 46 pages of drawings, poems and philosophical gems. In December of 1996 she decided to part with many of her beloved paintings; the result was an exhibition at her home at Carlyle Court and from the sale of her paintings she raised £1500 for the Royal National Lifeboat Institution.

Doris Ann Goodchild was a lady of such diverse interests she defies a title. She inherited her father's homespun philosophy (her books are full of short homilies and quotations) and her mother's practicality and busy activity. Never a moment was wasted.

In her 92nd year, on 31 December 1998, she was deservedly appointed to Membership of the Most Excellent Order of the British Empire (MBE) for her work in the arts and education. Sadly she had little time to enjoy it; she died suddenly at her home in Carlyle Court, Haddington on 19th September 1999.

SIR ALISTAIR GRANT KB

A strong leader imbued with Celtic common-sense and vision

Haddington born Sir Alistair Grant is Chairman of Scottish and Newcastle plc. He was honoured in 1994 in his elevation to knighthood (KB) and by Napier University, Edinburgh (1996) with the honorary degree of Doctor of Business Administration, this addition to his other honorary doctorates from Edinburgh University, Robert Gordon University, Warwick University, Cranfield Business School, De Montford University and Strathclyde University where he is a visiting professor.

Courtesy of Sir Alistair Grant. Photo by Jane Brown of The Observer

The Grant family first arrived in Haddington in 1866 to live at St Martin's Gate. His Irish born great-grandfather was Patrick Grant, but his great-great grandfather who lived in Ireland and probably emigrated there from Scotland was affectionately known as the "Heiland man". Patrick, a physically strong man, worked as a hewer in Edinburgh. He walked from Edinburgh to Haddington every Saturday and returned, again on foot, every Monday morning. He joined the army and was promoted to the rank of sergeant of the Queen's Army serving finally in the Boer War. His thirty-two years of distinguished army service earned him the privilege of wearing the Queen's uniform after his retirement. There is a famous photograph of him standing, stately and erect, by the entrance to Sandybed Castle (known as Bothwell Castle) in the Hardgate (sadly, the castle was demolished in the 1960s). Sergeant Grant died in 1915.

Alastair Grant was born on 6th March 1937 and remembers his childhood, the eldest of six children, as idyllic. He left Haddington at the age of nine years when his father, John Grant, a well-known professional athlete had obtained employment as a Remedial Gymnast at Bradford Royal Infirmary.

Young Alistair received his early education at Woodhouse Grove School in Yorkshire where he preferred sport to academic study. He played rugby for the 1st XV and was captain of the athletics team.

Instead of going on to university (he gained entrance to Edinburgh Univerity; English was his forte) he chose to complete his National Service. He joined the Royal Signals and was commissioned a 2nd lieutenant.

The following extract from his laureation, given by the Assistant Principal of Napier University, Professor G T Fielding, gives a brief resume of his career:

> *After military service in Cyprus and Aden he joined Unilever's management training scheme after which he worked for Batchelors Foods, J Lyons and the advertising agency Connel, May and Stevenson. In 1968 he joined James Gulliver at Fine Fare. These appointments gave him a broad view and a clear insight of the retail food trade in all its aspects which led to his close involvement in the formation and development of the Argyll Group with its many Safeway outlets of which he became chairman in 1988.*

In 1963 he married Judith May Dent, the physiotherapist daughter of a Lincolnshire farmer and they have two sons and a daughter. It was in that year that he moved from Unilever to J Lyons and in 1968, having the experience of a three-year spell with Connel May and Stevenson, he answered an advert of James Gulliver, the head of Fine Fare supermarkets. This gave him his first opportunity in the realm of the 'future chief executive' and young Alistair grasped it with alacrity. This was the start of eighteen years of hard but rewarding work. The two men became not only business colleagues but friends, the charismatic Gulliver being the 'boss' - at least initially. They were joined by David Webster to form the Argyll Group of which Alistair eventually became Chairman. After a failed bid and a fierce battle for the Distillers Company during which Alistair was the Argyll company spokesman they sold their food and drink manufacturing interests and bought the Safeway Supermarket chain for £680 million. Alistair became its Deputy Chairman and two years later Chairman, successfully amalgamating Safeway with Presto.

His interests are not confined to business matters alone; as well as a sports enthusiast (he loves athletics and cricket), he was Chairman of the Biotechnology and Biological Sciences Research Council, President of the Institute of Grocery Distribution, President of the Royal Show (1996), a trustee of the Heritage Lottery Fund and a trustee of both the National Museums of Scotland and the Scottish Business Achievement Award Trust. For his services to industry he was knighted in 1994 and in 1997 he was elected a Fellow of the Royal Society of Edinburgh (FRSE).

He is by no means a stuffy city type, in fact, he is rather difficult to place - he has a rare ability to fit himself into any company with complete ease and to the great comfort of his listeners. Although he submits facts to critical analysis he has no compulsion to 'hold the floor', but he is no 'push-over', he is a strong leader imbued with Celtic common-sense and vision combined with the romanticism of the Scot - a man to be trusted.

His literary interests include his active membership of the Sir Walter Scott Club and the Trollope Society. In 1997 he provided the libretto and commissioned the cantata 'The Jacobite Rising' by Sir Peter Maxwell Davies; the text being taken mainly from Gaelic poetry including Sorley McLean's *Hallaig*.

Most recently he was appointed Chairman of Scottish and Newcastle plc and Governor of the Bank of Scotland. Sadly due to illness Sir Alistair has had to retire from his appointments. His Scottish home since 1990 is at Tyninghame House, the previous residence of the Earls of Haddington since 1628. The old 19th century house was transformed by William Burns in 1828 for the 9th Earl and the name 'The Library Wing' gives a clue to Grant's love of Scottish literature and his deep interest in the preservation of the Scottish tongue and having returned to his roots in East Lothian he was delighted to be appointed Deputy Lieutenant of the county in 1997.

THE EARLS OF HADDINGTON

The **1st Earl of Haddington** was **Sir Thomas Hamilton** whose Earldom dates from 1627. His connection with East Lothian was through his mother, Elizabeth Heriot, a daughter of James Heriot of Trabroun. The first of Heriots of Trabroun was John Heriot who had the lands granted to him by the Earl of Douglas in 1423. Heriot is a well-known name in Edinburgh through George Heriot's School and Heriot-Watt University each endowed by the extremely rich jeweller to James VI, George Heriot, maternal uncle of the 1st Earl of Haddington.

The 1st Earl's father was Thomas Hamilton of Priestfield in Duddingston, Edinburgh who was a Lord of Session, Lord Priestfield. Thomas Hamilton was born in 1563 and was educated at Edinburgh's High School and the University of Paris. He became an advocate on 1st November 1587 and was appointed a Lord of Session as Lord Drumcairn in 1592 until 1626. With his maternal uncle, George Heriot, he was a favourite of James VI who appointed him King's Advocate and referred to him as 'Tam o' the Cowgate' in Edinburgh where his mansion was situated. According to Court of Session records his title was 'Lord Advocate'. This was the first time that this title was used in Scotland. [It is the present day title of the first law-officer of the Crown and Public Prosecutor for Scotland.]

Thomas, 1st Earl of Haddington (Courtesy of the Scottish National Portrait Gallery)

Thomas Hamilton was one of the 'Octavians' - an eight man Commission of the Treasury set up in 1596 to sort out the financial chaos of the Royal finances and to raise £100,000 a year for the royal purse. Their powers were formidable and wide ranging, even the king himself could not spend without the sanction of five out of the eight men. But James VI borrowed large sums from Sir Thomas's uncle,

'Jinglin Geordie' Heriot. Even the Scottish kirk felt the pinch through the James's excesses and complained to him to have the Commissioners removed, emphasising their discontent with the notion that Catholics were among them.

When King James acceded to the throne of England as James I in 1603 he knighted Thomas Hamilton; the sale of knighthoods was another of the king's methods of raising money. Sir Thomas now received a succession of appointments: Lord Clerk Register (21st April 1612), Secretary of State of Scotland (October 1612 - February 1626), a Lord of Parliament as Lord Binning (19th November 1613), a Privy Councillor (1615-16) and Lord President of the Court of Session (1616-1626). These appointments and his closeness to the king gave him extraordinary power in Scotland. Fortunately, his power and influence was matched by his competence and efficiency, although he was not always popular.

The origin of the Earldom of Haddington is explained after the death of the Viscount of Haddington, Sir John Ramsay who died in February 1626. He had no family and Sir Thomas Hamilton, who had been created Earl of Melrose in 1619, now applied to have his title changed to Earl of Haddington which took place on 17th August 1627. Two months later he was appointed Lord Privy, an appointment he held until his death on 29th May 1637. In 1628 he acquired the estates of Tyninghame. He was succeeded by his eldest son, Thomas, by his second wife, Margaret, who was the daughter of James Foulis of Colinton.

The **2nd Earl of Haddington, Thomas Hamilton**, was born on 25th May 1600 and styled Lord Binning at the age of nineteen until he succeeded his father in 1637. In 1615 he travelled abroad for six years and returned home to take part in the pageant at the opening of the Scottish Parliament on 25th July 1621. His next official appearance was his attendance with his father at the funeral of James VI (I of England) in Westminster Abbey in 1625.

In February 1621 he married Lady Catherine Erskine, the fourth and youngest daughter of the Earl of Mar; her dowry was 20,000 merks. They had six sons and one daughter. His second wife was Jean, third daughter of the 2nd Marquis of Huntly. They married in June 1639/40 and her dowry was 30,000 merks.

He was the Colonel of a Covenanting regiment when General Alexander Leslie invaded England reaching Newcastle in August 1640. The Earl of Haddington was asked to remain in Scotland with a defence force of 10,000 men. On 29th August he beat back an English attack on the garrison of Berwick and returned to Dunglass Castle. That night an English servant, enraged by a remark passed against the English, stuck a red hot poker into a barrel of gunpowder which blew up the castle killing himself and most of the occupants including the forty-one year-old Earl of Haddington and his step- brother, Robert. The 2nd Earl was buried at Tyninghame.

His second wife, the Marchioness, gains a somewhat ignominious reputation as the "the painted harlot" of Aytoun's *Lays of the Scottish Cavaliers.* (66 p.33) She was present at the wedding of Lord Lorne to Lady Mary Stuart, daughter of the Earl of Moray, at Moray House in the Canongate, Edinburgh. During the wedding celebrations the Royalist Marquis of Montrose was being taken by cart up the Canongate to his execution on 21st May 1650 and the bridal party ordered the cart to which he was tied to be stopped so that they could jeer him but such was the calm steadiness of Montrose's gaze, 'Jean Gordon, Countess of Haddington, did (alone) publicly insult and laugh at him' (66 p.41); she leaned over the balcony and spat at him. An onlooker from the crowd surrounding the cart shouted, 'that it would become her better to sit in a cart for her adulteries.' (66 p.41) The Marchioness died in 1655.

The **3rd Earl of Haddington, Thomas Hamilton** was born in 1625 the son of the 2nd Earl by his first wife, Catherine. He was styled Lord Binning in 1637 until he inherited the Earldom in 1640 after the murder of his father and two uncles at Dunglass. His tenure of the title was cut short by his early death from consumption (tuberculosis) on 15th February 1644 at Holyrood Palace. His marriage to Henrietta de Coligny, daughter of Count de Coligny, a Marshal of France, and granddaughter of Admiral Coligny, took place at Chatillon only seven months before his death. She was a celebrated beauty and died on 8th February 1645.

The **4th Earl of Haddington, John Hamilton**, the brother of the 3rd Earl, was born in 1626. During the occupation of Scotland by Cromwell, the 4th Earl was a strong adherent of Episcopacy which, with Catholicism, was banned and the 4th Earl was fined £555 for his belief and encouragement to others. On 13th April 1648 he married Christian, second daughter of the 17th Earl of Crawford, 1st Earl of Lindsay, at Holyrood. This Earl sold Barnbougle for 160,000 merks (about £9000 Sterling) to Sir Archibald Primrose and in 1622 Tyninghame now became the principal residence of the Earls of Haddington. By his second wife, Lady Jean Gordon, third daughter of the Marquis of Huntly, he had a daughter who pre-deceased him. The 4th Earl died at the age of forty-three on 31st August 1669 and was buried at Tyninghame. His widow died on 26th October 1704; their only son Charles succeeded to the Earldom.

The **5th Earl of Haddington, Charles Hamilton**, was born on 1st

July 1650 at Struthers, near Cupar in Fife. He was styled Lord Binning until he inherited the Earldom in 1669. On 8th October 1674 he married Margaret, eldest daughter of the Duke of Rothes with a dowry of 40,000 merks. As part of the marriage contract he resigned his titles in favour of his second son. His wife became the Countess of Rothes and this Earldom was thus kept separate from the Earldom of Haddington. He died at Leslie House in Fife in May 1685 aged thirty-five. His widow died on 20th August 1700.

The **6th Earl of Haddington, Thomas Hamilton** was the second son and heir to his father's titles in accordance with the marriage contract of his parents. He was born at Tyninghame on 29th August 1680 and was five years of age when he inherited the titles. He was granted the charter of Hereditary Keeper of Holyroodhouse Park dated 23rd January 1690. He was a zealous Whig and promoter of the Union of the English and Scottish Parliaments.

Thomas Hamilton, 6th Earl of Haddington by Sir John Baptiste de Medina (Courtesy of the Scottish National Portrait Gallery)

At the age of eighteen he married his sixteen year-old cousin Helen, sister of the 1st Earl of Hopetoun. Under the influence of Adam Cockburn (Lord Ormiston) (1656-1735) *qv*, who was a Commissioner for the Union, he became a strong supporter of the House of Hanover and with his eldest son Charles he fought at the Battle of Sheriffmuir in November 1715.

The Earl of Mar raised the standard for 'King James VIII' (the 'Old Pretender') at Castleton and, having marched from Perth, he met the Duke of Argyle at Sheriffmuir near Dunblane. Although the outcome was inconclusive Mar's men had left the field when dawn broke and Argyle claimed victory over the rebels. The Earl of Haddington was wounded and on his return to Edinburgh he was made a Representative Peer (1716-34), Lord Lieutenant of Haddingtonshire (1716-35) and a Knight of the Most Ancient and Most Noble Order of the Thistle (KT) (1716).

The Tyninghame estate had been owned by the Earldom of Haddington since 1628 but little had been done to improve it, their principal residence being at Barnbougle at Dalmeny. This estate was sold by the 4th Earl to Sir Archibald Primrose for £9000. In 1705 the 6th Earl, being in residence at Tyninghame House, was strongly encouraged by his wife to improve the grounds. Doubtful at first, he took an keen interest in the work. They deserve the credit for its present day magnificence. He planted a 400-acre forest on Tyninghame Moor and named it Binning Woods (Lord Binning being the title accorded to the eldest son of the earldom). His experimental planting of trees on sandy soil, thought not to be capable of sustaining growth, was surprisingly successful and led him to complete a whole forest, the first of its kind in Scotland. In fact, the 6th Earl is credited as the originator of many hundreds of plantations in Scotland. His double rows of holly trees provided wide avenues of exceptional beauty. His publication *A Treatise on the Manner of raising Forest Trees* was written for his grandson's Christmas 1733 and published posthumously in 1761. He died on 28th November 1731 at New Hailes.

His eldest son Charles was born in 1697 and styled Lord Binning. He was something of a poet (as was his father whose *Ungrateful Nanny* was published in the *Gentleman's Magazine* after his death. He fought bravely with his father at the Battle of Sheriffmuir and was appointed Knight Marischal of Scotland and a Commissioner of Trade. He married Rachael, a daughter of George Baillie of Jerviswood, but he suffered poor health and, being advised to spend the winter in Italy, he died of consumption in Naples on 27th December 1733.

The **7th Earl of Haddington, Thomas Hamilton**, was the grandson of the 6th Earl. He was born in 1720/1 and styled Lord Binning in 1732. He was educated at Oxford and the University of Geneva. He was elected a Fellow of the Society of Antiquaries in 1740 and took no interest and played no part in politics. He succeeded to the title at the age of fifteen in 1735 and married Mary, the widow of Gresham Lloyd in 1750. She died in September 1785 and six months later he fell in love with and married the twenty-six year-old Anne, eldest daughter of Sir Charles Gasgoigne. He was sixty-six years old and his family did not hide their disapproval. He died in 1795 aged seventy-four. His widow married James Dalrymple of North Berwick in St Petersburg in February 1796. She died in 1840 in her eightieth year.

The **8th Earl of Haddington, Charles Hamilton**, was the only surviving son and heir of Thomas, the 7th Earl and of his first wife Mary. He was educated at Eton (1761-4) and styled Lord Binning. He was a Captain of the Grenadier Fencibles in 1778, Lord Lieutenant of

Haddingtonshire (1804-23) and a Representative Peer of Scotland (1807-12). Grant's *Old and New Edinburgh* records 'bitter complaints against the Earl of Haddington, who, as a keeper of the Royal Park, by an abuse of his prerogative, was quarrying away the craigs, and selling the stone to pave the streets of London; the immense gaps in the south-western face still remain as proof of his selfish and unpatriotic rapacity.' (13 Vol. II p. 311).

In 1779 he married Lady Sophia Hope, the fourth daughter of John Hope, 2nd Earl of Hopetoun, at Hopetoun House. Their only son, Thomas, was born in 1780. Lady Sophia died in March 1813 aged fifty-four and the earl died in March 1828 aged seventy-four and was buried at Tyninghame.

The **9th Earl of Haddington, Thomas Hamilton**, was born on 21st June 1780 and baptised at High Kirk of St Giles in Edinburgh. He was styled Lord Binning in 1795 and educated at Universities of Edinburgh and Oxford where he gained his BA degree in 1801. In the year of his marriage to Maria, the only surviving daughter of the 4th Earl of Macclesfield, he was elected Tory MP for St Germans in 1802 until 1806. A close friend of George Canning (1770-1827), he remained faithful to the Tories after Canning's death, whilst most of the Canningites deserted. As a contemporary of Sir Robert Peel (1788-1850) he followed his desertion of the Corn Laws in 1846 and, again with Peel, he opposed the Reform Bill in 1831 but finally he wavered to support it in 1832. From 1807 until 1827 he was MP for five different constituencies: Cockermouth, Callington, St Michael, Rochester, and Yarmouth (Isle of Wight). He was appointed a Privy Councillor in 1814 and Commissioner for Indian Affairs in 1809 and in 1814 until 1822.

In 1827 he was created Baron Melrose of Tyninghame and appointed Lord Lieutenant of Ireland from 1834 to 1835. In 1841 he rather astonished his contemporaries when he declined the high office of Governor-Generalship of India preferring instead the post of First Lord of the Admiralty with a seat in the Cabinet of Peel's second administration.

In East Lothian he was a patron of James Miller *qv*, the poet and author of *The Lamp of Lothian*, to whom Miller dedicated this work. The Earl showed great sympathy with the plight of Miller when his fortunes declined and he took to drink.

The Earl's honours included his creation as a Knight of The Most Ancient and Most Noble Order of the Thistle (KT) in 1843, his election, in 1844, to Fellowship of the Royal Society (FRS) and, in the same year, his admission as a brother of Trinity House. In 1846 he was appointed Lord Privy Seal but he lost the hereditary office of Keeper of Holyrood Park being paid £30,674 in compensation. He died without issue at Tyninghame on 1st December 1858 aged seventy-nine.

The **10th Earl of Haddington**: the Earldom passed to **George Baillie**, a cousin of the 9th Earl and great-great grandson of Thomas the 6th Earl. He was the eldest son of George Baillie of Mellerstain and Jerviswood, brother of Thomas the 7th Earl of Haddington. George Baillie was born on 10th April 1802 at Mellerstain and by Royal lineage he took the name Hamilton soon after he succeeded to the earldom in December 1858. He became a Representative Peer of Scotland in 1859 and was Vice-President of the Royal Company of Archers in 1860, a governor of the Bank of Scotland in 1863, High Commissioner to the General Assembly in 1867 and a Lord-in-Waiting in 1867. He married Georgina, daughter of Robert Markham, the Archdeacon of York, on 16th September 1824 and died on 25th June1870.

The **11th Earl of Haddington, George Baillie-Hamilton-Arden**, was born on 26th July 1827 the eldest son of George Baille, the 10th Earl. He was educated at Oxford and was styled Lord Binning in 1858 when his father succeeded to the Earldom. He married Helen, daughter of Sir John Warrender, the heiress of the Arden family and on 31st December 1858 he changed his surname to Arden by Royal Licence. He was Sheriff of Cheshire in 1871, a Scottish Representative Peer in 1874, Lord Lieutenant of Haddingtonshire in 1876, Brigadier-General of the Royal Company of Archers, Grand-master of the Freemasons of Scotland, 1892-94 and Yeomanry ADC to Queen Victoria in 1893 and to Edward VII in 1901. He died, aged ninety on 11th June 1917 and was buried at Tyninghame. The family estates were 6256 acres in Chester, 14,279 acres in Berwickshire, 8302 acres in Haddingtonshire, 4708 in Roxburghshire and 501 acres in Lanarkshire (totalling 34,046 acres). Family residences included Arderne Hall in Cheshire (from the Arden family), Mellerstain at Gordon (from Hamilton) and Tyninghame (from Baillie).

The **12th Earl of Haddington, George Baillie-Hamilton, KT, MC, TD** was born on 18th September 1894, son of Lord Binning, he succeeded his grandfather the 11th Earl in 1917. He was educated at Eton and Sandhurst and in 1923 he married Sarah, youngest daughter of GW Cook of Montreal. During the 1914-18 War he served with the Royal Scots Greys being wounded and awarded the Military Cross after which he was a Major of the 19th Lothians and Border Horse, Armoured Car Company. In World War II he served as a Wing Commander in the RAF Volunteer Reserve. He was Captain of the Queen's Bodyguard for Scotland (the Royal Company of Archers) and President of the Society of Antiquaries of Scotland. He died in his 92nd year in 1986.

The **13th Earl of Haddington, John George Baillie-Hamilton** was born on 21st December 1941. He was educated at Ampleforth. He married firstly Prudence Elizabeth Hales in 1975; this marriage was dissolved in 1981. His second marriage to Jane Hayworth took place in 1984; their family consists of a son and two daughters and they reside at Mellerstain.

The Earl of Haddington's residential connection with East Lothian ended when Tyninghame House had to be sold in the 1980s.

RICHARD BURDON HALDANE OM, QC, Viscount Haldane of Cloan

The MP for East Lothian who gave us the Territorial Army

Richard Burdon Haldane, 1st Viscount by George Fiddes Watt (Courtesy the Scottish National Portrait Gallery)

Richard Burdon, 1st Viscount Haldane, was the Liberal statesman and philosopher who represented East Lothian after the three East Lothian Burghs were combined following Gladstone's 1884 Reform Bill which was supported by all Liberals. This Bill gave the vote to rural labourers and Haldane ousted Lord Elcho (heir to the earldom of Wemyss) by 1528 votes from what was thought to be a safe Conservative seat in East Lothian. Haldane held the seat for over 25 years to attain high office - Secretary of State for War (1905-12), Lord Chancellor (1912-15) and minister of Labour (1925).

He was born in Edinburgh in 1856 and educated at the Universities of Edinburgh and Gottingen. Although his prime interest was in philosophy (he read Hegel for relaxation and translated Schopenhauer) he studied law and was called to the bar in 1879, entering parliament the same year. He practised law in London and was made a QC in 1890.

It was Haldane, in 1899, who was the brain behind the proposed teaching universities in London to be followed by Manchester and Liverpool. He was a founder of the London School of Economics and he helped with the setting up of the University Grants Committee (UGC).

He supported the war against the South African Boers (1899-1902) even when the conduct of the war was brought into disrepute through the neglect which caused the unnecessary deaths of hundreds of Boer women and children in Kitchener's concentration camps. This was the cause of an irreparable split amongst Liberals.

His pedigree as Secretary of State for War was formidable; he was related to Sir Ralph Abercrombie of Aboukir and Admiral Adam Duncan of Camperdown. Haldane overcame the anti-militaristic suspicions of his party which wanted an army on the cheap; in any case, the army itself seemed directionless. Haldane created the Imperial General Staff and appointed men of ability on his Army Council - Haig, Nicholson, French, Ewart and Grierson - and by army order he formed a general staff and created an expeditionary army of six infantry and one cavalry divisions. He amalgamated the yeomanry and the volunteers into a Territorial Force consisting of fourteen divisions and fourteen cavalry brigades. Haldane therefore deserves the credit for the formation of the modern Territorial Army.

He was convinced that Britain had to be master of the seas and that a professional striking force was essential. Haldane undoubtedly deserves full credit for Britain's ability to send four highly trained infantry and one cavalry divisions to the front in 1914 - these were the men who were dubbed contemptible by the Kaiser and became known as the 'Old Contemptibles'.

For his excellence of his service to the nation he was raised to the viscountcy of Cloan (near Auchterarder) in 1912 and appointed Lord Chancellor. His elevation to the House of Lords with the departure of James Bryce to the ambassadorship in America weakened the front bench at a time of vulnerability for Premier Asquith. Lloyd George and Churchill, leading the younger generation, were not dependable - this was Liberalism in its last stage.

Haldane was much more than a politician or even than a statesman, he was a philosopher of merit. Such was his reputation he was invited to give the Gifford* Lectures at the University of St Andrews between 1902 and 1904 and he published three philosophical treatises.

The 1914-18 War was going badly and Lloyd George feared a calamitous defeat. British armaments were sorely deficient, the retreat in France, the disaster of the Dardanelles, 300,000 casualties in 1914 alone - the sequence of defeats brought down Asquith's government. The new coalition government was useless and lasted less than two years. Fisher had resigned, refusing to send more ships to the Dardanelles. Haldane was not included in the cabinet and Churchill was demoted.

** The Gifford lectureships were endowed by Lord Gifford (1820-87), who was an Edinburgh born Scottish Judge. He endowed lectureships at Edinburgh, Glasgow and St Andrews for undogmatic studies in natural theology.*

Although no longer Lord Chancellor in 1915, Haldane was awarded the Order of Merit (OM), the most coveted and special distinction awarded to those supreme in the arts and literature. It is the sole gift of the Sovereign and in the twenty-six year reign of George V, from whom Haldane received his award, only two awards were given.

In 1924 he was again in the Cabinet, as Minister of Labour, under Prime Minister Stanley Baldwin but he went over to Labour (mainly because of Liberal Party indifference to his crusade for educational reforms) with some support while Churchill with the majority went over to Conservatism; the Liberals now had only 40 seats.

Haldane died in 1928 and was buried at Gleneagles.

SIR JAMES HALL of Dunglass

The first to show the igneous origin of rock in his laboratory

The idyllic hamlet of Dunglass on the border of East Lothian and Berwickshire was the birthplace of the world's first experimental geologist. He was East Lothian's Sir James Hall. He was as much a chemist as a geologist but he was the first to show the igneous origin of rock in his laboratory. In addition, he was a distinguished antiquarian having published works on the origin, history and principles of Gothic architecture. He was undoubtedly one of the geniuses of the 'Golden Age' of Scotland - *The Scottish Enlightenment.*

The science of geology was not yet born in the 18th century and Sir James, with the great James Hutton (1726-97), argued almost daily over the formation of rocks and minerals. Hutton was the master and founder of modern geology who, with his *Theory of the Earth*, first formulated the igneous origin of many rocks. Sir James, a mere lad of fifteen, having studied the rock formations in Scotland, the Alps, Italy and Sicily, discussed, almost daily, his findings with his old friend and mentor. It is interesting to note that until Hutton had published his *Theory of the Earth* it was still commonly believed that the date of Creation, as worked out by Archbishop Ussher, was 23rd March 4004 BC.

Sir James Hall was born in 1761 at Dunglass House, not far from Cockburnspath; this was on the invasion route from England. Scotland's poet, Robert Burns, during his tour, was to write of Dunglass as 'the most romantic sweet place I ever saw' and of his hosts Sir James and Lady Helen Hall, 'a pleasant happy couple.'

Dunglass House was built for Sir James in 1807 and was demolished after the fire of 1947; it had been sadly misused during the 1939-45 war; nothing of it remains and when the Usher family bought the estate a modern mansion was built on the site of the old house.

The Dunglass House in which Sir James was born was built on the site of the old castle of Dunglass, originally a strong fortress of the Earls of Home which was destroyed by the Earl of Somerset in 1548. The castle was rebuilt and enlarged and in 1603 James VI spent a few days there on his way to London. He returned to Dunglass in 1617 as James I of England and VI of Scotland when he enjoyed its generous hospitality. Dunglass Castle was blown up on 29th August 1640 when the 2nd Earl of Haddington with his step-brother were killed. An English servant, incensed with anger over an anti-English remark, stuck a red hot poker into a barrel of gunpowder to blow himself and all the occupants of the castle to death.

Returning to our subject, James Hall was the eldest son of Sir John, 3rd baronet of Dunglass and Magdalen and Lady Hall, daughter of Sir Robert Pringle. His ancestor, the 1st baronet of Dunglass (created in 1687), Sir John Hall, was a wealthy merchant in Edinburgh and became Lord Provost of the city in 1689 but he resigned the Lord Provostship prematurely.

James Hall's interest in geology seems to have been fostered by James Hutton at an early age. Hutton had come to Berwickshire in 1754 to study agriculture and chemistry having already graduated MD at Leyden in Holland, then the major centre of medicine in Europe. He had studied new farming methods in France and Norfolk and he brought the Suffolk plough from East Anglia to East Lothian. They were neighbours and met often through their mutual love of enquiry.

James Hall succeeded to the baronetcy in 1776, aged fifteen, when he met the forty year-old Hutton. Hall soon became fascinated with the study of rock formations and more particularly with Hutton's completely new theories of how these rocks had been formed. No-one had conceived of the idea that rocks could have been pushed up through the earth's crust in a molten state. Hall decided to try to prove Hutton's theory by experiment but his old friend exclaimed that 'to judge of the great operations of the mineral kingdom from having kindled a fire and looked into the bottom of a crucible' (25 vol. 4 p.68) was simply not possible. But Hall had discovered 'that basalt and even bottle-glass when fused and very slowly cooled, became stony and crystalline, and not glassy; that carbonate of lime, when heated under pressure, was not burnt into quicklime, but became crystalline marble; and that the vertical position and convolutions of strata in the neighbourhood of granite have been produced by intrusion in a molten state causing lateral pressure.' (25 vol. 4 p.68) These with many other observations he presented in a series of memoirs to the Royal Society of Edinburgh after the death of his old friend Hutton in 1797.

Sir James explained the formation of volcanic cores such as Vesuvius but he opposed Hutton and Playfair* in his explanation of the great boulders on Jura and at Corstorphine, attributing them to a 'great sea-flood' which we now know were glacial.

Hall's interests were not confined to geology, he was MP for the borough of Michael in Cornwall from 1807 to 1812 and he presented a 27-page essay on *The Origin and Principles of Gothic Architecture* to the Royal Society of Edinburgh of which he was President. In 1813 he enlarged his essay in the 150-page *Origin, History and Principles of Gothic Architecture* explaining that it began with stone reproductions of simple wattle buildings, that crocketing was derived from sprouting

* *John Playfair (1748-1819), Professor of Mathematics and afterwards Natural Philosophy of the University of Edinburgh who strongly supported the Huttonian Theory in Geology.*

buds on willow-staves and that cusps were derived from curling flakes of the bark of trees. He built a miniature Gothic cathedral in wattle-work to demonstrate his claims.

He died at Edinburgh on 23rd June 1832 and was survived by his wife Helen, second daughter of Dunbar Douglas, 4th Earl of Selkirk. Their family consisted of three sons and three daughters. Each of the sons attained distinction and appear in the *Dictionary of National Biography* whilst the daughters were, as was the practice of the time, given no opportunity or encouragement to develop their talents. The eldest son, John, succeeded to the baronetcy as the 5th baronet and achieved Fellowship of the Royal Society. The second son, Captain Basil Hall served in the Royal Navy for twenty-one years and became known as a travel writer on Korea, Chile, Peru, Mexico and North America. He demonstrated one of his father's inventions to the Geological Society of London - a machine for regulating high temperatures. The third son, James, was an advocate and amateur painter of considerable excellence who exhibited at the Royal Academy.

In the beautiful Collegiate Church of Dunglass the memorial plaques of the Hall family are to be found on a transept wall; that to Sir James Hall is inscribed:

Sacred to the Memory of
Sir James Hall of Dunglass Bart.
President of the Royal Society of Edinburgh
A philosopher distinguished amongst
the eminent men of an enquiring age
not less by the originality, boldness
and accuracy of his speculations
than by
the ingenuity and resolute perseverance
with which he substantiated
various important theoretical views in his
favourite science of geology
by a series of brilliant and convincing
experimental researches
born 17th January 1761. died 23rd June 1832

Dunglass Collegiate Church (St Mary) was developed from a chantry chapel dedicated to the Blessed Virgin. A charter of Alexander Home 23rd November 1423 granted priests an acre of land. On 12th March 1443 Sir Alexander Home, son of the above, founded the chapel with the consent of the Bishop of St Andrews and on 2nd January 1450-1 the erection of the church was confirmed by Pope Nicholas V.

14TH AND 15TH DUKES OF HAMILTON

The Premier Peers of Scotland;
World record holders and air aces

This noble family can trace its roots back to 1296 when Walter Fitz-Gilbert (Hamilton) owned land in Lanarkshire and swore homage and fealty to Edward I (the 'hammer of the Scots') with all the Scottish Clergy and nobility including Robert the Bruce, at Berwick in September 1297. However, Walter joined Bruce's party in 1314, the year of the Scots' victory over the English at Bannockburn.

In the years that followed the Hamiltons had many titles bestowed upon them:

Earl of Angus bestowed by Robert III in 1397
Earl of Arran bestowed by James IV in 1503
Duke of Chatelherault bestowed by Henry II of France in 1548/9
Marquess of Hamilton bestowed by James VI in 1599
Earl of Cambridge bestowed by James VI in 1619
Duke of Hamilton bestowed by Charles I in 1643
Duke of Brandon bestowed by Queen Anne in 1711.

The Hamiltons would have been king's of Scotland from their ancestry of the 2nd Earl of Arran. He was James II's great-grandson (James V's first cousin) and would have become king had Mary of Guise given birth to Mary Queen of Scots a week later (she was born on 8th December 1542 and was one week old when her father, James V, died). The Earl became Regent at the beginning of Mary's reign.

The East Lothian connection started in 1946 when **Douglas Douglas-Hamilton PC, GCVO, AFC, 14th Duke of Hamilton** and 11th Duke of Brandon purchased the lands and property of Lennoxlove from the Baird family in 1946. After the sad demolition of their ancestral home at Hamilton Palace in 1919, which was necessitated because of increasing damage due to subsidence of underground coalworkings, the family moved firstly to Dungavel House, Strathaven before finally purchasing Lennoxlove (previously called Lethington and owned by the Duke of Lauderdale (1616-82) *qv*.

The 14th Duke of Hamilton was born on 3rd February 1903 the eldest son of the 13th Duke. He was educated at Eton and Balliol College, Oxford. At the age of twenty-seven, he was elected MP for East Renfrewshire, a seat he held until his succession to the dukedom in 1940.

Apart from the fact that he was the Premier Peer of Scotland he became world famous when, as Marquess of Clydesdale and chief pilot of the Mount Everest Flight Expedition, he became the first man to fly over Mount Everest in 1932. In fact there were two two-seater planes, one piloted by the 30-year-old Marquess (he succeeded to the dukedom of Hamilton in 1940) accompanied by Colonel Stewart Blacker (the instigator of the expedition) and the other piloted by the 28-year-old Flight Commander David MacIntyre who was accompanied by the camera man, Sydney Bonnett. This photographic reconnaissance flight was made possible through funding by Lady Houston with the support of the Royal Geographical Society, the government of the day and the Air Council. The main purpose of the flight was to take photographs and to make maps. [Lady Houston also funded the Schneider Trophy Race which led to the development of the Spitfire.]

The whole venture was fraught with danger: flying at 30,000 feet (9144 m), the flyers' dependence on cylinders of oxygen, pipes and masks (there were no pressurised cabins then), the sudden losses in height due to down-draughts and the freezing cold. There was no question of an emergency landing in such inhospitable territory. Douglas Hamilton's plane suffered a terrifying 2000-foot drop hurtling towards the east ridge of Everest when he managed to regain height in the nick of time. McIntyre too went into a 1000-foot drop and his cameraman fractured his oxygen pipe but managed a temporary repair with his handkerchief. His photographs failed and against orders they repeated the flight to obtain a photographic record which would be used in future climbing expeditions. They were deservedly hailed the greatest heroes of their day. Douglas Clydesdale's publication, co-authored with Group Captain DF McIntyre, *The Pilot's Book of Everest*, 1936, describes this world record achievement in detail.

The Duke's interest in flying started long before his flight over Everest when he joined the 602 Squadron of the City of Glasgow Royal Auxiliary Air Force in 1927. He won his Air Force Cross in 1935 for his part in the squadron's performance in a bombing competition. In 1937 he was elected president of the British Airline Pilots' Association and appointed Chairman of the Committee on Pilot Training. On the outbreak of World War II in 1939 he volunteered for the RAF attaining the rank of Wing Commander when he was 'mentioned in despatches' for his reconnaissance of airfields during the Battle of France. The Commander-in-Chief of fighter command, Hugh Dowding (later Lord Dowding, Air Chief Marshal) asked Douglas Hamilton in June 1940 to fly to each of the French airfields to assess their capability for further combat. It was as a result of his recommendations that Dowding refused to sacrifice further British fighters preferring instead to prepare for the Battle of Britain which shattered the German air fleet in August/September 1940.

Early in the war, in 1940, having succeeded to the dukedom, he was made a Privy Councillor and appointed Lord Steward of His Majesty's Household.

Astonishingly, in 1941 Rudolph Hess, Hitler's deputy, landed by parachute near Glasgow to seek out the duke at Dungavel House in hope of negotiating a peace deal. Hess's position had been seriously undermined by Hitler's personal secretary Martin Bormann, and in desperation Hess imagined that he might re-establish himself in the eyes of his beloved leader, Adolph Hitler, whom he worshipped. He flew alone from Germany to Scotland on 10th May in an attempt to start negotiations for an Anglo-German peace with the Duke of Hamilton who knew the son of Hess's political advisor, Albrecht Haushoffer, whom the duke had met during the 1936 Olympic games. The duke was Lord Steward and Hess imagined him dining with the king every night. The duke immediately reported this to Prime Minister Winston Churchill and Hess, who was regarded as a rather weak-minded fanatic, was duly treated as a prisoner of war and a potential war criminal; he was imprisoned for life at the Nuremberg trials in 1946.

After the war in 1948 the Duke of Hamilton was elected Chancellor of St Andrews University and in 1959 he was given the honour of Honorary Air Commodore and was President of the Air League of the British Empire from 1959 until 1968. In 1963 he was appointed a Liveryman of the Guild of Air Pilots and Air Navigators.

His interests were not confined to flying: he was a noted Scottish boxer; treasurer of the Boys Brigade from 1938 to 1962 in which, in 1963, he was made Honorary President; a director of Scottish Aviation Ltd; president of Securicor (Scotland); chairman of the Building Societies Association from 1961 to 1965; Chairman of the Scottish Board of the Nationwide Building Society; the last Governor of the British Linen Bank (1963) before it became the Bank of Scotland. He was a member of the Royal Company of Archers, Hereditary Keeper of the Palace of Holyroodhouse and was four times High Commissioner to the General Assembly of the Church of Scotland (1953 to 1955 and 1958).

After the 1939-45 War the duke decided that Hamilton Palace was no longer tenable, he sold Dungavel House to the National Coal Board and decided to relocate to East Lothian. Lennoxlove had been vacated by Lady Hersey Baird having been inherited by her son Robert, the baronetcy and the estate at Newbyth having been inherited by her eldest son Sir David Baird. The duke purchased the lands and property of Lennoxlove in 1946 for the sum of £4,000. Today Lennoxlove is funded by a charitable trust and is open to the public. Nobody lives in the house but it is the home of , among other things, the Hamilton collection of historic artifacts and works.

His honours include:
Air Force Cross, 1940
Knight Grand Cross of the Royal Victorian Order, 1946
Knight of The Most Ancient and the Most Noble Order of the Thistle (KT), 1951
Royal Victorian Chain, 1964
Deputy Lieutenant Renfrewshire
Honorary Doctor of Laws of St Andrews University (1946) and of Edinburgh University (1954)
Honorary Fellow of the Royal College of Surgeons Edinburgh
Fellow of the Royal Geographical Society

He married Lady Elizabeth Percy, elder daughter of the 8th Duke of Northumberland in 1937. They had a family of five sons: Lord Angus Alan Douglas born 1938, Lord James born 1942, Lord Hugh Malcolm born 1946 and died 1995, Lord Patrick George born 1950 and Lord David Stephen born 1952. The **Duchess of Hamilton** took great interest in the local affairs of East Lothian, particularly of the Royal Burgh of Haddington: she was the inspiration behind the *Lamp of Lothian Collegiate Trust* which was formed in 1967 to bring the arts to Haddington. In this she was ably assisted by the internationally acclaimed actress Lennox Milne *qv* who became the *Trust's* organiser. In addition, she encouraged the restoration of Haddington House in 1969 when the house became the centre for the *Lamp of Lothian*. In 1971, she was a prime mover for the restoration of the choir and transcepts of St Mary's Parish Church which had lain derelict for four hundred years.

The 14th Duke died at Lennoxlove in 1973 and after his cremation his eldest son Lord Angus flew over Lennoxlove to scatter his ashes over his estate.

The present **15th Duke of Hamilton and 12th Duke of Brandon, Angus Alan Douglas Douglas-Hamilton MA, CEng, MIMechE**, was born on 13th September 1938 and lives at Archerfield Home Farm by Dirleton; the family seat is at Lennoxlove, Haddington. He succeeded his father as the Premier Peer of Scotland and Keeper of the Palace of Holyroodhouse in 1973.

Angus Alan Douglas Douglas-Hamilton was educated at Eton and Baliol College, Oxford. In 1956 he won a Flying Scholarship and was a member of the Oxford University Air Squadron for the next four years. His first solo flight in 1956 was in a Magister and after gaining his MA degree in Engineering in 1960 he became an RAF officer and in March 1962 he gained his wings. He passed through the Initial and

Advanced Flying Schools piloting Jet Provost Mk3s and the Vampire T11s. In addition he passed the Operational Conversion Unit to fly Canberra T4s and PR3s after which, in 1962, he served in Brunei, Sarawak, Sabah, Indonesia, the Philippines, Vietnam and in the South China Sea flying Canberras as a photo-reconnaissance pilot. During the Brunei revolt emergency he flew as a second pilot in Belvederes, the troop-carrying, twin-rotor helicopters. Returning home in 1965, as a flight-lieutenant, he qualified as a flying instructor and instrument rating examiner for Edinburgh University Air Squadron teaching on Jet Provosts at Syerston and Chipmunks at Edinburgh.

After he was invalided out of the RAF in 1967 he gained his senior commercial pilot's licence and in 1970 he became a test and demonstration pilot for Scottish Aviation Ltd at Prestwick. His responsibilities included the testing of production aircraft to ensure that they met the performance criteria for the issue of their certificates of airworthiness. In addition his expertise involved him in visits to military and other customers in Sweden, Denmark, Austria and in Malasia he taught the RMAF instructors to fly Bulldogs.

Shortly after leaving the RAF he became a professional private entrant racing-driver and won several land speed records Significantly, he and his colleagues secured the British one-hour record for diesel vehicles at 143.48 mph (previously 120.57 mph). To quote the duke: 'This was substantially faster than the record for petrol cars of the same size. Our campaign was to prove that diesel cars could go faster than petrol ones while using less fuel and generating less greenhouse gases. During the 1990s we did break over 150 British and International records but the 1-hour was the most important.'

The Duke of Hamilton is a qualified and highly-trained engineer being a Member of the Institution of Mechanical Engineers (MIMechE) and a Chartered Engineer (CEng). He has carried out several research projects as a consultant engineer investigating the effects of extreme high pressures on natural crystals with professor Lord Energlyn; heavy oil/water emulsion as a substitute for water injection boilers for NEI Ltd at Derby and Annan; the evaluation and selection of trainer aircraft for the RAF; development work on engine substitution of military high mobility load carriers for Croco UK, TAG, Carbodies Ltd, Norton Motors Ltd and Alvis Vehicles Ltd; development of a utility vehicle to replace the Australian Mini-Moke for both civilian and military use for Austin Rover Group Ltd, Kowari Motors Pty Ltd (Mining Equipment) and Partington Ltd; development of racing cars for Ibex Vehicles Ltd; it was the IBEX diesel-powered, four wheel drive in which he has beaten no fewer than thirteen national and international records one of which was a 200-mile endurance test.

His interest extended from cars to motorbikes from about 1970 when he started his collection by purchasing several of them from a garage in Kingston-upon-Thames. These and others are exhibited in the old kitchen of Lennoxlove.

He is a member of the Royal Company of Archers (the Queen's Bodyguard in Scotland), a Knight of St John (1975) and Prior for Scotland (1975-82), a Member of the Royal Scottish Pipers (1977), a council member of the Cancer Research Campaign (1978) and honorary Air Commodore, Maritime Headquarters Unit 2, Royal Auxiliary Air Force (1982-1993).

His deep interest in historical research of his family led to his publication of a learned history entitled: *Mary R.* in which he has further elucidated the mystery of the casket letters used as evidence leading to Mary's death sentence (her death mask and the 15th century French casket being on display in the Great Hall at Lennoxlove).

On 1st June 1972 he married Sarah Jane, only daughter of Sir Walter Scott 4th baronet of Beauclaire. They had two sons and two daughters: Alexander, Marquess of Douglas and Clydesdale, born 1978, Lady Eleanor, born 1973, Lady Anne, born 1976 and Lord John born 1979. His first wife died in 1994. His second marriage to Jillian, daughter of Noel Robertson of Sydney, New South Wales, Australia took place in 1998.

As the Premier Peer of Scotland and Keeper of the Palace of Holyroodhouse he carried the Crown of Scotland (first worn by James V for the coronation of his queen, Mary of Guise, on 22nd February 1540 in Abbey Church of Holyrood) (99 p27) from Edinburgh Castle to the Assembly Hall in Castle Hill in the Royal Mile, Edinburgh for the historic opening of the new Scottish Parliament on 1st July 1999.

His interest in flying has never diminished. Recently, he was invited by the Shuttleworth Trust in Bedfordshire to fly a Magister to various airfields in France to recreate and commemorate his father's special reconnaissance flights which saved many lives and planes at the end of the Battle of France.

JOHN HAMILTON, 2nd LORD BELHAVEN

He beseeched the House to save Scotland from extinction and degradation

John Hamilton, 2nd Lord Belhaven, was at the centre of 17th century politics - often a dangerous place to be during times of religious persecution and heated debate over the impending Union of the Scottish and English Parliaments. The Rev. William Whitfield in *East Lothian Studies* described him thus: 'One of the noblest and most patriotic Scotsmen that ever lived', whereas Macky in his *Memoirs* (p.236) describes him 'a rough, fat, black, noisy man, more like a butcher than a lord' but in his obituary he is portrayed as of 'of good stature, well set, of healthy constitution, black complexion and graceful manly presence, a quick conception ...steady in his principles both in politics and religion.' (25 vol. 11, p.198). Opinions of him were as polarised as the politics of the day.

John Hamilton succeeded to the title of 2nd Lord Belhaven in 1679, and became a member of the Scottish Parliament. Aware of the danger to his life, he spoke out against the Test Act of 1681 which was a complicated, self-contradictory piece of legislation by the vindictive James, Duke of York who was the Royal Commissioner appointed by his brother Charles II. Belhaven had described it as 'failing to secure our religion against a Popish or fanatical successor to the crown.' For this he was imprisoned at Edinburgh Castle with the Earl of Argyle. The latter escaped dressed as a page-boy but Belhaven had to kneel before Parliament and crave pardon. Had he been too proud to do so, he would undoubtedly have lost his head for treason.

John Hamilton was born on 5th July 1656 the eldest son of Robert Hamilton of Barncluith. His father was a judge of the Court of Session with the title Lord Pressmennan at the start of the second Civil War in 1648; he died in 1696.

John Hamilton's title as 2nd Lord Belhaven was inherited from his wife's grandfather, Sir John Hamilton of Biel, who was created Baron Belhaven and Stenton by Charles I in 1647.

John Hamilton and his wife, Margaret, lived in the mansion house of Biel in the parish of Stenton, and, having suffered a fall from grace and subsequent penitence over the Test Act, he resumed his seat in the Scottish Parliament which had been suspended for nine years. From 1685 he survived the so-called "killing time". This was the persecution of the Covenanters by the King's Commissioner, James Duke of York, who became king, James VII (II of England) in 1685 and being a staunch

Catholic he imposed his religion upon an unwilling nation. Belhaven kept a low profile until the Revolution of 1688 when James was deposed having gone too far with his 'Dispensing Power' - giving himself power to change the law as it suited him. In 1688 a message was sent to William of Orange and Mary (James's daughter) inviting them to Protestant rule over England. In November William and Mary landed in England and in January 1689 Lord Belhaven was one of the party of Scottish nobility to go to London to invite William and Mary to Scotland. On agreeing to the Scottish Convention's Claim of Rights, William and Mary were offered the Scottish crown.

In April 1689 Belhaven succeeded Andrew Fletcher of Saltoun (the 'Patriot') *qv* in command of a troop of horse, which was raised in Haddingtonshire, and led at the Battle of Killiecrankie on 27th July 1689 when the Highland supporters of James VII under Viscount Dundee fought and defeated William's army. That day Belhaven was appointed a Privy Councillor. However, Dundee was killed and the Highlanders were routed a year later.

In June 1689 Belhaven was appointed a Commissioner to the office of Clerk of Register. With Andrew Fletcher of Saltoun he was a strong supporter of the Darien Scheme in which William Paterson (the founder of the Bank of England) planned a colony at Panama from which the Darien Company would trade. There was no shortage of investors of whom Belhaven was one. He had invested £1000 hoping to make a fortune with hundreds of other Scots. The scheme was a hopeless failure and William III and English merchants were blamed for the loss of over £200,000 and 2000 lives; Scotland was almost financially ruined.

Belhaven continued as a Privy Councillor when Queen Anne acceded the throne in 1702 and in the new Scottish Parliament he strongly supported Andrew Fletcher's proposed Act of Security (1704) which he intended should give home rule to Scotland after the death of Queen Anne.

Belhaven was unjustly accused of taking part in Lord Lovat's 'Scots Plot' for a Stuart restoration to the throne and he (Belhaven) was dismissed as a Commissioner of the Scottish Treasury in 1705. With Fletcher, he was vehemently against the proposed Union of the Scottish and English Parliaments. He gained his place in history from his famous speech of 2nd November 1706 in which he denounced the proposed Union. James Grant, in his *Old and New Edinburgh* described the scene thus:

> 'As the Union debates went on, in vain did the eloquent Belhaven, on his knees and in tears, beseech the House to save Scotland from extinction and degradation.' (13 vol.I p.163)

The speech was the only one to be recorded in English collections of rhetorical masterpieces. It was a long impassioned speech in which Belhaven described his vision of 'our ancient mother Caledonia, like Caeser sitting in the midst of our senate, ruefully looking about her, covering herself with her royal garment, and breathing out her last', but Lord Marchmont dismissed him scornfully and briefly, with sarcasm, "Behold he dreamed, but lo! when he awoke, behold it was a dream." (25 vol. 11, p.198) Belhaven found himself ridiculed when two of his speeches were printed in Edinburgh and in London.

As a leader of the 'Country Party' he was thought to be sympathetic to the Jacobites. The 'Old Pretender', James Francis Edward Stuart, was still in France and the French king had proclaimed him James III of England and VIII of Scotland. Belhaven was suspected of supporting an invasion by the French and was imprisoned firstly at Edinburgh Castle then, in April 1708, he was taken to London to be interrogated by the English Privy Council. He was allowed bail but the imprisonment and the trauma of these events so affected him that he died in his fifty-first year on 21st June 1708, a few days after his release.

Belhaven's interests extended to farming in East Lothian with his *An Advice to the Farmers in East Lothian to Labour and Improve their Grounds* which was published posthumously in 1713. He was succeeded by his son, John, who was appointed Governor of Barbados but drowned on the outward voyage. His second son, James, became an advocate in Edinburgh.

CHARLES MARTIN HARDIE

of East Linton

Charles Martin Hardie is probably best known for two of his most famous paintings, prints of which could be found in many drawing rooms: *Meeting of Burns and Scott* and *Burns reading his Poems to the Edinburgh Literati.*

Hardie was born on 16th March 1858 at East Linton where he spent many hours drawing and sketching in the picturesque countryside of East Lothian during his youth. He was greatly influenced by his relative John Pettie RA (1839-1893), the Edinburgh born painter of historical and literary subjects.

After his early education at the local school in East Linton, Hardie was accepted for entry at the Art School of the Board of Manufacturers in Edinburgh and at the age of seventeen he entered the life class of the Royal Scottish Academy. He was a brilliant student who passed with distinction. His painting *The Baron's Jester* won the Stuart prize in 1879 and he followed this a year later with the Keith prize for the best painting, *The Swish of the Scythe*, of the Academy's exhibition of students' work. This was a young artist of talent; it was clear that he would reach the heights of success. As is always the case with those who achieve excellence, he admired and emulated greatness which for him was exemplified in the works of John Pettie (1839-1893) and Sir William Quiller Orchardson (1832-1910).

In 1886 Hardie was elected an Associate of the Royal Scottish Academy and justified his elevation with two great paintings: *An Unrecorded Coronation - Inchmahome, the Isle of Rest, 1548* and *A Royal Decoration.*

In the decade from 1890 his output was prodigious and included large paintings of Scottish subjects, several of which were reproduced by engravings and became popular abroad. His best known works were *Burns Reading His Poems to the Literati of Edinburgh* and the *Meeting of Burns and Scott*, the latter took place in the drawing room of Professor Adam Ferguson in Sciennes Road in Edinburgh. To students of the 'Scottish Enlightenment' this painting is a wonderful study of several geniuses of the era; it was Hardie's crowning glory. Deservedly he was elevated to full membership of the Academy in 1895.

His *Curling at Carsebreck* portrayed peers and peasants. Its success was immediate and it was photogravured for the Royal Caledonian Curling Club. Although famous for his portrait painting his landscape The Bather received 'Mention Honorable' at the Paris Salon in 1902 and his view of the Firth of Forth painted from his garden at Garthill in North Queensferry was another of his great landscapes. He died suddenly in his 58th year in 1916.

The Scottish National Portrait Gallery in Edinburgh has several of his paintings:
Alexander Anderson (1883)
Lord Balfour of Burleigh (1899)
Curling at Carsebreck (1899)
Victor Alexander Bruce, 9th Earl of Elgin (1849-1917) (1899)
The Very Reverend John Gillespie (1836-1912) (1899)
T.D. Thomson of Dirleton Curling Club (1899)

GEORGE HARLEY MD, FRCP, FRS

The world authority on liver and renal diseases who wrote Christmas stories for children

George Harley was born in Haddington on 12th February 1829. He was an eminent medical researcher whose work on diseases of the liver led the field in his day. He became Professor of Medical Jurisprudence in University College, London to become the acknowledged world authority on liver and renal diseases.

Harley's ancestry is long and distinguished: Father John Harley who died in 1377 was the Abbot of the Franciscan monastery in Haddington and, prior to the Reformation, several members of the Harley family held high positions in the Catholic Church. Adam Harley, the warden of the Franciscan Friary supervised the education of the young John Knox *qv* and through their close association with John Knox also born in Haddington, they changed to Protestantism. In 1553 the Rev. Dr John Harley was appointed a Fellow of Magdalen College, Oxford and Chaplain to James VI who appointed him as the first Bishop of Hereford; his cousin, the Rev. William Harley (born c1500) was the first legally inducted minister in Scotland at St Cuthbert's, Edinburgh in 1560 and was a member of the first General Assembly on 20th December 1560. His son, Nathaniel Harley (born 1567), was minister at Ormiston and was one of the original students of Edinburgh University (founded as the 'Tounis College' in 1583) where he took his MA in 1587. He died in 1637.

George Harley's childhood was spent at his father's house in the grounds of the old Abbey overlooking the Tyne. His father, George Barclay Harley, was sixty-three and his mother was forty when George, their only son, was born.

'His life was one long struggle, mental strength battling with physical weakness' (34), but his phenomenal will-power and insatiable curiosity drove him to look continuously for the scientific bases of old empirical practices in medicine. He specialised in diseases of the liver and wrote *Jaundice: its Pathology and Treatment* in 1863 which influenced and advanced medical opinion. In 1883 he published the results of years of experience and research in his *Diseases of the Liver* which was reprinted in Canada and America and translated into German.

His early education at the Burgh School of Haddington, the rector of which was Dr Gunn, was a thorough and good grounding for his entry to Edinburgh University where he took his MD degree, aged twenty-one. Even before his graduation he amazed senior medical men by single-handedly performing an emergency Caesarean section after the death of the mother from heart disease and saved the baby boy. James Young Simpson, of chloroform fame, highlighted the case in the *Edinburgh Journal of Medical Science* in 1850.

George Harley was appointed Resident Physician of the Royal Infirmary of Edinburgh and after valuable experience he went to Paris to pursue his researches and there he discovered how to stimulate the nerves of the liver to produce diabetes, experimenting on dogs and on himself. Astonishingly, he demonstrated that by living on a diet of asparagus for three days he could upset his digestion sufficiently to make himself diabetic. He did not repeat the experiment. He published his findings and in 1853 he was elected Annual President of the Parisian Medical Society.

Courtesy of Eric Groome of Haddington

He continued his researches at the German Universities of Wurtzburg, Giessen, Berlin, Vienna and Heidelberg. At Wurtzburg Professor Scherer publicly complimented Harley on his discovery of iron in normal urine, a finding with which he had previously disagreed. Scherer now requested the Academy to honour Harley with its corresponding membership which, with his work on histology, gained him the Lectureship of Practical Physiology and Histology at University College, London. His published work in German gained him a grant of £50. He had worked under Professor Robert Bunsen (1811-99), inventor of the Bunsen burner) who, with Professor Gustav Kirchhoff (1824-87), the German physicist who discovered spectrum analysis (all electrical engineers are familiar with Kirchhoff's Laws). Their study was gas analysis and this enabled Harley to research the Chemistry of Respiration, part of which he read before the Royal Society and gained him the coveted Fellowship (FRS) in 1865 - the highest academic honour in the land.

By 1856 his output of scientific publications was prodigious but his practice was on the point of financial failure until he was consulted by Sir Thomas (then Dr.) Watson who was impressed by Harley's new and ingenious theory relating to the duodenum and gall-bladder. From then Dr Watson, who was President of the Pathological Society, consulted Harley in liver and renal cases and his practice prospered.

In 1858 Harley was elected a Fellow of the Chemical Society. Two days after he wrote his paper on the effects of nitro-glycerine for the *Medical Times and Gazette* he took a few drops of it as part of an experiment on himself which sent his pulse soaring to 130 and down again to 40 per minute. Simultaneously, he became paralysed but remained fully conscious. He then took ammonia and brandy which brought him back to normal in about ninety minutes - such was the bravery of this dedicated man of medical science.

At the age of thirty, when he was appointed Professor of Medical Jurisprudence and Physician to University College Hospital, he published his *On Oxygen of the Blood* which overturned previously accepted theory.

He moved his practice from Nottingham Place to Harley Street in 1859 and continued his researches into the digestive system on which subject he published several papers. In 1862 his *The Pathology and Treatment of Jaundice* showed for the first time that jaundice was not a disease but a symptom. The Royal College of Surgeons awarded him its triennial prize. He was by now the acknowledged world authority on liver and renal diseases and treatments; he had published dozens of research papers.

Sadly there was a price to be paid for his continuous use of the microscope for fifteen years. It had caused a severe acute retinitis and glaucoma, and removal of the affected eye was recommended. He refused the operation and instead he subjected himself to total darkness for nine months, after which his vision was restored but he was colour blind and had lost the ability to judge even short distances. This led him to the conclusion that judgement of distance is not intuitive but developed, and Harley now explained why infants continually knock things over on attempting to grasp them. He published his findings in *Lancet* in 1868. Even during his period of darkness he continued his work by employing a secretary to whom he dictated the text of his book, *The Urine and its Derangements* which was published in 1872.

In 1854 he was elected a Fellow of the Royal College of Physicians of Edinburgh and in 1864 he was elected to Fellowship of the Royal College of Physicians of London. In this year he became active in the formation of the Edinburgh University Club and was President of its first council. Also in 1864 he proved his versatility by reading a paper to the British Association at Bath entitled *The Poisoned Arrows of Savage Man* in which he demonstrated that North and South America were originally populated from Asia. His article, *Ecclesiastical Buildings of Haddington* was written in 1878 for the *Haddingtonshire Courier*; this was mainly a reference to the Abbey Church in which several of his ancestors were closely associated. He wrote *My Ghost Story*, a Christmas story for Mrs Riddell's *Home* in 1879-80. He invented the Harley microscope and even became involved in orthography when the Spelling Congress met in London. This led him to write another book, *The Simplification of English Spelling*. But his great achievement for which medical science owes most to him was his *Diseases of the Liver* which opened up a new epoch in this area of medicine. It was reprinted in Canada and America and translated into German. It became a classic.

Two years after his return to England in 1861, he married Emma, youngest daughter of James Muspratt of Seaforth Hall in Liverpool. They had four children: his eldest son, Dr Vaughan Harley, followed him into the medical profession and his eldest daughter, Ethel, married Dr. Alexander Tweedie FRS who became Physician to the London Fever Hospital and editor of *The Library of Medicine*.

George Harley the man was genial, courteous to his opponents and quick to recognise and to praise sound scientific work. The great medical researcher died on 27th October 1896. His eldest daughter, who admired and loved him dearly, spent many years in writing his biography. It is interesting that she was helped in this by her father's friend, Samuel Smiles *qv* also of Haddington.

George Harley was buried at the church of his ancestors, St Mary's Parish Church, Haddington. His gravestone is still decipherable and is simply inscribed:

GEORGE HARLEY FRS
Professor of Medical Jurisprudence
in University College, London
born at Haddington 12th February 1829
died on the 27th October 1896.

SIR JOHN HEPBURN of Athelstaneford

the founder of the Royal Scots

Sir John Hepburn, a kinsman of the Hepburns of Waughton, was a famous and brave Scottish soldier of fortune who commanded Scottish companies in Germany, Belgium, Holland and in Sweden winning the admiration and favour of King Adolphus Gustavus (1594-r.1611-32).

In 1625 Hepburn was made colonel of one of his Scottish regiments; this was the old 1st foot, the direct representative of the Royal Scots regiment. He is therefore credited with the distinction of being the founder of the Royal Scots as the first colonel of the "Royal Regiment". He allied himself and his regiment to the king of Sweden during the European power struggles.

He was born in Athelstaneford in 1598, the second son of George Hepburn of Athelstaneford, and educated at St Leonard's College, St Andrews where he matriculated in 1615. He then travelled to Paris and Poitiers with Robert Munro, a school friend.

At the age of about 22 he became embroiled in the Wars of Religion in the Holy Roman Empire between Protestants and Catholics when he joined the Scottish force of Sir Andrew Gray to fight for the Protestant Elector Palatine of Bohemia. In 1622 he fought with extraordinary bravery at the Battles of Bergen-oop-Zoom (July) and Fleurus (August). He led the Scottish companies in Sweden where the king made him colonel of the Scottish regiment which eventually became the Royal Scots. At Mewe during the invasion of Polish Prussia he served with distinction under Sir Alexander Leslie (1580-1661), later 1st Earl of Leven, at Danzig. In 1627, Hepburn's regiment was involved in the invasion of Prussia and Hungary and the following year he was in the thick of fighting in Poland. During the siege of Ruegenwalde, Hepburn relieved another Scottish soldier, Monro, and took over as governor of the town.

In 1631 King Gustavus Adolphus of Sweden only just saved the German Protestants from complete collapse when he arrived with military aid giving Hepburn overall command of four Scots regiments which was known as the Scots brigade to assist in the siege of Frankfort-on-the-Oder. Almost at the instant he blew up the town gates to lead his men into the town he was shot in the thigh but undeterred he had the wound bound up quickly and resumed his command. He cleared the Imperialists out of Pomenaria capturing Landsberg and charging on to victory at the Battle of Leipzig on 7th September 1631. He then stormed Marienburg, Oppenheim and gained the surrender of Mentz in December to remain with King Gustavus for the next three months.

He captured Donauworth during his march to Frankfurt-on-the-Main; the king, overjoyed, thanked him publicly. His brigade was first to enter Munich and was bodyguard to the king. He then joined the Swedish camp at Nürnberg but because of some real or imaginary insult he refused to 'draw his sword' again on behalf of the king. His parting from his men was sorrowful and he returned to Scotland about September 1632. King Gustavus was killed at Lutzen before the year ended but Sweden had become a great international power and had made many territorial gains by the end of the Thirty Years War in 1648 - due in no small measure to Sir John Hepburn.

His offer of service to France was accepted with alacrity and on 18th March 1633 he left Louis XIII at Chantilly to raise a force of 2000 men in Scotland, known in France as *Le Regiment d'Hebron.* By August he was in Boulogne with his men, 'mostly gentlemen' who amalgamated with the Scots Archery Guard to become the oldest regiment in France - a claim disputed by the Picardy regiment which had been raised in 1562 and nick-named 'Pontius Pilate's Guards.'

As Marechal-de-camp (Brigadier-General) Hepburn fought in the conquest of Lorraine and in 1634, under the Duc de la Force, he took part in the capture of Hagenau, Saverne, Luneville and La Motte. He was then sent to relieve Heidleberg and Philipsbourg against a superior force of imperialists. In 1635 he took part in the capture of Spires, the defeat of Duke Charles of Lorraine and several other battles. However, he was captured by the Imperialists while arranging the encampment of the rear-guard. With impeccable command of the German language and his haughty orders he was mistaken for a German and released.

About this time Duke Bernard of Weimar joined the French with the remainder of the Scots Brigade bringing its strength up to 8,300 which delighted Hepburn's regiment. Hepburn himself now requested that 'Meternic' be considered his prisoner (bringing a ransom of 4000 crowns) and that his brigade should take precedence over others. Both requests were granted but before the ransom arrived Hepburn was killed while assisting Duke Bernard in a reconnoitre of fortifications of Saverne on 8th July 1636.

Cardinal Richelieu, minister of state to Louis XIII, thought highly of Hepburn and considered his death a dear price to pay for Saverne. Hepburn was buried at Toul Cathedral in north east France where a monument with a recumbent effigy was erected in his honour and the Meternic ransom was paid to his nephew, a page to Richelieu. The monument was destroyed during the French Revolution.

THE REV JOHN HOME

Minister of Athelstaneford, author and friend of David Hume

John Home, although not a son of East Lothian, has strong associations with the county. He was born in Quality Street, Leith on 22nd September 1722 and became minister at Athelstaneford in 1747.

During his ministry Sir David Kinloch the 5th baronet of Gilmerton *qv* and he became great friends and Sir David let the land and barony of Athelstaneford for thirty-eight years to him. John Home built Kilduff House on the land and Sir David was eternally grateful to Home for procuring from the crown the gift of the lands of Mantle.

It was at Kilduff that he wrote his tragedies *Agis* and *Douglas*. The latter was produced with enormous success in Edinburgh in 1756, but at that time such activities as play-writing and acting were strongly disapproved of by the church, the City Council and the magistrates. It was considered dangerous being thought to inflame the ordinary people. The Edinburgh Presbytery objected strenuously and John Home resigned his ministry in 1757 rather than suffer the indignity of reprimand and dismissal. His play did indeed excite his audiences at the Canongate Theatre in Edinburgh where it provoked the often quoted, "Where's your Willie Shakespeare noo?"

Rev John Home by William Miller (Courtesy of the Scottish National Portrait Gallery)

His father, Alexander Home, was Town Clerk of Leith and his grandfather was a native of Berwickshire, a descendant of the Earl of Home. His mother was Christian Hay, daughter of an Edinburgh solicitor. John Home was educated firstly at the local Grammar School in the Kirkgate then at the University of Edinburgh where he graduated with distinction and was licenced to preach on 4th April 1745. As a student he was imaginative and gushing in his friendships among whom were many of those who would become the 'literati' of what came to be called the *Golden Age*.

A life-long friend was David Hume who became the greatest historian and philosopher in Europe; he was the first to write a *History of England* in six volumes. Of course, any who were friends of Hume had to know how to argue, and two matters over which Home and Hume never agreed were: the spelling of their surnames, and the merits of claret over port! Another friend of Home was Robert Adam (1728-1792) who would become Scotland's most famous architect; they often travelled together on horseback to London.

John Home was a young man of energy and verve who imagined himself a figure of chivalry; he longed for military glory. His opportunity arrived with the Jacobite Rising. An ardent Presbyterian and Whig he was vehemently against Jacobitism and Prince Charles Edward Stuart's invasion of Edinburgh was an offence to his sense of chivalry. He volunteered his services with Hanoverian army - the Royal Corps, which, much to his frustration and anger, dissipated into nothing as soon as the Highlanders appeared in Edinburgh.

John Home now decided to study the enemy and to report to Sir John Cope, commander-in-chief of the army in Scotland; in effect he had become a spy. In January of 1746 he rejoined the Hanoverian forces at Falkirk during the retreat of the Chevalier. Cope's successor, Hawley, was ignominiously defeated and Home was captured with several others. They were incarcerated at Doune Castle in Monteith in the charge of a nephew of Rob Roy MacGregor. Home escaped with his fellow prisoners by tearing their blankets into strips to lower themselves from a high window. They made their way to Alloa where they were welcomed aboard the sloop *Vulture* and taken to Queensferry.

This was sufficient adventure for the time being. At his father's house in Leith he returned to his studies and was soon presented to the church and Parish of Athelstaneford by Sir Francis Kinloch, the patron of the parish. He settled at Kilduff to complete the writing of *Agis*. In 1749 he travelled to London, full of his achievement, to present his play to the great actor David Garrick (1717-79) who was the manager of Drury Lane Theatre. Home was mortified when his play was deemed unsuitable. Dejected, he sat at the tomb of William Shakespeare at Westminster and wrote:

Image of Shakespeare! to this place I come,
To ease my bursting bosom at thy tomb;
For neither Greek nor Roman poet fired
My fancy first - thee chiefly I admired;
And day and night revolving still thy page,
I hoped, like thee, to shake the British stage;
But cold neglect is now my only meed,
And heavy falls it on so proud a head.
If powers above now listen to my lyre,
Charm them to grant, indulgent, my desire;
Let petrification stop this falling tear,
And fix my form for ever marbe here.

His tragedy *Douglas* was written between his duties as a minister. After six years and the favourable opinions of his friends he set off on horseback, full of high hopes, again to London carrying his manuscript in the pocket of his great-coat. Again it was rejected as 'totally unfit for the stage'. Home and his friends refused to accept this opinion of the English critics. Through the eyes of Scotsmen they 'beheld it something quite superior to the ordinary run of English tragedies'. They decided to stage the play in Edinburgh; they, being members of the literati - William Robertson (1721-93) who became Principal of the University of Edinburgh, Hugh Blair (1718-1800) who was minister of the High Church and became Regius Professor of Rhetoric and Belles Lettres at the university, David Hume (1711-76) the great philosopher and historian, Adam Ferguson (1723-1816) Professor of Natural Philosophy and Moral Philosophy, the father of Sociology, Adam Smith (1723-90) the father of Economics and several others equally talented. The play was an astounding success and an early report in *The Edinburgh Weekly* gave the *dramatis personae* as:

Lord Randolph	Dr Robertson, principal, Edinburgh
Glenalvon	David Hume, historian
Old Norval	Dr Carlyle, minister of Musselburgh
Douglas	John Home, author
Lady Randolph	Dr Ferguson, professor
Anne (the maid)	Dr Blair, minister, High Church

This was a secretly performed rehearsal but the fact that the play was written by and acted in by ministers of the church was as astounding as its success. Several eminent legal figures were in the audience - Lords Elibank, Milton, Kames and Monboddo, and several ministers of the church, the latter preferring not to be seen - such was the passion for drama. But the Church disapproved and no less a figure than Dr Johnson, of dictionary fame, was heard to say, "this merriment of parsons is very offensive." John Home resigned his ministry of Athelstaneford to escape the inevitable censure of the church.

After the success in Edinburgh he returned to London in 1757 and was cordially received by the Earl of Bute, George II's first minister and tutor to the Prince of Wales. Bute prevailed upon a reluctant David Garrick to perform *Douglas* at Drury Lane. It was an unqualified success; Home was overjoyed. Through the influence of Lord Bute, Home obtained the sinecure of Conservator of Scots privileges at Campvere. He felt that he could now sit back and enjoy the fruits of his fame as a poet and dramatist. Even his previously failed *Agis* was performed by Garrick himself and was almost as successful as *Douglas* but his *Siege of Aquileia* was what would now be termed a 'flop'. Again, through the good opinion of the Earl of Bute, Home enjoyed the favour of the Prince of Wales having dedicated his three latest tragedies printed in one volume to the Prince. When he acceded to the throne in 1760 as George III, Home was granted a pension of £300 a year which when added to his income, also £300, as conservator, made him comparatively affluent.

By 1767 George III was busily engaged in one crisis after another, Bute was out of favour in Parliament and Home left London to return to East Lothian to build himself a villa not far from Kilduff. He married in 1770 and settled happily in East Lothian for the next twelve years to write three tragedies all of which were well received but only for a short time.

John Home cultivated the friendship of all the literary men of his day but none more so than with David Hume whom he accompanied to Bath in April 1776 only four months before the death of the great man. David Hume was ill and had been advised to visit the spa. Home, good friend that he was, attended to his old friend's every need. These two men-of-letters sparkled with intellect and wit and enjoyed each others company. During one of their banters David Hume, referring to their old dispute over the spelling of their names suggested that they should draw lots to settle the matter. John Home answered, grinning from ear to ear: "Nay, that is a most extraordinary proposal, indeed, Mr Philosopher, for, if you lose, you take your own name, whereas, if I lose, I take another man's name." In a codicil to his will, added only eighteen days before his death, David Hume left a mischievous challenge to his old friend:

"I leave to my friend Mr John Home of Kilduff, ten dozen of my old claret at his choice; and one other bottle of that other liquor called port. I also leave him six dozen of port, provided that he attests, under his hand, signed John 'Hume', that he has himself alone finished that bottle at two sittings. By this concession he will at once terminate the only two differences that ever arose between us concerning temporal matters."

Home moved to Edinburgh in 1779 and spent the remainder of his life in the complete enjoyment of his literary friends indulging in quite lavish entertainment of them. He attempted a *History of the Rebellion of 1745* but the combination of a fall from his horse which dulled his mental state and the restriction of his royal pension meant that the result, published in 1802, was sketchy and incomplete.

This generous, friendly soul who never expressed ill of anyone died in Edinburgh nine days before his eighty-sixth birthday and was buried in South Leith Churchyard where his gravestone bears the inscription:

In Memory of
John Home
author of the tragedy of 'Douglas,' &c
Born 13th September 1722
Died 4th September 1808

GEORGE HOPE of Fenton Barns

He was dedicated to the improvement of farming

George Hope of Fenton Barns made his name in East Lothian through his dedication to the improvement of farming. In fact, the name Fenton Barns became famous as far afield as America and on the continent as an exemplary farm on which all farms should be modelled.

George Hope was born on 2nd January 1811, the second son of Robert Hope and Margaret Buchanan, the second generation of tenant farmers of Fenton Barns. His early education took place at the village Parish School of Dirleton. He had not intended to follow in his father's footsteps by becoming a farmer. Instead, he had set his sights on becoming a lawyer. He had worked in a law office in Haddington for four years when his ageing and exhausted father, Robert Hope, asked him to take over the farm at Fenton Barns of which he was a tenant of Hamilton Ogilvie of Archerfield.

Robert Hope had struggled to keep it going. The land was tough clay soil; it was an unrelenting struggle which had taken its toll of the old man who simply could not conceive of giving up the tenancy so he asked his eighteen year-old son George to make the change from law to the land and to help him run the farm.

It was 1829 and this young man, probably without realising that farming was in his blood, took over the farm. The Duke of Wellington had become Prime Minister; it was a time of reform and young George took a strong stand against the punitive Corn Laws. He joined the Anti-Corn Law League in 1839 and became a firm friend and ally of statesmen John Bright (1811-1889) and Richard Cobden (1804-1865) both of whom were ardent supporters of the League. George Hope wrote a brilliant essay in 1842 and gained a £30 prize from the League.

He had no sooner taken over the management of the farm when he received news of the first show appearance of Aberdeen Angus cattle at Perth. Watson's herd was something to aim for and George Hope was determined to improve the quality of his scrawny beasts at Fenton Barns.

George Hope's aim was to become numbered amongst the 'Improvers'. In 1690 John Walker had been the first to practice 'fallowing'. This wasteful runrig system, in which narrow strips of land were allocated to peasants, was replaced by separate holdings from about 1650. In 1723 *The Society of Improvers of Knowledge of Agriculture* was founded in Edinburgh and the society published works on fallowing, ploughing and manuring, the use of clover and methods of management. James Hamilton of East Calder, a schoolmaster, had produced his theory of husbandry,

James Meikle of Saltoun brought fanners from Holland in 1710 but many years passed before they were accepted. Andrew Rodger built his winnowing machine from an old Dutch fanner which sold in England for £3 a machine. Then Meikle, after another visit to Holland, built his mill for Andrew Fletcher *qv*, the 'Patriot. By 1776 Andrew Meikle, James's son, built his threshing machine. Ploughing had not changed for several centuries until, in 1791, John Small from Berwickshire, constructed his two-horse swing plough; it was more readily taken up. These were the innovations in farming when George Hope took over Fenton Barns in 1829; the latest being that of a young divinity student, Patrick Bell, who demonstrated his new reaper.

Farming was not something to which young George Hope had to adapt. With the drive and energy of the young he threw himself into the creation of a modern farm. His day started at 6.0 a.m. and on market day in Edinburgh he had to be out of bed at 1.0 a.m. to walk almost twenty miles to be there at 6.0 a.m.

As many as 100 men and women were employed to shear, bind and stook the harvest at Fenton Barns. There were many Irish families in East Lothian who carried out this back-breaking work. The youthful George Hope decided at the outset to drain the land. He set up a kiln and used the plentiful supply of clay for tile making. Tile-draining was a new innovation and had the effect of drying the land more quickly at sowing time. So successful was this practice that farmers throughout East Lothian followed his example and bought their tiles from Fenton Barns. The additional income was a much needed bonus for the farm.

Something had to be done to improve the unyielding soil. The produce per acre was poor, the work was back-breaking and the age of the machine had not yet arrived. The answer as far as George Hope was concerned lay in breaking up the soil with great loads of manure. To many of his contemporaries this additional, equally back-breaking work seemed unnecessary but the extra effort paid him tenfold. Now, he introduced sheep and cattle, moving them from one enclosure to another to maximise feeding. His cattle became healthy and fat - the best in Scotland.

His reputation grew beyond East Lothian to England and to the continent. Many farmers sent their sons to Fenton Barns to learn of his methods. By now he had invested in one of the new reaping machines and was able to cut oats at four times the rate of his teams of men and women. This was the invention of a student of divinity, Patrick Bell, a farmer's son, who, having observed the action of hedge shears, invented a reaper which was given its first public trial in 1828. It was slow to be adopted; only ten machines existed in Scotland by 1832.

George Hope farmed at Fenton Barns with extraordinary success until 1872 when he was forced out by his Tory landlord, Hamilton Ogilvie of Archerfield. Hope had become involved in politics and was a strong Liberal voice in support of land reform, the Anti-Corn Laws League and in opposition to game laws and the law of hypothec in which a farmer could lose his crop and his property as security against impossible loan conditions.

He stood for Parliament, firstly in 1865 for Haddingtonshire and again in 1875 for East Aberdeenshire he was defeated on both occasions; this was due mainly to his outspoken opinions on religion which were too broad for the established church and were regarded as verging on heresy. He refused to give in to the threats of his landlord to change his political opinions and he paid the price; he was evicted after forty-three years of dedicated and enlightened farming. The Hopes had been at Fenton Barns for over 100 years. There was an uproar at the sheer bullying unfairness of his eviction which reverberated from as far afield as Canada and USA. The press took up his cause but to no avail. He published an article: *Hindrances to Agriculture from a Tenant Farmer's Point of View* and he contributed to Recess Studies edited by Sir A Grant. (25. p.314)

He had to move to an upland farm at Broadlands in Berwickshire where he purchased a small estate and East Lothian lost its most successful farmer. He was now over sixty years of age and lived only another four years. He died at Broadlands on 1st December 1876, one month before his sixty-fifth birthday, and was buried in the family plot at the ancient and beautiful Dirleton Churchyard. His gravestone is inscribed:

To The Memory of
GEORGE HOPE
For many years tenant of Fenton Barns.
He was the devoted supporter of every movement which
tended to the advancement of civil and religious liberty and
to the moral and social elevation of mankind born
2nd January 1811 died 1st December 1876
with his honoured name is united that of his beloved wife
ISABELLA PETERKIN
who in all his aims was one heart and one soul with him
whether her own path lay through joy or sorrow she ever tried to
lighten others' burdens; she was the light and joy of her home
and her sympathies were strong enough and wide enough
to reach far beyond it to all the suffering and oppressed.

Isabella Hope survived her famous husband by 15 years and died on 16th June 1891.

SIR JOHN HOPE, 4th Earl of Hopetoun

The Hopetoun Monument on Byre's Hill -

" the ablest man in the Peninsular army." Duke of Wellington

Sir John Hope, although not born in East Lothian, deserves a place here if only because his great monument stands high in the Garleton Hills overlooking Haddington and the Lammermuirs to the south and over the Forth to the kingdom of Fife looking north.

The Hopetoun Monument is a well-known landmark to every Haddingtonian. It stands 560 feet, (171 m) above sea level and is 3inches less than 100 feet high and mighty on top of Byre's Hill in the Garletons just north of Haddington. Its foundation stone was laid on 3rd May 1824 on land owned by the Earldom of Hopetoun and which was bought from the Hope family in 1960 by Sir James Miller, Lord Provost of Edinburgh and Lord Mayor of London who, in 1977, gifted the land to East Lothian District Council 'for the enjoyment of the people.'

The Hopetoun Monument is inscribed:

This Monument was erected to the Memory
of
the Great and Good
John - Fourth Earl of Hopetoun
by
His affectionate and grateful tenantry
in East Lothian
MDCCCXXIV

The 4th Earl of Hopetoun, Sir John Hope, was genuinely well-loved and respected in East Lothian not only for his sound common-sense and integrity but as a heroic soldier during the Napoleonic and Peninsular Wars. During the latter (1808-14) he took over command of the army at Corunna when Sir John Moore (the great Glasgow general) was killed just at the moment of his victory over the French. Sir David Baird of Seringapatam *qv* took over the command but he was severely wounded and lost his arm in the battle. Hope was now in overall command.

The vastly out-numbered British had been forced to retreat 300 miles over the snow-covered mountains of Spain. Their last stand at Corunna in Spain in 1808, the 'Dunkirk' of this war, was commanded by Major-General Sir John Hope who refused to leave until he had personally seen to it that every last soldier was safe. Astride his horse he searched every narrow street of Corunna until he was satisfied that all of his men were taken to the safety of the ships which awaited them . The great 'Iron Duke' - Wellington, was heard to say of Hopetoun: "he is the ablest man in the Peninsular army."

The Hope family can be traced back to 1537 when John de Hope came to Scotland from France. He accompanied Magdalen de Valois, daughter of Francis I, who married James V. It was John de Hope's great grandson who was the first to use the name Hopetoun when he was elevated to the Bench as Lord Hope of Hopetoun, but it was not until 1702 that the 1st Earl was created - Charles Hope (1681-1742). He was a strong supporter of the Union of Scottish and English Parliaments and it was he who commissioned Sir William Bruce, who had redesigned the Royal apartments of Holyroodhouse, to build Hopetoun House near Queensferry; it was altered later by William Adam whose sons Robert and John designed the interior in 1767. His connection with East Lothian was through the purchase of the Cockburn estates of Ormiston for the bargain price of £12,000. John Cockburn *qv* was in dire straits and having been declared bankrupt he was forced to sell to the only buyer, the Earl of Hopetoun.

The 4th Earl, John Hope, was born on 17th August 1765 at Hopetoun House; his father, also John Hope the 2nd Earl, married three times and it was by his second wife, Jane Oliphant, that John was born. He succeeded to the title as 4th Earl in 1816 on the death of his step-brother James the 3rd Earl.

He was educated by tutors at Hopetoun House and during his tour of Europe he was accompanied by his brother and Dr John Gillies who became Historiographer Royal. John Hope started his army career, aged eighteen, as a cornet (sub-lieutenant) in the 10th Light Dragoons and he rose steadily in rank to become lieutenant-colonel of the 25th Foot at the age of twenty-seven, having been elected MP for Linlithgowshire during this period.

At the start of the war with France in 1793 John Hope was stationed at Plymouth and for the next two years he itched for action. In 1795 he sailed to the West Indies in charge of ten companies but he was invalided home from Grenada. He returned a year later as Adjutant-General under Sir Ralph Abercrombie who commended him for bravery under fire at the destruction of French and Spanish West Indies.

Hope's army service included North Holland (1799), the Mediterranean (1800) and Egypt (1801) where he was badly wounded at the Battle of Aboukir on 21st March when his commander, General Abercrombie, was killed by a stray bullet. Hope had commanded two of the most distinguished regiments of the British Army - the 28th Foot and the 42nd Highlanders. After their victory it was Hope who was chosen to arrange the surrender of the French who were finally driven out of Egypt. But 1801 was a disastrous year for him; not only was he severely wounded but his wife, Elizabeth Hope-Vere had died during his absence.

In 1803, he was promoted to Major-General in command of a brigade stationed at the east coast of England to defend against the threatened French invasion. The invasion never took place and during this period of relative inactivity for him he met Louisa Dorothea Wedderburn, daughter of Sir John Wedderburn. Their happy marriage gave them eleven children. Hope had been appointed Lieutenant-General of Portsmouth in 1805 but he was now anxious to join the expedition to Hanover and he resigned his appointment to do so. The great sea victory of Trafalgar was followed by Napoleon's victory over the Austro-Russian army at Austerlitz and in despotic style he gave each of his brothers a kingdom: Joseph became king of Naples, Louis king of Holland and Jerome king of Westphalia.

In 1808 Hope regained his rank of Lieutenant-General and was sent to Sweden and then to Portugal under Sir John Moore. Hope, in Command of a division, joined Moore at Salamanca, but the odds against them were too great. Moore marched his 29,000 men over the frozen mountains between 25th December and 11th January to Corunna (La Coruna) in Spain. Conditions were horrific: bitterly cold, lack of provisions and almost total exhaustion; only their rearguard action saved them. They scored a last victory through cunning use of the reserves but Moore was mortally wounded and Hope took command following the severe injury of Sir David Baird. Hope successfully evacuated his men. His bravery earned him a Knighthood of the Order of the Bath from George III and the thanks of Parliament.

Sir John Hope was appointed Commander of the forces in Ireland in 1812 and a year later he succeeded Sir Thomas Graham (later Lord Lyndoch) in the Peninsular army to command a division under Wellington at the Battles of Nivelle and Nive where he was again wounded. Wellington described him:

> 'I have long entertained the highest opinion of Sir John Hope....every day more convinces me of his worth. We shall lose him if he continues to expose himself as he did during the last three days. Indeed his escape was wonderful. His coat and hat were shot through in many places, besides the wound in his leg. He places himself among the sharpshooters, without sheltering himself as they do.....'

In February 1814 Hope blockaded Bayonne with stubborn skill until the end of the war. He had his horse shot from under him and, wounded again, he was captured but soon released. After Wellington's magnificent victory at Waterloo, which marked the total and final defeat of Napoleon, Hope was raised to the peerage as Baron Niddry of Niddry Castle in Linlithgowshire.

In 1816 he succeeded as the 4th Earl of Hopetoun and was promoted to full General in 1819. He was appointed Colonel of his old regiment, the 42nd Highlanders - an honour he held in great affection. He was appointed Lord Lieutenant of Linlithgowshire, a governor of the Royal Bank of Scotland (his statue stands in the garden of its headquarters in St Andrew Square in Edinburgh), he attended George IV during his visit to Scotland in 1822 when he entertained the King at Hopetoun House to celebrate this historic visit - the first since that of Charles II in 1651.

His death was sudden - it occurred during a visit to Paris only ten days after his fifty-eighth birthday on 27th August 1823. He was mourned by his wife and family and nationally as a man of great integrity, strong common sense and as a courageous soldier.

DR JOHN IMRIE of Oldhamstocks

The friend of researchers of historical documents

When John Imrie died in February 1996 in Edinburgh, Scotland lost one her foremost and dedicated scholars. John Imrie would have denied this for he was modest in the extreme. His was not a false modesty; he was quite simply devoted to scholarship and to helping fellow researchers. His monumental contribution to the world of historical records and archives, although well enough known to specialists through his encyclopaedic knowledge and his kindliness, seemed only to become generally known after his death.

It was perhaps something of a surprise to his neighbours in Bonaly, Edinburgh to learn that in their midst they had met and socialised with a man who had not only a first class honours degree in history from Edinburgh University, a Bachelor of Laws with distinction but two honorary doctorates and a well-deserved CBE with a string of erudite publications to his name. He never spoke of these achievements and insisted on being known as simply "John".

Dr John Imrie CBE (Courtesy of Mrs Valerie Imrie)

John Imrie was born on 15th December 1923 at Oldhamstocks where his father, David Imrie, was the estate manager and his mother, Mary, cared for her family of four children of which John was the eldest. He immersed himself in books at an early age and at Dunbar Secondary School he excelled to become dux of the school in 1939. On the outbreak of war he enlisted for the Fleet Air Arm to gain the rank of pilot officer observer serving in India and Ceylon naval base in readiness for a German attack on Egypt or a possible Japanese attack on Singapore (Japan had not yet entered the war in 1940).

At the end of the war in 1945 he was conscious of having lost time. He was a young man in a hurry and he gained entry half way through the academic year of the history faculty having to make up a considerable workload. This was the only faculty which gave some time exemption and it was this which led him towards the study of Scottish history. Under the guidance of Professor W Croft Dickinson, John Imrie gained a First Class Honours degree in Scottish history in 1948.

It seemed to John that he should become a teacher so that he could give back something of his learning to young people and to this end he took his Teacher Training Certificate at Moray House College of Education and was appointed a teacher of history at Ayr Academy. However, he soon recognised that his less than extrovert personality was not suited to the needs of the young, most whom looked for fun rather than scholarship.

Returning home one weekend he discussed his doubts about remaining in the teaching profession with his father who was the estate manager to Sir James Fergusson of Kilkerran, the Keeper of Records at Register House in Edinburgh. Sir James, who took an interest in the progress of his estate manager's children, was aware of John's academic abilities and suggested that John should apply for a post in General Register House as an Assistant Keeper of Records. His application was successful and John took up his new appointment at the Scottish Record Office in 1950.

He became immediately absorbed in his new work and such was his dedication, Sir James, encouraged him to add to his qualifications by studying Scots Law. This he did by part-time study taking the degree of Bachelor of Laws with distinction in 1953.

He became totally committed to the development of archives so that the records should become more and more accessible. His promotion to Curator of Historical Records (Deputy Keeper) was the inevitable result of his dedication and expertise in 1961. Sir James came more and more to rely upon John's sound and entirely reliable historiography and it was natural that he should succeed Sir James on his retiral in 1969.

Immediately, John set out to make Register House even more friendly and more accessible; in this he most certainly succeeded. He had already dealt with the records of the Scottish Office, the Court of Session and Sheriff Courts and he encouraged the setting up of archives for Health Boards in Scotland. Now, he turned his attention to the drafting of new regulations in the Local Government (Scotland) Act 1973 and was responsible for the insertion of a clause to ensure the safe transfer of local authority records to the Scottish Record Office; in the process he gained the admiration of colleagues and officials alike; his was the guiding light, although he would vehemently deny this. Another of his special interests was the encouragement of the preservation of Scotland's archival heritage through the National Register of Archives

(Scotland) which is based in the Scottish Record Office. These documents are mostly in private hands and John Imrie took great pains and gentle persuasion to ensure meticulous recording and preservation.

John was a teacher at heart and in this respect he assisted dozens of research students in their work for their PhDs and in recognition of this he was awarded an Honorary LLD by Glasgow University in 1974; with typical modesty he answered only to 'Mr', refusing to be called 'Doctor'.

He was far ahead of his time in his encouragement of his young colleagues at Register House to become conversant in the use of the computer and information technology as applied to historical records. This was new ground in record-keeping and John sent several young men and women on many courses at home and abroad thus establishing valuable world-wide contacts. The legacy of this is of great benefit today, so much so, that the Scottish Record Office is now considered to be one of the most experienced and forward-looking archives in Europe. He gained new and highly respected status for the Scottish Record Office such that Scotland was given an independent presence on the International Council on Archives alongside the Public Records Office (the latter had previously represented the whole of the UK). It was mainly for this international work and recognition that John was honoured in 1984 in being made a Commander of the Order of the British Empire (CBE). From 1971 to 1981 he was a member of the Council of the British Records Association and was elected its chairman

So far, this account of John's life gives an impression of one with singular interest and activity and, whilst his overwhelming interest was undoubtedly in historical records and research, in assisting many students in their research and in making the Scottish Records office as friendly and as widely accessible as possible, he was known to be fond of Western films. Colleagues who were privy to this 'secret' would often leave notes on his desk such as: "John Wayne tonight, Channel 3" or " *High Noon*, Sunday 3.0pm!" At an international conference in Bonn, John, who was almost completely tone deaf, was persuaded to take the stage with the German National archivist, Hans Booms, and sing *By Yon Bonnie Banks* - an indication of his sense of fun and adaptability.

At home at Bonaly in Colinton, Edinburgh, he with his wife Valerie had three children: Barbara (born 1954), the eldest who is a college lecturer, Richard (born 1958), who is a solicitor in Perth and Christopher (born 1961), who is a psychiatric nurse.

In his retirement in December 1984 John continued his research and writing and was unanimously elected the first Chairman of the Colinton History Society; no history society in Scotland could have wished for a more eminent historian for its inauguration. In 1986 the University of Edinburgh made him a Doctor *Honoris Causa* and the Royal Society of Edinburgh elected him a Fellow (FRSE) in 1987.

In 1994 John became seriously ill and after several operations he returned home to Bonaly. For a short time he seemed to recover his health and on a visit to Colinton village to buy flowers for his wife Valerie he collapsed in the street. He died soon afterwards on 19th February 1996. He bore his long illness with stoicism and bravery. Touchingly and deservedly, many tributes from research students, officials of all grades in the Scottish Office and eminent academic historians arrived at his home.

ELEONORA JENKINSON
of Harperdean
East Lothian's Lorimer Medallist for popular astronomy

Nora Jenkinson is one of those rare beings who leaves you with a feeling of well-being after meeting and talking with her. To quote the Earl of Lauderdale "she is greatly under-rated in East Lothian." She is a lady of over eighty years of age with the mental energy of any of half her age. On 4th May 1993 she was awarded the coveted Lorimer Medal making her one of a small band of eminent astronomers.

This award was instituted by the Astronomical Society of Edinburgh in 1939 for notable contributions to popular astronomy. Only nine people have been honoured with the Society's gold medal during the fifty-six year span of its existence and Nora Jenkinson's name deservedly appears alongside: Harold Spencer Jones, Astronomer Royal; Professor W.M.H. Greaves (Astronomer Royal for Scotland); Professor William Smart; Reverend Dr. Martin Davidson; Reverend Dr. Hector MacPherson; Patrick Moore; Norman Matthew and Harry Ford.

In 1997 she was astonished to receive a telephone call from New Zealand where the Siding Springs Observatory announced that an asteroid was to be named in her honour - "the Nora Jenkinson Asteroid". This was a truly wonderful surprise and with typical self-effacement she asked, "why do I deserve this for something that I love doing - teaching children a love of the stars."

Mrs. Nora Jenkinson of Harperdean observes the heavens with the wonder of a child. The stars never cease to amaze her. Astronomy is her love and her solace from the tribulations of this world. From her observatory, only a few paces from her front door in her garden at Harperdean, she runs a Tuesday class in astronomy for local children, many of whom continue their observations using Nora's telescopes into adulthood. There is no charge for her lessons, only the love of sharing her enthusiasm for the heavens. She started this class in 1974. She remembers well her first pupil, Sarah Wood, the daughter of the Rev. John and Sheena Wood, "she was so keen she encouraged me to encourage others." Soon there were twenty pupils and she takes justifiable pride in having missed only six Tuesdays during these twenty-one years - "two Christmases, two New Year's days and two Tuesdays snowed in." This Tuesday class now appears in the Index of the British National Space Centre as *Harperdean Astronomical Society* - an educational entry.

Nora's love of the stars started at the age of eight when as a child her father used to send her each evening to collect the *Edinburgh Evening Dispatch* from the local Post Office in Dolphinton. It was a half-mile walk - "there was no thought of being attacked in those days." On many a dark and frosty winter's night she would stop at the old Kippet Bridge and gaze up to the stars in astonishment and admiration. Even as a busy young nurse in Edinburgh's Royal Infirmary her love of the stars was to become a solace at times of stress. A few minutes on the balcony of her ward gazing skywards brought immediate relaxation and somehow gave her energy to continue her hard and rewarding work.

Nora is convinced that her love of astronomy is inherited from her paternal grandfather, James Laurie of Berwickshire, who was a keen amateur astronomer in the 1860s.

In 1936 Nora married a farmer, William Jenkinson, a descendant of Alexander Jenkinson, the China Pottery and Glass Merchant at No.10 Princes Street, Edinburgh, a founder of The Edinburgh Crystal Glass Company who was active in the religious life of Edinburgh through his superintendance of the Sunday School of 150 pupils of the Carrubber's Close Mission in the Royal Mile (now the Carrubber's Christian Centre). While Nora looked to the stars her farmer husband had his eyes on the ground; he had not the slightest interest in astronomy. He had farmed at Hawthornbank, Gladshot and Gladsmuir. He and Nora took up residence in the farmhouse of Hawthornbank in the days of the great Clydesdales.

In 1946 Hugh Craig of Harperdean (Provost of Haddington in 1959) offered the tenancy of his farm to the Jenkinsons and after eight years Craig decided to sell the farm. This posed an enormous problem for the young Jenkinson family. However, they worked relentlessly to pay off their loan to the bank. Nora describes her memories of her hard working husband in her essay, *The Lone Furrow*. Her happy married life was blessed with two boys, James and Ian. The Jenkinsons sold Gladshot, but life was hard at Harperdean and at Hawthornbank, where they owned a total of 450 acres. There were no washing machines, no 'Hoovers', no microwave ovens *etc*. In her story, *A Way of Life No More*, in which 'a man and his horse ploughed just over an acre a day,' Nora describes the gradual and sorrowful replacement of their majestic Clydesdales with the internal combustion engine.

After thirty-eight years at Harperdean her husband, William, died and their son, Ian, took over the farm. His brother Jim, now a doctor and anaesthetist at the Western General Hospital, observing the possibility of loneliness in his mother, suggested that she should follow up her interest in astronomy by attending adult education classes at the University of Edinburgh. Reluctant at first and imagining that age might be a barrier (she was now over sixty) Jim offered to accompany her. Soon she made friends and Jim left the class after a month knowing that all was well. After three years of study and simply to check that she had learned well she sat the Scottish Certificate of Education in Astronomy and passed effortlessly; she had been rewarded for her hard work.

Her first telescope was purchased from a legacy of Willie Aitchison who had lived with his mother on the farm all his days. Willie, a crippled lad, was confined to a wheel chair and thought that his happy days at Harperdean would end when his mother died. Nora would hear of no such thing. She insisted that his rented house should be remodelled so that Willie could fend for himself. Nora 'phoned or visited him twice each day for many years until the end of his life and Willie's way of thanking Nora for her concern and care was his gift of the 4-inch refractor telescope. Her second and larger telescope (it is a 14-inch reflector telescope) was a legacy from her brother. He had suffered a stroke and again Nora looked after him.

Nora's activities are not by any means confined to astronomy, she is an enthusiast on old maps of East Lothian, she is imbued with curiosity about placenames and name changes over the centuries. With her friend, Margaret McKinlay, she writes for magazines under a pseudonym which, she insists, must remain a pseudonym. Sadly, her *History of St Mary's Church, 1063-1983* remains unpublished. Their latest work, in course of preparation, is the story of the Jenkinson family, *A Farming Family in East Lothian over 100 years.*

Her diary contains a continuous stream of visitors and her brilliant conversation enlightens their day. In her interview for this brief story she had no wish to talk of the past; she becomes positively animated when she talks of the progress of her pupils. A wonderful and gracious lady of East Lothian - a star of the stars.

THE KINLOCHS of Gilmerton

Lairds of Athelstaneford; Baronets of Gilmerton

This story of the Kinloch family of Gilmerton in East Lothian and their lairdship of Athelstaneford starts in Edinburgh early in the 16th century when James V was king. **David Kinloch** was the deacon of bakers in Edinburgh from 1538 to 1556; he was the great-grandfather of the **1st Baronet, Sir Francis Kinloch of Gilmerton**.

David Kinloch married Margaret, daughter of William Cathkin a burgess of Edinburgh and lived at Blacklock's Close (later renamed Kinloch's Close) in the High Street of the Royal Mile. They had five sons the eldest surviving of whom was **William**. He was succeeded by his young brother **David**, a baker burgess who built the houses at Kinloch Close. David married firstly Elizabeth, daughter of William Blacklock (after whom Blacklock's Close was named) and secondly Margaret Adamson by whom he had six sons and five daughters. **Andrew**, their fourth son, a saddler, inherited his father's estate and married Elspeth Miller in 1594. They had five sons and one daughter. The first of his three sons predeceased their young brother **Francis** who became the 1st baronet. (94 pps. 105 & 122-3)

The **1st Baronet, Sir Francis Kinloch of Gilmerton** was born in December 1604 and baptised on 26th December 1604. He is regarded as the founder of the family being the first to be knighted. 'He was a merchant-tailor in Edinburgh of which city he became a wealthy and influential citizen' (94 p.123) He became a burgess of Edinburgh on 1st September 1647, MP for the County of Edinburgh in 1678 and Lord Provost of Edinburgh in 1677 and 1678. He inherited Blacklock's Close, renamed Kinloch's Close in the High Street (on the east side of Niddry Street) Edinburgh in 1627, and lived there when he was a merchant councillor (95 p.373).

Francis Kinloch was one of the commanders under David Leslie who led the Scottish army against Cromwell at the Battle of Dunbar in June 1650. Charles II had sworn an oath of loyalty to the Covenant in Edinburgh and Oliver Cromwell marched north to capture Charles. On reaching Edinburgh Cromwell was forced to retreat back to Dunbar. Leslie's army of 11,000 Scots outmanoeuvred Cromwell who was hemmed in between the Lammermuirs and the sea but rashly the Scots moved from their favourable position on Doon Hill and were ignominiously defeated by 3000 English troops. Three thousand Scots were killed that day, 3rd September 1650. Exactly one year later Charles, having crossed the border, established himself at Worcester but Cromwell outnumbered the Scots by three to one and again, at the Battle of Worcester, defeated the Scots. Charles II fled to France and Francis Kinloch was taken prisoner.

On his return to Scotland his business flourished and he amassed a sufficient fortune to purchase the Gilmerton House and the lands at Athelstaneford from Hepburn of Waughton in 1655 (where the Battle of Athelstaneford was fought at the beginning of the ninth century) and the adjoining lands of Markle and Drylaw from Dame Mary Seton of Hailes (his charter of the barony of Markle is dated 24th June 1664) (94 p123).

He was created a baronet of Nova Scotia on 16th September 1686 by James II (VII) for his services to the crown - he had lent £300 to him when he was the Duke of York for his tour of Scotland. This is the origin of the Baronetcy of Kinloch of Gilmerton.

Sir Francis married Magdalene McMath of Newbyres and had three sons and three daughters. Sir Francis died in December 1691 and was succeeded by his eldest son, Francis.

The **2nd Baronet, Sir Francis Kinloch of Gilmerton**, was born in 1650, the year of the Battle of Dunbar. On 29th April 1675 he married Mary, daughter of the famous Covenanter general, David Leslie, 1st Lord Newark. They had nine children, five sons and four daughters. His fourth daughter, Elizabeth, married Andrew Fletcher of Salton *qv*, (a nephew of Andrew Fletcher *qv*, 'The Patriot'), who became Lord Milton when he was appointed a Senator of the College of Justice in 1724.

His father-in-law gained fame in the history of Scotland when he defeated the Covenanter turned Royalist the Marquis of Montrose at Philiphaugh on 13th September 1645.

Francis Kinloch succeeded his father in 1691 and died in September 1699 (94 p.125).

His son, **Sir Francis Kinloch, the 3rd Baronet**, was born on 23rd June 1676. He married, in 1699, his cousin the Hon. Mary, co-heiress (with her brother) daughter of Sir James Rocheid of Inverleith in Edinburgh. They had five sons and three daughters. The eldest son Francis, born in 1702, predeceased his father and the second son James became his heir; he married illicitly and fled the country. Their third son, Alexander born in 1712, succeeded to the estate of his maternal grandmother and took the name Rocheid (13 Vol.II p.94). He received the dignity and title of baronet on 4th June 1704.

Sir Francis was served heir to the lands and barony of Gilmerton in 1676 and owned a mansion house in Haddington - Kinloch House (or Gilmerton House) in Market Street which dates from about 1700. It is rubble built with crow-stepped gables and a front-facing Dutch chimney. He purchased the barony of Athelstaneford in 1706; he died on 2nd March 1747 at Gilmerton House.

Sir James Kinloch, 4th Baronet was born in 1705 being baptised that year at Athelstaneford. He lived most of his adult life in Switzerland and married firstly Margaret Foulis of Woodhall but had an illicit affair with a Swiss lady, Marguerite Wild of Bern. They married and fled the country and had three sons and five daughters none of whom were naturalised British citizens and thus could not inherit the baronetcy. 'By a contract with his father, dated 10th October 1741, he renounced all right, as his eldest son, to the estate at Gilmerton and afterwards consented to a deed of entail of that estate and others in favour of his younger brothers. He died in Switzerland on 25th March 1778.

Sir David, 5th Baronet was born in 1711. He was educated by a tutor, Alexander Matheson, the "doctor" of the Haddington Seminary. Matheson became Rector of the High School of Edinburgh when Dugald Stewart was one of his pupils (50 p.136). Sir David qualified for the Scottish bar and was one of the commissioners 'for the encouragement of British Fisheries and Manufacturers' (94 p.128).

On 16th January 1746 he married Harriot, daughter of Archibald Cockburn of Langton, they had five sons and three daughters - (i) Francis, his successor; (ii) Archibald Gordon-Kinloch, an army major who adopted the name Gordon on succeeding to an estate but was incarcerated insane for the murder of his elder brother; (iii) David who served under Cornwallis in the American War; (iv) Alexander, a Collector of Customs at Prestonpans and (v) John who died unmarried in India. (13 Vol.III p.344) and (i) Mary (ii) Janet and (iii) Harriet

Sir David succeeded to the Gilmerton estates in 1747 and, on the death of his brother in 1778, to the baronetcy. He commissioned the building of Gilmerton House about 2km east-north-east of Athelstaneford by mason John Aitken. The 50-room house was built during the 1750s on the site of the original house of 1530 to a design of William Adam, although an east wing was added in 1828 by William Burn who designed the porch, its coupled pilasters and balconies and the matching west side (30 p.215).

Sir David let some land and the barony of Athelstaneford for thirty-eight years to his close friend the Reverend John Home *qv*. Home built Kilduff House and had to resign his ministry for daring to write and perform a play at a time when works of drama were severely disapproved of by the Church. Sir David was eternally grateful to Home for procuring from the crown the gift of the lands of Mantle

According to Martine's *Reminiscences*: 'the late Sir David Kinloch, Baronet of Gilmerton, obtained from the Crown a perpetual lease of these lands at the rent of forty-six bols (bushels) of wheat, fifty-one of barley, thirty-five of oats, one dozen kainfowls, two dozen chickens.

The rent is doubled for one year at every singular succession of the family of Kinloch of Gilmerton.' (59 p.21). Sir David died on 18th February 1795 and was buried at Greyfriars Churchyard in Edinburgh.

Sir Francis Kinloch, 6th Baronet was born on 10th August 1747 and succeeded his father in February 1795 but he was shot dead by his brother, Archibald, only two months after succeeding to the title.

He was Governor of the British Linen Company and Writer to the Privy Seal of Scotland. A little known fact is that Sir Francis has a fair claim to be the inventor of the threshing machine. In 1784 he displayed his mechanical prowess in designing a model threshing machine which he had made by William Veitch, a watchmaker of Haddington. The model was then sent to the Agricultural Society of Bath where it received approbation. A full sized version was built from the original design of Sir Francis at Kilbargie by Andrew Meikle *qv* who then received the credit for its invention. [Meikle was reputed to have found a fault in Sir Francis's machine which he tested to destruction and rebuilt it with modifications curing the fault - thus the Meikle claim for the invention].

Sir Francis Kinloch took up residence at the family's town house in Haddington, the old Gilmerton House having fallen into disrepair. He was a heritor and Laird of the Parish of Athelstaneford where he owned about 1300 acres and became well-loved for his concern for the people of village where he set up a butchers' market (East Lothian Life, Issues 4 and 9)

Sir Francis was shot on 14th April 1795 and died two days later, aged forty-eight, by his brother, Major Archibald Gordon Kinloch, who was imprisoned in the Tolbooth and taken to the High Court of the Judiciary on 29th June 1795 in Edinburgh for trial for murder. Sir Francis never married and the baronetcy was now inherited by his brother, Archibald.

Sir Archibald Gordon Kinloch, the second of the five sons now inherited the title and estates as the **7th Baronet** in 1796 from the brother he shot. He was born on 31st December 1749 and entered the army serving in the West Indies in command of his regiment in 1780. He left Scotland a healthy and bright young man 'beloved and esteemed in his own regiment by both officers and men, respected by the whole line and in every point one of the most amiable characters they ever knew' (93 p.127). He returned from that 'grave of millions' a changed man.

Having been imprisoned in Haddington jail and in the Tolbooth of Edinburgh he was brought to trial at the High Court of the Justiciary where the indictment by Robert Dundas, the king's advocate, was read to him:

'You, the said Sir Archibald Gordon-Kinloch, being on the 14th day of April 1795, in the house of Gilmerton, belonging to the deceased Sir Francis Kinloch of Gilmerton, baronet, Your Brother-german, ... did ...come down from your bed-chamber...to the parlour ...You did then and there Murder the said Sir Francis Kinloch, Your brother, by wickedly and feloniously discharging one of the said pistols at your said brother, by which he received a mortal wound....And the said Sir Francis having languished in great pain till the evening of the 16th of the said month of April, did then expire.....' (93 p.4)

Letters written by Sir Archibald and the pistols were produced as evidence; he pleaded 'Not Guilty' on the grounds of 'having scarce any knowledge or remembrance of what passed .... If unluckily it shall appear and be shown, that the pannel's [prisoner's] hand has been the unhappy cause of the death of his brother - then, my Lord and in that event his plea must be understood to mean....... That at least his heart and purpose have not been in the deed, but his hand only, - that it was not the work of malice and design, (without which there is no murder) but of pure fatality and misfortune, which he could not avoid, and for which he is not the object of punishment, but of sympathy and commiseration' (93 p.5). This was a plea of insanity.

Witnesses attested to his good character and bravery as a soldier. Mr Hope gave a long and impassioned plea on his behalf. The Lord Justice Clerk's charge to the jury concluded with the words:

If you are convinced that he knew right from wrong, you will return a verdict of guilty. On the other hand, if it shall appear to you that he was not able to distinguish between moral good and evil, you are bound to acquit him. I think you ought to return a special verdict of not guilty, finding that the pannel was guilty of taking the life of his brother, but finding also that he was insane at the time. (93 p.151)

On the 30th June the jury delivered its verdict after 35 minutes of deliberation and unanimously found 'it proven that the pannel killed the deceased Sir Francis Kinloch, his brother-german, in the way and manner mentioned in the indictment; but find it proven, that, at that time the pannel was insane, and deprived of his reason' (93 p.152).

Robert M'Queen, the Lord Chief Justice Clerk, Lord Braxfield delivered his judgement on 15th July: '...Sir Archibald Gordon Kinloch be ... detained and confined prisoner during all the days of his life; or at least, ay and until he is delivered to any friend or other person... to secure and confine him in sure and safe custody, during all the days of his life, and that under the penalty of L.10,000 Sterling.... receive and detain him prisoner....' (93 pps. 156-7).

Sir Archibald was given into the custody of Dr William Farquharson and he died at Greenlaw House on 24th October 1800. The baronetcy passed to Alexander, the fourth son of Sir David Kinloch, 5th Baronet, his third son Captain David Kinloch having died unmarried in 1790.

Sir Alexander Kinloch, 8th Baronet was born c1775 and succeeded to the estates and title on the death of his brother on 24th October 1800. He was married on 20th January 1801 to Isabella Stowe co-heiress of John Stowe of Newton, Lincolnshire. They had four children one son: David (born 1st September 1805), and three daughters: Maria Ann (born 8th February 1803), Harriet (born 4th September 1804) and Isabella (born 14th August 1809).

In 1811 he produced a pamphlet entitled: *The Threshing Machine - an address to the public but more particularly to the landed interest of Great Britain and Ireland* disputing the attribution of the invention of the machine which had been claimed by Andrew Meikle *qv*. Twenty-seven years had passed since Meikle's invention and the dispute came to nothing. Sir Alexander died on 12th February 1813

Sir David Kinloch, 9th Baronet was born on 1st September 1805 and succeeded to the title on 12th February 1813 at the age of eight. Aged twenty-one he entered the East Lothian Yeomanry as a cornet. In 1827 he became a member of the King's Bodyguard, the Royal Company of Archers and in 1831 he was commissioned as Deputy Lieutenant of the County. He married Eleanor Hyndford Carmichael, the eldest daughter of Sir J Gibson-Carmichael of Stirling, on 5th June 1829 and had four children, one son, Alexander and three daughters. He died 23rd February 1879.

The **10th Baronet, Sir Alexander Kinloch** was born on 1st February 1830. He was promoted from lieutenant to captain in the Grenadier Regiment of Foot Guards in 1853 and served in the Crimean War. At home he was appointed Deputy Lieutenant of the County of Haddington and commissioned captain of the 1st Company of the Haddington Volunteers in 1859 but he resigned his captaincy in the autumn of 1860 after he commanded the contingent of County East Lothian in the review of the Scottish Rifle Volunteers which was held in Edinburgh in the presence of Queen Victoria on 7th August 1860 (50 p.76).

He succeeded his father in 1879. He married, on 12th August 1852, Lucy Charlotte, daughter of Sir Ralph Anstruther of Balcaskie. They had four sons: David Alexander (born 20th February 1856), Henry Anstruther (born 7th November 1859), Francis (born 6th October 1863), Alexander Carmichael (born 11th June 1866) and two daughters: Eleanor Ann (born 5th July 1853) and Mary Anna (?-1898) He died at Gilmerton House on 11th March 1912 and was buried in Athelstaneford

Churchyard beside his wife who died on 14th November 1908 and to whom he was married for fifty-one years.

The **11th Baronet, Brigadier-General, Sir David Alexander Kinloch CB, MVO**, was born at Gilmerton on 20th February 1856 soon after the return of his father from the Crimean War.

His boyhood at Gilmerton was followed by his schooling at Cheam where his outstanding success was marked with a half day holiday. After Eton and Oxford, where he studied history, he joined and distinguished himself in the 96th Regiment of Foot. In 1876, he joined the Grenadier Guards and was promoted second in command of the 3rd Battalion in 1897.

This was the year of his marriage to Elinor Lucy, the youngest of the three daughters of Colonel Bromley Davenport of Capesthorne, Cheshire. They had one son, Alexander Davenport (born 17th September 1902) and two daughters: Jean Mary (born 3rd November 1898) and Katherine Hariot (born 5th March 1906).

He served in the Boer War from 1899 to 1900 and was present at the relief of Kimberley in February 1900 when John French (then a dashing cavalry officer who would become Earl of Ypres and Field Marshal) lifted the siege. He took part in the Battles of Belmont, Graspan and Modder River and was mentioned in despatches. Sir David attained the rank of Lieutenant-Colonel when he took command of the 1st battalion of the Grenadier Guards in June 1900. He was summarily retired on half pay in 1903 following a complaint made against him by the fathers of three subalterns who had suffered bullying and beating following a mock 'court-martial' by fellow subalterns. The colonel knew nothing of these events and the bullying and unfairness of his dismissal became a cause-celebre; there were almost 300 articles in many newspapers and lengthy heated debates in both Houses of Parliament. As commander of the battalion he had received no complaints from the victims and Lord Roberts acted at the behest of the fathers: the Duke of Wellington, Lord Belhaven and an uncle Lord de Saumerez. Lord Belhaven later denied having drafted any letter to Lord Roberts.

Courtesy of Sir David Kinloch 13th Baronet

He never lost his enthusiasm for military life and played an important part in the training of the newly-formed Territorial Army in 1908. He succeeded to the baronetcy in 1912 becoming the Laird of Athelstaneford where he gifted land and subscribed generously for the erection of the village hall. In 1914 at the age of 58 and with the rank of Brigadier-General he took command of a brigade in Kitchener's new army serving at the front line in France. On his return home he commanded a reserve brigade until the end of the war.

With the help of Lady Kinloch and the patronage of the king he spent much of his time in helping destitute artists to find work. Lady Kinloch was herself a talented artist and soon the work of her team of artists was in demand. In December 1929 he was elected President of the East Lothian Agricultural Society.

During World War II Lady Kinloch was active in many parish events and took a particular interest in the Red Cross. She died suddenly on 22nd November 1943 aged 73 years and eleven months later Sir David died on 27th October 1944 aged 83 years. He was buried beside his wife Nelly at Athelstaneford. A memorial window in their honour can be seen at Athelstaneford Church.

The **12th Baronet of Gilmerton, Sir Alexander Davenport Kinloch** was born on 17th September 1902. He was educated at Eton where his athletic prowess was such that he won the coveted 'Eton Mile'. After a spell of about three years in USA he returned home with his valet having married Alexandra, daughter of Frederick Y. Dalziel of New York in 1929.

During World War II he, as Deputy-Assistant Quartermaster General (Movements), was based at Plymouth and was involved in the extensive preparations and detailed and secret planning for the mounting of the Expeditionary Force for 'Overlord' - the invasion at Normandy on D Day, 6th June 1944.

After the war he was appointed a Member of the Queen's Bodyguard for Scotland and a Major of the Special Reserve Grenadier Guards. His business activities for the next thirty years included grass-drying and the manufacturing of pellets and meal for cattle feed.

His marriage to Alexandra Dalziel was dissolved in 1944; they had two daughters : Emi-Lou, born 1930 and Jean Kinloch, born 1934. In 1946 he married Anna, daughter of Thomas Walker of Edinburgh; they had three sons: Ian Kinloch born 1942, Francis Kinloch born 1944 and David, his heir, who was born on 5th August 1951 and three daughters: Victoria born on 22nd December 1947, Harriet born on 14th October 1949 and Ann born on 5th August 1951. By Ann Maud White he had Jamie born 1973.

He died aged eighty at Gilmerton on 22nd November 1982 and was buried at Athelstaneford Churchyard.

The present **13th Baronet, Sir David Kinloch**, was born in Edinburgh on 5th August 1951. He was educated at Gordonstoun where he was given a schoolboy project which would lead him into the business he manages today - Gilmerton Land Services. His school project required him to use a metal detector and to report his findings. He discovered what he thought to be disused cable and he proceeded to dig it up. Having recovered a short length of it he returned next day to find the area fenced off and under military guard. He had accidentally cut the lighting and communications cable which were connected to the RAF Station at Lossiemouth. This was not only a shock to him but a salutary lesson which would never be forgotton. His company, founded in 1965, now makes use of sophisticated equipment and location devices for site investigations and the removal and recovery of decommissioned oil-filled and gas-filled high voltage and other cables, and gas pipelines in chemical works, factories, old estates, farmland and Ministry of Defence properties. In this work Sir David has performed a valuable public service in unearthing many tonnes of live ammunition and bombs which have remained undiscovered having been buried after two world wars. It is therefore conceivable that he has saved developers, treasure hunters and members of the public not only a great deal of money but many lives from injury and death.

He succeeded his father in 1982. He married firstly Susan daughter of Arthur Middlewood of Kilham in 1976 and they had two children: Alexander (born 1978) and Alice (born 1976). They divorced in 1986. He married secondly Maureen, daughter of Robert Carswell in 1987; they have two children: Christopher Robert (born 20th December 1988 and Mathew Carswell (born 17th July 1990) (92 p.1599).

THE KINLOCHS of Gilmerton - family tree

David Kinloch, Deacon of Bakers, Edinburgh, 1538 - 1556

married c1538 Margaret Cathkin, daughter of William Cathkin, burgess of Edinburgh

sons: (1) Henry
(2) William
(3) David
(4) Francis
(5) Mungo

married: (1) Elizabeth Blacklock
(2) Margaret Adamson

sons: (1) Francis (baker burgess, died 1611)
(2) David (surgeon, burgess 1579-80)
(3) James (of Auldcambus, died 1639)
(4) Andrew (of Gilmerton, died 1647)
(5) Archibald (tailor, burgess 1597, died 1615)
(6) Samuel (died before 1647)
daughters: (1) Isobel
(2) Katherine
(3) Euphane
(4) Margaret (1607-?)
(5) Marion

married: 1594, Elizabeth Myller

sons: (1) David (1595-?)
(2) George (1598-?)
(3) Archibald (1601-26)
(4) **Sir Francis Kinloch, 1st Baronet of Gilmerton** cr.1686 (1604-91)
(5) Archibald (1610-25)
daughter: Margaret (1607-?)

married: 1664, Magdalene McMath of Newbyres

sons: (1) **Sir Francis Kinloch, 2nd Baronet of Gilmerton** (c1650-99)
(2) Andrew (1656-?)
(3) James
daughters: (1) Magdalene (married 1660 Sir James Rocheid of Inverleith)
(2) Elizabeth (1655-1686, married Sir James Fleming of Ratho)
(3) Mary (married James Charteris WS, her son was the infamous Col. Francis Charteris *qv*)

married: 1675, Lady Mary Leslie, 2nd daughter of General David Leslie, 1st Lord Newark

sons: (1) **Sir Francis Kinloch, 3rd Baronet** of Gilmerton (1676-1747)
(2) David (1677- died young)
(3) James (merchant in Carolina, America)
(4) Alexander (merchant in Carolina, America)
(5) Archibald (1686-96)
daughters: (1) Anne (1682-1698)
(2) Jean (1684-1726)

(3) Magdalene (1689-?)
(4) Elizabeth (married Andrew Fletcher of Salton, Lord Milton *qv*)

married: 1699 Mary Rocheid, his cousin, 3rd daughter of Sir James Rochied

sons: (1) **Sir James Kinloch, 4th Baronet of Gilmerton** (1700-1778) (relinquised title)
(2) Francis (1702 -1746)
(3) **Sir David Kinloch, 5th Baronet of Gilmerton** (1710-1795)
(4) Alexander (1712-1755, assumed name and arms of Rocheid)

daughters: (1) Mary
(2) Magdalene (1704—?)
(3) Janet (1706-1794)
(4) Elizabeth (1710)

married: (i) 1730, Margaret Foulis of Woodhall
illicit relationship with Marguerite Wild of Bern, Switzerland

sons: (1) James (2) Alexander (3) David
daughters (1) Marianne (2) Louisa (3) Katherine (4) Anne (5) Susanne
[children were not naturalised British subjects therefore incapable of succession; 4th baronet renounced lands and title to his brother David]

married: 1746 Harriet, daughter of Sir Archibald Cockburn

sons: (1) **Sir Francis Kinloch, 6th Baronet of Gilmerton** (1747-95, murdered by his brother)
(2) **Sir Archibald Gordon Kinloch, 7th Baronet of Gilmerton** (1749-1800), died unmarried.
(3) David (1751-90)
(4) John (died in India)
(5) **Sir Alexander Kinloch, 8th Baronet of Gilmerton** (c1750-1813

daughters: (1) Mary
(2) Janet (1755-1848)
(3) Harriet

married: 1801, Isabella Stowe, co-heiress of John Stowe of Newton

son: **Sir Alexander Kinloch, 9th Baronet of Gilmerton** (1805-79)
daughters: (1) Maria-Anne (1803-1820)
(2) Harriet (1804-?)
(3) Isabella (1809-?)

married: 1829, Eleanor-Hyndford, daughter of Sir Thomas Gibson-Carmichael

son: **Sir Alexander Kinloch, 10th Baronet of Gilmerton** (1830-1912)
daughters: (1) Isabella-Anne (1831-?)
(2) Eleanor-Janet (1832-1900)
(3) Harriet (1833-1925)
(4) Eliza-Napier (1835-)
(5) Anne-Minster (1839-40)
(6) Mary (1839-40)

married: 1852, Lucy-Charlotte, daughter of Sir Ralph A Anstruther

sons: (1) **Sir David Alexander Kinloch, 11th Baronet ofGilmerton**
(1856-1944)
(2) Henry Anstruther (1859-1903)
(3) Francis (1863-
(4) Alexander Carmichael (1866-70)
daughters: (1) Eleanor-Anne (1853-1925)
(2) Mary Anna (?-1898)

married: 1897, Eleanor Lucy, daughter of W Bromley Davenport

son: **Sir Alexander Davenport, 12th Baronet of Gilmerton** (1902-82)
daughters: (1) Jean Mary (1898-?)
(2) Katherine Hariot (1906-?)

married: (i) 1929, Alexandra, daughter of Frederick Y. Dalziel, New York (dis.1944)
daughters (1) Emi-Lou (1930-)
Jean Kinloch (1934-)

(ii) 1946, Anna, daughter of Thomas Walker of Edinburgh

sons: (1) Ian (1942-)
(2) Francis (1944-)
(3) **Sir David Kinloch, 13th Baronet of Gilmerton** (1951-)
daughters: (1) Victoria (1947-)
(2) Harriet (1949)
(3) Anne (1951)
and by Anne Maud White: son Jamie (1973-)

married: (i) 1976, Susan daughter of Arthur Middlewood of Kilham (div.1986)
(ii) 1987, Maureen, daughter of Robert Carswell in 1987

son: Alexander (1978-)
daughter: Alice (1976-)

sons: (1) Christopher Robert (1988-)
(2) Mathew Carswell (1990-)

Source: Unpublished family records: Genealogical Account of the Family of Kinloch of that Ilk in Fife and its Various Branches

JOHN KNOX

The illustrious leader of the Reformation 'who never feared the face of man'

The birthplace of this illustrious son of East Lothian is claimed by Haddington as well as Morham. However it is generally accepted that his early education took place at the Grammar School of Haddington where he is commemorated by the school named after him - Knox Academy, as well as Knox Court (originally built as a school in 1877), where his statue, by D.W.Stevenson, stands in an elevated niche on the central tower of this Gothic building by John Starforth in Knox Place.

Whether or not John Knox was born in Haddington, no less a literary giant than Thomas Carlyle (1795-1881) was sufficiently convinced of his birthplace to request that an oak tree be planted on the site of the house in Giffordgate where he was thought to have been born c1505 (some sources give c1513 as his birth year but this would make him eight years old when he attended Glasgow University in 1521).

John Knox attended the the Grammar School of Haddington to be educated as a friar in the Franciscan Monastrey of Haddington by its warden, Adam Harley (an ancestor of Professor George Harley *qv*). He attended the University of Glasgow from 1521 and he was ordained as a Catholic priest in 1529.

Peter Hume Brown *qv*, the Historiographer Royal for Scotland, explained Knox's choice of Glasgow:

> 'St Andrews was nearer his home, and possessed the more famous university; but he was probably drawn to Glasgow by the fame of the most distinguished Scotsman of his generation - John Major [*qv*]... ... What he learned from Major was the art for which that scholar was renowned throughout Europe - the

art of logical exercitation; and Knox's writings everywhere show that all through life he had a natural delight in the play of dialectic. He left the university without taking the degree of Master of Arts...'.(84 p.11)

During the next fifteen years, although a devout Catholic, he was very much aware of the corruption, cruelty and persecution perpetrated by the Church. He had studied the works of Martin Luther even though an Act of Parliament forbade their importation and he was filled with anxiety and foreboding over the religious persecution which had been practised since 1530. The burning of the first martyr, twenty-three year old Partick Hamilton in 1528, greatly affected Knox, and other such butchery served only to arouse his passion against injustices and for the cause of the Reformation.

By 1544 he had had enough of the cruelty and corruption in the Church and he surrendered his Orders. For Knox this was a deeply difficult decision but after George Wishart's inspiring sermon on the Lutherian doctrine in St Mary's Church of Haddington, Knox was convinced. He wanted to accompany Wishart to St Andrews but Wishart told him to return to Haddington. Wishart was accompanied instead by Cardinal Beaton's men who promised him safe conduct. When Knox was told that Wishart had been burned at the stake on 1st March 1546 at St Andrews his commitment to the Reformed Church was absolute. There was no turning back; there was no alternative; he would give his life to this cause. But Knox's life, as a known devotee of Wishart, was now in danger. Cardinal Beaton had ordered his assassination but Beaton himself suffered this fate only two months after Wishart's martyrdom as part of Henry VIII's 'Rough Wooing'. Beaton had refused to consent to the marriage of young Mary Queen of Scots to Henry's son Edward. He had spoiled Henry's ambition for union with Scotland.

Knox, thought to have been involved in Beaton's murder, fled with his pupils and took refuge in the Castle of St Andrews. The Scottish Catholic nobles sought assistance from the French and Knox was taken prisoner when the French fleet laid siege to the castle. With his fellow Reformers he was chained as a galley slave and taken to Rouen then to Nantes. The experience almost killed him. Meanwhile Henry VIII had died (1547) and his son, Edward VI, now twelve years old, interceded on Knox's behalf. Knox was set free in February 1549.

Meanwhile, Henry's 'Rough Wooing' was pursued by Protector Somerset to try to force an agreement. The Scots had been thoroughly defeated at Pinkie Hill near Musselburgh in September 1547 and an English garrison was stationed at Haddington. The French were pleased to be requested to drive the English out of Haddington. This was the

Siege of Haddington of 1548-49 which effectively kept a wedge between England and Scotland and, by prior agreement, young Mary Queen of Scots was sent to France to marry the Dauphin. The French now talked of Scotland as a dependency; the Scots regretted this arrangement and Knox dared not return home. He remained in England as one of King Edward's Chaplains in Ordinary. The ways of the English Court displeased him and no-one escaped his stern reproof. He made enemies, one of whom was the Duke of Northumberland who cunningly arranged that Knox should be offered the Bishopric of Rochester in order to curtail his influence. Knox declined it risking criticism and accusations of disloyalty but he knew that Edward VI favoured him. However, Edward died on 6th July 1553, aged only fifteen years and Knox cleared out of London on the day that Mary I, a staunch Catholic, was proclaimed Queen.

Queen Mary, or 'Bloody Mary' as she became known, exercised repressive and vindictive authority by penalising Protestants as heretics but Knox steadfastly refused to leave the country. He wrote his *First Blast of the Trumpet against the Monstrous Regiment of Women.* It created great controversy in Court circles. The word 'regiment' meant 'government' and not any group of women and Knox was wrongly branded a misogynist. After his marriage to Marjery Bowes he was persuaded to travel abroad in January 1554. He arrived in Geneva where he and John Calvin (1509-64) became friends. Knox's two sons were born there and after two years he returned with his family to Scotland. He had been given the freedom of the city of Geneva where he had become greatly respected.

The Protestant nobles of Scotland had formed the 'Lords of Congregation' and in 1558, with their help, Knox made a new translation of the *Geneva Bible*. Mary I had died in 1558 and Protestant Elizabeth I reigned but when Knox arrived home the Queen Regent, Mary of Guise, James V's widow and mother of Mary Queen of Scots, treated Knox with undisguised hostility and he was proclaimed an outlaw and a rebel. Protestant ministers were put on trial for administering the Sacrament, even the Protestant nobility were threatened. After a riot in Perth and the burning of monasteries Knox was told that he would be shot if he attempted to preach. Ignoring all threats he proceeded to denounce the Papacy in the Cathedral of St Andrews where he gained the strong support of the Provost, the bailies and the inhabitants. They agreed to set up the Reformed worship and to strip the church of all its Catholic images.

Knox's influence spread rapidly. He was called to a meeting of nobles, barons and borough representatives in Edinburgh. It was agreed to suspend the authority of the Queen Regent until a meeting of a free Parliament took place. She sought reinforcements from the French and the fortifications of Leith were attacked. The Reformers, under the Earl of Arran, repelled the French from Fife and, for the first time in the history of Scotland, English troops were asked for their support against the French. In March 1560 they blockaded Leith and starved the French to surrender. However, Mary of Guise died suddenly and in July the Treaty of Edinburgh was signed between Queen Elizabeth and the French. It agreed to their withdrawal and a free Parliament in Scotland.

In December 1560 young Mary's French husband, the Dauphin, died and she, avoiding Queen Elizabeth's intercepting ships, landed at Leith on 19th August 1561. She was eighteen years old, tall, comely and beautiful. She had many offers of marriage but asked only to be left in peace to practice her religion. She promised not to interfere with the new Scottish Protestantism. One of Knox's early rows with her was over the land revenues of the Catholic Clergy, one third of which was shared between the Crown and the kirk. Knox, dissatisfied, claimed all of it, saying,

"Two parts freely given to the devil and the third divided between God and the devil." (84 p.90)

Protestantism was now formally established in Scotland and Knox, with four ministers, was commissioned by the Privy Council to plan ecclesiastical government. The result was *The First Book of Discipline* which demanded that a school for every parish be erected and that all monies should support the universities and the churches. This, however did not please the nobility; they had long enjoyed the rich revenues of the Catholic Clergy. Neither the First nor the *Second Book of Discipline*, compiled twenty years later, received legislative sanction.

The first meeting of the General Assembly of the Church of Scotland took place on 20th December 1560 in Edinburgh with forty members of which six were ministers. Knox was minister of the only Reformed Church in Edinburgh and he took Mary under his special charge. Her sympathy lay with the Catholic Princes of Europe who advocated universal extermination of Protestants. Knox badgered, argued, corrected and criticised her behaviour and public policy; she was often reduced to tears.

The Scottish Parliament met in May 1563, the first meeting since Mary's return. Mary cleverly blocked ratification of the Treaty of Edinburgh. Knox was so angry he severed his old friendship with the Earl of Moray and in his next sermon he preached against the deep ingratitude among the Lords for their deliverance from the bondage of Catholicism. The Queen was furious, and more so when Knox predicted serious consequences if she married a Papist. She had him brought to trial on the pretext of a letter he had written supporting two Protestants accused of rioting. He was begged to plead for the Queen's mercy. Knox would hear none of it. After long arguments the Lords voted that they could find no fault. The Queen and her 'flatterers' were enraged and commanded a second vote. The nobility, highly offended, absolved Knox of any offence.

In 1564 Knox, having lost his wife three years before, married Margaret Stewart, the sixteen year old daughter of Lord Ochiltree. Knox was now accused of ambitions to the throne, the Ochiltrees being of Royal blood.

Mary married her cousin, the odious and overbearing Henry, Lord Darnley, in June 1565. She proclaimed him king without even consulting the Estates of the Realm. Darnley set out to attack Knox. He found fault in one of Knox's sermons and demanded his arrest for an imaginary insult. Knox was ordered to stop preaching but he replied simply that commands to speak or abstain could be made only by the Church. The Queen and Darnley renewed their efforts to encourage Catholicism and Catholic ecclesiatics were restored to Parliament but they fled after the murder of the Queen's secretary, Rizzio, by the jealous Darnley. Knox had retired to Ayrshire to write his *History of the Reformation in Scotland*.

The year 1567 was a momentous one. Knox was out of the country having been given permission to visit his two sons in England. Darnley was murdered in his absence. The Queen was suspected of complicity with the Earl of Bothwell who was put on trial. He was found guiltless in a farcical trial at which he was not even present. After a pretended abduction he took the Queen firstly to his stronghold of Hailes Castle in the Parish of Prestonkirk and then to Dunbar Castle where they married on 15th May. The scandal was too much. Several lords joined against Bothwell who fled to the Orkneys after his defeat at Carberry Hill in June. Mary was jeered on her return to Edinburgh. She was imprisoned in Lochleven Castle and compelled to sign a deed of abdication.

Knox, having returned to Edinburgh, preached a sermon at the coronation of the one year old James VI in which he advocated that Mary should answer to the crimes of adultery and murder. The Earl of Moray became Regent and immediately summoned Parliament to ratify all the Acts of 1560. He worked assiduously for peace but he had his enemies - the family feud with the Argyles and the jealousy of the Hamiltons. He had to crush two revolts and his victory at Langside compelled Mary, who had escaped from Lochleven, to flee to England. However Moray was assassinated by the treacherous Hamilton of Bothwellhaugh. There was national mourning. Hamilton fled to perpetual banishment and Knox, overwhelmed with grief, preached the funeral sermon. Afterwards he had a stroke which affected his speech and he wrote that he would 'soon take his goodnight of the world'. But there was to be no rest for him. Leith was under attack from the Queen's forces, Protestants were harassed and assaulted and Knox was accused of complicity in the murder of Darnley. He defended himself easily and discredited his accusers, Robert and Archibald Hamilton, in the process. Ironically, the latter was hanged for his part in the murder.

Knox was weakening but he could still electrify his congregations. On 6th August 1572 he wrote a touching farewell to the General Assembly. By November he was dying. He asked to hear evening prayers after which Dr Preston asked him if he had heard the prayers. Knox replied,

"Would to God that you and all men had heard them as I have heard them; I praise God for that heavenly sound" (84 p.157). He lifted up his hand and died peacefully. The day was 24th November 1572, he was sixty-seven. He was interred in the Churchyard of St Giles in Edinburgh; his burial place is at car park No. 44. The newly-elected Regent Morton summed up his character,

"Here lies one who never feared the face of man."

SIR PETER LAURIE of Sandersdean

Lord Mayor of London

The Laurie family came from Kelso and arrived at Sandersdean on the Coulston estate on 28th May 1777. John Laurie, Peter's father was one of the Lauries of Maxwellton immortalised by Lady John Scott's *Annie Laurie*. Peter, born on 3rd March 1778, was the twelfth child and his upbringing was very religious. His father was an elder of the Burgher Church of Haddington under the inspiring and hardworking minister, the Reverend John Brown *qv* who baptised Peter. As far as his father was concerned, Peter too would be trained for the ministry.

His mother died when he was six years old and from then life became hard for the boy. His father had married again, a cousin of the minister of Morham, Isabella Carfrae, and the nine year-old Peter did not get on at all well with his step-mother. After completing his Primary education at Morham he was sent to the Grammar School at Haddington. However the idea of training for the ministry did not appeal to him and he took himself off in the middle of winter to Jedburgh where his elder brother was a saddler. The journey was horrendous. On his pony, in a thick snow storm, the boy lost his way on Soutra and but for a fortuitous meeting with a stranger he would certainly have lost his life.

He enjoyed the work as an apprentice saddler but he fell out with his cousin and again rode off to complete his apprenticeship with an Edinburgh saddler. However he found diversions in the theatre which, at that time, 1790, was strongly disapproved of by the city fathers and the Church, in the belief that play-acting would inflame the minds of the ordinary people. Young Peter Laurie was besotted with drama to such an extent that he learned the whole of 'Douglas', a play written and performed at the Canongate Theatre some thirty years before. Its author, John Home *qv*, the minister at Athelstaneford, was called to account before the Presbytery of Haddington and had to resign his ministry. Peter Laurie became an actor in the Theatre Royal in Shakespeare Square (which stood on the site of Register House in Edinburgh) but he was soon to learn that an actor's life was a precarious one and had even less pecuniary advantage.

In 1801 he left Scotland and obtained employment in London with David Pollock, the saddler to King George III; his workmanship was therefore of the highest standards and soon he became the foreman. After two years he met his future wife, Margaret Jack, at the Scotch Church in Swallow Street at Piccadilly Circus. Her father was a minister of the Church of Scotland and they married in 1803.

He decided to set up in business for himself in Oxford Street. His timing was excellent in that saddles and other military apparel were urgently required for the Indian Army. He gained a large and lucrative contract and through hard work and honest dealing his business flourished. He became very rich, as did most army contractors at that time - France had declared war on Britain ten years before and the Napoleonic War was still raging. Fortunes were to be made and Peter Laurie became well-known in high social circles. By 1812 he had made a fortune and became very popular having been admitted to the livery of the Saddlers' Company. In 1823 he was elected to the Shrievalty (sheriffdom) of the City of London and in 1824 he was knighted by George IV for his services to the City. Now *Sir* Peter, he was elected an Alderman in 1826. It was about this time that he decided to devote all of his considerable energy to public life and social reform; to do so he retired from business at the age of forty-nine.

As is not uncommon with expatriate Scots they take pleasure in meeting together in their adopted country. He renewed his friendship with Edward Irving (1792-1834) who was the master of the 'Mathematical School' in Haddington and who taught Jane Welsh. Laurie invited Irving and Jane and her illustrious husband Thomas Carlyle to Christmas dinner. The latter, in one of his acerbic moods, was to describe the event as 'very sumptuous, very cockneyish - strange and inadmirable to me.'

The climax of Laurie's career was his election as Lord Mayor of London on 9th November 1832. This was a year of great rejoicing: at last, the 'Great Reform Bill' was passed and Laurie's election seemed exactly right; he had promoted social reform and was now identified with prison reform. Such was his popularity that the illustrious novelist Charles Dickens characterised him as 'Mr Cute' in his Christmas story 'The Chimes'.

This popular and devoted servant of the City of London, having served as an Alderman for thirty-five years, died in his eighty-third year on 3rd December 1861 and was buried at Highgate Cemetery. His portrait, by Thomas Philips RA, in the regalia of the Lord Mayor of London hangs in the County Buildings in Haddington.

KING LOTH of Lothian

the grandfather of St Mungo

Whether or not the kingdom of Loth stretched beyond the Lothians during the 6th century is unknown but the origin of the name Lothian is said to be from Loth, the legendary king whose hill-top settlement sat in about 30 acres on the top of Traprain Law where the Votadini, were supposed to have ruled and traded with the Romans in AD 79.

No doubt King Loth considered that the extent of his kingdom was as far as he could see from the highest point of his domain. Traprain Law was a well-protected little kingdom with which the Romans were not averse to trade.

Christianity was a relatively new phenomenon in Scotland, then called Dalriada, but the eastern area, Bernicia, was that over which King Loth ruled. He was half pagan and although St Columba had arrived at Iona in 563, King Loth was still not quite sure that this new God was more powerful than his old pagan Gods. His doubts grew considerably after his Christian daughter, Princess Thanea (or Thenew), seemed to have been miraculously saved from the punishment of the death sentence he had pronounced against her for her disobedience and the disgrace she had brought to his Royal household.

The legend continues with King Loth and his Queen having chosen a husband for their daughter: the young man, a Prince from Galloway called Owen Ap. He was a pagan and an arrogant, conscienceless, overbearing bully. She disliked him from the moment he was introduced as her prospective husband. She could not bring herself to marry him and it was with a mixture of fear and sorrow that she refused her parents' request even to their betrothal.

To disobey one's parents, especially the King and Queen, was an unthinkable act and such was the duty of a king, King Loth, in a mixture of anger and tears, had no option but to banish her from his home. She was said to have become a shepherdess in the Lammermuir Hills and, while her father and mother worried about her welfare, she astonished herself when she found that this new life of tranquillity suited her well. St Cuthbert would shepherd his sheep in these same hills many years later and the princess felt the same peace and the Spirit of God.

Meanwhile, one can imagine that King Loth tried to pacify the rejected prince with lavish entertainment and feasting but his childish anger and aggravation seemed to grow in proportion to the king's attempts to mollify him. As far as he was concerned the princess should have been forced to marry him; his overbearing pride was hurt and he doubtless considered her punishment insultingly lenient. When he heard that the princess was actually enjoying the summer months in the lovely Lammermuirs he felt that her enjoyment was meant to taunt him. He grew even more paranoid and promised himself that he would hunt her down and punish her.

He was a cunning young man. He pretended to accept the king's apologies and made his preparations to return to his father in Galloway. The thought of meeting his father without a bride was shameful to him. She would pay for this. King Loth and the spurned prince parted amicably enough but had the king been able to read the young prince's thoughts he would certainly have held him prisoner.

Prince Owen Ap rode off into the Lammermuirs and as soon as he was out of earshot of the king, he ordered his servants to scour the hills until Princess Thanea was found. Within a matter of hours a servant reported her whereabouts. Quickly, he rode off to confront her. The princess's instinctive reaction was one of horror but she recovered her composure quickly and greeted him with cold politeness. His servants formed a ring around her to prevent her escape and he grinned while dismounting from his horse; he walked slowly towards her. Like lightening, he struck her down and crashed on top of her. Shocked and winded she struggled but he tore at her clothing and amid the laughter of his servants he raped and beat her with a terrible vengeance - the vengeance of his warped mind.

They probably rode off laughing and she lay on the hillside, broken and sobbing. She was alone, her parents had banished her, she could not return to them. She prayed for spiritual help and received comfort and peace. The days and nights passed until she met an old shepherd who gave her comfort and sympathy. He gave her shelter and food and when it became obvious that she was pregnant the king and queen, learning of her condition, fumed with anger.

"Go after them, hunt them down, kill them - and stone her to death." the king commanded his servants, weeping sorrowfully.

Prince Owen Ap was never found and Princess Thanea was brought before him in shame, and he, in a state of the most terrible anguish, pronounced the death sentence over her. She was to be tied to a stake and stoned until she was dead. What he had not reckoned with was the love of his people for his gentle daughter. No one would lift a stone.

Now, he was in a state of complete quandary. He knew only too well that any woman who conceived without his consent had to be put to death. He could not make an exception of his daughter. The firm hold which he held over his kingdom would be loosened irrevocably. He would be no longer fit to rule. For several days he paced his palace and argued with himself and with the queen. He had to decide. On the third day he appeared and pronounced that she was to be taken to the cliff's edge by two of his most trusted bodyguards and thrust into space and to her death. On the appointed day she was ceremoniously taken by unwilling hands and pushed from the edge of the cliff. The people wailed in misery but as she fell her voluminous dress became entangled by the protruding branch of a tree and to the astonishment of the onlookers her calls for help were heard. This was surely the work of the Lord, people knelt and prayed in thankfulness to God. She was carefully lifted to safety amid the cheers and tears of gratitude. A miracle had been witnessed.

The legend continues that King Loth was now visibly afraid. Was this the work of the Christian God? Again, he agonised over what should be done. Ultimately, he decided that she should be bound to a coracle made of animal hide and set out to sea. The pagan god Lamannan, god of the seas, would surely decide her fate. Sorrowfully, the people of Traprain watched her float away on the tide. They were never to see her again and they wept. But this is not the end of this story. She was washed up on the opposite coast and the monks of the monastery at Clackmannan under St Serf* took her in and cared for her. Her son was born there in 518 and was named Kentigern (meaning 'chief lord'). [A recent archaeological excavation which unearthed a medieval shrine on Traprain Law is now thought to be the birthplace of Kentigern.]

He was brought up in monastic tradition and soon proved to be not only a bright scholar but was well loved by everyone. As a young man he was sent to the west of Scotland where he founded a monastery called Cathures - the ancient name of Glasgow. His popularity grew and he was made Bishop of Glasgow. In 543 he was consecrated Bishop of Cumbria and as so often happens, popularity leads to jealousy, Kentigern suffered gossip and persecution. He fled to Wales in 553 where he met St David and founded another monastery and a bishopric. In Scotland Rederech Hael had become a king and he recalled Kentigern in 573. He met St Columba about 584 and conversed with him at the Molendinar Burn where they exchanged pastoral staffs. Such were his good works this grandson of King Loth was sanctified St Mungo, the patron saint of Glasgow where he died in 603 and was buried in Glasgow Cathedral. King Loth is said to have been buried at Standing Stone near Morham which takes its name from the standing stone supposed to commemorate this burial place.

* *St Serf founded the church as Culross in 697-706 - an anachronism*

WILLIAM DARLING MCKAY RSA

Scotland's pioneer of Pastoral Art in East Lothian

The idea of painting outdoors was still fairly new when William Darling McKay painted his *An October Morning* in 1878. To leave the studio and to work out-of-doors was deemed to be artistically unnecessary. Only a few decades before 'plein-airisme' (open-airism) had become an innovation by artists Corot, Courbet, Boudin, Jongkind and the Barbizon School with Millet, Rousseau and Diaz de la Pena had retired to the small village of Barbizon in the Forest of Fontainbleu during the 1830s to escape the artificiality of Paris. McKay did exactly this in East Lothian. He escaped from the bustle and the politics of the city to concentrate on painting farmworkers and country folk in the peaceful simplicity of the countryside.

William Darling McKay was born in 1844 in the village of Gifford where his father, Peter McKay, was the Parish schoolmaster. At the age of sixteen he was accepted as a student by the School of Art in Edinburgh and afterwards he attended the Royal Scottish Academy Life School where his early painting was greatly influenced by Hugh Cameron RSA, RSW (1835-1918), William McTaggart RSA, RSW (1835-1910) and George Paul Chalmers RSA (1836-1878).

During his journeying through Holland he was influenced by the work of Anton Mauve (1838-1888) and the Maris brothers and on his return to East Lothian he decided to paint out-of-doors; in fact he became one of the first in Scotland to depict the country life of his birthplace. In 1877 he was made an Associate of the Royal Scottish Academy and his highly praised An October Morning painted in 1878 was exhibited at the Royal Scottish Academy that year; thirty years later it received added admiration and recognition when it was exhibited at the Scottish National Exhibition of 1908, the British Exhibition in Japan of 1908, the Royal Scottish Academy in 1919 and the Exhibition of Scottish Art in 1939.

His other pastoral works included his *Sheepshearing* and *Turnip Shawing* in 1882 and his *Village Gossips* were exhibited the following year at the Royal Scottish Academy. In 1883 he was elected to full Academician of the Academy (RSA)

In 1896 his extensive knowledge was recognised in his appointment as Librarian of the Royal Scottish Academy and it was during this period that he strongly supported James Guthrie as President of the Academy in 1902. McKay with Guthrie were followers of the Glasgow School; Guthrie was knighted in 1903 and held the Presidency for the next 17 years. In 1907 McKay was appointed the Academy's Secretary, a post he held until his death in 1924. But it was his literary work which gained him deserved recognition from the University of Edinburgh with an honorary LL.D in 1919. He published his learned and exhaustive study: *The Scottish School of Painting* in 1906 in which he described such as 'The Forerunners 1600-1750', 18th century painters - Raeburn and Wilkie through to the 'Young Men of the Forties' covering no fewer than 142 painters. In 1916 he published *The Royal Scottish Academy 1826-1916*.

He died in 1924 aged 80 years. Three portraits of William Darling McKay, one of which is a self-portrait, are to be found in the Scottish National Portrait Gallery in Edinburgh.

PROFESSOR JOHN PITCAIRN MACKINTOSH

East Lothian's intellectual Member of Parliament

On the wall of the old manse at Gifford there are two commemorative plaques side-by-side: one commemorating the Rev. John Witherspoon (1723-1792) *qv*, the only Scot to sign the American Declaration of Independence who was also Principal of Princeton College USA, and the other commemorating Professor John Mackintosh MP, an inspiring teacher and original-thinking politician whose ideas and aims in politics were not entirely shared by the Prime Minister of the day, Harold Wilson; in fact the two clashed on numerous occasions.

In the normal course of events Mackintosh would at least have achieved ministerial office but Wilson vetoed it. Mackintosh's loss of high office was, in one sense, a gain for his constituents of Berwick and East Lothian who had the pleasure of more of his attention than they might otherwise have enjoyed. In another sense his coruscating intellect was denied to the Cabinet in no.10 Downing Street, in the Commons as a Minister of the crown and therefore in policy-making for his country.

John Mackintosh was born on 24th August 1929 in the beautiful mountain resort of Simla in northern India where his father was a salesman of cotton goods, whisky and finally insurance. His mother, Mary Pitcairn, was a lecturer at the Simla College of Education. He inherited his father's fast-talking, quick-thinking articulacy and his mother's intelligent love of academia - a formidable combination in politics.

At the outbreak of war in Europe and after eleven years in India the family returned to Scotland. Young John Mackintosh attended Melville College and then the University of Edinburgh where he gained a first class honours degree in history. He followed this with a BA degree at Balliol College, Oxford, but this was an unhappy experience for the young Scot. He was not a little annoyed that his first class honours degree of Edinburgh merely gave him entry to an undergraduate course at Oxford. His annoyance was compounded when his degree at Oxford was second class. This led to a lifetime of scepticism and disparagement of the English system and its 'Oxbridge' products. His razor-sharp wit led him irresistibly to counter, with stinging effect, the somewhat haughty arrogance he seemed to invite from those 'Oxbridgers' in high places. Any who dared to patronise or to talk down to John MacIntosh received their 'come-uppance' with compound interest.

In 1952 he was awarded a John Dill Memorial Fellowship which took him to Princeton USA for post-graduate work. This was the university of which Gifford born John Witherspoon became Principal 186 years before. It seems an incredible coincidence that the commemorative plaques of these two great academics of Princeton sit next to each other on the manse wall at Gifford.

Initially, he followed a purely academic career becoming a lecturer of history at the University of Glasgow in 1953 and at the University of Edinburgh from 1954 until 1961. His lectures were brilliant with the added attraction of subtle humour. It was during this period, probably the happiest of his life, that he married one of his students, Janette Robertson.

In the general election of 1959 he stood as the Labour candidate for the Pentlands division of Edinburgh but was defeated in this Tory stronghold. It was clear to the Labour Party in Scotland that this young, articulate academic would become a great asset and George Middleton, the Secretary of the Scottish Trades Union Congress, backed him for the vacancy at Paisley. However, Mackintosh felt that his time was not yet ripe; he had, in any case, been offered a senior lectureship in government at the University of Ibadan in Nigeria. During this period he wrote his *The British Cabinet* which was published in 1962. This received approbation from its reviewer Richard Crossman, a leading Labour politician, who went so far as to suggest that it was comparable to Walter Bagehot's *English Constitution* (1876). This was praise indeed because the latter had been used for the instruction of future monarchs. In addition he wrote his *Nigerian Politics and Government* (1966) whilst in Nigeria.

John Mackintosh returned to Britain in 1963 to take up a senior lectureship in Politics at Glasgow and his reputation as an inspiring lecturer with the excellence of his publications led to his appointment, in 1965, as Professor of Politics at Strathclyde University. His marriage to Janette Robertson had come under severe strain due to his absence in Nigeria and his need to concentrate on his writing - each at the expense of his wife and two children. Their marriage was dissolved in 1963 and shortly afterwards he married a lecturer in social medicine, Catherine Maclean.

He was now working hard on his next publication: *The Devolution of Power: Local Democracy, Regionalism and Nationalism* during the writing of which he was elected MP for Berwick and East Lothian, winning the seat from the Conservatives. His book was published in 1968, it was undoubtedly the authoritative source for serious consideration towards devolution. He had resigned his professorship in order to give his full attention to his constituents and Parliamentary duties. In the trend towards Scottish and Welsh nationalism he should have been the natural choice for a post in Cabinet, but his scathing criticism of the Scotland Bill negated his chances. Prime Minister Harold Wilson, although radical and reforming in his early government, disagreed with Mackintosh, who, true to his beliefs, might be said to have sacrificed high office.

However, he was too good a man to be ignored. He was appointed to the select committee for the oversight of government and the committees on agriculture and Scottish affairs. Tam Dalyell MP recalls, in his biographical outline of Mackintosh *(Dictionary of National Biography 1971-1980)*, the 'verbal clash of arms' between Mackintosh and the leader of the House, Richard Crossman over the proposal to disband the agriculture committee. It was a battle of brilliant minds: articulate, sharp, witty and erudite but Crossman won the day; one suspects because of his seniority. Mackintosh had no equal in debate and discussion on parliamentary reform; he loved a good argument and the stiffer the opposition the more he relished the debate.

It was sad for the Labour Party that he was not given a post in the shadow government of 1970 for he would have been brilliant in opposition. At the general election of February 1974 Mackintosh lost his seat but he regained it in October. He published his *British Government and Politics* in 1970 and he accepted a part-time professorship of politics at Edinburgh in 1977 but by then his health was failing. Cancer had been diagnosed and for many months he worked as hard as ever taking his students to heights of inspired thought - a reincarnation perhaps of the great Dugald Stewart (1753-1828) also adored by his students. He discussed his illness with no-one; he sought no pity or privilege; he worked even harder until the day of his death on 30th July 1978, aged forty-eight, at the Western General Hospital in Edinburgh.

His wife Dr Catherine McLean Mackintosh donated 40 boxes of his papers - memoranda, letters, notes for speeches etc, to the National Library of Scotland for the future use of researchers.

Such was the high esteem in which he was held, his colleagues in East Lothian District erected the memorial on the wall of the old manse at Gifford. It is inscribed:

1929 - 1978
To the Memory of
JOHN PITCAIRN MACKINTOSH
buried at Yester Churchyard
Academic, Politician, Humanitarian
Three times returned as
Member of Parliament for
Berwick and East Lothian
1966-1978
erected by his colleagues and friends
in East Lothian District

LENNOX MILNE McLAREN OBE, MA, LRAM, ELOC

Organiser of the Lamp of Lothian Collegiate Trust

Lennox Milne Court, off the Poldrate on the way to the Waterloo Bridge in Haddington, was named after Lennox Milne McLaren in 1980 to commemorate her contribution to the culture and well-being of the Royal Burgh of Haddington and especially her unstinting work as the Organiser of the *Lamp of Lothian Collegiate Trust* in Haddington in which capacity she was the energy behind the opening of the newly-restored Haddington House in 1969. The naming of this lovely little court was the proposal of the Dowager Duchess of Hamilton, a friend and admirer of Lennox Milne. Also, at the instigation of the Dowager Duchess, a plaque in the beautiful garden of Haddington House was erected in her memory shortly after her death in 1980.

Courtesy of Lord Douglas-Hamilton

Lennox Milne was born on 9th May 1909. She was educated at the University of Edinburgh where she graduated with a Master of Arts degree in 1932. She studied music to qualify as a Licentiate of the Royal Academy of Music (LRAM) and she trained for the stage with Ann Turner-Robertson at the Royal Academy of Dramatic Art in London.

She became a school teacher and this experience gave her a clear insight into the needs and learning processes of children. It seemed a natural progression for her when she was appointed the producer of the BBC Schools Department in Scotland during the 1939-45 war.

Shortly after the war she met the talented author Moray McLaren who became the BBC's first Programme Director for Scotland. They met through the theatre - he had agreed to stand in for John Laurie for one night in his own play at Perth Repertory Theatre. The experience, although not entirely novel, was nightmarish for him. It was on this stage and in that play that he met his future wife, Lennox Milne. Their marriage in 1946 was the start of a wonderful twenty-six year partnership of theatre and authorship.

During her acting career between 1946 and 1949 she played many leading roles as a member of the Citizens' Theatre Company in Glasgow. In 1948 her portrayal of *Veritie* in Tyrone Guthrie's production of *The Thrie Estaites* was so successful it was repeated many times.

With actor, director and commentator Tom Fleming she was a co-director of the Edinburgh Gateway Company having co-founded the Company in 1953. This happy association was to last for twelve years during the last five of which she was Director of Productions. Fleming and she played several major roles together in such as: *The Flouers O' Edinburgh, A Singular Grace* and many others. On one memorable occasion her husband, while taking his stage call as author of *One Traveller Returns*, kissed his wife's hand in congratulation and respect for her impeccable performance as Sister Chisholm.

Another husband/wife success occurred in 1955 when she played the lead in her husband's award-winning play *Heather on Fire*. He had written it for her and he won the *Charles Henry Foyle New Play Award* - a £100 prize. Her vast contribution to her profession was given royal recognition in 1956 when she was honoured with the award of the OBE - Officer of the Order of the British Empire. In 1959 her solo performance at Stratford, Ontario in Kemp's *The Heart is Highland* was again received with acclaim.

Between her engagements she loved to travel with her wanderlust husband; in an article *Actress Wife Spotlights her Husband* written for the *Edinburgh Evening Dispatch* of 6th March 1954 she wrote:

> I have 'sat in boats paralysed with cold, cowered in motor cars starved and miserable, slept on river banks, waded in icy Shetland estuaries, and still the man will fish, hour after hour, without food, soaked to the skin....I find myself on a small Icelandic cargo-boat making for the Arctic Ocean or standing in the Palais des Papes in Avignon or sitting in the Tivoli Gardens at Copenhagen, while the Scottish man of letters tears round the scenic railway yelling like a schoolboy.'

In 1967 she received an invitation from Broadway in New York. This was further recognition of her now international stature as an actress of the highest merit. Her portrayal of the Headmistress, Miss Marcia Blaine, in the stage version of *The Prime of Miss Jean Brodie* earned her another award for her performance; it was a sell-out. Her magical portrayal of eccentric comedy characters had again endeared her to her public.

Much to the great benefit of Haddington she settled with her husband at Pegh-de-Loan in Station Avenue. She was soon to become a well-known and popular figure in the Royal Burgh. At the formation of the *Lamp of Lothian Collegiate Trust* in 1967 in Haddington the Duchess of Hamilton, the prime mover of the Trust, was looking for someone who could give inspired leadership to its development and administration; the wise choice was Lennox Milne who had by now retired from the stage. She became 'Lamp Organiser' and was responsible for the opening of the newly-restored Haddington House.

Two years later, on the bicentenary of the birth of Sir Walter Scott, she wrote and produced the *Young Scott*, which was performed in the Corn Exchange of Haddington with school children from all over East Lothian. It was acclaimed in the national press as, 'the most animated of all the Scottish Bicentenary programmes.' At the first meeting of the Haddington Literary Society at the Bridge Centre the first speaker was Lennox Milne. In the words of artist and author Doris Ann Goodchild *qv* who witnessed her speech, 'her face and eyes were so alight, she was a flame of interest.'

She threw herself into work for the Edinburgh International Festival of 1971. She with Tom Fleming and Richard Todd performed *A Singular Grace* - another bicentenary tribute to Sir Walter Scott. At the Gateway Theatre, in the learned Robert Kemp's *The Other Dear Charmer* she played Miss Nimmo (it was of course at Miss Nimmo's house at a tea party she introduced Robert Burns (Tom Fleming) to Mrs McLehose - Clarinda (Iris Russell).) Such was Lennox Milne's superb acting ability she appeared in eight of the first ten Festivals (41).

In 1971 she retired as Organiser but continued to serve the 'Lamp' as arts adviser and committee member. She was appointed to the Lamp's Board of Trustees in 1980 but by now she had become ill, suffering from cancer and within a few months she died.

On 20th June 1980 Lennox Milne McLaren OBE, MA, LRAM, ELOC died. Hers was a full and excitingly active life. She bore the dreaded cancer with bravery. 'It ought never to have happened so soon; she was too great a loss.' said Pamela Roberts, her colleague and successor. One sentence contained in her obituary and composed by the Dowager Duchess of Hamilton sums up the sense of loss felt by all who knew her, "In whatever success we may have achieved or to which we may aspire, her influence remains a potent factor."

Dr William Farquhar McLean MC, MB, CHB, MD

of the Hollies and Hilton Lodge, Haddington

A new doctor arrived in Haddington shortly after the 1914-18 War. There was some speculation about this new medic - he was a high ranking, highly decorated war hero almost straight from the front line in France. He had been awarded the Military Cross and had held the rank of Lieutenant-Colonel in the Royal Army Medical Corps.

Would he be snobbish? Would his tough war experience make him intolerant of the illnesses of elderly Haddingtonians? There need have been no fear this was a son of the manse. Dr William Farquhar McLean was from the north of Scotland. He had no snobbish accent but had that straightforward openness which is characteristic of the Highlander. The people of Haddington took to him immediately.

Courtesy of Mrs Mary Barlee

He was born in the manse of Boddam, near Peterhead on 25th May 1888. His father was the Reverend William George Green McLean (1858-1938) and his mother, Mary Gordon Farquhar, was a teacher. The family consisted of seven children of whom William was the second child and eldest son. His childhood under his strict but kindly parents was spent amongst the fishing and farming folk of the north and, as the eldest son, he had to wear an Eton collar to Church Service every Sunday under the observant eye of his father - much to the amusement of the younger members of the family. In addition to the Church service, attendance at Bible Class and teaching in Sunday School were part of the routine of their strictly observed Sabbath day.

William was exceedingly bright at Fordyce Academy where he gained the Redhyte bursary giving him a place at Aberdeen University but he chose an Arts course at Edinburgh University. However, after one year he transferred to the Medical Faculty and undoubtedly found his forte - he won six medals and achieved the hitherto unknown distinction of taking both the Junior and Senior Surgery medals in 1912. He just missed the highest award in medicine, the 'Ettles Scholarship' being *proxime accessit* (next to the prizewinner).

He was appointed house surgeon to Professor Caird. At that time house surgeons were unpaid and in order to save for further training he took a job as a ship's medical officer for a year, travelling all over the world. He returned home in 1914 causing quite a stir in quiet Cullen when he appeared with a green Amazon parrot on his shoulder. He had intended to continue his studies but war was imminent and any thoughts of becoming a surgeon were now brought to an abrupt end.

In August 1914 he was commissioned a lieutenant in the Royal Army Medical Corps Special Reserve and went to France with the Original Expeditionary Force. After the retreat at Mons in 1915 he was second in command aboard the hospital ship *Asturias*, a cross-channel ship. During one of these harrowing trips, the ship being packed with wounded and dying men, he found his brother, Douglas, on deck among the flea infested wounded. In later years Douglas McLean recalled the enormous relief he felt in being removed to his brother's cabin to have his first wash for many weeks and to be free of fleas at last.

McLean was promoted Medical Officer in charge aboard the *Panama* during the Gallipoli evacuation in 1915 and he served in the Mediterranean for the next nine months. For his meritorious bravery with the Field Ambulance Guards Division he was awarded the Military Cross. Finally, he commanded the 51st Field Ambulance with the rank of Lieutenant-Colonel up to the Armistice in 1918. He was Mentioned in Dispatches three times and the citation of his Military Cross reads:

> "Captain WILLIAM FARQUHAR MCLEAN - For conspicuous devotion to duty as DADMS Guards Division, during the past year. During the operations from 8th. to 16th. October, 1917, in BROEMBEEK Sector and at FLESQUIERES on 27th November 1917, he displayed the greatest energy and ability in co-ordinating the evacuation of the wounded from the Advanced Dressing Station, and by his initiative and disregard of danger and fatigue, assisted materially in the rapid evacuation of the wounded. His ability and initiative in organising the medical arrangements to meet the varying conditions of the fighting during the enemy advance at GOUZEOUCOURT were of the greatest assistance to the Division."

He returned home to Cullen to the great joy and relief of his young wife Mollie and his family. His first priority was to find a suitable job and a home. This was to be in Haddington - a terraced house in Wemyss Place, next to the bowling green. He entered General Practice in partnership with Dr Henry H Robarts *q.v.* With his brother Rev. Douglas McLean and his wife Jessie, who lived at that time in Manchester, the two couples travelled together to Buckingham Palace where William was presented with his Military Cross by King George V. But their celebrations were short-lived when Mollie, expecting their first child, died of eclampsia. Dr McLean immersed himself in hard work for his new community who shared his grief and took him to their hearts.

There are many stories of this kindly, caring, competent family doctor, but he was no push-over. For example, while attending a mother and her new-born baby whose husband was known for his frequent bouts of drunkenness, he noticed bruising on the young mother's face and on enquiry she turned her face away. Her sardonic husband was spread out on a chair. Dr McLean asked him to "get up" whereupon he felled him with a single blow. On his way home he called in to the Police Station and reported that he had assaulted one of his patients. Nothing more was heard of the matter. It was the first and last time he raised his hand in anger. When a passing motorist asked him for directions in Haddington, he did not simply point the way, he escorted him to his destination and on another occasion a child in distress over her 'injured' doll asked the doctor for help - this busy man took the time to sit with the child and patiently sew up the doll - his payment was the huge delight and admiration of a child. His daughter, Mary, recalled, "father used to come to our room somewhere around November/December and pick up toys and books at random, stating 'you have finished with these now and I know someone who would love them.'"

The year 1920 was a busy one for Dr McLean. He spent many twilight hours in study to complete his thesis for his MD degree and during that summer he spent a holiday with his parents at the manse in Cullen. He met Edith Lumsden, a brilliant scholar of mathematics who could equally have made a career in music. She was a 1st class honours graduate and gold medallist in mathematics of the University of Aberdeen and assistant to the Professor of Mathematics there. They met at the tennis club in Cullen and William, without preamble, asked:

"Edith, can I see you home?" As she was to say in later years: "Of course, I ignored him, he should have called me Miss Lumsden!" But he persisted: "Come on Edith, I ken fine you heard me." On their way home he asked her to marry him. She was completely taken aback.

This was the start of a year long correspondence between them during which he purchased 'The Hollies' in Station Road, Haddington. Her father died in the Spring of 1921 and they delayed their wedding until the Autumn.

They settled in Haddington where their family of three children were born - James who was born on 8th August 1922, and twins Edith Mary and Ian Ross were born on 1st December 1926. William McLean was elected an Elder of St Mary's Parish Church. His wife and family never missed a Sunday and although he had to miss some services through pressure of work he never missed Communion Sundays. Each Sunday after lunch the three children were catechised severely on the contents of the service to make sure that they had not only listened to the sermon but that they understood it. The minister, Rev. James Thompson, was heard to remark with kindly modesty that he felt superfluous in the community as most people in Haddington took their worries and fears to Dr McLean.

He was a crack shot and became captain of Haddington's Miniature Rifle Club when the club won the Scottish Cup. He represented Scotland at Bisley as a member of the 'Scottish 20' and qualified for a place in the 'King's Hundred' on five occasions. He won many trophies including the *Graphic* Cup of 1926 and the *Times* Cup of 1928. He was the natural choice as President of the Rifle Club. In addition he was a keen golfer and became captain of Haddington's Golf Club.

During World War II, he trained Voluntary Aid Detachment workers in First Aid. In addition he was Chairman of the East Lothian Medical Committee under the National Health Insurance Act for 12 years before the advent of the National Health Service in 1948 when he was appointed Vice-Chairman of the Lothians and Peebles Local Medical Committee. He was appointed a member of the Lothian & Peebles Executive Council, President of the East Lothian Medical Practitioners' Society, Medical Superintendent of the East Lothian Mental Hospital in Haddington and Medical Officer of Alderston Convalescent Home.

In May 1934 the family moved to Hilton Lodge in Court Street His wife, Edith, was a tower of strength to his labours and had the help of Miss Walker, governess for Ian and Mary. During the 1939-45 war Ian and Mary were 'evacuated' for two years to live in the manse with their aunt Jessie and uncle Douglas at Innellan, a few miles south of Dunoon. Meanwhile, Edith acted as treasurer of *Haddington's Women's War Work Fund* from 1939 to 1946 (the records of which are held in the archives of Haddington' Library) and she organised 'Coals for the Poor' of Haddington for which she collected what became known as the 'ladies shilling' from those who could afford it so that coal could be distributed to poorer people. These war years were tough for the hard-working doctor. Dr Robarts had had to retire through illness and Dr McLean, almost single-handedly, had to care for the whole of Haddington and the surrounding districts; he worked night and day to almost total exhaustion.

When Ian and Mary returned to Haddington from Innellan they resumed their school studies at Knox Academy. James, the eldest son, transferred to Melville College for his last three years of schooling and was accepted as a medical student at Edinburgh University in 1939. After one year he joined the RAF and was sent to South Africa for training as a Pilot Officer. On being posted to Cairo he found a surplus of pilots and on discovering that he had completed three years of medicine he was given a job in hospital administration and promoted to Flying Officer, Acting Flight-Lieutenant. After the war he returned to Edinburgh to complete his medical studies to find himself in the same year as his bright young sister Mary; she had been dux girl of the Knox Academy in 1944. They graduated together in 1949.

Meanwhile, Mary's twin brother, Ian, having been a member of the University Naval Division, enlisted in the Royal Navy to be posted to the flagship of the Southern Fleet, *HMS Nigeria.* While berthed at Durban Docks in South Africa he was selected as one of the Guard of Honour for the arrival of King George VI and Queen Elizabeth. After his 'demob' in 1948 he became a student of dentistry at the Edinburgh Dental College qualifying as a dentist in 1952. He settled in Essex where he practised dentistry for the next 42 years, until his death on 16th July 1994.

The war years had taken their toll of Dr William McLean and he was delighted when his eldest son, James, joined him in Haddington in 1951. Mary became House Surgeon to Dr E C Fahmy at the Simpson Memorial Maternity Pavillion and subsequently she joined the practice of Dr James Robart *q.v.* in Haddington.

It seemed unbelievable to Haddingtonians that their cheery doctor William McLean had become ill and was taken to the Royal Infirmary, Edinburgh. His death on 28th May 1951 was a stunning blow to his family; all East Lothian mourned. His wife, Edith, presented a beautiful lectern and Bible to St Mary's Church in memory of her beloved husband an elder of the church for 28 years. Tributes poured in:

> "Many of us had a true friend and confidant, as well as a skilful and trusted physician. We came to know to our benefit how great were his understanding and sympathy, how infectious his hopefulness and cheerfulness, and how almost unlimited his kindness.......always when we think of him, we think of strength of character and buoyancy of spirit, magnanimity and large heartedness, ungrudging and unwearying helpfulness and a life

that was a constant self-sacrifice for others."

"It was with deep grief that I learned of Dr McLean's death. That grief is shared by so many who have been his patients and who had been privileged to have come within the radius of his radiant and kindly personality. He had many virtues, more than most of us - an intensity and industry to his profession, an unwearied gait for those who were in dire need, a resounding correction for those who warranted it, and a kindly, cheery word for all."

His wife, Edith, continued to live in Haddington until her death on 21st June 1964. She was cremated at Warriston Crematorium in Edinburgh and her ashes were scattered in the garden of remembrance where the ashes of her husband had been scattered thirteen years before.

The McLean family served the population of Haddington as medical practitioners for a total of 64 years through father to son and daughter between 1919 and 1983 when James retired to the Isle of Seil.

PROFESSOR JOHN GORDON MCVIE BSc(Hons), MB,ChB, MRCP, MD, FRCP, FRCPS, FRCPE, FMedSci, DSc(hon)

He fights for a cure and the elimination of cancer

This eminent physician, the Director-General of the Cancer Research Campaign, arrived in East Lothian in 1947 at the age of two when his father, John McVie, joined a long established law practice, now McVies WS, in Haddington's High Street. The McVie family settled firstly at Gifford and moved to Haddington in 1950 when John McVie was appointed Town Clerk of the Royal Burgh.

Young John, known in the family as Gordon, born in Great Western Road, Glasgow on 13th January 1945, received his Primary education at Yester Primary School in Gifford and Knox Primary School in Haddington before going to his father's famous old school in Edinburgh, the Royal High, in 1956. He did not pursue his academic studies with enthusiasm preferring instead his activities in drama and the arts.

His choice of career from an early age was medicine and he has certainly proved that the earlier in life you decide on your career the more successful you are likely to be. His choice of a caring profession was sparked when he lived at the home of his grandparents in Edinburgh while attending the Royal High School. The slow demise of his favourite aunt Jean MacAuslan fashioned his later career path.

His career is an astonishing and fast-moving story of unrelenting work rewarded with enormous success and recognition. He entered the faculty of Medicine of Edinburgh University in 1962 where he studied for his first degree, BSc(Hons) in Pathology in which he won the Gunning Victoria Jubilee Prize before qualifying MB, ChB in 1969. He was appointed a House Officer at the Royal Hospital for Sick Children and at the Royal Infirmary, Edinburgh. He recalled with admiration the work and the excellence of the lectures of Frederick Robarts MB,ChB,FRCSE *qv*, the Haddington born Senior Paediatric Surgeon at the Royal Hospital for Sick Children, who was one of his lecturers when he was a student at the University of Edinburgh.

In 1970 his work load was enormous - as a Medical Research Fellow in the University's Departments of Pathology and Therapeutics he lectured in Therapeutics and simultaneously he was appointed Honorary Registrar of Lothian Health Board. Two years of devoted research and clinical experience earned him Membership of the Royal College of Physicians (MRCP) and led to his appointment as Senior Registrar of the Royal Infirmary, Edinburgh, working initially in general medicine, haematology and gastroenterology. He was not yet thirty years of age.

In 1973 he was appointed to a full lectureship in therapeutics of the University of Edinburgh and three years later he became a senior lecturer in Clinical Oncology at the Cancer Research Campaign Unit of the University of Glasgow and Greater Glasgow Health Board appointed him their Honorary Consultant in Medical Oncology - the first in Scotland and at the age of 31 years. He was now a leading authority in the study of tumours. In 1977 as a consultant he led a team of researchers who developed a new treatment for testicular cancer. He had already submitted his thesis *Clinical and Laboratory Studies in Human Lymphoma* to the University of Edinburgh which gained him the degree *Medicinae Doctor* (MD). That year, 1978, he was invited to become a visiting Fellow in the Department of Medical Oncology at the University of Paris and, in 1979, a Visiting Fellow to the Netherlands Cancer Institute.

His reputation having spread to the Continent, he was 'head-hunted' in 1980 to become the head of the Clinical Research Unit for the Netherlands Cancer Institute in Amsterdam. In addition to his consultancy work he was appointed Chairman of the Division of Experimental Therapy in Amsterdam and after four years of exemplary leadership it was not unexpected that he should become the Institute's Clinical Research Director. Meanwhile, he was a consultant for the International Agency Research in Cancer for the World Health Organisation in carcinogenesis of cytostatic drugs, and a visiting professor to the University of Sydney, New South Wales, Australia. This was a Scottish physician in demand world wide.

In 1981 he was elected to Fellowship of the Royal College of Physicians of Edinburgh (FRCPE) and by now his service on a wide range of committees and his membership of examination boards constituted a valuable contribution to the advancement of the research in and treatment of cancer.

His appointment as Scientific Director of the United Kingdom Cancer Research Campaign in 1989 followed from his nine years in the Netherlands and his appointment in 1990 as Visiting Professor of the British Postgraduate Medical Federation of London University were deserved recognitions of his devoted teaching and research. Deservedly in 1994 he was given the high honour of the Presidency of the European Organisation for Research and Treatment of Cancer and he was appointed the first European Editor of the Journal of the National Cancer Institute of the United States of America. In April 1996, aged 51, he succeeded David de Peyer as Director-General of the Cancer Research Campaign, the first medic to hold the top post with responsibility for a £50 million annual income and its remarkable record of piloting the use of fifty-five new anti-cancer drugs.

Courtesy of Professor John Gordon McVie

His published works include a total of five books, thirty-five chapters for other books, 215 articles in Scottish, British and European medical journals and 200 abstracts for medical journals and proceedings. He has accepted no fewer than a hundred invitations to address national and international academic bodies in Holland, Germany, Italy, Singapore, Taiwan, Sydney, New York, Maryland etc.

He is committed to find the elusive cures for all kinds of cancer. He lives in Bristol with his wife Claudia Danby and commutes to London daily; although, as part of his work, he visits and encourages the workers in the forty Cancer Research Campaign units around the country as well as giving talks to supporters, politicians and other groups, always seeking their support in his work to defeat the scourge of cancer.

A family man, he has three sons by his first marriage to Evelyn Strang: Malcolm, a computer scientist, Tammas who works in the insurance industry and Douglas who works in a pharmacy. His contact with East Lothian is frequent through regular visits home to Haddington where his parents, Lindsaye and John McVie live in happy retirement.

Professor Gordon McVie takes his message of the fight against cancer far and wide. He is continuously covered by the media - radio television and national and local newspapers - no opportunity is missed. His message is often alarming but never alarmist. He rightly brings to the attention of politicians and the public the scourge of cancer in our lives by giving often unpalatable details of his researches in the occurrence of various types of cancer in various locations and in various social groups. It makes tough reading but it has led to a vast increase in high quality research, new treatments and hope to sufferers. His most recent campaign was his dire warning of the scourge of lung cancer laying the blame firmly at the feet of the tobacco industry whose massive profits he regards as immoral and unethical. Equally unacceptable to him is the annual European agricultural subsidy of 1 billion euros to southern Mediterranean tobacco growers. How is it possible that so much of taxpayers money can be given to produce a cancer-producing plant when less than one per cent of that subsidy is given annually for cancer research?

He has been awarded three honorary doctorates by three universities for his valuable work: Abertay in Dundee, Nottingham and Portsmouth. He is never content that enough is being done and his mission in life - and he has devoted his whole life to it - is to bring an end to that which we all fear most - the dreaded cancer. If one were to try to sum up his work and his career in the briefest of terms: it is in Professor McVie's motto for the Cancer Research Campaign: 'Research Cures Cancer'.

He was overjoyed when a young man who was given little hope as a "half dead man" with testicular cancer was cured using the drugs pioneered by Professor McVie - his name - Lance Armstrong, the winner of the 2000 *Tour de France* cycle race - an astonishing athletic achievement for one of the ninety per cent of men who have been cured.

THE MAITLANDS of Lethington,

The Earls of Lauderdale

The earliest mention of this ancient family occurs in 1058 when **Robertus de Lavedre** aided Malcolm III (Canmore) (1057-1093) in asserting his kingship by the rule of premogeniture against Macbeth (1040-1057) for which he was given large grants of land. The Maitlands, on the other hand, probably originate from France being of Anglo-Norman origin on their arrival in Scotland during the 12th century when **Thomas Mautalent** witnessed a charter of the monks of Melrose in 1227. He was probably an ancestor of **Sir Richard Maitland** who acquired the lands of Thirlestane through his marriage to Avicia, the heiress of Thomas de Thirlestane. His son **William Maitland** died c1293, and his grandson, **Sir Robert Maitland** added to the family estates on his acquisition of the lands of Lethington from Sir John Gifford of Yester when David II confirmed the grant on 15th October 1345. Sir Robert was killed during the defeat of David II's army at the battle of Neville's Cross 17th October 1346; ironically, it was this battle which finally brought him recognition as king of Scotland. Sir Robert married a sister of Sir Robert Keith, Marischal of Scotland their son **John Maitland** of Thirlestane and Lethington married Agnes, sister of the 9th Earl of Dunbar/March. He died c1395 in the reign of the kindly man of justice Robert III. His son **Sir Robert Maitland** was born c1369 was succeeded by his son **William Maitland** who died c 1471 and **John Maitland** born 14th August 1464 and married a daughter of the Laird of Dundas.

Their son was **Sir William Maitland** fought and died with his king James IV at the disastrous Battle of Flodden on 9th September 1513. Sir William married a daughter of 2nd Lord Seton and his son **Sir Richard Maitland** of Lethington, who was born in 1496 and educated at St Andrews and Paris, was a man of great integrity and became an eminent historian, jurist and statesman. Throughout his life he advocated moderation during the troubled times of James V and Mary of Guise. James V died shortly after the 'Rout of Solway Moss' (24th November 1542) and in 1532 he had established the Court of Session in Edinburgh. In 1551 Sir Richard Maitland was appointed an Extraordinary Lord of Session. In 1561 he was an Ordinary Lord and was appointed Lord Privy Seal in 1562.

This remarkable man lost his sight in 1584 and retired from the Court. He then wrote one of his best known works: his *History of the House Seyton* and he became known as a poet of great merit. He died

1586 and his collection of Scottish poetry, many of which he wrote himself, was published in 1828 by the Maitland Club, the originals are held in Magdalene College, Cambridge. He had three sons and four daughters by his wife Mary, daughter of Sir Thomas Cranstoun.

His eldest son, **William of Lethington** was born in 1528 at Lethington (now called Lennoxlove) near Haddington and as the 'cleverest statesman then living in Scotland' (61 p.185) he became the celebrated *Secretary Lethington*, that is Secretary of State to Mary Queen of Scots. In 1558 he was Secretary of State to the Queen Regent, Mary of Guise, widow of James V and mother of Mary Queen of Scots, but a year later he turned against her when he joined the Lords of Congregation supporting John Knox. Mary of Guise died suddenly during the Siege of Leith (1560) when the French were starved into submission and Maitland became the Speaker in the Convention of the Estates representing the Protestants at the English Court.

When Mary Queen of Scots arrived from France, Maitland in association with the Earl of Moray supported her against John Knox and he represented her several times at the Court of Queen Elizabeth I. Protestant one year and Catholic the next, Maitland connived against Rizzio, Mary's talented secretary, who was murdered in 1566 by the odious and overbearing Lord Darnley, her husband. Mary was deeply hurt and angry but in 1567, at Whittingehame Tower, Maitland, with Douglas Earl of Morton and the Earl of Bothwell, plotted the murder of the despised Lord Darnley. Maitland, again in royal favour, became Mary's counsellor and a friend of Bothwell. The two were involved in the murder of Darnley but when Mary married Bothwell (her third husband), Maitland turned against them and supported the insurgents who defeated Bothwell at Carberry Hill.

Mary was now imprisoned at Lochleven Castle and forced to abdicate in favour of her one year-old son who was now James VI. After her escape to England, Maitland supported the new government under the Regency of the Earl of Moray, but secretly he was still sympathetic to the exiled Mary Queen of Scots. In 1568 he was appointed one of the Commissioners who, with Regent Moray, presented the indictment against Mary. The devious Maitland was, almost simultaneously, plotting against Regent Moray in the formation of a party in support of Mary. Meantime Regent Moray had been killed and Maitland joined William Kirkcaldy of Grange who commanded Edinburgh Castle. The latter conceived a plan to kidnap the new Regent, the Earl of Lennox, with the King's Lords at Stirling. They failed and during the chase Regent Lennox was shot.

The new Regent, the earl of Mar, agreed a truce during which he died. The next Regent was the Earl of Morton who tried to starve out Kirkcaldy and Maitland and, with the help of Elizabeth I's cannons, they surrendered on 29th May 1573. Kirkcaldy was executed and Maitland died in prison in Leith a few days after Kirkcaldy's execution on 9th June. His son **James Maitland** died in 1620 and had no family.

William of Lethington's young brother **Sir John, 1st Lord Maitland of Thirlestane**, was born in 1545 and educated at St Andrews and in France. He was Keeper of the Privy Seal for Scotland in 1567, the year of Mary Queen of Scots' imprisonment in Loch Leven Castle. He was appointed a Lord of Session in 1568-71 and Secretary of State in 1584-91, being knighted in 1584. In 1585 he survived the royal backlash and the fall of Regent Arran after the Ruthven Raid and as Lord High Chancellor of Scotland (1587-95) he successfully and painstakingly managed a coalition until 1592. He married Jean, the daughter and heiress of 4th Lord Fleming in 1582/3. He died in 1595.

Their son **John, Lord of Thirlestane, 1st Earl of Lauderdale** succeeded to the peerage on the death of his father and he was created Viscount of Lauderdale on 2nd April 1616. He was a Lord of Session from 1618 until 1626, a Commissioner of Parliament in 1621 and created Earl of Lauderdale on 14th March 1626 for his support of Charles I who had succeeded to the throne on 27th March 1625. In honour of his elevation and of his monarch he had his new-born third son christened Charles. He was commissioner of Taxes in 1634 and President of Parliament from 1644, the year of his death at Lethington. He married Isobel, second daughter of Alexander Seton, 1st Earl of Dunfermline and Lord High Chancellor of Scotland. They had fifteen children; three sons and twelve daughters; only one son and one daughter survived.

Lord John Maitland, the 2nd Earl, the only surviving son of the 1st Earl who became the **1st** and only **Duke of Lauderdale**, was the most famous and most powerful of the Lauderdales. His other titles were Marquess of March, Viscount Maitland, Lord Thirlestane, Musselburghand Boulton, 1st and last Earl of Guildford and Baron Petersham. During his eighteen year 'reign' of Scotland (1662-80), 'John Red', as he was known, formed several alliances to gain control of Scotland during a period of dissent. The nobility were seriously in debt after a dozen years of Cromwellian rule, the Covenanters rebelled against the imposition of Episcopacy and the intrigues of the Court were all held in check by the clever manipulations of Lauderdale until the smallholders (not the landowners) rebelled.

Lord John Maitland was born on 24th May 1616 at Lethington at Haddington. His father, the 2nd Lord Maitland of Thirlestane, was created 1st Earl of Lauderdale in 1624 and his mother was Elizabeth Seton. She was the second daughter of the Earl of Dunfermline, the High Chancellor of Scotland. The 1st Earl's grandfather was Chancellor to James VI and his grandmother, Dame Jane Fleming, Lady Thirlestane, had the lands of Brunstane (from Brunstane Castle near Penicuik). Lord John Maitland's ancestry was therefore impeccable for a brilliant future.

Lord John was nine years old when Charles I became king in 1625 and in 1638 he married Anne, daughter of the Earl of Home, having had the estates at Brunstane passed to him in 1632, he remodelled the late 16th century Brunstane House as a lodge in 1672. The north-east stair tower door has a segmental pediment with the arms of Maitland and Home and the monogram 'IMAH' carved into the stone for 'John Maitland and Anne Home'. He became an ardent Covenanter but this was a role he was to discard as he donned the mantle of 'Master of Scotland.'

Lauderdale was one of the Scottish Commissioners at the Westminster Assembly when Charles I raised his standard at Nottingham in 1641; but Scotland kept out of the Civil War during its first year. Lauderdale, as one of the Commissioners of the Solemn League and Covenant, sought to reform the English and Irish churches - 'according to the word of God and the example of the best Reformed Churches' - to preserve the Scottish Reformed religion, to exterminate Catholicism and Episcopacy and to agree a uniform religion. The English swallowed all this in exchange for an army of 20,000 men. In any case Charles I never felt bound by any agreements but he did firmly believe in the divine right of Kings. The Assembly, attended by Lauderdale, had little power but it produced the confessions of faith which still bind the Scottish Kirk.

Charles was handed over to Parliament by the Scots following his surrender in March 1646; he had reneged on paying for the Scottish army but the Scots accepted about half their due and left England. Even after Charles had been seized by the English army he met the Scottish envoys - Lauderdale, Loudon and Lanark to make the 'Engagement' but Charles would not take the Covenant and refused Lauderdale's offer of help to escape. The Engagers had agreed to fight the English for a religious settlement but were beaten at Preston in 1648 by Oliver Cromwell. The new ruling party, led by the 8th Earl of Argyll, passed the Act of Classes which excluded Lauderdale from office and Parliament.

After Charles was executed Cromwell took the initiative and attacked north via the east coast with an army of 16,000 men which had assembled on the Braid Hills in Edinburgh. David Leslie forced him back to Dunbar but was surprisingly beaten on 3rd December 1650. Meantime, Charles

II, having been declared King by the Scottish Parliament, had joined the Royalists of the north but Lauderdale prevailed upon him to return to join with the Committee of the Estates. Charles was crowned at Scone but the English army held the border country and Edinburgh. General Monck finished the conquest of Scotland and Lauderdale, with several other nobles, was imprisoned after the battle of Worcester in 1652. He was kept at the Tower of London, at Windsor and at Portland until 1660, the year of the Restoration.

Most of the Scottish nobility now turned up at Court. Lauderdale was already there and had found the favour of the King who kept him in London as a companion and Secretary of State. Argyle (the 8th Earl) however found himself spurned and arrested for treason for his support of Cromwell. He was put to death with Archibald Wariston, the main Remonstrant leader, in 1661.

With the dissolution of Cromwell's Union, Lauderdale insisted that Scotland must now be free of English rule, English law and the English army. His rival for control of Scottish policy was the rough, hard-drinking old soldier, General Middleton whom the king appointed as Commissioner in Scotland. Twelve years of Cromwellian rule had denuded the Royalist Scottish nobility of their estates and power; restitution was sought and Lauderdale explained his discontent to the King, but there was no money in the coffers of the Crown. Lauderdale's struggle for power, particularly against Middleton, came to a head when Middleton tried to have Lauderdale excluded from any position under one of the 700 exceptions to the 1662 Act of Indemnity, but Middleton himself, his scheme being obvious, was ousted and sent off to govern Tangiers. His replacement as Commissioner was the heavy-drinking, ill-educated Earl of Rothes, a friend of Lauderdale.

Lauderdale, as a leading Presbyterian politician, was hated by the unpopular 1st Earl of Clarendon partly through jealousy because of his unrivalled ability in debate but mostly because of Clarendon's overbearing Anglicanism. With skilful mental agility and powerful patriotism he presented an irrefutable case for Scotland. With complete loyalty to the King and expert knowledge of religion he built up and kept his party by a mixture of praise, threat and favouritism.

Scotland had gained a million pounds from fines to compensate Royalists but this was mishandled as was Parliament's insistence that the Oath of Allegiance be taken by Presbyterian ministers and that patronage be restored for all ministers appointed since 1649. The ministers, 262 of them, refused to go 'cap in hand' to their patron to ask to be allowed to return to their congregations; they left the church in protest.

The imposition of Episcopacy upon Scotland led Lauderdale to give up his Covenanting past - as a member of the Cabal ministry (an acronym for Clifford, Arlington, Buckingham, Ashley-Cooper and Lauderdale) he wished to prove his loyalty to Charles II. Covenanters in Fife, Galloway and Edinburgh held secret prayer meetings and the Privy Council feared an uprising which might support the Dutch against the English in their war of 1665-67. He gave orders to quarter 4500 Highlanders on the western shires of the Lowlands in the hope that their arrogant and warlike presence would intimidate the Covenanting Presbyterians to accept Episcopacy. The Highlanders pillaged and plundered at will and after a month they returned to the hills laden with everything they could carry.

The Covenanters' rising, when it came in 1666, was too late. Edinburgh was fortified and well-prepared; three-thousand ill-equipped peasants trekked through Lanarkshire to be slaughtered at Rullion Green in the Pentland Hills. Rothes over-reacted with numerous rebel hangings but in spite of this an amnesty was granted and Rothes was given the Chancellorship. Lauderdale with Rothes and Archibald Campbell, the 9th Earl of Argyll held power.

Less repressive policies meant a change of leadership. Lauderdale was still in control and, with the Earls of Tweeddale and Kincardine and Sir Robert Murray, a good measure of intelligent, indeed intellectual and efficient government was provided. Meanwhile London suffered the Great Plague in 1665 and the Great Fire of 1666. Clarendon had been dismissed and Lauderdale had the complete trust of the King.

During the next six years of dangerous English government Lauderdale trampled over deeply held beliefs in Scotland. The Covenanters hated him to such an extent that they were said to have bestowed their curse upon him: 'may you never rest in peace.' However, in 1672 he was made Commissioner to Parliament and given a dukedom. He took up residence at the newly rebuilt Palace of Holyroodhouse. The Duke of Hamilton led the intrigues against him, but Lauderdale, now very rich and aided by the King, attempted to effect Parliamentary Union, but opposition in Scotland forced him to dissolve the Scottish Parliament.

Covenanters now held their meetings openly and Lauderdale with the Bishop of Dunblane, Robert Leighton, offered a compromise - the 'Indulgence' - to entice the old Resolutioner party back into the church. Forty-two 'outed' ministers returned, but not the complaining Archbishop Burnet of the Glasgow Synod who was replaced by Leighton. Lauderdale's leniency was repaid with a resurgence of armed conventicles which, in 1678, culminated in an attack on Lauderdale himself. This was too much, he arranged 'free quarter' for 800 Highlanders which meant they could confiscate whatever they wanted. It developed into riotous looting and the reaction against Lauderdale was a furore.

In May 1679 the Archbishop of St Andrews, James Sharp, was murdered by a group of horsemen which signalled the start of the rebellion. They gathered strength as they travelled west. John Graham of Claverhouse ('Bluidy Clavers') in his attempt to break up a large prayer meeting found himself against a superior armed force and he had to retreat to Glasgow which itself was a rebel stronghold. In June the Duke of Monmouth (Charles II's illegitimate son), with English troops, defeated the rebels at the Battle of Bothwell Brig and this marked the end of Lauderdale who was now sixty-three years old. He resigned his Commissionership, his friends deserted him and he died in 1682. The 'killing time' had started under James VII.

Lauderdale may have been deserted but he was certainly held in great respect. From the unlikely source of a conventicle minister, Robert Law, came this message:

> "truly a man of great spirit, a most daring man and a man of great success, and did more without the sword than Oliver Cromwell did with it, was a man very national, and truly the honour of our Scots nation for wit and parts" (11).

His marriage to Elizabeth Murray, Countess of Dysart, was a disaster, she being described as 'the evil genius of himself and family'. She was a spendthrift and disposed of large sums on her son from her first marriage to Sir Lionel Talmash. She berated the Town Council of Edinburgh even after the Council had bestowed the sum of £6200 on the duke and his friends and 'threatened the magistrates in great wrath for not giving her a present notwithstanding all the good she said she had done them' (71 p.168). In addition when married to the widowed Duke she greedily denuded Thirlestane Castle to furnish her Castle of Ham. The Duke died without a son and the Dukedom of Lauderdale and the Earldom of March became extinct. Thomson in his *Lauder and the Lauderdales* summed him up: 'his heart was hardened through lust of rank, riches and honours. He died "rolling in wealth". He lives in all time the evil genius of Scottish Presbyterianism' (71 p.176).

As a postscript, folklore in the Royal Burgh of Haddington tells of the Covenanters' curse on Lauderdale - "may you never rest in peace" - during the flood of 1948 the waters seeped into the vault in St Mary's Parish Church, the only coffin to move was that of the Duke of Lauderdale.

The Earldom and the titles of Viscount Lauderdale (1616), Viscount Maitland (1624) Lord of Thirlestane (1590) and Lord Thirlestane and Boulton (1624) were inherited by the Duke's brother, **Charles, 3rd Earl of Lauderdale**, who also became Lord Hatton through his marriage to Elizabeth, the second daughter of Richard Lauder of Hatton. He was born in 1626 and, to celebrate the crowning of Charles I, his father, who was created the 1st Earl that year, named his third son *Charles* in honour of his elevation.

He was appointed Captain-General of the Mint from 1660 to 1682 and a Privy Councillor (Scotland) from 1661 to 1682 after Charles II was restored to the throne. He a was Member of the Scottish Parliament for Midlothian from 1669 to 1672, Hereditary Royal Standard Bearer of Scotland in 1671 and Treasurer Depute in 1672. As a Lord of Session from 1670 to 1682 he was removed from the Privy Council during the 'black year' at the start of the 'killing time' in the reign of James VII when Covenantors were mercilessly hunted down and shot. In 1686 he was resworn as a Privy Councillor. He died on 9th June 1691 and Richard, the eldest of his six sons inherited his titles.

Richard Maitland, 4th Earl of Lauderdale, the eldest son of Charles, 3rd Earl, was born on 20th June 1653. He followed in his father's footsteps becoming MP for Midlothian in 1678, the year in which he was appointed a Privy Councillor. He was Lord Justice General from 1681 until 1684, General of the Mint in 1685 to 1689, a Commissioner of the Treasury in 1687 to 1689. As a Roman Catholic and a Jacobite he supported James VII (II of England) during the revolution when his son-in-law William of Orange replaced James as king. Richard Maitland accompanied the dethroned king to St Germain in France and was outlawed on 23rd July 1994. Not surprisingly, he quarrelled with the exiled impatient and arrogant James and, having been exiled from England and Scotland, Richard was forced to live in poverty in Paris where he died aged forty-two years in 1695 leaving no children.

John Maitland, 5th Earl of Lauderdale, the second of the six sons of the 3rd Earl, was born c1655 and inherited the titles of his brother Richard in 1695. He studied law and became a member of the Faculty of Advocates on 13th July 1679. He was created a baronet in 1680, the year of his marriage to Margaret, only child of the 10th Earl of Glencairn; they had three sons and one daughter. In the family tradition he became MP for Midlothian in 1685 to 1686 and again from 1689 to 1696 being a heritor of Currie Parish near Edinburgh. He was a Privy Councillor in 1688/9, a Lord of Session, first as Lord Raveling (1689) then as Lord Halton until his death. He was the colonel of the Edinburgh Militia and a strong supporter of the Treaty of Union of 1707. In *Macky's Characters* (1707) he is described as 'a gentlemen that means well to his country'. He died aged 55 on 13th August 1710.

Charles Maitland, 6th Earl of Lauderdale, the second son of John the 5th Earl, was born in 1688. He was an officer during the battle of Sheriffmuir on 13th November 1715 on the side of the Royalist 2nd Duke of Argyle against the Jacobite 11th Earl of Mar, an indecisive battle but one which put an end to the 1715 rebellion. Charles Maitland inherited his titles at the age of twenty-two in 1710 and he was Lord Lieutenant and Sheriff of Midlothian, Captain general of the Mint and a Representative Peer from 1741 until his death on 17th July 1744. He married Lady Elizabeth Ogilvy, daughter of the 1st Earl of Seafield; they had six sons, James the second son inherited the titles in 1744. The sixth son, Frederick Lewis Maitland, distinguished himself in a naval career reaching the rank of Captain RN.

James Maitland, 7th Earl of Lauderdale was born on 28th January 1718. He joined the army in 1740 and reached the rank of Lieutenant-Colonel by 1745 during the rising of Charles Edward Stuart and the Jacobite Highlanders. He resigned his commission in 1765 and was a Representative Peer from 1747 to 1761 and from 1782 to 1784. He was Commissoner of Police in 1766 and Lord Rector of Glasgow University in 1780. He married Mary daughter of Sir Thomas Lombe, an Alderman of London, which brought a fortune of £60,000 to the Lauderdale estate. He died on 1789 aged seventy-one years. His second son James inherited the titles and the earldom.

James Maitland, 8th Earl of Lauderdale was born at Ratho on 26th January 1759. He matriculated at Trinity College, Oxford and attended the Universities of Edinburgh, Glasgow and Paris. After studying at Lincoln's Inn he was admitted to Membership of the Faculty of Advocates in 1780 but he gave up the law to enter the House of Commons when he became MP for Newport, County Cornwall. He was a staunch Whig and a friend of the popular Edinburgh Judge, Lord Advocate for Scotland and Dean of the Faculty of Advocates, Henry Erskine (1746-1817). In the Commons Maitland admired and followed Edmund Burke (1729-97) and Charles James Fox (1749-1806), the great antagonists of Prime Minister William Pitt (1759-1806). Maitland was a manager of the impeachment of Warren Hastings (1732-1818), the governor of Bengal, who was accused of fraud and whose trial lasted seven years leading to his eventual acquittal but financial ruin.

When he succeeded his father in 1789, at the start of the French Revolution, Maitland was elected a Scottish Representative Peer but he was so aggressive he was not re-elected. He had become a passionate Jacobite during the French Revolution, insisting on the title 'Citizen Maitland'. He was a founder of 'Friends of the People', a pro-Revolutionary Society, membership of which often led to imprisonment and deportation during Pitt's so-called 'Reign of Terror' (1793-94). During the French Revolution he visited Paris and witnessed the attack on the Tuilleries. He surrendered his peerage and tried without success to re-enter the House of Commons (69 p.128). He was honoured by Glasgow University with an LLD (1804) and on the dissolution of the

Pitt ministry he was a created a peer of the United Kingdom as Lord Lauderdale and Thirlestane (22nd February 1806). He was appointed a Joint Commissioner to France in 1806 and became a Privy Councillor that year and was resworn in 1826; he was by now a rabid Tory. This 'sagacious, clear-sighted and most wily Scotchman' (Sir Charles Bagot) died at Thirlestane Castle on 15th September 1839 aged eighty. In 1782 he married Eleanor, daughter of Anthony Todd Secretary of the General Post Office who gave her £50,000 on her marriage and promised a further £10,000 for the birth of each child. This brought them a further £90,000 with the births of their four sons and five daughters.

James Maitland, eldest son of the 8th Earl, succeeded as the **9th Earl of Lauderdale** in 1839. He was born in London on 12th February 1784 and educated at Eton and at the University of Edinburgh. He became Whig MP for Camelford in 1806-7 and for Richmond in 1818 and finally as a Tory MP for Appleby in 1826. He was Lord Lieutenant for Berwickshire and died unmarried on 22nd August 1860 at the age of seventy-six at Thirlestane Castle. His brother **Anthony Maitland** succeeded him as **10th Earl of Lauderdale**. He was born at Walthamstow in Essex on 10th June 1785 and entered the Royal Navy being severely wounded at the age of sixteen during the attack on the Boulogne flotilla in August 1801 and after the Battle of Trafalgar in 1815 he was made a Companion of The Most Honourable Order of the Bath (CB). He was MP for the Haddington Burghs in 1813-18 and for Berwickshire in 1826-32. He was ADC to William IV for the whole of his reign (1830-37) and to Queen Victoria from 1837 to 1841. He earned several honours for his naval heroism - KCMG in 1820, KCB in 1832 and GCB in 1862 when he was appointed Admiral of the Red. He died unmarried at Thirlestane on 22nd March 1863 aged seventy-seven.

Thomas Maitland, grandson of the 7th Earl and cousin of the 10th Earl, was born on 3rd February 1803 in County Cork and inherited the Scottish titles to become **11th Earl of Lauderdale** (the UK Barony of Lauderdale of Thirlestane having become extinct). He was the only surviving son and heir of General the Hon. William Mordaunt Maitland (fifth son of the 7th Earl) and Mary, widow of John Travers of Co. Cork.

Thomas Maitland entered the Royal navy aged thirteen and was promoted to Lieutenant aged twenty, Commander aged twenty-four and Captain aged thirty-four. As commander of the *Sparrowhawk* in in 1832 he brought home 589,405 Mexican dollars and other booty (11. Vol.VII p.31). He commanded the *Tweed* in 1835 and for his effective command on the coast of Spain during the Civil War he was made a knight of the Spanish Order of Charles III. In 1838 he commanded seamen and marines to quell the insurrection at Malabar in India and in

1839 he was involved in the operation of the Persian Gulf. In 1840/41 he distinguished himself in China and was made a Companion of The Most Honourable Order of Bath (CB) and was knighted in 1843. He was Captain of the Gunnery School at Portsmouth 1854-57, Commander of the Pacific Fleet 1860-62, made a KCB in 1865 and first naval ADC to Queen Victoria 1866-73. In 1868 he was promoted to the rank of Admiral. He was elected a Conservative Representative Peer (Scotland) in 1867-78 and was awarded the Knight Grand Cross of the Most Honourable Order of the Bath (GCB) in 1873. He married Amelia, third daughter of William Young of Rio de Janeiro in 1828 and had one son Thomas Maurdant who predeceased him. They also had two daughters: Isabel Anne who died in 1854 and Mary Jane who died in 1918. The 11th earl died at Thirlestane Castle aged seventy-five on 1st September 1878 and the earldom passed to a distant cousin.

Charles Barclay-Maitland, the second cousin once removed of the 11th Earl inherited the titles to become the **12th Earl of Lauderdale** in 1878; his great-grandfather was a brother of Charles, the 7th Earl. The 12th Earl was born on 29th September 1822. Little is recorded of his life except that he never married and was struck down and killed by lightning on Braidshaw Rigg Moor near Lauder in his 62nd year.

Frederick Henry Maitland was a great-great-grandson of the 6th Earl and succeeded to the titles becoming **13th Earl of Lauderdale** in 1884. He was born on 16th December 1840 the son and heir of Major-General Frederick Colthurst Maitland and Anna Dering daughter of Stephen Williams. Frederick Henry joined the 8th Hussars in 1861 and was promoted lieutenant in 1866, Captain in 1873 and attained the rank of Major in the Bengal Staff Corps in 1881. He retired from the army as a Lieutenant-Colonel to become the Political Agent in Central India. In July 1885 he claimed his peerage and was Representative Peer (Scotland) from 1889 to 1920 having been Lord Lieutenant of Berwickshire from 1889 to 1901. He married Charlotte in 1864; their sons were Frederick Colin and Sydney George William. His wife died in 1879 and four years later he married Ada, fourth daughter of the Reverend H Trail. He died aged 83 on 5th September 1924.

Frederick Colin Maitland, 14th Earl of Lauderdale was born 12th April 1868. His mother Charlotte died when he was eleven years of age and he decided to follow in his father's footsteps by joining the Royal Scots Fusiliers in 1886. He was transferred to the Scots Greys in 1887 and to the Scots Guards in 1889-94. He was mentioned in despatches and gained a medal and four clasps in the South African War of 1900-01. In 1903 he was appointed to the Honorary Corps of Gentlemen-at-Arms and Assistant Director of the Auxiliary Forces

Headquarters staff in 1904-08. During World War I he was wounded, attained the rank of temporary Lieutenant-Colonel of the 3rd Battalion of the Royal Fusiliers in 1916 and was awarded the OBE for his military services in 1919.

He married Gwendoline Lucy, daughter of the Rt Hon Sir Edward Vaughan Williams on 16th April 1890. He died aged sixty-three in 1931.

Ivor Colin Maitland, 15th Earl of Lauderdale was born on 30th January 1891 and educated at Eton he succeeded his father the 14th Earl in 1931. He served in the World War I with his father and attained the rank of Major. He was ADC to the Lord Lieutenant of Ireland in 1915-16 and again in 1918. He married Ivy, daughter of JJ Bell Irving in 1912 but had no family. He died on 17th February 1953.

The Reverend Alfred Sydney Frederick Maitland, 16th Earl of Lauderdale was born on 17th April 1904, son of the Reverend Sydney George William Maitland who was the second son of the 13th Earl. He was educated at Sydney Sussex College, Cambridge and graduated BA in 1925 and MA in 1938. He was appointed Deacon in 1927, Priest in 1928 and Curate at Worthing in 1951-53 and Woking in 1953-56. He was Rector of Catsfield in Sussex from 1957 to 1960. He died on 27th November 1968 and was succeeded by his brother Patrick Maitland.

The present and **17th Earl of Lauderdale, Patrick Maitland**, is well-known in Haddington for his work of reconciliation in encouraging pilgrimages from Whitekirk to St Mary's Parish Church - over 3000 pilgrims from many traditions join together to attend the annual pilgrimage for fellowship, prayer and healing. Until recently the Earl himself led the pilgrimage from Whitekirk to St Mary's, a distance of 12 miles (19km).

This kindly, caring and religious gentleman set out to befriend all factions of the huge family of Maitlands by inaugurating the Clan Maitland Society. He has spent much of his life in healing old wounds and bringing together various sections of the family. His aim is to earn relief from the old so-called 'Covenanter's Curse' supposed to have been bestowed on the 1st Duke of Lauderdale when, around 1670, he forsook the Covenanters to please the king, Charles II, in pushing for Episcopacy in Scotland. An old Highland minister advised the present Earl that relief from the effects of the curse could best be achieved through a life of reconciliation.

"I am the only person alive to have seen the great Duke" said the Earl in relation to the decision to restore the Lauderdale crypt beside the Lauderdale Aisle at St Mary's Collegiate Church, Haddington. The year was 1965 and the crypt was in a dreadful state. It had been under water during the flood of 1948. Every coffin had to be uplifted and that of the Duke had been damaged beyond repair. His skeleton had even to be hosed down and encased in a new coffin. The Earl supervised this grisly task with reverence and care. He noted that the Duke's hair was not, as commonly believed, red but was indeed black. The coffin of the 12th Earl, who had been killed by lightning in 1894, had even floated off its ledge suggesting that the old curse was still at work. The Duke's coffin lay at a hideously rakish angle.

The Earl believes that 'Secretary Lethington' (William Maitland 1528-73, Secretary of State to Mary of Guise when she was Queen Regent of Scotland and to her daughter Mary Queen of Scots), is buried below the aisle floor as are other ancestors. But the water table had risen over the centuries and it became necessary to drain the entire crypt and to waterproof it altogether.

The restoration was finished in 1978 and the Aisle was then rededicated as 'The Shrine of Our Lady of Haddington' to be called 'The Chapel of the Three Kings'. It is truly ecumenical; its formal dedication was an historic event in that several religious traditions took part - the Bishop of Edinburgh (then Primus of the Scottish Episcopal Church), who presided at the dedication represented the Episcopalian Church, Dr Roy Sanderson, an ex-moderator, represented the Church of Scotland; the Abbot of Nunraw represented the Catholic Church and the eastern Orthodox Church was represented also. The Holy Table in the Chapel was rebuilt from stones from Maitland houses all over Scotland and from other Holy places.

The present Earl, Patrick Maitland, was born a son of the manse at Walsall in Staffordshire on 17th March 1911. Religion is strong in his family: his father was the vicar of St Paul's Church at Burton-on-Trent, his maternal grandfather and his elder brother, Alfred Maitland - the 16th Earl - were vicars and his youngest son, Sydney Maitland, is a non-stipendiary priest in charge of St George's Episcopal Church, Maryhill, Glasgow.

The Earl's childhood holidays were spent at Thirlestane Castle, Lauder and he recalls with affection, a boyhood escapade when at the age of seven he climbed from his bedroom window at dawn to sit by the Leader Burn. Such was the enchantment of that moment he resolved to live and work for Scotland.

After school at Lancing in Sussex he gained his BA(Hons) at Oxford in 1933. Penniless and out of work at the bottom of the 1931/33 slump he and a student friend took to the streets of London to earn a precarious living from busking. They worked the pubs around the Charlotte Street area near Tottenham Court Road and on a good night their income would reach perhaps thirty shillings or so. He soon saw that there was no great future in busking.

At Oxford he had met and fallen in love with a young Yugoslav lady, Stanka Lozanitch. She had returned home to Belgrade and he borrowed just enough money from his father for his fare and a few meals to go and find her. He travelled firstly to Vienna having obtained employment with the *Daily Express* as a correspondent. Later on he was appointed *The Times* correspondent for South-East Europe with headquarters in Belgrade where he was reunited with Stanka. Together they returned to Britain in July 1936.

War threatened and Patrick Maitland was sent to Warsaw to cover the threat of German invasion in 1939. Stanka on a visit to Belgrade remained there while Patrick found himself trapped in Poland by the Germans on one side and the Russians on the other. He made his escape through Czechoslovakia, Hungary, Romania and Yugoslavia to Greece but when the Italians invaded Albania he found himself in the midst of a highly dangerous conspiracy in which his assassination was planned. Fortunately, friends warned him and took him into hiding. His first safe-haven was a harem which was full of very fat, scented women. He got out of it quickly to flee to Durresi (Durazzo) on the coast of Albania. Later on, having reported on the Greek front in Albania for *The Times*, he was eventually among about 100 prisoners exchanged with Italy in return for the safekeeping and handing over of the Italian Crown Prince Umberto who had been held by the Abyssinians and under threat of being horribly maimed. When the Albanians let him go free, the British party, which had been captured in Yugoslavia and interned in Italy, were allowed their freedom and Patrick Maitland was among them.

On 7th December 1941 the Japanese attacked Pearl Harbour and Patrick was appointed War Correspondent in the Pacific for the *News Chronicle*. He had earlier sent his wife and first-born son, Ian, to New York while he finished his work in Belgrade but was now sent by the *News Chronicle* to join the U.S. Navy in the South Pacific. The Japanese had captured most of the islands in the Pacific by that time and he witnessed and reported many battles including that of the Coral Sea, Guadalcanal and many others, when serving with the US Navy, the US Airforce, the Australian and New Zealand Army and Navy.

After the war he returned to London to revive the *Fleet Street Letter* - a monthly newsletter which he had started in 1938. In addition he wrote for *The Scotsman* whose editor, Murray Watson, introduced him to politics. The Rt. Hon. James Stuart, who became Secretary of State for Scotland and later Lord Stuart of Findhorn, put him forward as a

Tory candidate when the late Lord Home of the Hirsel (then Lord Dunglass) succeeded to his earldom on the death of his father and a by-election was pending. He recalled his eight years (1951-59) as MP with great affection for his constituents, particularly the miners who, although they heckled him without pity, respected him and treated him with tolerant admiration. In 1964 he stood for Caithness and Sutherland but he was defeated by John Maitland Mackie - a very distant kinsman.

On 27th November 1968 his brother, the Reverend Alfred Sydney Frederick Maitland, the 16th Earl, died and Patrick succeeded to the Earldom. He entered the House of Lords and was eventually made Chairman of the House of Lords Energy Committee to study directives and documents passed by the European Union Commission in Brussels.

In 1996 he celebrated 60 years of happy marriage to Lady Lauderdale. They have two sons and two daughters: Ian, Master of Lauderdale (Viscount Maitland), is a London banker with much expertise of the Middle East, especially the Gulf. Lady Olga Maitland, MP for Sutton and Cheam is his second born. She was quickly elected Secretary of the Northern Ireland Committee of the Conservative Party in Parliament and had made a name for herself by founding a movement 'Women and Families for Defence'. Her youngest sister, Lady Caroline Militsa Maitland, is a psychological counsellor and the youngest of all, Sydney Maitland is, as already mentioned a non-stipendiary priest in charge of the Episcopalian Church of St George's, Maryhill, Glasgow while otherwise working as a Town Planner.

Today the Earl's main concerns are for his large family of Maitlands world wide through the Clan Maitland Society for which he has had the Maitland tartan checked and approved by the Lord Lyon King of Arms in 1960 as a protected tartan. The Earl's consent is required before the tartan can be bought or worn by anybody and the wearer must agree to use only the Maitland tartan and forswear any claim to wear or be entitled to any other clan tartan. This undertaking is insisted upon with every Maitland who joins the Clan Maitland Society. The Earl himself edits the Clan Maitland Yearbook and a half-yearly Newsletter. These circulate to clan members in USA, Canada, Australia and New Zealand and elsewhere. It is through the Society and the annual Pilgrimage at St Mary's Church that he achieves his mission in life - to try and get people reconciled and to be content with one another - he is a "sincere Christian and noble gentleman".

Maitland - Earldom of Lauderdale - family tree (male line):

Thomas de Matalant (Anglo-Norman origin) living 12th century
Sir Richard Maitland
married Avicia, daughter and heiress of Thomas de Thirlestane

son: William Maitland of Thirlestane, (c1258 - c1293)

son: Sir Robert Maitland of Thirlestane and Lethington (killed 1346)
married sister of Sir Robert Keith, Marischal of Scotland

son: John Maitland of Thirlestane and Lethington (died c1395)
married Agnes, sister of 9th Earl of Dunbar/March

son: Sir Robert Maitland of Thirlestane and Lethington (1369-?)
married daughter of Sir John Scrymgeour

sons: William Maitland of Thirlestane and Lethington (died c1471)

son John Maitland of Thirlestane and Lethington (1464-)
married a daughter of the Laird of Dundas

son: Sir William Maitland (died at Battle of Flodden, 1513)
married daughter of 2nd Lord Seton

son: Sir Richard Maitland, Lord Lethington (1496-1586)
married: Mary, daughter of Sir Thomas Cranstoun

sons: (1) William of Lethington 'Secretary Lethington' (c1528-1573)
(2) John, 1st Lord of Thirlestane, Lord High Chancellor of Scotland (1545-1595)
(3) Thomas (c1550-1572)

daughters: (1) Helen, married Sir John Cockburn of Clerkington
(2) Margaret, married William Douglas of Whittinhame
(3) Mary, married Alexander Lauder of Hatton
(4) Isabel, James Heriot of Trabroun

married: (i) Lady Menteith
(ii) 1567, Mary, daughter of 3rd Lord Fleming

son: James (died 1625) barred from inheritance
married Agnes Maxwell

2 daughters : Margaret

married Jean daughter and heiress of 4th Lord Fleming

son: Sir John, 2nd Lord Maitland, **1st Earl of Lauderdale**, cr 1624 (d.1645)
married 1638 Lady Isobel Seton, daughter of **1st Earl of Dunfermline**

15 children, only two sons and one daughter survived their father:
(1) John, **2nd Earl of Lauderdale** and 1st Duke of Lauderdale (1616-1682)
(2) Charles, **3rd Earl of Lauderdale**, (1626?- 1691)

married (i) 1632, Anne, 2nd daughter of 1st Earl of Home (died 1671)
(ii)1671, Elizabeth, Countess of Dysart (died 1682) no family

married 1652, Elizabeth, daughter Richard Lauder of Hatton (died 1691)

sons: (1) Richard, **4th Earl of Lauderdale** (1653-1695)

married 1678, Anne, 2nd daughter of 9th Earl of Argyll, no family
(2) Sir John, **5th Earl of Lauderdale** (c1655-1710)
(3) Charles
(4) Alexander
(5) William
(6) Thomas

daughters: (1) Isabel (married John, 8th Earl of Elphinstone)
(2) Mary (married 4th Earl of South Esk)

married c1680 Lady Margaret Cunningham, only child of 10th Earl of Glencairn

sons: (1) James, Viscount Maitland (c1680
(2) Charles, **6th Earl of Lauderdale** (1688- 1744) eldest surviving son
(3) Alexander

married: 1710, Lady Elizabeth Ogilvie, daughter of 1st Earl of Seafield

sons: (1) James, **7th Earl of Lauderdale** (1718-89)
(2) Charles Barclay-Maitland (died 1795)
(3) Richard Maitland (1724-1772)
(4) Sir Alexander 1st Bt.
(5) Frederick Lewis of Rankeillor (1730-86)
(6) Patrick, of Freuch (1734-97)

married: 1749, Mary, daughter of Sir Thomas Lombe, London

sons: (1) Valdave Charles Lauder (1752-54)
(2) James, **8th Earl of Lauderdale** (1759-1839)
(3) Sir Thomas (died 1824)
(4) William Mordaunt Maitland (general ,died 1841)

daughters: (1) Hannah Charlotte (married 7th Marquis of Tweeddale)
(2) Jane

married: 1782, Eleanor, only daughter and heiress of Anthony Todd

sons: (1) James Maitland, **9th Earl of Lauderdale** (1784-1860)
(2) Anthony Maitland, **10th Earl of Lauderdale** (Admiral) (1785-1863) died unmarried

daughters: Eleanor (married James Balfour of Whittinghame)

married: (i) Mary, daughter of Rev.Richard Orpen of Killowen
(ii) 1819, Jane, daughter of Rev.Thomas Walker

son: Thomas Maitland, **11th Earl of Lauderdale** (1803-1878) married: 1828, Amelia, 3rd daughter of William Young of Rio de Janeiro

son: Thomas Mordaunt (1838-44)
daughters: (1) Isabel Anne (died 1854)
(2)Mary Jane (died 1918)

married: (i) 1761, Isabel daughter and heiress of Sir Alexander Barclay of Towie
(ii) 1765, daughter of Patrick Haldane of Gleneagles

sons: (1) Charles of Tillicoutry (died 1816)
(2) Alexander; Lt. 100 Regt. (died 1794)
four daughters

married: 1786, Elizabeth Mary Hale

son: Charles (Rev.) (1789-?)
married: 1810, Anne, daughter of Thomas Knott of Stockland

sons: (1) Charles (1821-22)
(2) Charles Barclay-Maitland, **12th Earl of Lauderdale** (1822-1884)
daughter: Maria Anne (died 1845)

married: 1772, Mary McAdam of New York

sons: (1) Richard (1768-1802) no family
(2) Patrick of Kilmaron Castle, Fife (1770-?)
married: 1807, Anne, daughter of Colthurst Bateman

son: Frederick Colthurst Maitland, (1808-76)
married: 1837, Anne Deering, daughter of Stephen Williams

sons: (1) Frederick Henry Maitland, **13th Earl of Lauderdale** (1840-1924)
(2) George Thomas (1841-1910

married: (i) 1864, Charlotte Sarah, daughter of Lt-Col BWA Sleigh
(ii) 1883 Ada Twyford daughter of Rev Henry Traill

sons: (1) Frederick Colin Maitland **14th Earl of Lauderdale** (1868-1931)
(2) Sydney George William Maitland (1869-1946)

married: 1890, Gwendoline, daughter of Judge R Vaughan Williams

son: Ian Colin Maitland, **15th Earl of Lauderdale** (1891-1953)
married: 1912, Ethel Mary, daughter of James Jardine Bell-Irving of Kelso

son: Ivor Colin James (1915-1943) killed in action
daughters: (1) Mary Helena
(2) Anne Priscilla (The Lady Anne Eyston)
(3) Elizabeth Sylvia (The Lady Elizabeth Maitland)

married: 1899 Ella Francis daughter of Rev James Richards

sons: (1) Alfred Sydney Frederick Maitland, **16th Earl of Lauderdale** (1904-1968)

(2) Patrick Frederick Maitland, 17th and present Earl of Lauderdale (1911-)
daughter: (Ella) Mary (1906-?)

married: (i) 1938, Norah Mary, daughter of William Henry La Touche (died 1938)
(ii) 1940, Irene Alice May, daughter of Rev Charles Percy Shipton (no family)

married: 1936, Stanka, daughter of Prof Milivoje Lozanitch of Belgrade

sons: (1) Ian, Viscount Maitland (1937-)
(2) The Rev and Hon. Sydney Maitland (1951-)
daughters: (1) The Lady Olga Hay (1944-)
(2) Caroline, The Lady Militsa Maitland (1946-)

[Source: *Burke's Peerage and Baronetage*]

JOHN MAJOR

the theologian and historian who taught John Knox

In one of a group of small cottages in the 15th century village called Gleghornie, about two miles inland from Tantallon Castle, was the boyhood home of John Major who was born there in 1469. This son of a tacksman (a tenant) became a distinguished and highly respected theologian and historian. This cottage and indeed the village was owned by the 5th Earl of Angus, George Douglas *qv*. John Major's parents were held in great respect in the village being deeply religious and of some social standing.

John Major's early education took place at the Franciscan Friary in Haddington, a generation before John Knox (c.1505-1572) *qv*. To this early education Major owed much; he was given a thorough grounding in Latin in which he conversed with ease, but then all pupils of the friary could do so; they were threatened with physical punishment for speaking in their mother tongue.

In Major's time Tantallon Castle near his home was occupied by the 5th Earl of Angus, 'the Great Earl' or 'Bell-the Cat', who undoubtedly learned of this young scholar through his own equally scholarly son, Gavin Douglas (1474-1522) *qv*. Although five years older than Major, Gavin Douglas became a lifelong friend. Their interests were alike and Gavin Douglas became patron to John Major which enabled him to study at God's House (which was renamed Christ's College), Cambridge. In 1493 Major continued his studies in Paris, firstly at St Barbe's College and then at 'his true nursing mother', as he called it, the College of Montaigu of which he always spoke in the most reverential terms. He graduated Master of Arts at the University of Paris in 1496.

One of Major's specialist studies was the work of the 12th century Italian theologian Peter Lombard who was Bishop of Paris in 1159. Major wrote several dissertations on his works and was appointed a regent of the college. His lectures on Philosophy and Theology were controversial in his opposition to the up-and-coming Renaissance. He detested this move away from the medieval world and described the Reformation as 'Lutherian heresy'; Martin Luther (1493-1546) being the German religious reformer who attacked the church of Rome continuously and excited a huge assembly of intellectuals and citizens in Wittenberg when he burned the papal bull against him in front of them.

Major became a Fellow of the College of Navarre where his fame as a teacher soon became known and his intolerance of anything new seemed only to increase his popularity with his students one of whom described him as "a man who flies on his own wings higher than the clouds would carry him, till he passes above all spirits in sublimity".

In 1503 he published his first work on logic and gained his Doctorate of Divinity in 1505. The next thirteen years were among his most productive: by 1508 he had published his lectures on logic and his magnum opus of theology, *A Commentary on the Four Books of Peter the Lombard's "Sentences"*, was published in parts between 1509 and 1517.

In 1509 his boyhood friend, Gavin Douglas, now Dean of St Giles in Edinburgh, had secured for him the treasurership of the Chapel Royal in Edinburgh but he declined the offer because of his dedication to his literary work in France. However, in 1518 he accepted the post of Professor of Philosophy and Divinity at Glasgow University and, to give him a salary, he was made Vicar of Dunlop in Ayrshire and Canon of the Chapel Royal at Stirling. Among his students were two young men who were to make history - one was John Knox who was to become the great leader of the Reformation and the other, Patrick Hamilton, who was to write his *Patrick's Places* propounding the doctrine of Luther and for which he was burned at the stake in St Andrews.

Major had written most of his history of England and Scotland, *Historia Maioris Britanniae*, before leaving France. He completed this in 1521 and had it published in Paris. It was the first critical history of Scotland in which he rejected many of the old fables and concentrated on the actions of rulers and church leaders drawing moral lessons from their actions. He gave an insight of the customs and behaviour of the day in England and Scotland and advocated the union of the two countries whilst greatly praising the land of his birth. His 'History of Greater Britain is, in part a plea for a better understanding between England and Scotland' (60 p.100).

In 1522 he left Glasgow to follow his friend, Archbishop James Beaton, to St Andrews. Beaton had been promoted from the diocese of Glasgow to that of St Andrews and Major taught logic and theology at the University. One of his students was George Buchanan who was to become tutor to the young Mary Queen of Scots and to her son, James VI. (Today, graduates of the University of Edinburgh are said to be capped with 'Geordie Buchanan's breeks'). In 1525 Major returned to the University of Paris and in addition to his lectures at his beloved Montaigu he published eight *Books of Physics*, *Logical Questions* and the *Ethics of Aristotle* which he dedicated to Cardinal Wolsey from whom he had received generous hospitality on his journeys through England as well as the offer of a well-paid post in the new college he founded at Oxford. Major continued to publish many commentaries and was now 'the veritable chief of the scholastic philosophy' and 'the prince of Paris divines' (25 p.387). Before leaving Paris he published his *Commentary on the First Book of Sentences* referring to the 'execrable heresy of Luther.'

Major returned to Scotland to become Provost of St Salvador's College, St Andrews from 1533 until his death in 1550. He lectured in theology but wrote little and took no part in the events leading to the Reformation except in defence of a friar. The friar was saved from death because, according to John Knox, Major's 'word was then holden as an oracle in matters of religion.' By 1547 John Knox had surrendered his Orders as a Catholic Priest and Major, although still a devout Catholic, attended the Parish Church of St Andrews to hear him preach. Many of Major's friends and former students had accepted the doctrines of the Reformation. This must have affected him deeply in his old age as he firmly held to the Church of Rome and was stubbornly opposed to theological change. This great teacher, theologian and historian died at the birth of monumental change - the Reformation; he was in his eightieth year when he died in 1550 at St Andrews.

JOHN MARTINE of Haddington

the story-teller and author of Haddington

John Martine is probably known to most Haddingtonians as the author of his *Reminiscences and Notices of Fourteen Parishes of the County of Haddington* which was published in 1883. This covered fourteen of the twenty-five parishes of the county of Haddington - 'an elucidation of old times, events, and manners...' (59 p.6). A second volume: *Reminiscences of Ten Parishes of the County of Haddington* was published 1894 shortly after he died. The two volumes were amalgamated in alphbetical order with sixty-four illustrations and published in one volume by East Lothian Council Library Service in 1999 from which the bulk of this account Martine's life has been gleaned.

John Martine, the second of ten children, was born on 10th April 1811 in Sidegate at Haddington where his father was a currier (leather-dresser) and three times Provost of the town in 1807, 1813 and 1817. His mother, Alison Forrest, inherited the farm at Morhambank.

Although working in leather had become something of family tradition (his grandfather was a tanner and became postmaster of Haddington and Provost in 1781), John decided to learn the art of brewing and he became an apprentice brewer in the west of Scotland. [The tannery in which John's father and grandfather worked was situated approximately opposite Haddington House in Sidegate]. Eventually, John Martine set up his own brewery in Sidegate, a two-storey building with projecting dormers above. It was demolished as recently as 1946 (hence the name of Brewery Court, off Sidegate). His decision to abandon the brewing business was most probably because of the competition of the big breweries in Edinburgh (William Younger & Co. founded in 1749 and William McEwan founded in 1856).

He operated his brewery until 1863 and left Haddington that year when he accepted a grain commission agency at Portobello. He married Jane Thompson from Gateshead in 1864 and four years later, having inherited the farm at Morham from his mother, who died in 1868, he and his wife moved to Morham Mains. Farming proved difficult not only for him but for many other farmers who were forced to relinquish their farms to their landlords. He gave up farming in 1875 and moved to Edinburgh.

John Martine had, over a period years, written several newspaper articles which had been well received; the public liked his new style of writing his stories of country tales and events. He obtained his material through listening to old Haddington worthies and he re-told many of these old stories which had been gleaned during his regular visits to the markets at the Corn Exchange in Haddington. Of course, as a boy in Haddington he was enthralled by stories of the adults around him who talked almost incessantly of the sea battles and the land victories of the Napoleonic war.

His newspaper articles, when edited and put together, formed his *Reminiscences of the Royal Burgh of Haddington and Old East Lothian Agriculturists* which sold out quickly - 'a work such as this is bound to maintain its popularity with the natives; while Haddingtonians abroad place it on the shelf beside the Bible, and swither which of the two to take down first' - so wrote 'TC' in the *Memoir of the Author* (59 p.7).

This success encouraged him to write another entitled *Reminiscences of the Town and Port of Leith*. His *Reminiscences and Notices of Fourteen Parishes of the County of Haddington* was published in 1883 but with a condition that he would complete a companion volume if the first paid for itself. He need not have feared the possibility of failure; it too was sold out quickly and he proceeded to collect and collate the material for his second volume. He had almost completed it when he became seriously ill and he died in Edinburgh on 29th December 1891. Thankfully, his unfinished manuscript was completed by EJ Wilson and published by William Sinclair of the *Haddingtonshire Courier*.

JAMES, ANDREW AND GEORGE MEIKLE of Saltoun

Agricultural Engineers of East Lothian

When 'The Patriot', Andrew Fletcher *q.v.* of Saltoun, had become thoroughly disgusted with his fight against the Union of the Scottish and English Parliaments of 1707 he turned his attention to agriculture and set off an agricultural revolution. At that time flails were used to thresh corn; it was laborious and tedious. Winnowing was a process of simply letting the wind blow through an open-ended barn. Through the skill and inventive genius of **James Meikle** and his son Andrew, Fletcher mechanised many processes and pulled agriculture into a new era.

During a visit to Holland Fletcher had been greatly impressed by the modern machinery he saw there and the idea of a machine which could remove the husk from barley was very attractive to him. He was aware of the cleverness of a local millwright, James Meikle, and he sent him to Amsterdam to study this machinery. Meikle had to work covertly and on his return to Scotland in 1710 James Meikle brought Dutch fanners to winnow corn indoors; natural ventilation was no longer required but this change from the old method was thought by those resistant to change to be 'making the devil's wind and taking the power out of the hands of the almighty' (37 p.171). An extract from John Martine's *Reminiscences* refers to the Articles of Agreement between the Laird and Andrew:

> *It is agreed betwixt Henry Fletcher, brother to the Laird of Saltoun, and James Meikle...in the name of his said brother...The said James Meikle shall go to Holland with the first fleet that sails thither....and there learn the art of sheeling barley...and how to accommodate, order, and erect mills...That Saltoun shall pay all the said expenses in going and coming, and learning such arts. (Signed) H. Fletcher, Js Meikle. 17th day of April 1710.* (59 pps. 190-1)

Meikle now set about building a new barley mill at Salton, the first in Britain; in fact it was to be the only one of its kind in Britain, Ireland and America for the next forty years. He was said to have used a drawing made from memory by the eminent architect, William Adam. Such was the success of Meikle's mill 'Salton Barley' became a household name throughout the country. Andrew Fletcher's sister-in-law, a very enterprising lady, managed the mill and made sure that no-one gained entry; she kept this profitable monopoly in the family.

Andrew Meikle was born in 1719 and clearly inherited his father's inventive skills and became a millwright at Houston Mill on the Rennie family's Phantassie estate. He became a farmer in East Saltoun and spent laborious hours in making his new invention, the threshing machine; it was more of a clever piece of development work than a completely new invention but he is credited with the first working machine and is therefore regarded as the inventor. With Robert Mackell he had, in 1768, already invented and patented a machine (No. 896) for dressing grain at Houston Mill near Dunbar. He patented his improved spring sail for windmills in 1772 which gave greater safety in high wind speeds.

His first threshing machine in 1778 was a copy of another patented in 1734 by Michael Menzies. In fact, several farmers in England had experimented with 'thrashing' machines - Elderton at Alnwick, Oxley at Flodden and Smart at Wark. A trial of Meikle's 1778 machine was demonstrated to several farmers of East Lothian who signed a report which was published in Wright's *Present State of Agriculture in Scotland*, but the machine was not a success. One of the signatories of the report was George Rennie of Phantassie, the brother of the John Rennie (1761-1821), the eminent civil engineer whose bridges, canals and harbours are his memorial; he served his apprenticeship under Andrew Meikle.

Six years passed before Andrew Meikle resumed work on another machine. He was asked by a gentleman farmer, Sir Francis Kinloch 6th baronet of Gilmerton to look at a model of a threshing machine made from another machine which he had seen at Wark in Northumberland. Sir Francis Kinloch had tried it several times without success and finally gave it to Meikle who tested it at speed. This was a test to destruction and one can imagine the look of horror on Kinloch's face, but the observant engineer in Meikle could see where the fault lay. He strengthened the drum and fixed scutchers or beaters to it so that the corn was beaten rather than rubbed. The rubbing action of Kinloch's machine had caused excessive friction which led to overheating when the machine speeded up. Meikle's new threshing machine, adapted from Kinloch's machine, was an immediate success, but then followed an argument about the true originator.

Most inventions are adaptations of old and sometimes defective designs; credit is usually given to the designer of the final working machine, and so the name Meikle became synonymous with this invention. His new machine separated grain from straw and threshed and winnowed it. It could be powered by horses or water-power and it handled up to forty bushels an hour (a bushel being a dry measure of 8 gallons of grain). Every corn growing area from the Borders to the Moray Firth soon had Meikle's threshing machine.

Andrew Meikle married a local lady, Marion Merilees. They had eight children and as Andrew had inherited his inventive skills from his father the same skills were passed on to his second son, George Meikle. Robert Meikle, either an elder brother or a cousin of George, though less well-known, was equally industrious in building mills throughout Scotland and in surveying an alternative route for the Forth-Clyde Canal in 1767, in collaboration with James Watt (1736-1819) of steam-engine fame. Robert died in 1780.

In 1788 Andrew Meikle now designed and made a horse-driven machine for George Rennie. He patented the invention in England that year but it had been used in East Lothian which meant that it could not be patented in Scotland. However, he started the manufacture of threshing machines in 1789 - his advertisement in the *Scots Magazine* of May 1789 -

In all its essential parts, and in the principle of its construction,
it remains as it came from the hands of its inventor.

Andrew Meikle did not make much money from his inventions or from his business. In fact, he must have come upon hard times about 1809 when Sir John Sinclair started a subscription for his relief. He raised £1500, of which £85 was given in England including £21 from his two friends James Watt of steam engine fame and John Rennie. Meikle lived his remaining two years in relative comfort; he died on 27th November 1811 at Houston Mill, aged ninety-two years and was buried in Prestonkirk graveyard at East Linton.

George Meikle was born in 1756. In 1787 he made a water-raising wheel to drain the moss of Kincardineshire for Mr Stein, a distiller and farmer of Kilbeggie in Clackmannanshire. Meikle's design was adopted instead of Whitworth's pumping-machine.

The inscription on George Meikle's gravestone (he died two days after his father) at Prestonkirk was composed by the East Lothian author Samuel Smiles *q.v.*

GEORGE MEIKLE
(d1811)
son of Andrew was also a millwright.
Besides assisting his father in working out
the details of the thrashing-machine
he invented a water-raising wheel,
which was used in draining
the moss of Kincardineshire in 1787
being adopted in preference to
Whitworth's pumping machine.
He died on 29th November 1811

JAMES MILLER

the author of 'The Lamp of Lothian'

James Miller is best known to us in East Lothian as the author of *The Lamp of Lothian or, The History of Haddington* which was first published in 1844. He was born in Dunbar in 1792, one year before the French declared war on Britain. His father, George Miller, was a publisher and bookseller who set up the first printing press in East Lothian at Dunbar in 1795. A few years later the Miller family moved to Haddington complete with printing press which he named "Lamp of Lothian" and produced Miller's "Cheap Magazine" from his small printing shop in No.5 High Street (now the Carlyle Cafe). This was a high quality monthly magazine at four pence per issue and was highly praised in the literary circles of Edinburgh.

At school in Dunbar young James Miller was soon showing signs of literary talent in his authorship of a tragedy which was staged in a garret by some of his school friends. His father, recognising his son's abilities, put him to work in the publishing department of the magazine at Haddington. James wrote and published several poems but his real interest was in history. In the little spare time he was given from his father's business he collected material for his first book, *History of Dunbar*, which was published in 1830.

At work he had to keep accounts and visit far-off customers in all the towns between Dumfries and Berwick; on one occasion he was storm-bound for three weeks at Carfrae Mill during which he composed sixty verses of a poetical narrative *The Gudewife of Tulloshill and the Lord Lauderdale*.

He had become a well-known and well-respected figure locally and was duly promoted to the Council Board. After long research in the Burgh records and charter chests he presented a record of the ancient Burgh history. A Council banquet was arranged in recognition and gratitude of his services. Miller, not knowing in advance, was so overcome and amazed that he was struck almost dumb. In reply he could only mutter that he was "much obliged."

The frequency of his attendance at Garvald Church increased markedly after he met a certain Miss Craw, a most beautiful member of that congregation. In 1820 they were married and she became his helpmate in the best sense, so much so, that the great Thomas Carlyle was heard to remark that she "assisted him in all she best could." Their happiness seemed as assured as their prosperity until he agreed to sell the writings of an East Lothian farmer. This publication was vilified in every pulpit in the County; it was too imaginative and might stir the masses, and, to add to Miller's impending downfall, he began to enjoy the conviviality of the demon drink. Sadly, he had a long way to fall. Soon he was broken, friendless and homeless; he lived in any lodgings which would accept him but during periods of sobriety he found work in various printing offices and produced occasional pieces of writing.

He was still comparatively young, at forty, when he worked steadily on his *magnum opus* - *The Lamp of Lothian.* The wood engravings of the ancient Royal Palace in Court Street (then called King Street) in Haddington and several other places of interest were the work of Adam Neill and the text was a revelation of the military, ecclesiastical and civil history of East Lothian. Miller himself set the type and made corrections but he could be short-tempered if any dared to help. He dedicated it to:

The Right Honourable THOMAS, EARL OF HADDINGTON, Baron of Binning and Byres, Lord Melrose, etc. First Lord of the Admiralty, THIS VOLUME, is inscribed, with the highest respect. By the author.

Haddington February 12, 1884.

After the subscribers had received their copies and demand had diminished the unbound sheets lay for several years until they were bought as scrap by a tobacconist who used the paper to wrap tobacco. However, in a few years it became a collectors' item and second-hand copies were sought after at £1 to £1.10s per copy (the original cost was 8s.)

After the collapse of his business he was unable to settle for any length of time at any job. Occasionally, he would disappear for weeks on end and turn up again in a dreadful state only to be helped by the kindly 9th Earl of Haddington who, taking pity on the debauched soul, supplied him with food and new clothes. The Earl used his influence several times to obtain financial help for him from the Literary Fund but ensured that sums were given in small instalments. When it was suggested to him that he might apply for parochial relief, he replied angrily, "I can make more money with a scrape of my pen in one hour than your income's worth for a month." On another sad day he was discovered lying in a stream by the sister-in-law of the Provost who remarked,

"Eh, me! but the Lamp's burnin' low the day." Immediately, she sought help from the Provost who sent two men to drag him out of the burn. They were thanked with curses and a blow with a stick. Youngsters took perverse pleasure in teasing him to hear his curses interspersed with Hebrew, Greek or Latin. As old age caught up with him his friends became his enemies, he floated in Glenlivet and somehow he dragged out his existence to end his days at Queensberry House in the Canongate of Edinburgh. Again the Earl of Haddington and a few friends organised a small annuity from the Literary Fund and he found peace and warmth while by day he wandered the streets of the Capital. Poor James Miller died, aged seventy-three, on 23rd May 1865.

[Adapted and summarised from a Biographical Sketch of James Miller by Thomas Cowan written for the 1900 edition of the *Lamp of Lothian.*]

ANDREW FLETCHER, LORD MILTON

the able co-adjutor with his friend Archibald the great Duke of Argyle

Travelling in to Edinburgh from East Lothian through Musselburgh to Joppa, the main road to the city is Milton Road which takes its name from a son of East Lothian - Andrew Fletcher, a nephew of 'The Patriot', who became Lord Milton when he succeeded Sir John Lauder of Fountainhall as a Senator of the College of Justice in 1724.

Andrew Fletcher was born at Salton Hall, the family seat in East Lothian, in 1692, the year of the Massacre of Glencoe. He was the eldest son of Henry Fletcher of Salton. His mother was an active and enterprising lady who brought, in secrecy, the art of weaving and dressing linen (called holland) from Holland to Salton; she was the daughter of Sir David Carnegie. His uncle, Andrew Fletcher *qv*, was the great statesman who resolutely opposed the Union in 1707 and left Scotland with the words,

"It [Scotland] is fit only for the slaves who sold it."

After completing his legal studies in Edinburgh young Andrew Fletcher was admitted an advocate on 26th February 1717 and nominated a cashier of the excise in 1718. He replaced James Hamilton of Pencaitland as a Lord Justiciary in 1726, was appointed a Commissioner for improving the fisheries and manufacture of Scotland, succeeded James Erskine of Grange as Lord Justice Clerk in 1735 and was appointed Principal Keeper of the Signet in 1746.

Andrew Fletcher became a Lord of Session, Lord Milton, in 1724 when he was thirty-two years of age, succeeding Sir John Lauder of Fountainhall. James Grant, in his *Old and New Edinburgh* (13 Vol. II, p. 34) describes him:

> *Andrew Fletcher of Milton....was an able coadjutor with his friend Archibald the great Duke of Argyle, during whose administration he exercised a wise control over the usually-abused Government patronage in Scotland. He sternly discouraged all informers, and was greatly esteemed for the mild and gentle manner in which he used his authority when Lord Justice Clerk after the battle of Culloden.*

Lord Milton was the judge who appeased public opinion when he presided over the trial of Captain Porteous in 1736 when he sentenced him to be hanged for murder. The background to this celebrated event in Edinburgh was the public hanging of two thieves. The City Guard, commanded by Porteous, had, on the order of Porteous, fired on threatening rioters at the hanging of a horse-stealer who, by sheer strength, had held off three guards while his accomplice made his escape. The assembled crowd were vociferously on the side of the prisoner and Porteous was furiously angry. He grabbed a gun and shot a ring-leader. He ordered his men to fire above the heads of the crowd but several people in the crowd and some gazing upon the scene from their windows were killed.

Porteous was arrested and Queen Caroline, who was acting as Regent (George II being in Germany), ordered Porteous's reprieve pending a pardon. This caused such a furore in Edinburgh that a well-armed group of rioters stormed the Tolbooth, wrested Porteous from his hiding place (he was cowering with fear in a chimney), marched him through the streets and hanged him from a dyer's pole. The Government ordered the arrest of Lord Provost Wilson who was released after three weeks and Lord Milton was examined at the bar of the House of Lords; he acquitted himself effortlessly.

Lord Islay (who became 3rd Duke of Argyle) knowing of Milton's vast knowledge of the law of Scotland and of his sound judgement, made him his confidential agent or chief executive. George II sarcastically described Islay as 'Vice Roy in Scotland'. As the uncrowned king of Scotland Islay dispensed his favours to over half of the Scottish judiciary who owed him their appointments. Milton was a prime example who acted with discretion and with leniency during and after the 1745 Rising.

In 1746 Scotland was in a thoroughly depressed state and Milton worked energetically to improve trade and agriculture. The Islay-Milton duo exerted its influence over many important institutions - the Convention of Royal Burghs, the Town Council of Edinburgh, the General Assembly of the Church of Scotland and many new boards and commissions. Their function was not so much to create new policies but to ameliorate and to pacify troubles but gradually their influence diminished. Previously, they could guarantee 30 out of the 45 Scottish Parliamentary seats for Walpole; this reduced to 19 and consequently they were powerless against the punitive laws passed in Parliament which effectively dismantled Highland society in 1746. Jacobites lost their estates and tartans and bagpipes were proscribed.

Lord Milton married Elizabeth, daughter of Sir Francis Kinloch 2nd baronet of Gilmerton. Their daughter, Miss Betty Fletcher married Captain Wedderburn of Gosford at Milton's manor-house of Brunstane in 1758. Brunstane House, originally house of Gilbertoun, was enlarged for John Maitland, Duke of Lauderdale in 1672 and was completed by William Adam for Lord Milton in 1735-44 (23 p.125).

Lord Milton was not simply a stuffy Law Lord and Chief Executive he was the beloved guardian of the six beautiful daughters of the Countess of Eglinton from the time of the death of his friend, the Earl of Eglinton. A mark of the affection in which he was held was humorously described by the daughters in their "Petition of the six vestal virgins of Eglinton" which was signed by each of them and sent to him.

Lord Milton, in spite of a long illness, continued to preside as a judge until his death, aged seventy-four, at Brunstane manor-house near Musselburgh 13th December 1766.

ROBERT MOFFAT of Ormiston

the world's foremost translator-linguist and missionary

The monument to Robert Moffat in the town centre of Ormiston, the Moffat Arms and Moffat Road, commemorate a man who, had he been alive when the first Nobel Prizes were awarded in 1901, would surely have been a recipient. The great man was Robert Moffat who, from humble beginnings as a gardener in Ormiston, became a missionary and the world's foremost translator-linguist.

As a missionary in Africa he was determined to bring Christianity to the African natives. But how do you bring the Bible to people who speak to one another in an entirely strange tongue and who neither read nor write in their own language? Robert Moffat not only learned their language, Tswana, but he mastered the dialects, Tlhaping and Rolong. He lived among the natives and studied, in minute detail, every aspect of their lives and speech. He then devised an alphabet and a grammar in each language and proceeded to teach the natives to read and to write in their own languages. But his prime purpose was to see to it that every native should be able to read the Bible in their own language. So, he set about translating the Bible. A monumental task of such proportions that Moffat became the foremost translator in the world. A feat which has gone unnoticed for generations.

Courtesy of the Killie Campbell Africana Library, Durban, South Africa

The story of Robert Moffat starts on 21st December 1795, the day of his birth in Ormiston. He was the third son of a family of seven children. His father, Robert, was firstly a ploughman at Ormiston Hall and then a customs official at Portsoy and Carron near Falkirk. His mother, Ann Gardiner, was a stern but kindly and religious lady who proved the little appreciated fact that a mother's influence on her children is of vital importance in the formation of their future accomplishments. She was determined that her children should be educated properly. Her Christian faith took her to the local minister who took on the task of teaching young Robert. He was a slow but very thorough learner but later he taught himself Latin, elementary mathematics and blacksmithing. At this stage he showed no particular bent towards academic attainment and became an apprentice gardener firstly at Polmont then at Aberdour in Fife and afterwards in Manchester where he worked for James Smith. But the religious influences of his earlier years gnawed at his heart - he was determined to become a missionary especially after listening to the preaching of the evangelist Rev. William Roby who taught young Robert the basics of theology.

The daughter of his employer, Mary Smith, shared his burning ambition. They fell deeply in love, but things were not to run smoothly for them; her father resolutely refused to allow his daughter to accompany the young, newly trained missionary to Africa. The danger of the unknown seemed a fearful risk.

Robert Moffat, having been accepted and trained by the London Missionary Society, set out alone and sailed for Cape Town in 1816. At first he was refused permission to journey to Great Namaqualand, north of the Orange River, but he used the waiting time of ten months learning to speak Dutch. This was a discovery of himself - learning another language came easily to him. At last, he was allowed to journey into the unknown and he formed an amazing friendship with the notorious freebooter Jager Afrikaner who accompanied and doubtless ensured the safety of the man he came to revere. Together they travelled over 2500 km to the far north of South-West Africa but Moffat could find little hope of setting up a mission station there and they continued their journey eastwards to Griquatown and Dithakong in Bechuanaland. This adventurous missionary suffered many privations and dangers but his knowledge of the languages and customs of the people was growing. He was a pace-setter for those to follow; it has to be appreciated that his journeys were made twenty-three years before David Livingston arrived in Africa. The tribes he encountered had never seen a white man and their cruel superstitions and human sacrifices were a continuous challenge to this intrepid man.

He returned to Capetown to a joyous reunion with his fiancee, Mary Smith. Her father, realising his daughter's sincere love for Robert Moffat, now relented in his refusal to allow her to go to Africa. The young couple were married two days after the Christmas of 1819 and settled at Dithakong. Life, however, was anything but idyllic; their mission was attacked by refugee bandits who had themselves been ravaged by the warriors of the feared and tyrannical Zulu King, Shaka. Moffat was forced to enlist the aid of Andries Waterboer's mounted riflemen to chase them off. These years, 1820 to 1828, were dishearteningly troublesome; marauding tribes harassed the mission, the local population remained aloof to Moffat's teaching and many left in fear of their lives. Then, almost as if by some miracle, peace reigned and the first baptisms took place.

The Moffat family moved on to the famous 'eye of Kuruman' where the waters of an underground river appeared on the surface. Moffat's previous training as a gardener led him, quite naturally, to use this phenomenon to irrigate the land and he taught the natives the principles of agriculture. The success of this led to a lifetime friendship with the chief of the Matabele, Mzilikazi. It was, however, a rather one-sided friendship; the chief admired Moffat to the point of reverence but Moffat, on the other hand, had often to chastise the chief for his barbaric punishments. He changed his laws to please Moffat but never became a Christian. This was an astonishing relationship when one considers that Mzilikazi, as the toughest and most vicious commander of one of Shaka's Impi (regiment), was promoted by Shaka to become the supreme commander of all his armies. Moffat kept meticulous records of his meetings with Mzilikazi between 1854 and 1859. These records were discovered in 1942 and published in 1945 to give a first hand account of the lives and customs of the natives tribes.

Moffat had been working on his translation of the Bible for several years. He had already produced a Tswana spelling and reading book to be followed by the first Tswana catechism. His Bible and other books had been printed in London but the delays worried Moffat. He therefore bought a hand-printing press and loaded it on to his ox-wagon at Cape Town for the trek to Kuruman. He had learned, from BJ van de Sandt, to set up type and to bind his newly translated Bible, a book on Bible lessons and a collection of hymns. His reputation had reached the French missionaries and he was asked to produce literature from French language to the Rolong dialect of Tswana for the Paris Evangelical Mission Society at Mothito. In November 1857 he presented his translation of the Bible to Sir George Grey, Governor of Cape Colony - this was the first full translation of the Bible in any South African language - a monumental piece of devoted work. Moffat had more than earned his place as the world's greatest translator.

He returned to Britain in 1839 to write, lecture and preach. His publications were in great demand in both English and French. It was during this 'sabbatical' that he met the young David Livingstone who was studying for his ordination in London and he persuaded Livingston to come to Africa. Moffat returned to Kuruman in 1843. By now Livingstone had explored the unknown but had been savaged by a lion and was convalescing at Kuruman. There, he was nursed by Moffat's daughter, Mary. They fell in love and married in 1844.

In 1857 Moffat again visited Chief Mzilikazi to try to persuade him to release Matsheng, the Chief of the Ngwato, who was held in military servitude. Mzilikazi, out of his immense respect for Moffat but against his better judgement, agreed and Matsheng proceeded to wreak havoc among his tribe. More trouble was in store for Moffat's proposed mission: some renegade Tlhapings attacked the Boers in the Orange Free State and because of Moffat's friendship with the tribe the Boers accused him of aiding the Tlhaping and threatened to attack Kuruman. Moffat sought the help of the Cape Governor, Sir George Grey, who in turn received assurances from President Marthinus W Pretorius that Kuruman would be left in peace and that the mission to Matabele could proceed unhindered. In August 1860 Moffat embarked on this, his last mission accompanied by his son, John S Moffat.

He preached his last sermon in Kuruman on 20th March 1870 and left his beloved Africa with a heavy heart. He and his dedicated and loyal wife Mary returned to Britain to retire but sadly she died within a year. Moffat devoted his last years to preaching throughout Britain. He worked on the revision of the New Testament and his translation of the Bible was published in 1872 when he was honoured by the University of Edinburgh with the honorary degree of Doctor of Divinity.

Tragically Moffat had suffered the deaths of several of his children. He and Mary had ten children three of whom died in infancy. His eldest daughter, Mary, who married David Livingstone, died in 1862 and he attended Livingstone's funeral at Westminster Abbey in 1874.

Robert Moffat died aged eighty-eight on 8th August 1883. He was buried beside his wife in Norwood cemetery. His life had been devoted to teaching the 'poor heathen to know the Saviour'.

Dr DAVID MACBETH MOIR

The Musselburgh Physician and author 'Delta'

David Macbeth Moir was an author as well as a busy physician in Musselburgh he wrote under the pseudonym 'Delta'. He is commemorated in Musselburgh by two street names: Macbeth Moir Road and Delta Place.

He was born on 5th January 1798 in Musselburgh. His father was Robert Moir and his mother Elizabeth Macbeth who arranged an apprenticeship under Dr Stewart of Musselburgh for their son when he was thirteen years of age. The boy had attended school at Musselburgh and he found his new work so interesting that he decided he wanted to be a surgeon. He studied medicine at the University of Edinburgh and gained his Surgeon's Diploma in 1816.

His first articles were accepted for publication by *The Cheap Magazine* in Haddington when he was a mere fourteen year old and in 1816 the *Scots Magazine* accepted his anonymous article, *The Bombardment of Algiers and other Poems*. His confidence growing, he now wrote several witty articles for the Constable Edinburgh Magazine and for *Blackwood's Magazine*. It was at this stage he signed himself 'Delta' and through Blackwood he met Professor John Wilson (1785-1854) "Christopher North" and John Galt (1779-1839), two writers of genius who were to become good friends. In fact it was Moir who wrote the last few chapters of Galt's *The Last of the Lairds*. In 1824 Moir's magazine articles were reprinted to become *The Legend of Genevieve with other Tales and Poems* and in 1829 his best remembered novel *The Autobiography of Mansie Wauch* was published from his magazine articles It was the life-story of a tailor from Dalkeith which according to Augustus Muir in his *Scottish Portrait*, 'ought never to be out of print' (44 p. 269).

In 1831 he published *Outlines of the Ancient History of Medicine* which was written as the first instalment of a complete history but a serious outbreak of cholera in Musselburgh in 1832 and the retiral of his partner, Dr Brown, added to his already considerable work load and the *History* was abandoned, but as Secretary to the Board of Health he wrote a pamphlet: *Practical Observations on Malignant Cholera* in 1832. This was followed by his publication of *Proofs of the Contagion of Malignant Cholera*.

In the autumn of 1832 he travelled to Oxford to attend the meeting of the British Association after which he travelled on to Cheltenham and London where he met his friend John Galt of whom he wrote his Memoir of Galt published in the Literary Life in 1834.

Blackwood and many of Moir's friends tried to coax him to leave Musselburgh and come to Edinburgh. In his partnership with Dr Brown of Musselburgh Moir was so busy he never ventured beyond the boundary of the town for twelve years. In 1829 Blackwood offered him the editorship of the *Quarterly Journal of Agriculture* but he was not tempted by this generous offer.

JH Dawson's *Statistical History of Scotland* of 1853 says of him:

...the distinguished 'Delta' of Blackwood's Magazine, who, amidst all the harassing duties of the medical profession, had found time to embody in many chaste and touching strains those 'high imaginings' which visit the mind of genius, as well as to stray into the paths of richest and broadest humour - witness 'Mansie Waugh's' irresistible drolleries; whose laborious history of the art which he has himself so successfully studied, forms a most valuable acquisition to the practitioner; whose songs in the recent republication of Burns's lyrics with music, take a deserved place beside those of the illustrious minstrel.... (33. p. 355)

This well-loved doctor practised medicine in Musselburgh from 1817 until he died aged 61 on 6th July 1851. He was buried at St Michael's Churchyard, Inveresk where his family gravestone inscribed:

DAVID MACBETH MOIR
born 5th January 1798
died 6th July 1851
Catherine Elizabeth Bell
his wife
born 4th June 1809
died 30th October 1889
Oswald Bell Moir
born 5th August 1847
died 22nd June 1930
also his neice
Catherine Elizabeth Orr
eldest daughter of Major General Orr
Indian Army
born 25th October 1857
died 2nd October 1936

JOHN MUIR

The John Muir Country Park, Dunbar commemorates this leading authority on forest conservation in America

It is evident that every man loves himself better than any other person, he is naturally impelled to extend his acquisitions as much as possible; and nothing can restrain him in this propensity but reflection and experience, by which he learns the pernicious effects of that licence, and the total dissolution of society which must ensue from it.

David Hume (1711-1776)

These words, by Scotland's greatest philosopher and historian, might well have been reiterated in 1867, one hundred years after they were written, by John Muir himself after he witnessed the wanton destruction of his beloved forests in America.

John Muir Country Park is an eight-mile, 1760-acre stretch of coastal magnificence at Dunbar and commemorates the man who was proclaimed 'East Lothian's Man of the Millennium'*, the intrepid explorer and ecologist who saved the Yosemite Valley in America from destruction.

The John Muir Country Park is Scotland's largest 'Site of Special Scientific Interest' and was named after a Dunbar boy, John Muir, who was to become the leading authority on forest conservation in America. He would undoubtedly have approved of the care in conserving the flora and fauna as well as the ornithology of this special environment in which visitors, sportsmen and scientists are encouraged.

John Muir was born in 126/128 High Street, Dunbar on 21st April 1838, but there was nothing romantic or sentimental about his life in Dunbar; it was hard and harsh. This was partly due to his father's uncompromising discipline over his family of five daughters and three sons of which John was the eldest son. His strict father was Daniel Muir who had been an army recruiting sergeant. His first wife was a rich heiress who helped him to buy himself out of the army. After she died he married Anne Gilrye in 1833; she was John Muir's mother.

The Muir household was a regime of rigid discipline. After school John's father insisted on additional homework and long hours of Bible reading; each child had to memorise several verses each day and failure to recite them was punished with regular whipping.

Fortunately, his mother was a lady of loving kindness who, when she knew that young John was 'in for a hiding', would sneak him off to bed before her husband returned home; he was not so cruel as to waken a sleeping boy for punishment. But life was not completely miserable;

* As published in *East Lothian - Focus News from your Council*, Summer 1999

walks with his grandfather to Lord Lauderdale's gardens gave the boy his first glimpses of the marvels of nature.

The first eleven years of his life in Dunbar may have been unpleasant at times but worse was to come in America after the Muir family emigrated there in 1849. They lived at Fountain Lake, Wisconsin. John Muir tells of his early life in his *The Story of My Boyhood and Youth* which was published the year before he died in 1914. His father had bought a farm and young John was put to work. Not one hour of daylight must be lost. As a small boy the most arduous of hard labour was demanded of him - rail splitting, fencing, ploughing, hoeing maize, etc. In 1855 the Muirs moved to Hickory Hill. Yet another farm had to be worked with unrelenting labour, but in spite of this young John Muir had developed a thirst for knowledge and, incredible though it may seem to a school pupil today, he asked permission of his tyrannical father if he might be allowed to study during the early hours of each morning. His father agreed on condition that he got to work at daybreak. In order to waken himself the boy invented a machine which tilted him out of bed in the middle of the night to give him a few hours of study. In this way he gained sufficient knowledge for entry to the University of Wisconsin in 1860.

Statue of young John Muir in Dunbar; sculpted by Valentin Znoba, 1997.

John Muir found the prescriptive curriculum of the medical course too restrictive for his fertile mind and he chose subjects which interested him - chemistry, geology and especially botany. He continued to work on his inventions and exhibited some of them at the Wisconsin State Fair. The penalty he paid for choosing his own subjects was his degree; he left the university without it.

In 1867, while working in a wagon factory, he accidentally injured his eye. He gave up his inventions and instead he decided to devote the rest of his life to 'the inventions of God' - nature. He explored the country which he described in his *A Thousand-Mile Walk to the Gulf.*

In fact, he reached Cuba and his journal gives detailed descriptions of the flora and forests and makes observations on man's attitudes to nature - largely unfavourable. In 1868 he travelled to San Francisco and worked on a sheep ranch to finance his exploration of the Yosemite Valley; this occupied him for the next six years. He was appalled by the destruction which had been perpetrated by man and he resolved to campaign for the conservation of this magnificent valley. Another of his all-consuming interests was glacial erosion and he travelled to Alaska to study the glaciers, one of which, the Muir Glacier, was named after him.

On his return, in 1880, he met, fell in love and married Louie Wanda Strentzel, the only surviving daughter of Dr John Strentzel who had escaped the Polish revolution of 1830 to settle in America. Dr Strentzel had become an expert in horticulture and leased part of his Californian fruit ranch to the young couple. John and Louie worked hard for the next ten years to make a success of the ranch which he bought from his father-in-law. The Muir family then settled in Martinez, a delightful town north of San Francisco. His house today is the *John Muir National Historic Site* and the town is appropriately designated a "Sister City" of Dunbar.

At this stage of his life he had little time for travel or writing but his aim was to save sufficient money to pursue his real work - conservation. In 1891 he sold part of his ranch and leased the rest. He was now able to provide for his wife and two daughters while he explored his glaciers; happily, with the full support of his family.

He was the first to show that the Yosemite Valley had been formed by glacial erosion; this was contrary to the scientific opinion of his day. He discovered the residual glaciers in the Sierra Nevada and other great glaciers in Alaska. He studied trees, especially sequoias and pines, not only in America but in Australia, Africa and South America. The fact that the giant redwoods are a conserved species is due entirely to John Muir.

In 1889 John Muir and Robert Johnson, an editor of the *Century Magazine*, went on a camping trip to the Yosemite and Muir showed him the damage caused by vast herds of sheep and indiscriminate tree-felling. Johnson suggested that they should collaborate to campaign to have the Yosemite designated a National Park. With Muir's expertise and Johnson's flair for publicity they gained the support of influential men throughout America. The result was the passage of the Yosemite National Park Bill through Congress in October 1890, and, not content with this, another Bill of 1891 empowered the President to create forest reserves. A National Commission was appointed 'to inquire into the fearful wastage of forests, to make a survey of existing forest lands in public ownership, and to recommend measures for their conservation'.

John Muir was delighted. In 1896 (exactly twenty years after he had first proposed the formation of a National Commission), he was invited by the Commission's Chairman, Charles S Sargent, to accompany the survey team - he was a natural choice. He had already published his *Mountains of California* and his *alma mater*, the University of Wisconsin, had honoured him with an honorary doctorate. In 1897, as a result of Muir's work and the Commission's recommendations, President Cleveland created thirteen forest reservations totalling 21 million acres. But there were enemies of conservation whose commercial interests led them to oppose and to have the reservations annulled - they failed because John F Lacey, the chairman of the Public Lands Commission, placed Muir's judgement ahead of all others. This established Muir as the acknowledged leader of the forest conservation movement in USA.

During President Theodore Roosevelt's first term of office he asked John Muir to take him on a short camping trip to the Yosemite. Impressed by Muir's easy conversation, quick repartee, subtle humour and, most of all, his absolute sincerity, the President created another 148 million acres of forest reserves during the next six years and to Muir's delight he doubled the number of National Parks.

John Muir, never satisfied that he had done enough, fought valiantly to save the stunningly beautiful Hetch-Hetchy Valley from flooding. He was saddened when it was converted into a huge reservoir. John Muir was honoured many times for his dedicated work in conservation: he was Fellow of the American Association for the Advancement of Science, a Member of the American Academy of Arts and Sciences and he received honorary degrees from the universities of Harvard, Wisconsin, Yale and California. Parks, lakes, gorges, a glacier, passes, mountain peaks, trails and a college all bear his name. A butterfly, *Thecla muiri* and a plant, *Ivesia muiri*, found in the Sierras, have been named after him and a 5c postage stamp was issued in 1965 to commemorate his great achievements.

After his wife's death in 1905 he published four books including *Stickeen* (1909), a loving appreciation of his faithful mongrel dog, My *First Summer in the Sierra* (1911), *The Yosemite* (1912) and *The Story of my Boyhood and Youth* (1913).

He died in his beloved Martinez in 1914 having struggled for most of his life to save the forests of the West from man's insatiable and pernicious propensity to ruin natural beauty. His letters illustrate the heartbreak of his struggle; he died not a little sad being dissatisfied that he not achieved more - this in spite of his great achievements to mankind. He was buried beside his wife in Martinez.

ALEXANDER MUIRHEAD
of Barleymills, Saltoun
the co-inventor of radio

We have all been taught that the inventor of radio was Guglielmo Marchese Marconi (1874-1937) and it is true that he was hailed as such when he patented his system of practical radio signalling and formed his Wireless Telegraph Company in 1897. However, a Scottish engineer, scientist and inventor, Dr Alexander Muirhead, is now recognised with Sir Oliver Lodge (1851-1940) as the true inventor of radio.

Their experiment in sending a Morse code message over the 'air' from a physics laboratory at the Oxford University to a room in another building approximately sixty metres apart took place only ten weeks after Muirhead had listened with rapt attention to Lodge's memorial lecture on Hertzian Waves on 14th August 1894 at the Royal Institution in London. This was two years before Marconi had demonstrated electric telegraphy on Salisbury Plain. The Muirhead/Lodge experiment was successfully recreated on 15th May 2000 at an exhibition at Oxford University to commemorate the pioneering work of these two great men. At last the academic establishment have given their full recognition to Muirhead and Lodge.

Courtesy of Oxford University Museum of Natural History

Alexander Muirhead was the second son of a family of six children. He was born at Barleymills in the village of Saltoun in May 1848. His father, John Muirhead, was a tenant farmer and his mother was Margaret Muirhead nee Lauder. As a child his nurse dropped him on his head while crossing a bridge on the farm and the fall caused his total deafness in one ear with partial deafness in the other for the rest of his life. It was this handicap and his continual questioning of everything he observed during his boyhood which led his parents to believe that he was a backward child. Even his boyish experiments seemed to confirm his oddity; he would bury small items, such as a spade or a poker, in the garden to see if they would grow! Little did they realise that his curiosity and his childish experimentation were the prelude to brilliant scientific work.

His father's real interest was in science rather than farming. He left his farm in the 1850s and moved the family to London where he employed a tutor for young Alexander. Meanwhile, John Muirhead had become involved with the cable telegraphy business which was being rapidly expanded after Samuel Morse received a huge grant from the American government in 1847 for a telegraph line between Washington and Baltimore.

To the surprise of the Muirhead family young Alexander made excellent progress under his new tutor and his father now encouraged the boy to study chemistry and engineering rather than his first preference, medicine. To quote Alexander's great-great nephew, Patrick Muirhead: "Alexander was unsure of what to do until, one night in bed, he sensed the blood pulsing in his temple which seemed to spell out in Morse Code the word electricity. His future was instantly decided."

Alexander continued his studies and after gaining a first class honours degree he took his Doctorate of Science at London University. A powerful influence in his students days was that of his mathematics professor whose insistence on accuracy was exemplified with the words: "to mislead another is a greater crime than to murder, for killing stops with its accomplishment, whereas to state what is not true is to spread errors that may lead generations astray." This rigorous and disciplined approach would lead to Alexander's reluctance to publish his scientific work until he was confident of 'absolute accuracy' (88).

Alexander joined his father's cable telegraphy company and soon made his presence felt with several new innovations the most notable of which was his invention of the *duplex* system in which two-way signals could be sent over a telegraph line simultaneously.

On 14th August 1894 Alexander attended a lecture to commemorate the life of Heinrich Hertz (1857-1894), the German physicist, given at the Royal Institution in London by the eminent physicist Sir Oliver Lodge. His subject was *Herzian Waves* and Alexander realised immediately that with his expertise in cable telegraphy and Lodge's vast knowledge of Hertzian waves their collaboration could lead to a new discovery in electrical telegraphy - radio signalling. Within ten weeks of the memorial lecture Muirhead and Lodge demonstrated their 'wireless' apparatus by sending a radio message between two buildings approximately sixty metres apart at Oxford University - the date is important - 1st June 1894.

This was indeed a scientific breakthrough but the two scientists simply regarded it as an experiment and considered that it needed additional work before it could be patented. They had used their own money to finance their project and wanted to perfect their invention before releasing it to the public. They sought neither fame nor fortune, they were scientists and gentlemen whose quest was for truth through experimentation; scientific precision was a matter of honour.

At the meeting of the British Association for the Advancement of Science held at Oxford on 14th August 1894 Lodge and Muirhead demonstrated again what was regarded as the world's first radio transmission by sending a morse code signal over a short distance. They registered an electrical telegraphy patent on 23rd April 1895 but probably because they considered it to be capable of improvement they suspended it. Two years passed before Lodge wrote to Muirhead:

> *May 4th, 1897*
>
> *Dear Muirhead,*
>
> *Let us go shares over this entire business if you feel inclined to take pains and trouble about making it a working telegraph scheme. My own notion was rather to leave that to others and meanwhile to secure some sort of a bottom patent for the main ideas which have to be applied subsequently in detail. I want to be considerably guided by you whose interests, just as much as mine, are mixed up with the question, and without whom I should be helpless to do anything practical in the matter.* (88)

Lodge's lecture of 1st June 1894 on Hertzian waves had been published and was widely read in the scientific communities world-wide. In Italy Gugliemo Marchese Marconi (1874-1937), although not a scientist, quickly visualised the commercial possiblities of 'wireless' and after explaining his proposals to the Post Office in Britain he received generous sponsorship. He registered his first patent on 2nd June 1896 and demonstrated his apparatus on Salisbury Plain, two years **after** the Muirhead/Lodge demonstration at Oxford and over one year **after** the Muirhead/Lodge patent. Marconi's demonstration was given much publicity and hailed as a completely new discovery. When the Marconi supporters made further rather exaggerated claims Lodge was prompted to write to The Times:

Sir, It appears that many persons suppose that the method of signalling across space by means of Hertz waves ...is a new discovery by senor Marconi who has recently been engaged in improving some of the details. It is well known to physicists and perhaps the public may be willing to share the information that I myself showed what was essentially the same plan of signalling in 1894. (88)

This was the start of a long dispute over patents. Lodge applied for an extension of his 1897 patent and won, thus making Marconi's patent of 1900 illegal. Marconi could not now expand his business world wide. He was now forced to offer to buy the Muirhead/Lodge patent. This was a clear admission that Muirhead and Lodge were the first to invent radio and Marconi's offer to buy was accepted. The Muirhead/Lodge business was now wound up.

Alexander married at the age of forty-five. He had no family and he died at Shortlands in Kent on 13th December 1920 aged 72. He was buried beside his father and mother and his two brothers in West Norwood Cemetery, London. The family vault is identified by its 25-foot grey granite obelisk and the inscription reads:

Sacred to the Memory of
JOHN MUIRHEAD and MARGARET
and their eldest son
JOHN
and their second son
ALEXANDER, Doctor of Science,
Fellow of the Royal Society,
died December 13th, 1920 age 72
highly esteemed and much beloved

To quote his great-great nephew, Patrick Muirhead, who said at the end of a BBC Radio 4 broadcast *Making Radio Waves* on 15th May 2000:

'His maxim was "absolute accuracy" and therein was his failing. Possibly had he not been such a stickler for accuracy, had he expounded his theories more loudly earlier, then perhaps he'd be the one remembered today and not Marconi' (88).

WILLIAM NICOL FRSE of Humbie

Scientist, Inventor and Collector

William Nicol, born in Humbie about 1776, became well-known in Scotland and England through his popular lectures on science, a subject he never tired of promoting. However, his important contribution to science was his invention, at the age of eighty, of his prism which made it possible, for the first time, to identify minerals by optical means. But it was his pioneering work in the preparation of thin slices or sections of fossils and minerals for use with the microscope which laid the foundations of the science of minerology and petrology.

Little is known of William Nicol's childhood at Humbie except that he was the son of Walter Nicol and his wife Marion (nee Fowler) of Humbie. The geatest influence on young William appears to have been his astonishment and wonder on hearing a public lecture on the subject of science presented by his uncle, Henry Moyes (1749-1807), who was blind. This so inspired the boy, he decided to follow in his uncle's footsteps and to become his assistant.

Dr Henry Moyes of Edinburgh (left) and William Nicol. Engraving by William Ward from the portrait of John Rubens Smith, 1806. Courtesy of The British Museum ©

Whether or not the inspiring Dr Henry Moyes was a blood relation is unknown and young William may have adopted him as an uncle to become his devoted and conscientious assistant at the age of fifteen, when, in 1786, Moyes had returned from a successful lecture tour in America.

Moyes not only taught the intelligent William Nicol but he valued his assistance before and during his lectures; young William became his eyes. It was during a series of lectures at Doncaster in December 1807 that Moyes became suddenly ill and died. The local newspaper printed a glowing appreciation and offered for sale prints of a portrait by John Rubens Smith and engraved by William Ward of Moyes and Nicol both seated with Nicol reading to his blind mentor.

Although grievously saddened by the loss of his wise and generous teacher, William Nicol, now aged twenty-six, decided to continue the good works of Moyes by giving his own lectures on science. He returned to Edinburgh to settle the affairs of his uncle. Nicol is not mentioned in the Will and he purchased Moyes's 'Philosophical Apparatus' valued at £11.8.2 (72 p.125) with the intention of completing the interrupted lecture series in Doncaster. Such was the success of this he was reported as a worthy successor to Dr Moyes in the local press and was invited to repeat the series of lectures in Nottingham. He repeated his set of twenty-two lectures at Sheffield, Derby, Leeds, Lincoln, Nottingham and Edinburgh. The newly created Mechanics' Institutes, founded by Leonard Horner (1785-1864), welcomed his lectures and in Edinburgh he was elected a Fellow of the Royal Society (FRSE) in 1838.

Nicol befriended the Professor of Natural History at Edinburgh University, Robert Jameson (1774-1854), who had founded the Wernerian Natural History Society in Edinburgh. Jameson was a strong supporter of the work of the German scientist AG Werner who had propounded the theory of the origin of rocks through sedimentary action. Nicol gave several lectures to the Society between 1814 and 1835 and his papers were published along with those for the British Association for the Advancement of Science. Being impressed with Nicol's work Professor Jameson encouraged Nicol to accept a professorship at the university but Nicol refused the offer on the grounds that his earnings were already more than he would earn as a professor and that whilst his present work is 'a mere amusement the other would harass my soul with destructive anxiety' (72 p.127). Clearly, he preferred to be free to travel and to pursue his own interests.

He settled in Edinburgh at the age of fifty to concentrate on publishing his papers and to organise his collection of minerals. It was about this time that Jedburgh born Sir David Brewster (1781-1868), the famous researcher on the polarisation of light and inventor of the kaleidoscope, consulted Nicol and acknowledged his help. Nicol published a short but vitally important paper announcing his optical 'prism'. It was hardly noticed at the time and little use of it was made during his lifetime. However, the nineteen year-old James Clerk Maxwell, about to leave Edinburgh in 1850 to take up his studies in mathematics at Cambridge, took Nicol's (polarizing) prisms with him having been presented with them by the inventor himself (78 pps.170-177). The Edinburgh pioneer photographer William Henry Fox Talbot (1800-1877) used the prism in his early microscope and Henry Clifton Sorby

FRS (1826-1908), the chemist and geologist, also used and acknowledged Nicol's prism. In addition, Sorby used another of Nicol's clever inventions: that of Nicol's thin-section technique in which he had pioneered the new and technically advanced method of preparing thin sections of minerals and fossils for examination under the microscope. However, the geological experts of the day had insufficient knowledge to use the prisms in identifying minerals from the optical characteristics of their crystal structures.

Another of Nicol's consuming interests was conchology - the study of molluscs and their shells. Such was the vastness of his collection that the Zoologist James Wilson (1775-1856) in his *Illustrations of Zoology* named one of Nicol's shells *Conus Nicolli* in 1831; it became known simply as 'Nicol's Cone' (72 p.128).

This inspiring lecturer, inventor and collector from Humbie died in September 1851 and his collection of shells can be found in the Royal Scottish Museum in Edinburgh.

CHARLES NISBET

of Long Yester and Dickinson College, New Jersey

Is it a coincidence, or was the environment of Calvinist scholarship in Gifford and Long Yester such that two men who lived within a mile of each other followed almost identical paths of distinction in theology and scholarship? The Rev John Witherspoon (1723-94) and the Rev. Charles Nisbet (1728-1804) were the men in question. Witherspoon was the son of the local minister and Nisbet the son of the local schoolmaster. Both were called to the ministry, both were strict Calvinists, both went to America, both were sympathetic to the Revolutionary cause, both settled in America and became, indeed they were begged to become, Principals of colleges - Witherspoon of Princeton and Nisbet of Dickinson.

Charles Nisbet was born at Long Yester on 21st January 1728, where his father, William Nisbet, was the schoolmaster. Young Charles was sent to the High School in Edinburgh whereas his contemporary, John Witherspoon, was sent to the Grammar School in Haddington but both completed their degree level education at the University of Edinburgh. Charles Nisbet graduated at the age of eighteen years and continued his studies at Divinity Hall for the next six years. He was licenced to preach by the Edinburgh Presbytery in September 1760 and for the next two years he preached at the Gorbals in Glasgow. His first charge, in 1764, was at Montrose and soon he was to become an influential voice at the General Assembly of the Church of Scotland. In 1766 he married Anne Tweedie, daughter of Thomas Tweedie of Quarter, near Motherwell.

The American War of Independence had many sympathisers in Britain; Charles Nisbet was ardent in defence of the American cause. Nisbet and others like him were none too popular but they questioned the morality, if not the right of the British Government to impose heavy taxes to pay for the 10,000 British troops garrisoned there. Nisbet's sympathies, his excellence in scholarship and his strict Calvinistic theology brought him to the attention of Benjamin Rush (1745-1813) who had, in 1766, already recruited John Witherspoon. Nisbet had visited America where his preaching carried a clear message of sympathy for the American Colonies as a result of which he was made a Doctor of Divinity of the College of New Jersey in 1783. Benjamin Rush and John Dickinson now prevailed upon him to accept the Presidency (Principalship) of the newly established college - Dickinson College at Carlisle, Pennsylvania which had received its charter in 1783. Nisbet had not forgotten his responsibilities at home and needed considerable persuasion before he accepted this new challenge. His standing at home had become the subject of some speculation and discomfort. He had absented himself from his charge at Montrose for some time and it was deemed desirable on 5th October 1785 to declare it vacant.

He brought an entirely new kind of teaching to America; he was a first rate classical scholar and his lectures on logic, belle-lettres (elegant literature including poetry, fiction, criticism and aesthetics) and philosophy were new innovations. Apart from his excellence as a classical scholar he had a phenominal memory. He could recite the whole of Virgil's epic poem *Aeneid* and Edward Young's *Night Thoughts on Life, Death and Immortality*. He remained President (Principal) of Dickinson until his sudden death on 18th January 1804. Nisbet left no published works of any importance. Some of his notes were published as a 'Memoir' by Samuel Miller in 1806 and his extensive library was presented by his grandson to the Theological Seminary at Princeton thus completing the East Lothian connection.

SIR JOHN NISBET of Dirleton, Lord Dirleton

Sir John Nisbet of Dirleton, as Lord Advocate of Scotland during the reign of Charles II, was a loyal servant of the crown but a detested and despised tyrant as far as the Covenanters were concerned. His reputation for cruel and cunning 'justice' almost equalled that of his illustrious successor, Sir George Mackenzie ('Bluidy Mackenzie').

John Nisbet made his early reputation as an erudite and eloquent lawyer during his defence of the Marquis of Montrose when the latter was imprisoned in Edinburgh Castle for his abandonment of the Covenanters' cause and his support of the detested Charles I. Nisbet pleaded his case with eloquence and legal expertise, obtained the release of Montrose and enhanced his reputation in the eyes of the crown. This defence of Montrose in 1641 was to stand him in good stead in later years but after the execution of Charles and during the Interregnum, when Cromwell occupied Scotland, Nisbet had to maintain a low profile especially as Montrose became the scourge of the anti-royalists to the great anger of Cromwell. Charles I was executed in 1649 and to show the slightest support in defence of Montrose after his capture in 1650 would have been tantamount to professional suicide and even worse, an accusation of treason which would in turn have meant imprisonment and death.

John Nisbet's father, Patrick Nisbet, was an ordinary lord of session with the title Lord Eastbank. He was knighted by the king's commissioner, the Marquis of Hamilton, in 1638. John was born on 1st July 1610 and followed in his father's footsteps by studying civil law. He was admitted to the Faculty of Advocates on 30th November 1633. This was a momentous year in Edinburgh; Charles I had been on the throne for eight years and had at last decided to come to Scotland to be crowned. That year he made Edinburgh a City and decreed its recognition as Capital of Scotland.

John Nisbet's law practice in the capital grew and in 1639, a year after the signing of the National Covenant, he was appointed Sheriff-Depute of the County. He was the obvious choice of the Marquis of Montrose in his defence against the charge of treason against the Covenant and an accusation as one of the 'Plotters' in 1641. Nisbet defended him with the competence of a seasoned lawyer and obtained his release.

Nisbet was horrified when the execution of Charles I was announced at the Mercat Cross of Edinburgh on 30th January 1649 and after Montrose was finally defeated and captured in 1650 his defence was impossible; he had already been condemned to death and Nisbet dared not speak out for him.

Cromwell's rule over most of Scotland was detested but unchallenged for the next nine years. He died in 1658 and Charles II returned to Scotland in 1660, having been crowned at Scone in 1651. Charles had been forced to accept the Covenant at his crowning but now he hated the Covenanters as much as his father had done and Nisbet now began his persecution of them as crown prosecutor.

Nisbet's law practice became very successful so much so that he could easily afford to purchase the estate and castle of Dirleton. Its previous owner was Lord Dirleton of the Maxwell family who was a zealous Royalist and lost his estate during Cromwell's occupation when the castle was destroyed.

On 14th October 1664 Sir John Nisbet was appointed Lord Advocate and was simultaneously raised to the Bench as Lord Dirleton. His dual appointment was the last time that the Lord Advocate of Scotland simultaneously served as a Judge. As the King's Advocate he administered the law as his own instrument of punishment and persecution against the Covenanters; he had the protection and complete support of the crown. By 1666 the Covenants had been declared unlawful but, heedless of their danger, the Covenanters attended the services of the 'outed' ministers. The simple expedient of passing an Act to make it unlawful for ministers to come within twenty miles of their Parishes led to open rebellion, firstly at Dumfries, then in Ayrshire and in Lanark.

The Covenanters marched towards Edinburgh but were routed at Rullion Green in the Pentland Hills by the King's army under the command of Sir Thomas Dalziel. Fifty of them were killed and another fifty taken prisoner. Nisbet put them on trial in their absence and pronounced their death sentences. Knowing perfectly well that this was contrary to law, he prevailed upon the Scottish Parliament to pass an Act in retrospect to change the law to suit this injustice.

Nisbet was now the most feared of the judiciary; stories of his legal skullduggery spread and the law of Scotland was in disgrace. The Scottish church historian, Robert Woodrow, added to Nisbet's unsavoury legal reputation in his *Sufferings of the Church of Scotland, 1660-88* with the story of the case against Robert Gray who was accused of treason. During cross-examination Gray refused to divulge the whereabouts of his fellow Covenanters. Nisbet, without a qualm, ordered the gold ring on Gray's finger to be removed and to be sent to his wife to assure her 'that her husband had revealed all that he knew, and had sent the ring to her as a token that she might do the same' (13 Vol. II p.10). The unsuspecting lady revealed all that she knew and when Robert Gray was informed of this he became so disgusted and depressed he died soon afterwards.

Most of the stories against Nisbet were of course told by enemies of the state. The king and Parliament thought highly of him and in 1670 he was appointed a Royal Commissioner and sent to London to give advice on the proposal to unite the English and Scottish Parliaments. Nisbet was completely against such a proposal and clashed with Charles Maitland, brother of the all-powerful Lauderdale. He was now expected to resign his high office and, because of his refusal to do so, the establishment now conspired against him. He was accused of bribery in the case against his cousin who had been accused of perjury before the Privy Council. Nisbet was alleged to have advised his cousin to pay off his accusers but there was no proof of such action. In the case of the Leven estates, Nisbet was now accused by Lord Hatton, brother of the Duke of Queensberry and a strong supporter of the Union of Parliaments, of taking fees from both sides. During the investigation which followed Nisbet could foresee the outcome. He could no longer depend upon the support of his judicial colleagues and he decided to resign. Only one steadfast friend stuck by him, Sir George Mackenzie. He had been asked to succeed Nisbet but Sir George refused the appointment and offered to fight the case against Nisbet. However, Nisbet held to his resignation and in 1677 Sir George was to become an even greater scourge of the Covenanters and became known as 'Bluidy Mackenzie'.

Sir John Nisbet, Lord Dirleton, retired to his estates at Dirleton and died in 1687 at his house in the Canongate of Edinburgh. Opinions for and against him differ widely. Omod in his *Lord Advocates* castigated him:

> *At a time when bad men were common, he was one of the worst; and it does not appear that, in the course of his public career, he ever did one deed which lightens the darkness of his servile and mercenary life.*

Gilbert Burnet, on the other hand, painted an entirely different picture in his *History of the Reformation: Nisbet was one of the worthiest and most learned men of his age.*

ROBERT NOBLE of East Linton

East Lothian seems always to have been a magnet for artists the foremost of whom was Robert Noble RSA whose richly coloured oil paintings of East Linton simply gushed from his brush. His introduction to East Lothian is thought to have been through his friend and fellow artist Charles Martin Hardie (1858-1916) who was born at East Linton and who shared the Noble studio at No. 5 Picardy Place in Edinburgh.

Other painters, his contemporaries in East Lothian, included his cousin James Campbell Noble who lived and painted at Coldingham, Robert McGregor the painter of people at work, Robert Hope the portrait painter who turned his talent to painting the doocots, mills and cottages of East Lothian, William Millar Frazer whose paintings of East Linton and the surrounding countryside spanned an 80-year period from 1880 (he lived to the ripe old age of 97) and William Ferguson the bicycling caravan dweller who lived near Knowes Mill, to mention only a few. Other painters influenced by Noble to come to East Lothian for shorter periods included, Austin Brown, Joseph Farquharson, Coutts Michie, James Paterson, Grosvenor Thomas and Fiddes Watt.

Robert Noble RSA

The most dedicated and constant of the landscape painters of East Lothian was Edinburgh born **Robert Noble** who lived and worked in East Linton for 30 years. His parents lived in a tenement at Abbeyhill in Edinburgh and Robert's father, Thomas Noble, was a blacksmith at the railway workshops of St Margaret's (on the site of which now stands Meadowbank House). His mother Janet Ingles, from Carrington in Midlothian, was the daughter of a farm labourer and they had eight children of which Robert was the second child, born on 17th January 1857.

Robert, with his elder brother James, worked at St Margaret's. His cousin **James Campbell Noble** lived almost next door and was to have a lasting influence on Robert's life and future career. James Campbell Noble was eleven years older than Robert and was employed by the lithographer J O Brown as a draughtsman. He took over the business for a few years after Brown died and he studied part time at the Trustees School and the Royal Scottish Academy. Robert followed in his footsteps becoming an apprentice lithographer in 1871 and a student at the Trustees School. He was a co-winner of the Keith prize in the RSA class for the best student painting in the RSA's annual exhibition and in 1877 he had his first full exhibition at the RSA when he sold *The Young Bird-catcher* for the princely sum of £6 (a month's pay had he remained a lithographer). When cousin James exhibited his work at the studio in Picardy Place Robert worked at the studio and exhibited there himself from 1880 to 1884.

Like all aspiring young artists Robert Noble visited Paris. During his first visit in 1879 he attended the life class of Carolus Duran. He was to return to Paris several times and he exhibited his landscapes of the French scene between 1879 and 1886.

On his return from Paris in 1886 he married Christian Greig, the daughter of the Provost of Methil in Fife and the happy couple decided to settle firstly at Drylawhill Farm just north of East Linton where his first son was born. He merged effortlessly into the life of the village through his membership of the Tyneside Curling Club of which he became secretary. He was a keen angler and enjoyed golf. His house in Preston Road became the focal point of painters. There he heartily welcomed many visiting artists who had been attracted to the area by his paintings. Such was his love of East Linton he rarely ventured beyond the county boundary, but his paintings from Surrey were exhibited at the RSA in 1894 and 1896. In Fife his *Falkland Palace, St. Monans Kirk, The Burn Mill Leven* and *The Saw Mill Leven* were exhibited in 1900. However, from 1888 his paintings of East Linton, Prestonkirk and the Tyne were his favourite studies. His *Preston Mill* and *At Prestonkirk* were soon exhibited at the Royal Scottish Academy and in the next twenty-nine years he had over one hundred East Linton paintings exhibited at the RSA. In 1900 his reputation had spread and he was awarded a bronze medal at the Paris International Exhibition.

In 1891 he was elected the first President of the newly-formed Society of Scottish Artists; he was elected an Associate of the RSA in 1892 and became a full Academician in 1903, again following in the footsteps of his cousin James Campbell Noble who had attained RSA five years earlier.

Robert Noble's death was sudden. One spring day in May 1917 he was seen at his easel in the countryside and the next day he was dead. The loss to his family and to the community was devastating. He was sixty years of age when he died at his home in Preston Road, East

Linton and was buried in Prestonkirk graveyard at East Linton.
The Noble family gravestone is inscribed:

Robert Noble, R.S.A.
born January 27th 1857 died May 12th 1917

Christian Balfour Greig, wife
born October 18th 1859 died April 2nd 1924

Isobel Margaret Noble
daughter
born September 14th 1889 died December 27th 1913

William Balfour Noble, son
Lieutenant The Royal Scots
born June 28th 1891 died December 25th 1918
at Matlock, Derbyshire from illnes contracted
on active service
in the Great War 1914, 1918

MARGARET OLIPHANT nee Wilson

Mrs Margaret Oliphant by Janet Mary Oliphant (Courtesy of the Scottish National Portrait Gallery)

The East Lothian novelist Margaret Wilson was born in Wallyford, near Musselburgh on 4th April 1828, the daughter of Francis Wilson and Margaret Oliphant. Her childhood was spent in Glasgow and Liverpool. At the age of twenty-one years she had her first literary success with her first novel *Passages in the Life of Mrs Margaret Maitland*; its keen perception of the Scottish character were so popular it ran to three editions. Two years later, in 1851, she wrote *Caleb Field* which was followed by *Merkland* in the same year.

When that favourite literary journal of its day, Blackwood's Magazine, decided to serialise her next novel, *Katie Stewart*; this was the start of a life-long and successful relationship. Blackwoods was an old established publishing house which conducted its business from No.17 Princes Street, Edinburgh and Margaret Oliphant joined several distinguished writers who contributed to it. These included Professor John Wilson ("Christopher North"), Sir Walter Scott, Henry Mackenzie (the Man of Feeling), J McCrie, Sir David Brewster, Thomas de Quincey, Thomas Hamilton, Professor William E. Aytoun, John Gibson Lockhart, Samuel Warren, James Hogg ("The Ettrick Shepherd"), David Macbeth Moir (*qv*) and many others.

On 4th May 1852 she married her artist cousin, Francis William Oliphant, and they lived in London. She had three children and continued writing as industriously as before, producing several novels which were serialised in Blackwood's: *A Quiet Heart* (1854), *Zaidee* (1856) and *The Athelings* (1857).

Following the death of her husband in 1857 she was left with considerable debts and in order to pay them off and support her children she took on a formidable programme of work in writing novels on English provincial life. This was a series of seven novels entitled *The Chronicles of Carlingford* (1863-1876): *Salem Chapel* (1863), *The Rector and the Doctor's Family* (1863), *The Perpetual Curate* (1864), *Miss Marjoribanks* (1866) and the last in the series, *Phoebe Junior* (1876). She adopted the style of Anthony Trollope who considered that "a novel should give a picture of common life enlived by humour and sweetened by pathos."

At an early stage of this series she suffered the death of her daughter (1864) and her sister-in-law. Her widowed brother was left with four children and she took over their care. The added pressures on her time affected her writing which from then on did not receive the critical acclaim of her earlier novels. However, her output was prodigious; she wrote over one hundred novels, thirty works of non- fiction including her *Autobiography and Letters* published posthumously in 1899 and over two hundred articles for Blackwood's Magazine (52 Vol.I p.537).

She died in London on 25th June 1897 and is commemorated by means of a brass plaque between those of the poet Robert Fergusson (1751-1774) and Professor of Greek John Stuart Blackie (1809-95) in St Giles Cathedral, Edinburgh.

JOHN PETTIE RSA

John Pettie was born at the artists' paradise of East Linton on 17th March 1839 where his parents, Alexander and Alison Pettie, had settled after they left Edinburgh. Although his father was a successful tradesman who might well have expected his son to follow his trade he was wise in encouraging young John in his love of painting.

After his early education in Haddington, John Pettie became a pupil of Robert Scott Lauder (1803-1869), the inspiring teacher at the Trustees' Academy of Edinburgh who taught his students to use their imagination as well as their brushes and paints. Lauder was well-known for his paintings of imagined subjects from the works of Sir Walter Scott and from Scripture. Several of Lauder's students would become distinguished painters: William Orchardson, John McWhirter, William MacTaggart, Peter Graham, Tom Graham, George Paul Chalmers and of course Pettie. In fact, these young men under the influence of Lauder would themselves influence the history of the modern Scottish school of painting. Their imaginative paintings brought a new and rich resonance of colour into the painting of their time; they were daring and they criticised constructively and encouraged each other.

John Pettie by George Paul Chalmers (Courtesy of the Scottish National Portrait Gallery)

In 1859, at the age of twenty, Pettie achieved his first exhibit at the Scottish Academy with The Prison Pet; this was quickly followed by *False Dice, Distressed Cavaliers* and *One of Cromwell's Divines* - an amazingly distinguished start to a promising career. Within twelve months of this initial success *The Armourers* was selected for exhibition at the Royal Academy in London. He took his next subject from Sir Walter Scott's *Fortunes of Nigel*; this was a study of the Scott's *Jenkin Vincent* and was immediately popular.

Pettie's friend Orchardson had installed himself in a studio in Pimlico in London and following Pettie's successes he encouraged the young painter from East Linton to join him and in 1862 Pettie decided to leave Scotland. For several years the two artists shared the studio before moving to 37 Fitzroy Square.

It was Pettie's 'daring and assertive harmonies which compelled attention' and gave him even earlier recognition than his friend Orchardson. Soon after his arrival in London another of Pettie's imagined scenes from Scott, *The Prior and Edward Glendinning*, was exhibited at the Royal Academy and in 1863 his *The Trio, The Tonsure* and *George Fox refusing to take the Oath* were exhibited. In 1864 he painted his At Holker Hall which was followed by his interpretation of dramatic events in such as his *Death Warrant, Drumhead Court-Martial* and *An Arrest for Witchcraft* in 1865-66. The latter was not only imaginative but vigorous and dramatic and it gained him his election as an Associate of the Royal Academy (ARA).

Pettie was a prodigious worker and his paintings sold well among dealers as well as private collectors. He now felt that his income was sufficient to support the young lady he had long admired and loved. In August 1865 he married Elizabeth Ann Bossom, the sister-in-law of another Scottish painter, C E Johnson, and he left his friend Orchardson to set up home with her and to bring up their family of three sons and a daughter. As his fame grew other young painters from Scotland arrived in London and Pettie not only encouraged them in their early struggles but he and his wife gave generously of their hospitality at their house in St John's Wood Road.

Pettie the man was almost self-effacing and not in the least assertive in total contrast to the dash and vigour of his work. He was modest to a fault and held to the belief that only unremitting work was the key to his success.

His diploma picture *Jacobites*, 1745 was submitted in 1873 when he was elected a full member of the Royal Academy succeeding Sir Edwin Landseer. Pettie's paintings of imagined literary and historical subjects continued unabated increasing his great popularity. Some of the best known are: *Terms to the Besieged* (1872), *The Flag of Truce* (1873), *Juliet and Friar Lawrence* (1874), *Sword and Dagger Fight* (1877), *A Death Warrant* (1879), *Before his Peers* (1881), *Monmouth and James II* (1882), *The Vigil* (1884), *Challenged* and *Sir Peter Teazle* (1885), *The Traitor* (1889) and *The Ultimatum* (1892). In addition to his paintings for private collections he sent over 130 pictures to the Royal Academy in the years between 1860 and his death in 1893.

Towards the end of his life he turned to portrait painting with almost equal success; several of his portraits are to be found in the Scottish National Portrait Gallery - 8th Duke of Argyll, William Black, George Paul Chalmers, Sir David Murray, James Campbell Noble and his old friend, Sir William Quiller Orchardson.

During 1891 he suffered increasing pain from earache and this affected his work which became coarse with violent colour contrasts. His affliction proved to be a tumour in the brain and led to his paralysis and early death on 21st February 1893 aged only 54. He was buried at Paddington cemetery and was survived by his beloved wife, three sons and his daughter.

There are two portraits of him in the Scottish National Portrait Gallery, one by James Archer and the other by George Paul Chalmers.

ALEXANDER AND NORMAN PORTEOUS

scholars of Haddington who becameUniversity Professors

Two Haddington boys destined for intellectual achievement leading to eminent scholarship were the Porteous brothers, Alexander and Norman, born in 1896 and 1898 respectively. Both attended the Knox Institute in Haddington, the Universities of Edinburgh and Oxford, took 1st Class honours degrees at each university and became University Professors. Their lives were immersed in the joy of study which, from an early age, was gently guided by their father, a born teacher and headmaster of the Knox Institute of Haddington.

Norman (L) & Alexander (R) Porteous
(Courtesy of Prof. Norman Porteous)

Their father, John Dow Porteous MA (1852-1937), born in Keith, Banffshire, was the third of four sons of a gardener who worked on various estates in Strathspey, Glenluce and finally at Lasswade. His parents were the recipients of a legacy from a distant relative in London and decided that the money should be used for the education of their sons. John Porteous became a pupil teacher at Loanhead about 1865. After teacher training at Moray House Free Church Teachers' Training College in Edinburgh he obtained a teaching post at Forres and remained there for six years. At Edinburgh University in 1879 he graduated MA and was appointed a junior master at the Knox Institute in Haddington in 1883 with an initial salary of £90 per annum.

In 1888, in order to qualify himself in German, he went to Saxony for two months so that he could introduce the teaching of German at the Knox Institute and after ten years of dedicated work he was appointed Rector (1894-1919). He could now afford to marry his fiancee, Agnes Paton Walker (1864-1952), the daughter of businessman WG Walker of Ayr who founded and ran a large construction company. The late Alice Burnett of Haddington, a contemporary of the Porteous brothers, described her as 'a lovely gentle lady who was so fond of music.'

Their first child was a daughter, Elizabeth, born in 1895 but she survived only for a few hours. Then followed their two sons, Alexander and Norman. John Dow Porteous gave his sons possibly the greatest gift a father can bestow - a love of literature, language, learning and ultimately scholarship. Their boyhood was one of happy simplicity in which their imagination was stimulated by Greek antiquity and a love of learning. Their father read the Bible to them every day after school; this was not in the least demanding but a pleasurable daily ritual. Occasionally, he interrupted their play with suggestions of a short reading from *Alice in Wonderland* and stories from *Robinson Crusoe*, *Gulliver's Travels* and simplified versions of Homer and Virgil; another favourite was Charles Dickens. Attendance at Church each Sunday was a matter of course and in addition to Bible reading on the Sabbath, the boys read *Pilgrim's Progress* and Milton's *Paradise Lost*, its sequel *Paradise Regained* and *Samson Agonistes*.

The elder of the two brothers was **Alexander James Dow Porteous** born on 22nd July 1896 at the family home, then at Parkside, Station Road, not far from the Knox Institute. Later, the family moved firstly to Belmont Villas and finally to Simla Lodge in Letham Drive, Haddington. His boyhood was spent in a home blessed with patient and loving parents who inculcated a love of learning, language and the classics. His boyish games with his young brother, Norman, consisted of re-enacting the tales of ancient Greece stimulated by wonderful story-telling by their father.

Professor Alexander Porteous (Courtesy of Lesley & Malcolm Porteous)

After an excellent early education at the Knox Institute Alexander intended initially to become a scientist but changed his mind in favour of classics with the aim of becoming a teacher. Following in his father's footsteps he became a pupil teacher at the Public School in Haddington whose head was Mr. Burnett (father of Miss Alice Burnett above).

Alick, as he was affectionately known in the family, had not had the opportunity to study Greek at school; this was an essential prerequisite for entry to a classics degree course at the university and he had to teach himself, with guidance from his father. He passed the Preliminary Examination in the autumn of 1912 and entered Edinburgh University in 1914 but war interrupted his studies in 1916 when he joined the Royal Scots Fusiliers as a private soldier. He was not a good marksman and was sent to Beachy Head near Eastbourne for further training. This delay probably saved his life - the soldier he replaced in the trenches had just been killed and after three weeks at the front he was given respite; his replacement was killed almost immediately and Alexander returned to the front line. He survived the horrors of trench warfare and in 1918 he was gazetted as a 2nd lieutenant in the Royal Scots Fusiliers to complete his army service in France early in 1919.

On his return home to Haddington he resumed his studies at the University and graduated with 1st class honours in Classics in 1921 having gained subject medals in logic, metaphysics and moral philosophy. A few months later he went into residence at Oriel College, Oxford where he was placed first class in *Literae Humaniores*. On his return to Edinburgh he continued his studies in philosophy and simultaneously attended classes at Moray House College of Education. In 1924 he gained 1st Class honours in Moral Philosophy and was appointed an assistant lecturer in the University's Department of Logic and Metaphysics until 1926.

It was in the honours philosophy class of Professor Norman Kemp Smith of Edinburgh University that he met his future wife, Eliza Ross, also a student of philosophy and a Carnegie Scholar. Each morning she could be found setting and lighting the fire in the Classics library; Alexander made a point of helping her and they became friends. After gaining their degrees Professor Kemp Smith recommended Alick for a teaching post at Smith College in Springfield Massachusetts, a finishing school for young ladies, and rather than leave Eliza behind they married before setting off for America. Two of their children, Agnes and Colin, were born there.

His inaugural lecture to the sophomores as the new Professor of Philosophy was prepared with his usual thoroughness; he arrived early at the lecture theatre and waited. No students arrived and imagining that they had boycotted his lecture he informed the Principal. He discovered that there were two lecture theatres and that the students had waited patiently in the upper one in vain.

In 1930, after four happy years at Smith College, he was appointed to the Chair of Moral Philosophy of McGill University in Montreal. Whilst at McGill Alick contracted typhoid and became so seriously ill it was thought that he would die. The children were to be sent home to their grandparents but with careful nursing he recovered and he returned to work.

In 1932 he was appointed to a lectureship in Ancient Greek Philosophy at Edinburgh University where he was appointed a Reader in 1937. Finally, in 1938, James Mountford, the Vice-Chancellor of Liverpool University, invited Alick to the Chair of Education, a post he held for the next 25 years, retiring in 1963. During the 1939-45 war when Liverpool suffered intense bombing, his department was moved to the WEA College at Harlech. After the blitz the family (there were now six children) returned to Liverpool.

After his retirement at the age of 67 years, he received a final honour from Edinburgh, his *alma mater* - he was invited to occupy the Chair of Moral Philosophy from 1963 to 1964 until the appointment of a new professor.

His work was well-known and highly respected not only through his teaching with special emphasis on Plato and Aristotle but from his numerous reviews and papers to philosophical journals. His contributions on the Greek philosophers Democritus, Empedocles, Epicurus, Parmenides and others were published in Chambers Encyclopaedia. He was joint editor of the publication of *The Credibility of Divine Existence - The collected papers of Norman Kemp Smith* and wrote numerous articles for the *Mind and Aristotlian Society*. His contributions to Philosophical Societies in Scotland and England earned him the accolade of scholarship. He died in Liverpool in 1981 aged eighty-five years. His son Colin Porteous, who became a consultant gynaecologist, recalled his father as 'a disciplinarian who spoiled us.' Alexander Porteous left his family a legacy of learning with the words, "I may not leave you money but I'll leave you educated." Of his mother and father Colin recalled that "theirs was truly a marriage made in heaven."

The younger son of Haddington's Porteous household is **Norman Walker Porteous**, born on 9th September 1898 - one week after Kitchener crushed the Khalifa's army at Omdurman to take Khartoum, as his father reminded him. He recalls his father reading aloud reports from *The Scotsman* of the Russo-Japanese War in 1904. But as a young schoolboy he was almost crushed to death under the wheels of a passing horse and cart driven by its drunken

Professor Norman Porteous (Courtesy of Lesley & Malcolm Porteous)

owner in Station Road; fortunately for Norman the cart had the new Dunlop pneumatic tyres instead of the old iron rims under which he would almost certainly have died. He was rushed to Dr Ronaldson and missed only a few days of schooling.

The Porteous household was entirely conducive to learning. It seemed a natural pastime in which study was as natural as eating and sleeping. At the Knox Institute Norman received no special tuition from his father who had a heavy programme of teaching Latin, English, history and German; he gave equal attention to all of his pupils.

A contemporary and school-friend of Norman Porteous was William Gillies *q.v.* who gained distinction as an artist and as Principal of the Edinburgh College of Art. Although their talents were quite different each was equally interested in the activities of the other, in fact, Norman enjoyed learning of Gillies's world of painting and colour.

Norman Porteous and William Gillies were dux medallists in successive years at the Knox Institute having sat next to each other in the same classroom for six years. They even attended Sunday School together at the United Presbyterian West Church which later united with St John's Church. It is perhaps a reflection of the quality of their education and a most interesting coincidence that these two Haddington boys were each to achieve the distinction of becoming Principal of the college in which they had been students - Gillies, a student of the Edinburgh College of Art in 1916, was appointed its Principal in 1959 and knighted in 1970; Porteous, a student of New College, Edinburgh in 1924, was awarded an honorary Doctorate of Divinity by St Andrews University in 1944 and became Principal of New College in 1964.

About the age of 15 years Norman Porteous decided that his future lay in the church and his father, quietly and without fuss, simply suggested that he should learn Greek. He provided the books and his brother Norman, having already mastered the fundamentals of Latin, taught himself Greek and studied the Greek classics.

He recalled his school days with enormous gratitude; "there was no nonsense, it was a good school with good results. My father introduced German into the curriculum which was very successful. I owe everything to my parents and to my elder brother for my happy childhood in Haddington." He recalled with affection a friend of the family, Richard Baillie, an exceptionally talented artist who built up a huge construction business. His near neighbours, the Somerville family, were good friends and Richard Baillie married their daughter Maggie. The family doctor was Dr Martine for whom the family had a high regard.

Aged 18 years, in 1916, Norman entered the University of Edinburgh having been first bursar in the entrance examination. He took his place among young men from the leading Edinburgh schools and he more than held his own academically. He travelled each day by rail to Longniddry to change trains there for Edinburgh and he used the journeys to study. After only two terms he was conscripted to the army.

Basic training at Kinross and Norwich was followed by officer-training at Oxford. As a 2nd Lieutenant he was sent to Ireland and then to France where he joined his regiment, the 13th Royal Scots serving in the campaign both in France and Belgium. He became infected with measles however and, although he wanted to rejoin his regiment at the front, he was sent home to Haddington to recuperate. By the time he returned to France two of his friends had been killed in the trenches. Shortly afterwards, with the retreat of the German army, the war ended and after the armistice was declared all thought turned immediately to the future.

He returned to his studies at Edinburgh University to gain a 1st Class Honours degree in Classics in 1922 which he followed with further studies at Oxford (Trinity College) in the 'Classical Greats' (Literae Humaniores) achieving another 1st Class honours degree. He had followed an almost exact parallel path to that of his elder brother Alexander - both brothers attained the distinction of being Ferguson Scholars in Classics, Alexander in 1922 and Norman in 1923. Norman's eldest son, Ian, continued the family tradition by winning the Ferguson Scholarship in Mathematics in 1955.

It was during his student days that he met his future wife, May Robertson of Kirkcaldy, who was a student of classics and was awarded a 1st Class honours degree at Edinburgh. She was a strong support to him in all he achieved throughout their 52 years of happy married life. Another powerful influence on his life was his professor of Greek, Professor Alexander Mair. In later life Norman and he were to become firm friends, a privilege greatly cherished and made even more precious to Norman when Professor Mair named his youngest son after him - Norman Mair later to distinguish himself in the world of sport and as a sports journalist.

Norman Porteous returned to Edinburgh to study for the ministry of the United Free Church of Scotland becoming a student of theology at New College, Edinburgh where he gained the degree of Bachelor of Divinity. During his studies at New College he described his feelings of privilege to 'study alongside men who were destined for mission work.' He had studied Hebrew and had read the New Testament in Greek prior to his entry to New College. This gave him time to attend the University for two years of study of Arabic under Dr Richard Bell.

During his final session at New College he was Assistant Minister at Lothian Road Church where the Minister was first Dr Drummond followed by the Rev. James Jardine, an old pupil of his father's at the Knox Memorial Institute in Haddington. There he gained not only the wise counsel of Mr Jardine but valuable pastoral experience which he still regards as a most important part of the work of the church.

In 1927 he gained a travelling scholarship and spent three semesters in Germany at the Universities of Berlin, Tubingen and Munster in Westphalia and was the first British student of Karl Barth (1886-1968), the renowned Swiss theologian, who became a brave voice against the use of Christianity in Nazi propaganda.

Following his ordination, shortly before the Union of Churches in 1929, he became minister at Crossgates, a mining community near Dunfermline, marrying May in September of that year. He recalled his two years with his congregation of miners and their families with enormous affection. As a student he had spoken out with other young ministers during the miners' strike in sympathy with the dreadful conditions they suffered.

He believed strongly in pastoral care and it was with sorrow that he left his church in Fife to accept the invitation of the Secretary of State for Scotland to become Professor of Hebrew and Oriental Languages at St Andrews University - a Regius Chair. After four years of strenuous work he was appointed in 1935 to the chair of Old Testament Languages, Literature and Theology at New College, Edinburgh, succeeding Professor Adam Welch. In 1937 he was appointed Professor of Hebrew and Semitic Languages, again at Edinburgh, a post he held for the next 27 years. Finally, in 1964 aged 66, he was appointed Principal of the college in which he had been a student 40 years before - New College, Edinburgh. For nineteen of his years of teaching he was Secretary to the Faculty, succeeding Professor Watt, and for over twenty years he was a member of the inter-denominational team of leading scholars of Hebrew which produced the New English Bible. He was an elder of the Church for over half a century. After four years as Principal of New College he retired at the age of 70, in 1968.

A new life opened up for him: he was in demand abroad - at Princeton University and at other colleges in the USA he lectured to teachers of theology and for five months he lectured in eight theological centres in SE Asia including Hong Kong, Thailand, the Philippines and Singapore and finally he completed a lecture tour in Melbourne, Australia and Fiji.

In 1981 he suffered the loss of his brother Alick and of his beloved wife, May. Alick's wife had died previously in 1972. Each of the

Porteous brothers had six children: Alick and Eliza four sons and two daughters, Norman and May three sons and three daughters. Norman's second son, Malcolm, who started his teaching career at Loanhead nearly a hundred years after his grandfather was a pupil-teacher there, and who recently retired after twenty-three years as Head Teacher of Bonnyrigg Primary School. Malcolm recalls his father's eager participation in the fun and enjoyment of family holidays. In 1938 the older members spent part of that summer on the German Baltic coast. Friendships formed then, and in previous years survived despite the war years and formed part of a world-wide circle of friends with whom Norman still maintains contact. Post war holidays were mostly to the peace and quiet of Strathspey and to Speyside which were especially memorable when, during the long summer evenings in their holiday cottage, Norman, just as his own father had done, told many wonderfully amusing stories to the great amusement of his children; there was of course no television and family fun was invented and imagined.

Professor Norman Porteous enjoyed his 102nd birthday at his home in Edinburgh on 9th September 2000 with the company and good wishes of his family and many friends. His son Malcolm accompanies him on short sightseeing journeys, sometimes to his birthplace in Haddington, and he enjoys his family around him with visits from many friends.

THE LAST PROVOSTS OF HADDINGTON -

Provost Alexander Fraser Spowage MBE, JP (1971-74)
Provost William Laird Grant JP (1974-5)

The last two Provosts of the Royal Burgh of Haddington who lived in the same Haddington street, Glebe Terrace, and who played together as boys, sometimes in the same football team and sometimes against each other have been friends for over seventy years: Alexander Fraser Spowage and William Laird Grant. Their working lives took different routes but they served together on their Local Council, firstly as Councillors, then as Bailies and Justices of the Peace and finally as the last Provosts of the Royal Burgh of Haddington.

Alexander Fraser Spowage was Provost of Haddington from 1971 to 1974. As well as a local conservationist his philanthropic acts have benefited both national and local charities totalling over £30,000 This beneficence was a promise faithfully kept to his late wife, Isabelle - that throughout the rest of his life after her death he would support their favourite charities.

He was born in Moncur's Buildings (now demolished) near the Tweedmill of Haddington on 14th November 1924, the third of five children. His father, John Spowage, was a gardener on the Duke of Portland's estate near Nottingham who enlisted for the army during World War I and was posted to Haddington where he met his future wife, Alison Fraser, daughter of the manager of an ironmongers's Shop, Davie & Co, in Market Street.

Fraser's hard-working father suffered an early death as a direct result of mustard gas poisoning while serving in France from 1915 to 1919.

Today, Fraser lives at Knox Court in Haddington which overlooks the entrance to the Knox Institute Primary School where he spent his Primary School days from 1929. Five years later he transferred to the imposing Gothic building, the Knox Institute, for his Secondary education; it is in this converted building he now lives. Having been built in 1877 it was too small for the increasing school roll and it was replaced in 1938. Fraser Spowage was thus one of the first to attend the new Knox Academy which he left, aged fifteen, in 1939 with a medal for elocution.

He became an oiler on a crusher at the noisy, dusty quarry of Traprain Law. He detested that job and soon left to become an apprentice butcher with R J & A R Craik. However, his heart was not in the butchery business and his next job was at the local tannery (now Tyne Court) where he spread the wool for drying in the kilns for a few months.

In 1943, aged eighteen, he was 'called up' to the army and posted to Fort George, the training depot of the Seaforth Highlanders, and, although selected for the Pioneer Corps, he was sent for training to Mablethorpe as a Heavy Anti-Aircraft gunner in the Royal Artillery. His first posting with the HAA Regiment was at Freshwater Bay on the Isle of Wight which protected Portsmouth and part of the South Coast. As well as firing on the German bombers and flying bombs ('doodlebugs') there was one occasion his guns were used not against enemy aircraft but against mine-laying German E-Boats to fire shrapnel shells above them; they made a hasty retreat.

Such was Fraser Spowage's expertise and accuracy he was selected as a gunnery instructor with the rank of Sergeant. This he enjoyed and during this time he probably developed further his clarity of speech with unambiguous instruction which was to serve him well in local politics.

In 1947, his army service complete, he returned to 'civvy life' and found a job at Drem loading 'pre-fabs' (pre-fabricated houses) on to lorries. But this was not for him; he decided to re-enlist in the army. He did not reveal his previous rank and after another ten weeks of 'square-bashing' at Slough, he was posted as a Private to the Regimental Paymaster of the Royal Engineers at Whitchurch. This was relentlessly boring work and soon he applied to return to his old Regiment. However, his Lieutenant-Colonel, not realising that he had previously held the rank of Sergeant, offered him his old rank if he agreed to stay at Whitchurch. He agreed and was promoted to Quartermaster-Sergeant to be posted to the Gold Coast (now Ghana), then known as 'the white man's graveyard'. He sailed out in a flat-bottomed banana boat which was tossed about in the Bay of Biscay before reaching Freetown in Sierra Leone where they took on coal for the rest of the journey to Accra. He contracted an eye infection which permanently affected his eyesight and brought an abrupt end to his army career; he was invalided out and found himself back in Haddington in 1949.

He obtained employment as a porter with the Ministry of Works at East Fortune and it was during this time, in 1952, that he decided to stand for election as a Councillor for Haddington Town Council. His late father, a close friend of Robert Fortune (who became Provost of Haddington on three occasions), had an interest in local affairs and Fraser Spowage, encouraged by Mr Fortune, was duly elected. There was no question of time off work for Council business, meetings were held in the evenings, twice per month in the old and decaying Town Hall which was threatened with demolition. Fraser supported the Council's decision to completely renovate it. He supported also the first 'Overspill Agreement' in Scotland; it was signed between Glasgow and Haddington; the result was a welcome influx of cheery, hard-working Glaswegians.

In 1958, the unthinkable happened: Fraser Spowage lost his place on the Council. Disheartened, he decided to give up local politics. By now he had been appointed a rent collector and it was during this time that he met his future wife, Isabelle Aitchison Gillan. This, he considered to be the turning point of his life and after three years of courtship they married on 29th September 1962. She was his guiding light. From then his life changed completely; everything he did was for his beloved wife, she was his mentor and his wise counsellor.

Five years were to pass before he was persuaded by Councillor William Grant, with encouragement from his wife, Isabelle, to re-enter local politics. And so, in 1963, he was re-elected to the Council being firstly appointed Dean of Guild and within a year he donned the scarlet robe of Bailie. As a Magistrate he took his oath of office with a zeal he has never lost. He was Senior Bailie for three years and his next appointment, in 1968, was as Honorary Treasurer when he, with his committee, had to agonise over the level of the Burgh 'rates'. Finally, his election as Provost in 1971 was a close run contest between he and William Grant. The result, seven votes to five in his favour, was a moment of some emotion for him; this lad from decrepit Moncur's Buildings had reached the position of first citizen.

The highlight of his Provostship was the visit, on 21st July 1971, of H M Queen Elizabeth II for the opening of the newly-restored St Mary's Parish Church and the buildings of the Lamp of Lothian Collegiate Trust; he chatted to her happily for almost an hour during which she received several guests who were introduced by Provost Spowage.

In 1974 the reorganisation of Local Government was coincident with the end of his term of office and he was delighted when Baillie William Grant JP, his old friend and adversary, who had been elected as Independent Councillor for Haddington in 1962, was elected Provost for the final year.

At this time he was Licencing Officer in charge of Motor Taxation for East Lothian but the taxation of cars had been computerised and

Fraser was offered a transfer to Cardiff. He could not contemplate the idea of leaving Haddington and so turned down the offer of a transfer. He was now offered the post of Housing Officer at Musselburgh; with alacrity he accepted and remained in this post until his retiral in 1986. He and Isabelle now enjoyed their freedom at their home in Abbots View but sadly it was to be cut short with Isabelle's death on 9th July 1991. Fraser was devastated but in keeping his promise to his late wife he immersed himself in helping good causes and in giving his support to any scheme which added to the improvement and amenity of the Royal Burgh.

Fraser Spowage JP completed thirty years on the Bench (1964-94), firstly in the old Burgh Court and latterly in the East Lothian District Court - he served his community well and without fear or favour and always with scrupulous fairness. For his generosity to many charities and his untiring interest in the welfare of the people of Haddington he was deservedly awarded the honour of Membership of the Most Excellent Order of the British Empire (MBE) in the Queen's birthday honours of 2000.

William Grant was the last Provost of Haddington succeeding his friend Provost A F Spowage in 1974 until the reorganisation of Local Government to Regional Government in 1975 which introduced Regional Councils and brought to an end the Local Councils and the title of Provost.

William Grant is a direct descendant of an old Haddington family which originated in Ireland. His father was Thomas Grant, a foreman of the Bermaline Maltings in Haddington, who served in the Great War as a Lieutenant in the Seaforth Highlanders and in the Rifle Brigade; he died at Roodlands Hospital in 1951. His mother, Janet Haggarty had three sons and three daughters: Thomas born in 1922, James born in 1924 and William born at Roodlands Hospital on 10th December 1928, Mary born 1918, Janet born in 1926, and Roseanne born 1932.

His grandfather, Patrick Grant, arrived in Haddington from Co Leitrim in 1866 and his large family consisted of six sons and two daughters. He found work as a hewer before becoming a professional soldier reaching the rank of sergeant. His army service lasted for thirty-one years and after his last action, during the Boer War, he returned home to be accorded the privilege of wearing his uniform and his medals when and where he pleased. There is an old photograph of Sergeant Grant standing near Sandybed (Bothwell) Castle (demolishd in the 1960s). He died at his house in St Martin's Gate, Haddington on 8th July 1915.

William Grant attended St Mary's Primary School in Haddington and St Martin's Secondary School at Tranent. He left school at the age of fourteen to become an apprentice joiner with a small firm of joiners, James Chisholm at Gifford. During his apprenticeship from age sixteen he attended evening classes, three nights per week, at Heriot Watt College (now University) in Edinburgh for his studies in building construction. He was a fully-fledged joiner at the age of nineteen and in moving from a small company to large organisations he gained valuable experience on large contracts while working for Crudens Ltd., The Scottish Construction Co. Ltd., Richard Baillie & Sons of Haddington and finally in 1956 with J Smart plc. The latter was the start of a long and distinguished career.

Courtesy of William Grant

Having gained experience and expertise through hard and conscientious work, with an eye for detail, always aiming for perfection, he was soon in charge of other tradesmen on large building projects becoming progressively: the site manager, contracts manager and finally, at the age of forty-one, contracts director in 1969.

Finding himself a member of the board of J Smart plc was a new and, at first, a somewhat strange if not daunting experience in that he was conscious of the fact that the other members of board were long-established 'professionals' - men with degrees in building construction and design, accounting, quantity surveying and architecture. William Grant had been given his place on the board because of his track record of sound practical work. He brought a wealth of site experience to the board and he made his presence felt in a quiet, modest but absolutely reliable way. John Smart, the chairman, was a trained quantity surveyor and, as far as William Grant was concerned he was a thoroughly excellent professional. Another who received William's admiration was the accountant member, Leslie Wood, who kept the company on a sound financial footing. Clearly William's admiration for his fellow directors was reciprocated in their confidence in his abilities to manage 1200 men, to appoint senior tradesmen and to cost large and often complex contracts including the new Comprehensive School at Livingston, the extension of Telford College, the Library and Computer Centre for Napier University at Sighthill and many hundreds of houses.

Among many of the buildings completed by J Smart plc was one which stands out in the mind of William Grant: it was Ferrylee Old Peoples' Home in Leith which was built on the site of David Kilpatrick's School behind the Town Hall. It won a Saltire Society award for the excellence of its construction and design by architect John Dewar of Ian Roland & Partners. William Grant was given the honour of accepting this award on behalf of the company in the Advocates' Library in Parliament Square in Edinburgh - a special award in a special place - a proud moment for William Grant and James Smart plc.

He was also a director of Cramond Real Estate Co Ltd and of C & W Assets Ltd, each for seventeen years. In addition he was a member of the Prison Visiting Committee for eight years.

His decision to enter local politics was born firstly from a love of the town of his birth. He had taken an active interest in community affairs for many years and during a conversation one Sunday evening with his brother, James, he was asked why it was that he had never thought of standing for the Council at a local election. It was then that he decided with encouragement from his wife Rena to allow his name to go forward. However, the elections for new councillors were imminent and nominations had to be submitted to the Town Clerk on the next day. Without delay he was proposed and seconded by two friends, William Hands and John Kelly and supported by six rate payers resident in the Royal Burgh. At the local elections of 1962 he won his seat as an Independent Councillor. Within three years he was elected Bailie and he was appointed a Justice of the Peace in 1974.

As a new and Independent Councillor he was gratified to be in the company of other 'Independents' including Bob Fortune (three times Provost), Harvey Gardiner (Provost 1962-65), John Wood (Provost 1965-68), John Scott (Provost 1968-71) and Fraser Spowage (Provost 1971-74). In those days there were no party 'whips' or prearranged voting with decisions made unofficially outside the Council meetings; each councillor spoke his mind and voted according to his or her conscience or belief for the good of the town's people. The outcome of a vote was never predictable.

One of Councillor Grant's many interests was in the recreational facilities for young and old. At that time the only recreational facility was at Neilson park and he was delighted when the Council voted to purchase the land at Millfield and Mill Wynd from a local farmer and to convert it from agricultural use to form football and rugby pitches and to build the swimming pool at Aubigny Centre. In addition, the field leading out to Amisfield Park was purchased from the Earl of Wemyss for £40,000 and converted to form a golf course with a new club house. Councillor Grant was also instrumental in starting the Haddington Festival in 1968 and was elected Convenor of the Festival Committee. He was also convenor of the Housing and Works committees and he served on the Dean of Guild Court and the Licencing Court. After thirteen years of devoted and uninterrupted service Bailie William Grant was elected Provost of the Royal Burgh during the final year of the Council's existence. This was a well-deserved and unanimous honour and although the Council had a mere twelve months of life remaining he carried out the duties of his office as first citizen with dignity and enthusiasm.

Town Councils throughout East Lothian were now replaced with a single East Lothian District Council and William Grant was elected as one of its first Councillors - the only Independent Councillor. Party politics now dominated the scene of local government and in spite of his long and distinguished local government experience and his background of the 'rough and tumble' of the construction industry, his first rude awakening was to find that the independence of members was replaced with prearranged decision making. The first Council meeting came as something of a shock when the Convenor announced "we have decided..." Councillor William Grant was on his feet immediately to object to that which had been decided before and outwith the Council meeting and without proper discussion with the Council. "Why bother to have a Council meeting at all if decisions are already made?" He was told simply that he could discuss anything he liked for as long as he liked, "that is the decision." Democracy seemed to have been replaced with majority factionalism - members were no longer individuals with minds of their own.

After three years of serving his constituents with an open and unbiased mind, always ensuring that his amendments or objections to predetermined policy continued to be minuted, he retired from local politics. This decision was determined simply and solely due to the pressures of business, the company having achieved several new and prestigious contracts which required his immediate and close attention.

In 1994, aged sixty-six and after thirty-eight years of dedicated work for J Smart plc, he made the decision to retire. He now lives happily with his wife Rena (they celebrate their forty-sixth wedding anniversary on 5th June 2000) in his beloved Haddington. He and Fraser Spowage still meet socially and he meets many of his retired colleagues of J Smart plc regularly in Edinburgh.

Between them, these two friendly Provosts have given a total of thirty-two years of unstinting and loyal service to their community.

WILLIAM RAE JP, FIANZ

of Greymouth, New Zealand

William Rae was born on 4th June 1831 at Haddington where he attended the old Grammar School during the disastrous headship of the Rev. William Whyte. As a youth William Rae left Haddington to serve an apprenticeship with a firm of accountants in Glasgow and shortly after his twenty-first birthday he emigrated to Melbourne in Australia where he found employment as an accountant with Edmund Westly & Co. (89)

His father, George Rae, and his mother, Marion (nee Donaldson), were straw bonnet makers in Haddington where George had, in addition, a business as a silk merchant. William was ten years of age when his father died and it was great credit to his mother that he and his elder sister, Margaret (born 19th September 1829) and his younger brothers and sister - John (born 7th September 1833), James (born 5th December 1836) and Marion (born 21st July 1839) - were well if harshly educated in Haddington, this in spite of the unpopularity and inefficiency of the headmaster who succeeded in reducing the school roll from almost three-hundred to eleven children; in fact, one of his pupils died some time after a blow on the head from Whyte - he was fortunate to escape a charge of murder (28 p.224).

Courtesy of Margaret Pringle

Life in Australia was good for William Rae. He was a hard-working young man and he enjoyed the climate. He must have transmitted this enjoyment and success in letters to his brothers and sisters in Haddington because the whole family emigrated in 1854 - two years after William.

The excitement of gold discoveries at Bendigo attracted William and he bought a share in a steam puddling mill. This was a very successful venture and he sold his share at a tidy profit with which he started a sawmill in partnership with G F Walker. This too was very profitable and, learning of gold discoveries at Gabriel's Gully in New Zealand, William opened another timber business in Dunedin. It was here that he met and married Margaretta Wilson on 7th December 1864 at St Paul's Church in Dunedin.

Again, following the riches of gold, he transferred his business assets to the West Coast at Hokitika with his Australian partner G F Walker. The connection here was more than simply a business one; George Walker married William's young sister Marion in Australia.

Farther up the coast in Greymouth he bought the leasehold of some land which was rented by another Scot, John Sewell. Sewell had started the *Dispatch* Foundry (named after a paddle wheel tug-boat *Dispatch* of which he was the engineer). In 1872 Sewell wrote to his boyhood friend in Scotland, A B Hughes a highly skilled pattern-maker, suggesting that he emigrate and join him in starting his foundry business. Hughes arrived in 1873 and at this crucial time, William Rae supported the fledgling business with a half share holding in 1873 (91 p.78).

This was the start of a successful 32-year partnership during which Rae was company secretary. They chose a site for their foundry near a tidal creek to be useful for barge transport. However, the creek was reclaimed but fortuitously a railway line was built nearby. Their first casting of half a ton weight was poured on 8th August 1873. One of William Rae's first acts was to change the 'one month work for nothing' arrangement for boys to a proper apprenticeship scheme. Hughes left the company to join the Anchor Company and Sewell gave up his job with the tug *Dispatch* to give his whole time to the foundry.

The quartz mining boom had taken off in Greymouth and orders poured in to the foundry but expansion of the company was beyond their means. The two pioneers decided to form a limited company with a capital of £10,000. It seemed that Rae had the magic if not the 'Midas' touch in business. The Dispatch Foundry Company Ltd flourished under his influence. The company continued to expand and to innovate, always keeping pace with modern demand. [It celebrated its centenary in 1973 and currently manufactures a wide range of machinery for mining, smelter, forestry and construction industries].

Rae became an influential figure in Greymouth where he wrote his *Reminiscences of Greymouth*, a valuable historical insight of the beginnings of a nineteenth century new town. He was also interested in astronomy and his great neice, Mrs Eunice Walker of Clifton Springs, Victoria, Australia, has a map of the stars drawn by William Rae showing the passing of Halley's comet 7th and 28th May 1910. He played an active part in the formation of the first Borough Council of Greymouth and in 1868 he was elected one of its first members (91 p.78). He was well read in science and literature and contributed many articles to newspapers. The community benefited from his generosity as Chairman of the Greymouth Benevolent Society and he gave unstintingly of his time and money to help the poor.

In 1905, at the age of seventy-two, he decided to retire and was accorded the special thanks of the directors of the flourishing Dispatch Foundry Company Ltd for his meritorious service.

He never lost touch with the town of his birth and with his wife, Margaretta, he visited Haddington residing firstly at the Crown Hotel in Market Street which was then owned by Mrs Richard Kemp (the great-great grandmother of Margaret Pringle of today's Haddington's History Society). After Mrs Kemp died in 1882 and after his retirement he and his wife visited Scotland regularly as the guest of Mrs Kemp's grandaughter and her husband, Mr and Mrs George Pringle of 16 Market Street in Haddington. Their last visit was in 1905 when he was seventy-four years of age.

At his home in Greymouth, New Zealand he became seriously ill and was nursed for many months by his devoted wife, Margaretta. He died aged eighty on 3rd February 1911 and was survived by his wife who died on 13th November 1918. *The Grey River Argus* newspaper recorded its appreciation of 'the most widely respected of the West Coast pioneers...[who]...did an inestimable amount of good, never hesitating to lend a helping hand to assist those in distress'.

THE RENNIES of Phantassie

The Rennies of Phantassie Farm near East Linton were an extraordinarily talented family of engineers whose fame spread over three generations from East Lothian to London.

The founder of the family was the forward-looking **James Rennie**, (c.1720-1766), who farmed at Phantassie where his sons **George** and **John** were born. He must have imbued a sense of entrepreneurship in his boys by his keen interest in their education and his faith in them to take on responsibilities at an early age. For example, he sent his elder son George, when he was sixteen years of age, to make a survey of a new farming system then in use by the gentry at Tweedside. Young John, who had shown early signs of inventive genius was sent to be apprenticed to Andrew Meikle (1719-1811) *q.v.* the inventor of the 'thrashing' machine and every new idea from the boy was analysed and discussed with enthusiasm.

George Rennie, born in 1749, was brought up on his father's farm at Phantassie where he worked during his schooldays. His father encouraged him in all aspects of modern farming and it was therefore not surprising that as soon as he left school at the age of sixteen young George was entrusted with a mission to investigate the new farming techniques which were being used by several of the landed gentry such as Lord Kames at Tweedside and the Humes at Ninewells, nine miles west of Berwick-on-Tweed (the family home of the great historian and philosopher, David Hume).

Almost as soon as young George had completed his survey his father gave him the superintendance of the brewery he had built some years before, but his father died in 1766 and the seventeen year-old George returned to the farm. From 1787 he expanded the brewery and simultaneously looked after the farm employing Andrew Meikle to erect his newly-invented water-driven drum thrashing-machine. When Meikle's claim as the inventor of this machine was disputed George Rennie wrote his: *A Reply to an Address to the Public but more particularly to the Landed Interest of Great Britain and Ireland, on the subject of the Thrashing Machine* in support of Meikle as the true inventor.

Such was George Rennie's reputation in farming matters he was asked by the Board of Agriculture in 1794 to contribute to a report entitled: *A General View of the Agriculture of the West Riding of Yorkshire*. He gave up his interest in brewing in 1797 and leased the brewery to a tenant.

George Rennie died at his farm on 10th October 1828. He was buried at Prestonkirk Churchyard where his gravestone is inscribed:

GEORGE RENNIE Esq
of Phantassie
died on the 10th October 1828 aged 79 years
in this county so celebrated for its fertile
soil, and the perfection of its cultivation
Mr Rennie was acknowledged by his
contemporaries to be the most skilful and
successful agriculturist, nor was the reputation
he so justly merited, confined to his native land.
He corresponded with, and was visited not only by
the leading agriculturists of England and Ireland
but by many noblemen and gentlemen from France,
Russia,Germany, Poland, Hungary and other European states,
seeking information to improve their domains
were hospitably received by him and instructed in
his theories and practise. He performed zealously
and impartially the duties as a magistrate
and was ever ready to advise or assist those
who sought relief from difficulties or misfortune.
Deeply lamented by his wife
family, friends and dependants
His memory will long be cherished and remembered.
On the 13th January 1853 died
MARION wife of the above aged 78 years
closing a life passed in the fulfilment of every
conjugal and maternal duty. Her loss is sincerely
regretted by her family and by attached and appreciated friends.
Many unostentatious liberalities and charities exemplified
the truly self-denying benevolence of her disposition.

His son, also George Rennie, was born in 1802 and became a distinguished sculptor and politician. He exhibited at the Royal Academy from 1828 until 1837 and at the Athenaeum Club of London. His sculptures included those of his uncle John Rennie and Andrew Meikle. In politics he represented Ipswich as a Liberal and promoted improvements in the state of the arts in Britain. In 1841 he was appointed to the Governorship of the Falkland Islands.

John Rennie FRS by Sir Henry Raeburn.
Courtesy of the Scottish National Portrait Gallery

John Rennie, the younger son of James Rennie, was born on 7th June 1761 at Phantassie. He became intensely interested in mechanical devices at an early age and he spent many of his boyhood days in the company of the great Andrew Meikle (1719-1811) *q.v.* who lived at Houston Mill on the Phantassie estate. Meikle, an exceedingly clever millwright, was the inventor of the thrashing machine; young John could not have chosen a better teacher from whom he learned blacksmithing, carpentry and masonry.

He was sent firstly to the local Parish school at Prestonkirk and then, at his own wish, he attended the Burgh School at Dunbar where he displayed a talent for mathematics far beyond his years. He left school at the age of twelve and began work at Andrew Meikle's engineering works at Houston Mill. He matriculated at the University of Edinburgh in November 1780 and studied there for the next three years being taught by Professors John Robison, Joseph Black and several others from 1780 to 1783 (49 p.47). He spent his vacations working as a millwright and during one vacation he improved the durability of the machinery when he substituted cast-iron pinions for the old wooden trundles - this was his first innovation.

Shortly after he left the university he decided to expand his horizons in engineering by travelling south to meet the great Glasgow engineer, James Watt (1736-1819), the improver of the steam engine after whom the unit of electrical power is named. Watt was obviously so impressed by the enthusiasm and the knowledge of young Rennie that immediately he offered him a job at the Boulton and Watt works at Soho near Birmingham. After a few months at the Soho works, twenty-three year-old John Rennie was entrusted with his first big responsibility, that of taking full charge of the installation of a new steam engine at the Albion Flour Mills at Blackfriars in London. This was a wonderful challenge for this young engineer. He set about designing the associated machinery and introduced the use of iron instead of hard wood for the shafting and framing. The result was not only very successful but it was the first of its kind and worked to perfection.

Rennie remained with Boulton and Watt for the next seven years until 1791 when he decided to go into business for himself as a mechanical engineer. At Holland Street in Blackfriars his business as well as his reputation grew and was such that he was elected a Fellow of the Royal Society (FRS) in March 1798, the highest accolade in Britain. In those days specialisation was unheard of; engineers turned their skill, their intellect and their imagination to almost any engineering project mechanical or civil. Rennie was no exception and he turned to bridge building, canal making, harbour improvements and dock design. His first civil engineering undertaking was the Kennet and Avon canal and as soon as the success of this was known he received the contract for the Rochdale Canal through difficult countryside to Todmorden. Then followed the construction of the Lancaster Canal and in 1802 he was asked to revise the plans for the Royal Canal of Ireland from Dublin to the Shannon.

Any work he undertook was stamped with thorough and painstaking analysis. He always visited the site and his drawings and estimates of cost were accurate and reliable. His workmanship was second to none; stability and strength were his bywords. Testimony to the durability of his work remains in his bridges at Kelso (1803), Musselburgh - the "New" Bridge (1806) over the Esk which was characterised by the flatness of its roadway. He built bridges at Leeds, Newton-Stewart, Boston and New Galloway. In London he built the Waterloo Bridge (1810-17) and Southwark Bridge (1815-19) and he planned the new London Bridge which was completed after his death by his son George in 1831. This fine bridge was sold on the open market and bought by an American in 1968 for over a million pounds. It was transported and rebuilt stone by stone at Lake Havasu City in Arizona.

His work on docks and harbours is also notable: East and West India Docks in London, Holyhead harbour, Hull Docks, Ramsgate harbour and the dockyards at Sheerness and at Chatham. At the Ramsgate harbour improvement he used his improved diving-bell and he invented a steam-driven dredging machine with a chain of buckets for the construction of Hull docks in 1803.

In 1807 an Act of Parliament was passed for the construction of the Bell Rock Lighthouse in the River Tay - a project long considered far too dangerous and impossible to achieve. It would take an exceedingly brave and skilled engineer to execute this task. Robert Stevenson (after whom Stevenson College in Edinburgh was named) was given this highly complex undertaking and Rennie was invited by the Northern Lighthouse Board in Edinburgh to advise him. Stevenson had been planning the work for several years because this piece of jagged rock in the River Tay had been the cause of hundreds of shipwrecks and to make the task especially difficult, the rock was submerged even at low tide. Rennie made some suggestions to Stevenson in the design and construction but these were not used by Stevenson; never-the-less, the two engineers remained on friendly terms.

In August 1811 Rennie began the construction of the famous mile-long Plymouth breakwater. He had planned and proposed it five years before. This was a monumental undertaking across the Sound and in deep water. It required 3.67 million tons of stone plus 22,000 cubic yards of masonry. It was completed in 1841, twenty years after his death (by his son **Sir John Rennie**).

John Rennie built the Crinan Canal, the Birmingham Canal and docks in Scotland, Ireland and Wales. Portsmouth, Chatham, Sheerness and Plymouth owe their dockyards to Rennie. He drained the fen-country in the east of England and invented a dredging machine for the River Clyde.

Two of his sons, George and John, were born in London and became eminent engineers. **George** (1791-1866), the eldest, became superintendent of the machinery of the Mint and **John** (1794-1874) succeeded his father as engineer to the Admiralty and was knighted by William IV in 1831 on completion of London Bridge.

John Rennie, the great civil engineer who started as millwright with Andrew Meikle, died in 1821 and was given the honour of burial in St Paul's Cathedral; he was laid to rest beside its architect, Sir Christopher Wren. Rennie's memorial, on the south side of the A1 at Phantassie, is a bas relief bronze plaque on stone with seating and a baluster from his Waterloo Bridge and was erected by local subscription in 1936. "A man of unbounded resource and originality."

George Rennie, eldest son of John Rennie, was born on 3rd December 1791 at Stamford Street, London. His early education was from a tutor, Dr Greenlaw at Isleworth, after which he was sent to the prestigious St Paul's School. He continued his studies at his father's *alma mater*, the University of Edinburgh, from 1807 to 1811. As soon as he had completed his degree he joined his father's business at a time when many great works were being executed of which the biggest challenge was the Waterloo Bridge.

After seven years of hard work and valuable experience and with recommendations from Sir Joseph Banks (1744-1820), the eminent botanist, and James Watt (1736-1819), the Scottish inventor, he was appointed the Inspector of machinery and clerk of the dies at the Royal Mint. He remained in this post until the death of his father in 1821 when he joined in partnership with his young brother John to complete many very large contracts previously initiated by their father.

In 1826 George Rennie took full responsibility for the construction of the new Grosvenor Bridge spanning the Dee at Chester. His wide experience as a railway engineer led to his planning of the lines between Birmingham and Liverpool, the Vale of Clwyd line, and in France the railways between Mons to Manege and between Namur and Liege; he was chief engineer of the latter in 1846.

However, it was his mechanical genius which distinguished him when he took over the manufacturing side of the family business in Holland Street in London. He was responsible for the design and manufacture of a wide range of machinery including the first biscuit-making machine in Britain. In addition he designed and manufactured the machinery for the corn and chocolate mills of the Deptford victualling yard and the machinery for the Royal William Victualling Yard at Plymouth.

Such was his reputation for excellence and the reliability of his designs he was invited by several overseas governments to supply many large orders of machinery. He supplied engines for the Royal Navy; in fact it was his firm which built the *Dwarf*, the first ship of the British Navy to be driven by means of the screw propeller. This was the age of the clipper ships and square riggers and George Rennie had long been interested in screw propulsion. An early twin-screw, steam-powered boat had been tried in America but its engine failed in 1804. Thirty years later George Rennie installed his new steam engine with its screw propeller which was designed by the Swede John Ericsson and Sir Francis Pettit Smith for the merchant vessel which was well-named the *Archimedes* after the Greek scientist and inventor of the endless screw who lived from 287 to 212 B.C.

In 1822 his enormous contribution to engineering at home and abroad was recognised through his election to Fellowship of the Royal Society (FRS), the highest academic honour in Britain. In 1829 he contributed several papers to the Royal Society on such as 'the friction of metals and other substances'. His output of learned papers was prodigious: he presented several more to the British Association and to the Institution of Civil Engineers (formed in 1818, its first president being another Scot, Thomas Telford in 1820) to which he was elected to membership in 1841.

In 1865 George Rennie suffered a street accident and died at his home in London on 30th March 1866. He was survived by his wife, Margaret Anne, daughter of Sir John Jackson, and two sons and one daughter.

George Rennie's young brother, **Sir John Rennie**, was the second son of John Rennie and grandson of James Rennie of Phantassie. He was born on 30th August 1794 at Stamford Street, London. His parents, John and Martha (nee Macintosh) sent him to Dr Greenlaw at Isleworth and then to Dr Charles Burney at Greenwich for his education. His father, insisting on the benefits of sound practical training, put young John to work in his factory at Holland Street, Blackfriars Road. When he was 19 years old in 1813 he was given his first responsibility, that of superintending the foundations of the new Waterloo Bridge over the Thames, the resident engineer being Mr Hollingworth. Two years later he assisted his father in the construction of Southwark Bridge and 1819 his far-sighted father sent him to Europe to study engineering structures and the methodology of construction.

After his father's death in 1821 his elder brother joined him in the family firm. John took responsibility for the civil engineering side of the business while George took over the mechanical side. One of the most prestigious projects was that of London Bridge the designs of which had been initiated by his father. This great landmark in London was opened in 1831 amid great splendour and congratulation during which John Rennie was deservedly knighted by William IV; only one other engineer, Sir Hugh Myddleton, had been so honoured.

Sir John succeeded his father as Engineer to the Admiralty and he completed several of his father's civil engineering projects at Sheerness, Woolwich, Ramsgate and the massive breakwater at Plymouth for which he wrote an 'abstract' in 1848. With the developments in maritime activity and trading during the latter part of the 19th century Rennie spent several years in enlarging and improving many harbours in England and in Ireland. He carried out the complete restoration of the harbour at Boston and completed the drainage works in the Lincolnshire Fens started by his father.

Although the railway section of the company was not large he, with his brother George, designed a line from Liverpool to Manchester in 1825-6. In 1852 he designed a railway system for Sweden and was awarded the Order of Gustavus Vasa. In 1855 he designed several harbours and railway systems for the Government of Portugal but his designs were never used.

He was elected to membership of the Institution of Civil Engineers in 1844 and such was his eminence that within six months he was elected its president, the office of which he held for the next three years. In his presidential address he described the history of civil engineering which was published in the Proceedings of the Institution. He contributed several other papers on such as the drainage of the level of Ancholme, Lincolnshire, the improvement of the navigation of the River Newry and the 'Theory, Formation and Construction of British and Foreign Harbours', 1851-4. And his 'Account of Plymouth Breakwater', 1848 (25 Vol. 2 p.21) .

Sir John Rennie retired in 1862 and died twelve years later on 3rd September 1874 in his eightieth year. So ended this great era of Civil Engineering but the Rennies with Smeaton*, Brindley*, and Telford* undoubtedly formed the link with the next generation of Stephenson* and Brunel*.

**John Smeatom (1724-92), James Brindley (1716-72), Thomas Telford (1757- 1834), George Stephenson (1781-1848), Sir Marc Isambard Brunel (1769-1849), Isambard Kingdom Brunel (1806-59).*

THE ROBARTS FAMILY

devoted doctors of Haddington

Henry H Robarts MD, DPH
Frederick Howard Robarts MB, ChB, FRCS(Edin)
James Robarts MB, ChB

The Robarts family of Haddington were dedicated physicians. **Dr Henry H Robarts** (1879-1951) arrived in Haddington in 1906. This was to become the start of a long and distinguished medical practice which was to last until 1977 when his younger son Dr James Robart left Haddington to retire to the Island of Barra.

Henry Robarts lived for a short time in Ireland where his father was the factor of a large estate. His father, who died in 1925, suffered a serious riding accident from which he never recovered to work again and the family of four children had to be split up and sent to relatives. His eldest daughter was brought up by an aunt in Finland while her sister and two brothers were sent to their Aunt Emma in Edinburgh. [Aunt Emma was a niece of Emma Robarts who with Elizabeth Fry (1780-1845), the Quaker prison reformer, founded the YWCA]. The boys were educated at George Watson's College while their sister went to Esdaile School.

Henry entered the medical faculty of Edinburgh University where he graduated with distinction in 1902 gaining his MD in a remarkably short time - one year later. In addition, he gained the Diploma in Public Health (DPH).

His first hospital appointment was as house doctor at the Royal Infirmary of Edinburgh. He was then appointed to the Royal Hospital for Sick Children in Edinburgh. After a short spell in General Practice at Musselburgh he arrived in Haddington as assistant to Dr Ronaldson and succeeded him after his retiral in 1909. He lived firstly in Wemyss Place and after his marriage to Charlotte (nee Low) (1884-1984) in 1910 the young couple took up residence at *Ennerdale* in Knox Place which became a well-known medical surgery in Haddington. He attended his patients throughout East Lothian firstly on a motor-cycle until he was able to purchase a car, registration number SS11; his predecessor, Dr Ronaldson, being the first car owner in Haddington with the registration number SS1.

They had five children: **Dorothy** who graduated MA at Edinburgh where she became a golfing blue and afterwards secretary to John Bartholomew the famous map-makers of Edinburgh; **Frederick** who became an eminent paediatric surgeon; **James** who joined his father's medical practice in Haddington; **Elizabeth** ('Bud') who became a nursing sister of the female surgical ward at Roodlands Hospital in Haddington after her nursing training at St Bartholemew's Hospital in London; **Anne** who studied design at the Scottish College of Textiles in Galashiels.

In addition to his medical practice at Ennerdale he was the Medical Officer of Health for Haddington and Medical Superintendent of the East Lothian District Asylum (now Herdmanflat Hospital). The latter appointment required his daily visits to supervise the care of many patients and, to add to his busy life, he was the prime mover of the proposal to build a new cottage hospital which was named after its principal benefactor, Haddington born John Vert *qv* who had made his fortune in America. Dr Henry Robarts was the medical advisor on the committee which was set up under the chairmanship of Lady Hersey Baird of Lennoxlove to oversee the planning, money raising and final completion of the hospital which was opened in 1929.

Dr Henry Robarts was widely respected for his medical expertise and skill not only by his patients and colleagues in East Lothian but by many specialists and consultants in Edinburgh.

During the 1939-45 war he worked himself to exhaustion and suffered a coronary attack in 1944. This forced his retiral and his daughter, Elizabeth ('Bud'), returned from her nursing duties in London to look after her father. Dr Henry Robarts died on 22nd March 1951 at his house *Viewfield* in Station Road.

The eldest son **Frederick Robarts** qualified MB,ChB (the Ettles Scholar of his year) in 1937 and as a surgeon in 1939, FRCSE. He achieved eminence in the field of paediatrics as Chief Surgeon of the Royal Hospital for Sick Children in Edinburgh. He pioneered new surgical treatment for children who were born with Spina Bifida (or 'split spine') and performed hundreds of operations to relieve pain and to improve the lives of children with many kinds of disfigurement.

He was born on 9th December 1913 at *Ennerdale* in Knox Place, Haddington. After his early education at Knox Primary School he was sent to Prep School as a boarder at Warriston in Moffat. Then followed schooldays at Edinburgh Academy travelling daily from Haddington.

At Edinburgh University Fred excelled, winning class medals in Anatomy, Physiology and Zoology, the Senior John Aitken Carlyle bursary and the Grierson bursary in pathology. He gained his MB, ChB with honours and all of Haddington were delighted when one of their sons won the Leslie Gold Medal in medicine and the coveted Ettles Scholarship in 1937. Dr William Farquhar McLean *qv* (affectionately known to the Robarts family as 'Doccie') of Hilton Lodge was specially pleased as he had finished *proxime accessit* (next to the prize-winner) himself during his student days at Edinburgh.

Fred's professor, Sir John Fraser, nominated his star student as the Van Dunlop scholar to the Mayo clinic in Rochester, New York State, but war had been declared and Fred joined the Royal Navy thereby losing this opportunity of further study and research. However, he had completed his research and his thesis for his Fellowship of the Royal College of Surgeons of Edinburgh (FRCSE) which he gained in 1939.

Dr Frederick Robarts receiving the congratulations of his father Dr Henry Robarts (Courtesy of Mrs E Beattie)

As a qualified surgeon and an officer in the Royal Naval Volunteer Reserve he was immediately commissioned ship's surgeon aboard the battleship *HMS Barham.* In November 1941 the *Barham* was attacked by a German submarine, U-331, off Solum (west of Alexandria) and sunk. Surgeon Lieutenant-Commander Robarts was fortunate to survive the attack after floating in the water for many hours, he was almost left for dead in the oily sea. He was almost sucked under when the great ship exploded and sunk within four minutes. However, his injuries were confined to his lacerated hands caused when he had had to slide sixty feet down the barnacle-covered side of the sinking ship. He managed to clamber aboard a raft and did his best to keep up the spirits of the occupants by conducting a series of sing-songs. Sadly the Ship's Captain went down with the ship.

They were eventually rescued by the Australian destroyer *Nizam.* Fred always regretted losing his medical notes, particularly those of Sir John Fraser's lectures. He suffered severely from pneumonia and from inhalation of fuel oil. He convalesced in Alexandria and in Durban, South Africa after which he was posted to *HMS Bacchanti* in Aberdeen.

It was at the Royal Naval Auxiliary Hospital, Kingseat (part of *HMS Bacchanti* about eight miles from Aberdeen) where he met his future wife Miss Monica Pout, a physiotherapist working in the hospital. Courtships during the war were necessarily short and they were married at Rothbury in Northumberland on 7th November 1944. Soon after their honeymoon they had to part; he was sent to the Royal Naval Hospital at Trincomalee of Ceylon (now Sri Lanka) where much of his time was spent in treating wounded Japanese prisoners. Finally, he was seconded to Assault Landing Craft for D-Day and he made several trips to the Normandy beaches to bring back casualties.

At last he was reunited with his wife Monica and, having been 'demobbed' on 3rd June 1946, he was appointed surgeon-in charge at Leith Hospital, surgeon-in charge at the Royal Hospital for Sick Children in Edinburgh and Paedriatric Surgeon at The Simpson Pavillion of the Royal Infirmary of Edinburgh. He loved working with children and was specially fond of teaching. He was given deserved praise for his work because of the fact that he had carried out his research in a small unused building in the grounds of the hospital in his spare time and without additional funding.

In 1965 he was appointed Senior Paediatric Surgeon and Senior Lecturer in Paediatric Surgery, University of Edinburgh. In 1968 he was invited to give the J Mason Brown Memorial Lecture at the Royal College of Surgeons, Edinburgh. His lecture entitled: *The Origins of Paediatric Surgery in Edinburgh* was published by the Royal College. In addition he published several learned papers on paediatrics including Surgical Paedriatrics for the 20th edition of Pye's Surgical Handicraft, 1977, *Neotal Perforations of the Stomach* for Zeitschr. Fur Kinderchirund und Grenzgebiete, 1968.

In 1969 he was elected President of the British Association of Paediatric Surgeons and presided over the international conference of Paediatric Surgeons in Sydney, Australia in 1970.

After thirty-three years of dedicated and highly skilled surgery and teaching he retired in 1979. A plaque at the Royal Hospital for Sick Children was placed at the entrance to the library to commemorate his work; it is inscribed:

This Resource Room was established
in memory of
FH Robarts, Senior Paediatric Surgeon
1946-1979 - a fine teacher

With his wife Monica they enjoyed nine happy years in retirement at Eddleston, near Peebles where he died peacefully on 1st March 1988, aged 74. Monica died on 7th October 1999 at Brighton.

James Robarts, was born on 1st July 1916 (the day of the Battle of the Somme), the second son and third child of Dr Henry and Charlotte Robarts. He attended the Primary school in Haddington and followed his elder brother as a boarder to Warriston in Moffat aged nine where his fondest memory was of his teacher of mathematics, Mr B K Bowers, who introduced the youthful James to the study of ornithology, a love of which he never lost. Again following his brother Fred, he attended Edinburgh Academy arriving there at the age of thirteen and because he arrived rather later than his fellow pupils he had the feeling of always being an outsider.

Courtesy of Dr James Robarts

However, with a school friend, Andrew Jamieson (the son of Sheriff Jamieson who was the Sheriff in the County Buildings of Haddington for many years) he thoroughly enjoyed their training with the school's Officer Training Corps.

The curriculum of Edinburgh Academy in those days emphasised the classics at the expense of the sciences which is surprising when one recalls that James Clerk Maxwell (1831-1879), the world-renowned Scottish physicist who encapsulated the laws of electrodynamics in a set of equations, was educated there. In order to prepare for entry to the Medical Faculty of the University of Edinburgh he was given private tuition in Physics and Chemistry; so far his studies had consisted of Greek, Latin and French with other arts subjects - he had hardly heard of physics or chemistry.

Again, following his brother, he studied medicine at Edinburgh University and qualified as a doctor in 1939. This was a double celebration in the Robarts household as his elder brother Fred had qualified as a surgeon in the same year.

He completed six months as a House Surgeon at the Cumberland Royal Infirmary in Carlisle with a further three months as House Surgeon and House Physician at Edinburgh's Deaconess Hospital when he volunteered to join the navy. Little did he realise that Dr Martine, a retired Haddington doctor who was now in charge of the selection of doctors for the armed forces, had been in touch with his father to enquire about the likelihood of James enlisting in the forces. His father advised against the idea and considered that James should have more experience.

However, by 10th October 1940 he joined the navy and was posted immediately to Devonport. After two weeks he was sent to Canada to join *HMS Ranpura*, an armed merchant cruiser ex-P&O liner and sister ship to the ill-fated *Rawalpindi*, and for the next two years he was in 'U-Boat alley' escorting convoys of ships in the north Atlantic to bring a life-line of food, supplies and arms to Britain at a time when the losses inflicted on merchant ships were at their most severe. James recalled the loss of forty out of ninety ships with phenomenal loss of life in one Halifax convoy. It was during one such hazardous and stormy voyage that he performed his first appendectomy.

In 1943 James, still aboard *HMS Ranpura*, was posted to the Indian Ocean and was based at Mombasa. His work broadened from purely medical duties to cipher duty, censoring letters and as wine caterer for the officers' mess. The latter caused most concern and occasional amusement; it was a serious matter to leave harbour in a beerless state. His ship had just unloaded several crates of empty Whitbread bottles on the dockside at Yorkhill basin on the Clyde in Glasgow when the order to leave harbour immediately was received. The empty bottles had to be hurriedly reloaded for the beerless voyage of escort duty and troop-carrying to Aden, Bombay, Colombo, Mombasa and Durban. However, Castles Brewery in Durban replenished the ship's stock of beer and accepted the empty Whitbread bottles which were returned duly filled with Castles beer - free of charge.

He was home again before D-day (5th June 1944). The preparations were vast and Lieutenant Commander James Robarts found himself still aboard *HMS Ranpura* in Invergordon in the Cromarty Firth with one thousand Royal Marines aboard. They were there to practise landing in preparation for 'Overlord' (the landing in Normandy in 1944) and James as medical officer had to harden his heart to send young men into tough battle training situations even though some complained of minor ailments. The ship now proceeded to Portsmouth and successfully landed the Royal marines on the Normandy beach on D-Day.

Shortly after D-Day *HMS Ranpura* was de-commissioned and James was now appointed medical officer in charge of *HMS Bacchanti* at the Royal Naval Sick Quarters at Aberdeen and by an extraordinary coincidence his brother Fred was at Kingseat where he had returned after his service on assault crafts on D-Day. This was the first time the two brothers had met since saying their farewells in 1939. It was here that James met his future wife, an attractive young Wren officer, Zoe Woolmore, a Londoner who had experienced the worst of the blitz. Little did she realise that she would settle in Scotland to become a doctor's wife in Haddington. They were happily married on 17th July 1945 at St Sepulchre's Church in London.

After the war ended James and Zoe came to live in Haddington in 1946 and James joined his father's medical practice. Their twin daughters Jacqueline Zoe and Rosemary were born in 1946 and their son Philip arrived in 1951. At first, James was an assistant doctor with Dr William McLean *qv* and Dr Oswald Jarvis. The most common ailments at that time, before antibiotics were used, were the infectious illnesses of diphtheria, whooping cough, measles, chickenpox and tuberculosis. James recalls the poor condition of many houses and on one occasion he recalled his attendance to a poor girl in labour. Her bed was soaking wet, the rain pouring in through a leaking roof, and James delivered the baby under an umbrella. Doctors worked seven days a week with one half day off and responded to call-outs any time of day or night. James's wife Zoe was tied to the house to ensure that the telephone was answered.

His father who had worked himself to exhaustion when his sons were at war suffered a coronary attack in 1944 and had to retire. James's younger sister Elizabeth ('Bud') returned from London to care for her father who died on 22nd March 1951 at his house Viewfield in Station Road.

After the sudden and tragic death of Dr Jarvis in a car accident on the 'coal road' on his way to Longniddry, James took over full charge of the practice and continued to serve his patients of Haddington until his retirement in 1977 when he and Zoe left Haddington to live in Barra where they still enjoy happy retirement. The Robarts family thus completed a total of seventy-one years of medical care for the people of Haddington and its many outlying villages.

The Robarts story continues today: the son of James and Zoe, Dr Philip Robarts, who was born in 1951 at the hospital his grandfather helped to create, the Vert Hospital, carried on the family medical tradition by studying medicine at Edinburgh University graduating MB,ChB in 1975. He specialised in Obstetrics and Gynaecology and was elected a Fellow of the Royal College of Obstetricians and Gynaecologists (FRCOG) in 1993 and now practises in Chelmsford.

'OLD' AND 'YOUNG' BEN SAYERS

of North Berwick

In the world of golf the name *Ben Sayers* is not simply a set of clubs, it is a tradition. Every golfer of experience knows the name and fame of Ben Sayers of North Berwick.

In every tradition there is a story and this one starts in 1857, the year of the birth of 'Old Ben', as he came to be known, at Leith. He had his first game of golf at the age of sixteen with an old club given to him by his uncle in Haddington. What he lacked in height, he was a mere 5 foot 3 inches (1.60 m), he more than made up in strength and dexterity. He had the notion that his stature could be compensated for by longer clubs, so he designed and made them himself. This was to be the beginning of a dynasty.

He decided to try to make his living by making clubs. He had developed new designs with new materials and, then as now, golfers were keen to try his tailor-made clubs to improve their game. He inspired confidence and made golf clubs to suit the individual.

He played at Leith Links and at Musselburgh but when these courses became overcrowded he moved eastwards to North Berwick in 1879. He made his home there and eventually built his house, Abbeyville, at No. 39 Dirleton Avenue where he settled with his wife, Kate and four children, Bernard, Blanche, Emily and George.

Having acquired golf ball moulds from the greenkeeper of North Berwick his first business venture was in making golf balls using a mould which he was given by David Strath, an old greenkeeper at North Berwick. These were the old gutty balls which he sold for a shilling (5p) each, but his main interest was in club making and in teaching. Two of his pupils, the Misses Orr, took first and second places at the 1897 Ladies Open Championship at Gullane. He was delighted and his reputation for expert tuition soon spread. In 1910 he was to tutor another champion, Miss Elsie Grant-Suttie, who won the Ladies Open that year at Westward Ho! (38 pps. 8-9)

One of his early shops was at Point Garry. It was here that players came for advice and encouragement, even for slight alterations to the club face or the grip or a little extra weight added to the putter. These small services were given with such supreme confidence it was no wonder that players felt bound to improve and, of course, being golfers they talked only of their successes! The secret of old Ben Sayers's success was individual attention; this became the hallmark of the company - clubs made specially for the customer. With the expert help and enthusiasm of his son, 'young Ben', he developed new methods used new materials, new tools and new designs. It was not long before the demand for a set of matched Ben Sayers clubs outstripped the supply. Golf clubs throughout Britain were anxious to stock his clubs, even Harrods in London ordered several sets but 'Old Ben' was not interested in bulk supply and most orders were consigned to the waste-paper basket. However, he did supply his brother, George Sayers, in Pennsylvania, USA who emigrated there in 1913 and to whom Ben would visit in 1914 again in 1915 defying German U-boats on the way.

Ben Sayers was a dapper little man with a twinkle in his eye, always immaculately dressed and sporting his bow tie, he was not only a tutor but a master golfer. He won his first major tournament aged twenty-two in 1879 and in the decade from 1894 he won no fewer than thirty competitions including five foursomes but the British 'Open' eluded him. In 1888 he was runner-up, losing the title by one stroke, then followed a string of near misses. (38 pps. 12,13)

After the rail link was completed in 1850 North Berwick became more and more popular. Sir Walter Dalrymple, the 8th baronet of North Berwick, a keen golfer, laid out the Burgh links. North Berwick became a mecca for golf for the rich and famous, and its fame seemed complete when the king, Edward VII, arrived, having been invited to partner Arthur James Balfour *qv*, when he was first lord of the Treasury and leader of the House of Commons. Ben Sayers was the regular partner of Earl Balfour in an early form of 'Pro-Am' competitions and he gave tuition to the earl as well as Edward VII, Queen Alexandra and dozens of other nobles and knights. There is a wonderful story of his meeting with the king, who asked Ben how the Grand Duke Michael of Russia, one of Ben's pupils, was progressing. Ben replied, '"I am sorry to inform your Majesty that he was one of the keenest and one of the worst." The king stroked his beard and burst into laughter' (38 p.41).

Ben Sayers prospered and meanwhile, one of his sons, Ben Sayers Junior, had, under the guiding eye of his father, become a champion golfer. Father and son were chosen for the Scottish Professional Team from 1906 until 1909. The most formidable pair, however, were the great rivals, Andrew Kirkcaldy and Ben Sayers senior who were undefeated between 1903 and 1909. Stories of their victories are legendary. Ben Sayers was a master tactician, nothing intimidated him, his spirit was indomitable. He was a teetotaller and his preparation for a match was meticulous.

For forty-three consecutive years he played the Open Championship until the year before his death in 1924, aged sixty-seven. All of Scotland mourned the passing of the great wee golf professional. Tributes poured in: his old partner, Andrew Kirkaldy, wrote, *Ben was a kind little man and will be sorely missed by all throughout the golfing world; the editor of the* 'Irish Times' said, *he was always immensely popular, not only with his fellow competitors, but with the crowd;* J H Taylor (five times Open Champion) wrote, *I will always remember him as a lion-hearted player, clean-living, civil, attentive in all his duties and pre-eminently representative of a glorious period of the game that is rapidly passing;* the editor of 'Golfing', *The golfing world will miss Wee Ben. Not the disappearance of Big Ben from Westminster would leave a greater gap;* the editor of 'Golf Monthly', *He radiated the spirit of the links, he loved the game, he delighted in the companionship, he revelled in the blue sky and the green fields as does the lark.* (38 pps. 58-9)

Ben Sayers junior was born in 1884 at North Berwick. In carrying on the family tradition, he too became a master golfer, club maker and tutor of renown. He started playing at an early age and, benefiting from the expert tutelage of his father, he beat a scratch golfer over thirty-six holes at North Berwick 10 and 9 at the age of sixteen. At the age of nineteen he partnered his father in an exhibition match at a new course which had been designed by 'old Ben' at Moffat. They raised £500, more than enough to pay for the construction of the course (38 p.61).

In 1904 he had offers of many engagements overseas and he was appointed the professional at the Royal Wimbledon Golf Club. After playing for Scotland in the years 1906 to 1909 he decided to concentrate on his business, although he still retained his captaincy of the Scottish Section of the Professional Golfers Association.

In 1909 he married Elizabeth Vass and their daughter Doreen was born on 5th May 1911 at Wimbledon and two years later the young family returned to North Berwick to be with 'old Ben'; young Ben's brother George had left for America. Young Ben, always keen to try new ideas, invented the 'ribbed iron' in 1911 but, whilst it was used in America, it was not yet 'legal' in Britain. The firm was now renamed *Ben Sayers & Son* and clubmaking was transferred to workshops in Station Hill. Orders poured in from several countries but war was declared in 1914 and young Ben volunteered for the army to be sent to the Dardanelles after the failure of which he spent over three years in Salonika in Greece. The British and French held the Germans in check but the enemy described Salonika as their 'largest internment camp' and Ben was 'locked up', as the Germans put it, with half a million allied troops until 1918. After the armistice his homecoming was delayed until he had completed the layout of a golf course for the occupying troops who remained there.

Old Ben had visited his son George in America in 1914 before the Great War and during his absence his wife Elizabeth and four year-old daughter Doreen looked after the shop at the first tee until 'old Ben' returned from his second trip to America in 1915 and until 'young Ben' came home in 1919. His second trip aboard the *Lusitania* was made in spite of the threat of German U-boat attack.

A new shop had been rented from Sir Hew Dalrymple with a large workshop and space to swing new clubs. Sir Hew's father, Sir Walter, designed the east links ('Burgh Links') on Rhodes farm and laid out the nine seaside holes of the golf course; it became the Glen Golf Club, founded in 1906 ('young Ben' would be invited to its 50th anniversary). Ben Sayers's shop on the first tee was a popular meeting place for caddies, players and professionals. In 1933 Colonel Hutchison and Ben Sayers drew up plans to extend the course on the West Links and the 9th to the 12th holes were eventually realigned.

North Berwick was again the place to be seen: Lady Astor waxed lyrical over her golfing holiday and the Horlicks family insisted on tuition from Ben Sayers. He partnered King Paul of Greece against the Earl of Warwick and his partner at Muirfield.

When 'old Ben' died in 1924 the firm reverted back to *Ben Sayers* and change was forced on 'young Ben' because of the increased demand for hickory clubs. The supply of rough turned hickory shafts from Gibsons of Kinghorn, personally selected by Ben, was becoming a problem. It was now necessary to consider the use of steel shafts, which had first been patented in 1895 by master blacksmith Thomas Horsburgh the captain of Baberton Golf Club. These steel-shafted clubs were well thought of by 'old Ben' in his day but they were mistrusted by golfers and Horsburgh eventually allowed his patent to lapse. The 'True Temper Corporation' of America manufactured them from 1925 and they were allowed in Britain from 1929; Tom Horsburgh made no money from them (38 p.80).

Ben Sayers now changed his techniques in golf club making. Gone were the days of the feathery balls, wooden niblicks and *one off* clubs. Instead of using only woods, irons were used as the balls became more durable and with the introduction of the new 'loft and lie' machine and the 'swing weight' machine, which were developed and designed by Ben, accuracy was ensured and matched sets were introduced. The old driver, brassie, spoon, baffy, mid-iron, jigger track iron, mashie and niblick were replaced with the Nos 1,2,3,4 woods and 1,2,3,4,5,6,7 and 8 irons, but Ben made special woods for ladies and special irons in addition to the standard set and great pride was taken in the manufacture of wooden putters (38 p.85).

Such was the enormous demand for steel shafted clubs after they became 'legal' in 1929 that Ben Sayers found his premises at the Links tee to be too small and in 1931 he purchased the property which stretched from the High Street to Forth Street in North Berwick, but the Links shop kept going until 1962. The new shop now became a favourite venue for golfers world-wide and remained open for the next thirty-five years.

In 1934 Ben set up his own forge and, instead of using heads from other forgers, he was now able to make his own. He planned his workshops with the same meticulous care that he used in club making. They consisted of the 'woods' shop, the 'iron head' shop and the forge with a power hammer added later. He could now make clubs for left-handed players, and ladies and he designed *one offs* for special customers - all within the rules laid down by the R & A.

One of the memorable gatherings at the High Street shop was that of the whole American Walker Cup team in 1959 when Jack Nicklaus ordered a special mild steel putter to the design of 'Old Ben's' favourite putter (38 p.105). It came to be called 'old Nick' and sold in huge quantities in America. Another favourite was the 'Benny' putter, another of Ben's designs, which was used by hundreds of golfers including the great Henry Cotton and the Prince of Wales (who became Edward VIII).

He still aimed to produce made-to-measure clubs which were especially helpful to women, many of whom became top class golfers. In fact, almost every top player, male and female, in the country visited Ben Sayers's shop in North Berwick gaining excellent advice towards the improvement of their game. His clubs were probably the most expensive available but his prices reflected the expertise, reliability and caring workmanship of his clubmakers. On each of his invoices he printed a short quotation by John Ruskin (1819-1900): *There is hardly anything in the world that some man cannot make a little worse and sell a little cheaper, and people who consider price alone are this man's lawful prey* (38 p.110).

Ben and his brother George maintained regular contact comparing ideas and trying new designs. Ben's daughter Doreen observed in retrospect that he must have played havoc with productivity when he disrupted the routine with yet another experiment, but the clubmakers - all dedicated golfers - were encouraged to try out their own new ideas. Clubmakers trained by Ben Sayers were arguably the world's best and were in demand at home and abroad. Some left to work with brother George in America others went to Calcutta, Corsica, Cannes, Lucerne, Capetown, Nairobi and elswhere 'to teach the rest of the world to play the game' (38 p.111) and as a result orders from overseas poured in; by 1962 exports to fifty-five different countries world-wide had been achieved.

Ben had always hoped that his daughter, **Doreen Sayers**, would join the firm and this came to pass in 1931. She was a golfing blue (her handicap was 4) and an MA of Edinburgh University and her previous experience in secretarial and organisational work would now be put to excellent use. She organised exhibitions, attended tournaments and championships, designed and set up advertising material and catalogues, worked out costings, maintained stock control and processed orders. Ben was now able to take some time off to play golf with his wife Elizabeth (a good golfer) and to fish and to tend his immaculate nine-hole putting green in his garden at 'Kileen' in Ware Road in North Berwick which he built in 1931.

When war was declared in 1939 the clubmakers were 'called up' and the machines in Ben's workshops were 'moth-balled'. The golf courses were deserted and Ben offered his workshops for war work; an offer which was turned down because of the risk to the town centre. Ben became an air raid warden, Elizabeth helped in the forces canteen for the soldiers of the anti-aircraft batteries and search-light stations and Doreen became an ambulance driver with one of 'old Ben's' pupils, Miss Elsie Grant-Suttie (the Ladies Open Champion of 1910). Doreen also drove the Mobile Canteen and used Lord Haddington's kitchen at Tyninghame House to supply tea and rolls to the search-light and defence posts.

After working for the BBC at Bletchington near Oxford and in London during the flying bomb era, Doreen married Dick Stephenson on 18th March 1943. He was the son of a Berwickshire farmer and an officer in King's Own Scottish Borderers who won the Military Cross at Heinsberg in Germany. After the war Dick joined the company and was very happy to be part of its post-war success.

A poignant memory contained in Doreen's scrap book is a photograph of a young sailor, Able Seaman NWA Haddow, who was killed in action at the sinking of *HMS Hood* on 24th May 1941. This photograph was sent to Ben Sayers with a brief note on its reverse side: *For BEN SAYERS who made so much of Alastair's happiness. With gratitude from his mother.*

The company had come to standstill during the war and Ben had to live on what little capital he had. Immediately after the war golf regained its popularity and the demand for Ben Sayers clubs was greater than ever. He had to restock, re-equip and find new premises. He bought five buildings and modernised them to form his new workshops. Times had changed, the nobility had gone and with them the caddies but the courses were now used by the new caddy-car young golfers who patronised the High Street shop in growing numbers. The 'iron heads only' market, in which the new professionals had their names stamped on them, were despatched to the pros so that they could make the clubs themselves. It was almost impossible to meet the orders from brother George Sayers in America whose business was enhanced when his son George joined him.

At the age of seventy-one Ben Sayers could still put in a round equal to his age but he was advised to slow down. He found this difficult because he had ideas for expansion and on his drives towards Dunbar he cast an eye over the cabbage field of Heugh farm as a possible site for a new factory but he became unwell in 1961 and died that year on 2nd March at his home. Charles Thomson, chief clubmaker of the firm recalled that day:

It was a sad day in March 1961 when Mrs Stephenson...arrived at the factory and told us that her father had died during the night. We were all very shocked and upset. Another great golfer and personality had passed on and left us all wondering what was going to happen now, because whatever did happen there would never be another Ben Sayers. (38 p.131)

Charles Thomson had been a clubmaker since 1929 and some of his early reminiscences give an insight of character and humour of Ben Sayers:

Young Ben asked me if I would like to work for him as a clubmaker. I accepted right away, although I wasn't too happy about the wages...five shilling a week for a fifty hour week, 'OK, start on Monday, 11th April, don't be late and remember to bring a white apron', Well the day arrived and I was right there on time but in my excitement I had forgotten to bring my white apron. Ben was there to meet me and his first words were, 'where is your apron, laddie?' I said, Oh, I've forgotten it Ben.' He replied, 'OK but remember to bring it with you after dinner, you might never become a clubmaker - but there's no harm in looking like one!'

On another occasion Ben had arranged to give Mr Willie McCartney, the great manager of Hearts and Hibs, a lesson and he asked Charlie Thomson to come out on the course to retrieve balls.

'After the lesson was over we were walking back towards the shop with me bringing up the rear, when Mr McCartney stretched out his hand behind him towards me. Hullo, a tip! Sure enough when I put out my hand and made a grab it was for four shillings! Later, I was working away at the bench, when Ben came through to the workshop and said to me, 'Just to keep the books right laddie, did Mr McCartney pay you anything this morning?' I replied, 'yes, he gave me four bob.' You should have seen the look on Ben's face and then he said, 'Right, tomorrow morning

you give the lesson and I'll collect the balls!' It so happened that at that time the professional got only 2/6d an hour!

Doreen received an offer for the firm even before Ben's funeral. Understandably, she refused and in fact she vowed never to sell to this insensitive buyer. With her husband she had been running the firm for some time and eventually in July 1962 Grampian Holdings took over with Doreen staying on as a director for the next four years; her husband Dick stayed on with the new company until his death in 1972. Ben Sayers Limited had moved into new premises at Tantallon Road on the very site which Ben had considered several years before.

THE SETON FAMILY of East Lothian

Magnae Nobilitatis Domini

The first mention of a Seton in East Lothian is in the reign of William the Lion (1165-1214) when he was resident in his palace in Haddington; he was **Philip de Seton** who was given a charter of the lands Seton and Winton. **Sir Alexander Seton** of Seton, a later relative, had two sons, Sir Christopher Seton (c.1278-1306) and Sir Alexander Seton (1311-1340). (25)

Sir Christopher Seton is recorded as paying homage (on pain of death) to the king of England, Edward I ('the Hammer of the Scots') on 4th October 1298-9. In this way Seton was able to keep his father's lands on condition that he entered the king's service. He married Lady Christina Bruce, the third daughter of Robert Bruce, Earl of Carrick, and he supported Bruce's claim to the crown of Scotland being present at his coronation on 21st March 1306.

At the Battle of Methven when Bruce was badly defeated at the hands of the English under Valence in June 1306, Bruce was unseated from his horse by Philip de Mowbray and was rescued from certain death by Sir Christopher Seton. Bruce became a fugitive and Seton took refuge in Loudoun Castle in Ayrshire. However, the castle was taken by the English army and Seton was imprisoned in London where he was hanged and quartered as a traitor. Bruce later erected a chapel to the Virgin Mary near Dumfries at the spot where he was informed of the fate of his faithful friend, Sir Christopher Seton, who had saved his life. (25)

Sir Alexander Seton, born in 1311, was one of the nobles who signed the 'Letter of Barons of Scotland to Pope John XXII' in 1320 ('The Declaration of Arbroath') (60 p.55). He was killed in battle aged twenty-one at Kinghorn 1332 (13 vol III p. 318).

The baronial residence of the Earls of Winton was Seton House until 1715 when, because of the allegiance of the last earl to the 'Old Pretender', Prince James Francis Edward Stuart, his estates were forfeited to the crown. However the Seton story starts much earlier when **Sir George Seton, 1st Lord Seton**, who built the choir and sacristy of St Mary and Holy Cross at Seton c.1478. **Sir George, 2nd Lord Seton** founded the collegiate church there in 1492 and **George, 3rd Lord Seton** roofed the choir with stone slabs 1513, the year in which he was killed at the Battle of Flodden. His widow Lady Janet Seton added the north and south transepts by 1545. She remained a widow for forty-five years and founded St Katherine's Chapel.

George, 4th Lord Seton built the first Winton House in Pencaitland in 1480 but it was destroyed in 1544 by the Earl of Hertford at the start of the 'Rough Wooing'. His second daughter, Katherine, refused all offers of marriage and became a nun at the convent of Sciennes in Edinburgh until her death at the age of seventy-eight. (13 vol.III p.53)

Seton Palace, described in its day as 'the most magnificently structured and furnitured house in Scotland' (51 p.863), was the residence of **George 5th Lord Seton** the loyal supporter of Mary Queen of Scots. He was born c1527 and married Marie Pieris, a French lady-in-waiting to Mary of Guise (mother of Mary Queen of Scots and second wife of James V). As Provost of Edinburgh in 1557 and in 1559 and as a staunch Catholic Seton was arguably the most unpopular Provost of Edinburgh during the Regency of Mary of Guise.

George, 5th Lord Seton with his family (Courtesy of the Scottish National Portrait Gallery)

Because of his part in the release of Cardinal Beaton his palace and gardens were devastated during the 'Rough Wooing' in 1544.

After the murder of Mary's devoted and talented secretary Rizzio on 5th March 1566 Mary, fearing for her life, fled to the restored Seton Palace where she was joined by Lord Seton to continue her journey to Dunbar. It was here that she nonchalantly took part in an archery competition the day after her murdered husband's funeral, leading to speculation that she must have been an accomplice.

When the charismatic Earl of Bothwell took Mary off to Dunbar to marry her the couple were considered to be implicated in the murder of Lord Darnley (Mary's second husband and co-conspirator in Rizzio's murder) and on their journey back to Edinburgh the couple spent their last night together at Seton Palace.

Lord Seton maintained his loyal support to Mary when she was imprisoned in the Castle of Loch Leven but he withdrew his support from the outlawed Bothwell during his trial.

The Seton family's support of Mary was further strengthened when Lord Seton's daughter Mary (one of 'The Four Marys'), a Lady-in-Waiting to Mary Queen of Scots, took the queen's place at the Castle of Loch Leven when the queen attempted her first escape dressed as a laundress. After Queen Mary's final escape from the castle she set off immediately to meet Lord Seton and his followers at Queensferry reaching Seton Palace by midnight (57 p.428). Her attempts to negotiate with her brother, Regent Moray, failed and with a superior force of 6000, commanded by Argyll, she opposed Moray's smaller force under the command of the more experienced and skilled Kirkcaldy of Grange and Morton at Langside. Argyll's illness at a crucial time during the battle led to Mary's defeat but still, the faithful and stalwart Lord Seton never flinched in his support of his queen. He was captured with Sir James Hamilton and eventually escaped to France. Mary Seton followed her queen into captivity in England. She remained with Mary for the next sixteen years until illness forced her to retire to a French convent.

In April 1583 the 5th Lord Seton was accused by the Synod of Lothian of entertaining a seminary priest and a complaint against him was made to the king. James VI politely ignored it and displayed his entire confidence in Seton by sending him on an embassy to France. The king is said to have offered the Seton an earldom which he declined deeming his title as 5th Lord a greater distinction. He died aged fifty-five on 8th January 1585 shortly after his return from France.

Robert Seton, 6th Lord Seton and 1st Earl of Winton was a special favourite of James VI and was elevated to the Earldom of Winton on 16th November 1600 for his services to the crown. He commemorated his monarch in a panel at the east entrance of Winton House which displays the Royal Arms and bears the inscription: JACOBUS PRIMUS MAGNAE ET FRANCIAE ET HIBERNIAE REX. He married Margaret, daughter of Hugh Montgomery, the 3rd Earl of Eglinton. They had two sons, Alexander and George born in 1584.

Alexander Seton, 2nd Earl of Winton resigned the title and estates in 1607 in favour of his young brother George. He took the surname of his mother's family - Montgomery, having been assured of the Earldom of Eglinton. He became the 6th Earl of Eglinton in 1611.

George Seton, 3rd Earl of Winton (1584-1650) was the second son of Robert Seton, 1st Earl of Winton by Margaret daughter of Hugh Montgomery, 3rd Earl of Eglinton. He succeeded his brother, Alexander Seton, in 1607 at the age of thirty-three. It was this Earl who transformed the 15th century **Winton House** in Pentcaitland into 'a Jacobean gem' in the years 1620 to 1627. The work was carried out by the King's Master mason, William Wallace. He added to the remains of the first house which was built about 1480 by the 4th Lord Seton (it was burned down in 1544 by the Earl of Hertford during the 'Rough Wooing'). This 'original and remarkably striking modification of Tudor architecture' (25 p.270) was, of course, an additional or junior residence; his principal one being Seton Palace where he entertained James VI of Scotland (James I of England) when the latter paid one of his infrequent visits to Scotland in 1617. Seton in accordance with the family tradition also entertained Charles I there in 1633.

George Seton did not distinguish himself in the affairs of state, preferring to keep a low profile during difficult times. However, he was a strong Royalist and with four-fifths of the nobility of Scotland he supported the 'Engagement' for the rescue of Charles I in 1648 (the Engagement was a secret treaty between Charles and moderate Covenanters but Cromwell defeated the Engagers' army at Preston in 1648 and marched on Edinburgh).

The 3rd Earl's first wife was Lady Anne Hay, eldest daughter of the 8th Earl of Errol by whom he had three daughters and four sons, George, Charles, Alexander and Francis. By his second wife, Elizabeth, daughter of Lord Herries, he had five daughters and four sons. The Earl's eldest son George, having been inspired by the Marquis of Montrose's run of glorious victories against the Covenanting armies of the Marquis of Argyle, joined the Royalist cause shortly after the Battle of Kilsyth (15th August 1645) but he was captured at the Battle of Philiphaugh on 13th September when Montrose was surprisingly defeated. His father paid a large bond for his release but he lived only a short time and died in 1648 leaving a son, also George.

The 3rd Earl suffered from palsy and after the death of his eldest son his condition worsened and he died at Seton Palace on 15th December 1650. He was succeeded by his grandson, George Seton.

George Seton, 4th Earl of Winton, born in 1640, was the eldest grandson of the 3rd Earl Seton and inherited the title at the age of 10 years. The boy was fined £2000 under Cromwell's so-called 'Act of Grace' for the family's support of Royal cause. He left Scotland to serve in the French army and on his return he served his monarch Charles I against the Covenanters. During the reign of Charles II he commanded a regiment in 1666 during the 'Pentland Rising' against the Covenanters. Again in 1679 he was in command of another regiment at the Battle of Bothwell Bridge when the Covenanters were cruelly defeated by the Duke of Monmouth, son of Charles II.

The 4th Earl died in 1704 and his son, also **George**, by his second wife, Christian, daughter of John Hepburn of Alderston in Haddington, succeeded him.

George Seton, 5th Earl of Winton was in France when he inherited the Earldom but, having lost touch with friends and family in Scotland, his right to the Earldom was questioned by his cousin Viscount Kingston. Doubt had been placed on the validity of his father's marriage but in 1710 George Seton successfully defended his rights to the title and estates. A strong supporter of the 'Old Pretender' he made preparations for the forthcoming uprising in 1715 by raising an army of 300 men. He joined the Earl of Kenmure at Moffat on 14th October when the 'Old Pretender' was proclaimed King James VIII (25 p.271).

Seton opposed the Jacobite advance into England preferring instead that the Jacobite army should strengthen itself by joining the western clans via Dumfries and Glasgow. However, when the Highlanders threatened mutiny he persuaded them, against his better judgement, to advance into England. He was captured at Preston on 14th November and was tried for treason. Of the captured nobility he alone refused to plead guilty. Never-the-less he was found guilty and sentenced to death. He escaped from the Tower of London by cutting the prison bars and fled to France. He joined the Chevalier in Rome to share in the tragedy of Culloden when the 'Young Pretender's' armies were massacred in 1746.

He died unmarried in Rome on 19th December 1749. The estates of Winton were confiscated after '45 Rebellion and thus ended the Seton family link with Winton House.

Alexander Seton, Earl of Dunfermline, the fourth son of the 5th Lord Seton became a highly talented administrator as High Chancellor of Scotland from 1605 until he died in 1622 (18 p.238). He was one of three prominent nobles in the politics of the early 17th century; the others being the Earl of Dunbar and the Earl of Menteith. Seton could be regarded as one of the new leisured landed class whose symbol of gracious living was Seton Palace built by a French architect. His chateaux at Fyvie and Pinkie were also symbols of his status as were his new arms of regality of Dunfermline through royal office.

In Lord John Napier's last letter written, in the year of his death, to Alexander Seton, Earl of Dunfermline, Lord of Fyvy and Urquhart, High Chancellor of Scotland, Napier described his new *Canon of Logarithms* and in return Seton advised Napier to publish his works ' lest they should be published in the name of another.'

ARCHIBALD SKIRVING

Haddington's Scottish Enlightenment portrait painter
'Raeburn's Rival'

Archibald Skirving was born in October 1749 on his father's farm at Garleton and became the unrivalled pastellist of his time. His romanticised red-chalk portrait of Robert Burns was his best known work and placed him among the foremost of his more famous contemporaries: Allan Ramsay (1713-84) and Henry Raeburn (1756-1823). But Skirving never attained their fame or popularity perhaps because he was thought to be an eccentric. However, in 1999 an exhibition of his works at the Scottish National Portrait Gallery in Queen Street Edinburgh brought him for the first time into the public eye; the exhibition was well-named *Raeburn's Rival*. The exhibition was repeated in North Berwick during July and August 1999.

His father, Adam Skirving (1719-1803), was a tenant farmer at East Garleton on the estate of the Earl of Wemyss. He was a sympathiser of the Jacobite cause and wrote songs about the '45 rising such as Hey Johnnie Cope in which 'he satirised a lieutenant Smith of Sir John Cope's army'. The lieutenant challenged him to a duel and Skirving sent his reply:

> *...tell Mr Smith that I hinna time to come to Haddington to gie him satisfaction; but say if he likes to come to Garleton, I'll take a look at him, and if I think I'm fit to fecht him, I'll fecht him, an if no, I'll just do as he did - I'll rin awa'* (59 p.24)

His ancestor 'Black' John Skirving of Plewland was the standard bearer of William Keith, 3rd Earl Marischal of Scotland at the disastrous Battle of Flodden in 1513. Black John was captured but saved the standard by wrapping it around him. A later relation, William Skirving, presented the standard to the faculty of Advocates in 1808; it formed part of the exhibition referred to above.

The gravestone of grandfather Archibald and father Adam Skirving at Athelstaneford Churchyard is engraved:

ARCHIBALD SKIRVING
Farmer Muirton
of the most athletic and best tempered
of men
died only 36 years

His son ADAM farmer Garleton
born 1719 - died 1803
In feature, in tongue, ability, mind
and happy wit rarely surpassed
With lofty or low could be plain or refined
Content beaming bright to the last.

Archibald's early schooling at the new Grammar School of Haddington on the south side of Church Street was forward looking and more vocational than that of the old medieval grammar school in that Latin and Greek were giving way to the teaching of English.

Courtesy of Scottish National Portrait Gallery

He arrived in Edinburgh in 1765 to work as a clerk in the Edinburgh Custom House and to study drawing at the Trustees Academy earning a modest income from painting miniatures. In 1777 he then decided to study and to make his fortune in London being supported by the de jure 7th Earl of Wemyss who lived at Amisfield House in Haddington and had become his patron.

He returned to Edinburgh 1780 to become known for a much sought after new style of portraiture and among his later admirers were Sir Walter Scott (1771-1832) and Thomas Carlyle (1795-1881). Skirving's patron, the Earl of Wemyss, paid for his studies in Rome in 1786 where he mastered the art of pastel work and drew his famous and dramatic self-portrait wearing a black beaver hat and an enigmatic half smile.

In Italy he became part of the community of Scots artists and his style developed into the neo-classical. It was during this sojourn to Italy that the French Revolution broke out in 1789 and the new French Republic declared war on Britain in 1793. Skirving was on his way home to Scotland in August 1794 when he was captured by the revolutionaries and imprisoned at Brest on suspicion of spying. For nine months he suffered degradation and deprivation and witnessed the executions of many aristocrats during the 'Terror' which had been master-minded by the feared Robespierre (1758-1784) who was himself sent to the guillotine. However, many French and Scottish artists petitioned the Convention of the Republic exclaiming that they too had been oppressed by the tyrannical English. This gained Skirving his release but he was badly affected by the inhumanity he had experienced. He had contracted unocular elipopia, a disease of the eyes, and he was no longer able to paint miniatures. He became nervous and suspicious of everyone and was thought to be eccentric.

Unlike Ramsay and Raeburn he had no fashionable studio in Edinburgh and he seemed not to rely on painting for a living in that he tended to please himself when and whom he painted. As he grew older he rarely produced more than one picture a year but his prices ranged from one hundred guineas (£105) and were often in excess of that charged by Raeburn. His chalk drawing of Robert Burns (54.9 x 42.5 cm) gives the bard a romantic, dream-like appearance and was executed partly from Alexander Nasmyth's famous portrait and partly from his own recollection of the poet whom he met in Edinburgh in 1786 before he left for Rome.

Others of his pastels in the Scottish National Portrait Gallery include two of Alexander (Jupiter) Carlyle (1722-1805) minister of Inveresk, Lord Craig (1745-1813) the Scottish Judge, the artist Gavin Hamilton (1723-98), Professor Dugald Stewart (1753-1828), the architect Sir

William Chambers (1726-96) and many others of equal merit.

He died suddenly at Inveresk in 1819 and was buried beside his father and grandfather in Athelstaneford where his gravestone is inscribed on the same stone as his father and grandfather:

His first son and most semblance
ARCHIBALD
born October 1749
By peculiar excellence attained eminence
as a portrait painter
and might have lived in affluence
had he not aimed at private independence
by simplifying the comfort of common life
To beauty, virtue, talent he would bow
But claims from birth or rank would not allow.
Kept friends and foes at nearly equal distance
Knew how to give but not to take assistance.
At threescore ten when scarce began to fail
He dropt at once without apparent ail.

SAMUEL SMILES

Doctor, Biographer, Social Reformer and Railway enthusiast

A plaque affixed to the wall at No.62 High Street, Haddington is inscribed:

Samuel Smiles born in Haddington
lived in this house
author of Self Help and other books.
He died in Kensington 1904.

Samuel Smiles was born on 23rd December 1812. Alison Smiles, his grand-daughter in her biographical essay (48), described some of his earliest memories including the celebrations at the end of the Napoleonic War in 1815 when the pipes and drums of the Militia paraded in the High Street of Haddington. As a boy aged ten, young Samuel joined the fun of the bonfires on Traprain Law to celebrate the visit of George IV to Scotland in 1822, the first since that of Charles II in 1651.

The early schooldays of Samuel Smiles, firstly at the private school in St Ann's Place and then at the Burgh School, were a bad memory. He described his schoolmaster, Patrick Hardie, as "a toady and a tyrant." In spite of the fact that his parents, Samuel and Janet Smiles, insisted that "a good education is equivalent to a good fortune" it was perhaps not surprising that he did not distinguish himself at school - Hardie ruled with threats such as:

> "I will flog you to within an inch of your life; I will dash your brains against the wall; I will split your skull into a thousand pieces; Smiles, you will never be fit for anything but sweeping the streets of your native borough!"

Young Samuel Smiles was relieved to be rid of Hardie when he found himself at the Classical School under the rector William Graham whom he described: "as much a gentleman as the other a tyrant." The tutored daughter of his neighbour on the opposite side of the street, Jane Welsh, was dux of St Ann's and Samuel, eleven years her junior, was not impressed either with her looks or her intelligence and especially not with the favouritism shown her; but then Samuel was a boy while she was a young and attractive lady eleven years his senior and a boy of Samuel's age is simply not attracted to, what to him seemed, a flighty and affected young woman. Her parents Dr and Mrs Welsh were firm friends of Samuel's father and mother.

The Smiles family were strict Covenanters and proud of their ancestor Samuel Drummond who was struck down by the Scots Greys in 1660 when he was field-preaching near the Pentland Hills; only the Bible in his bonnet saved him when he was struck on the head. Sundays were agonising for young Samuel Smiles. The day started with the Catechisms which had to be learned by heart and recited that night. The only exercise allowed was a walk to and from Church and, after family prayers and three Church services, the day was spent reading the Catechisms and the Secession magazine.

On many a cold wintry night young Samuel accompanied his father to the graveyard at St Mary's for their stint of guard duty. The newly buried had to be protected from the 'resurrectionists' who supplied the doctors' dissecting rooms in Edinburgh at sixteen guineas a body. This was the era of the infamous Burke and Hare who supplied bodies to Dr Robert Knox at the School of Anatomy. But there was little time for brooding in the Smiles household which was a home of constant activity: homework from school, tending the yearly new baby, looking after the shop, feeding the pigs in the byre, gardening and the ever-whirring spinning wheel.

Samuel loved books and became obsessed with the free 'itinerating libraries' started by Provost Samuel Brown (son of Haddington's well-loved and scholarly Rev John Brown *qv* of *Self-Interpreting Bible* fame), the praises of which he was to preach to any who would listen later in life at Leeds. The disciplinarian of the large family was undoubtedly his mother. Samuel recalled one Sabbath day when his father took his eldest brother, Willy, for a walk. On their return his mother, in high dudgeon, remarked disapprovingly to young Samuel,

"he's leading that bairn straight to hell!"

His studies in Medicine at the University of Edinburgh where he qualified MD at the age of twenty would have been supervised by Dr. Robert Knox, the famous teacher of anatomy who was discredited when he was known to have accepted dead bodies from the infamous pair of grave-robbers, Burke and Hare. It was a proud day for the Smiles family when Samuel returned home again in 1832 to become Haddington's doctor following in the footsteps of their revered family friend Dr Welsh who had died thirteen years before in 1819 from one of the diseases he had tried so hard to cure - typhoid.

Samuel Smiles was appointed a surgeon in Leeds where his literary talents became evident in his publication of *Physical Education* (1838) and when he took over the editorship of *The Leeds Times*. His love of railways led to his secretaryship of the Leeds and Thirsk Railway in 1845 and he was appointed secretary of the South Eastern Railway in

1854 from which post he retired in 1866. At Leeds he met the famous George Stephenson (1781-1848), the inventor of the locomotive, and Smiles wrote his biography (1857).

Samuel Smiles by Sir George Reid (Courtesy of Scottish National Portrait Gallery)

This was a new style of biography and was a classic. In 1859 he published his famous *Self Help, Thrift and Duty* which promulgated a philosophy of doing good work, building character and independence to lead to the preservation of happiness even in humble circumstances. He opposed privilege and detested the protective duties on corn but his interest in politics came to an abrupt end when free trade was won with the passing of the Corn Laws in May 1846 (which decisively split the Conservative Party). Smiles' cheerful optimism encouraged a spirit of 'make the best of it' was eventually considered by his critics as self-satisfied, sanctimonious and bourgeois. Never-the less, his *Self Help* sold in tens of thousands at home and abroad being translated into several languages. Others of his publications included: *Lives of the Engineers* (3 vols. 1861-62), *Character* (1871), *Thrift* (1875), *Thomas Edward, Cobbler and Naturalist* (1876), *Robert Dick, Baker and Geologist* (1878), *Duty* (1880), *Jasmin, Hairdresser and Poet* (1891), *The Autobiography of Samuel Smiles LL.D.* (1905).

He died aged ninety-two at Kensington in 1904.

ALEXANDER SOMERVILLE

a Social Reformer of Oldhamstocks

Alexander Somerville, although of humble birth, became a leading social reformer, soldier, editor and author of many works of social significance in his day. He was 'persistently devoted to public well-being and to the removal of antagonism between the extremes of society' - this was how he described himself towards the end of his days which ended in abject poverty; he died of starvation alone in a shed in Toronto in 1885.

He was, the youngest of a family of eleven sons, born on 15th March 1811 at Springfield, Oldhamstocks, the son of a carter. His mother was the daughter of a labourer, John Orkney. Alexander went to school at the age of eight at Birnynows and started work aged twelve as a herdboy. In 1828 he joined his brother in Edinburgh where he worked in a timber mill as a sawyer with a weekly wage of six shillings. He was a young man filled with curiosity, always asking questions, he spent his leisure hours in reading and studying the political questions of the day.

This was a time of industrial depression, the year of the great Reform Bill, 1832, and the country was in a state of civil disorder. The Bill had a difficult passage through Parliament from its introduction in March 1831 until it was passed in June 1832 after three attempts. Somerville published his first letter to a newspaper in support of Reform.

Finding it impossible to live on such a small wage he enlisted in the Scots Greys and found himself posted to Birmingham on the eve of the Reform riots. He was ordered with his fellow soldiers to 'rough-sharpen' his sword in preparation for an attack on the rioters. Somerville protested to army headquarters against this extreme action and for this he was given one hundred lashes.

Word of this cruel punishment reached the townsfolk and on his release from hospital he was greeted as a hero of the people and those who had ordered the flogging were reprimanded after an enquiry. A public subscription was taken up for him, but he refused to become involved in any demonstrations; never-the-less he received £300.

He left the army and returned to Edinburgh where he started a newspaper and after it failed he opened a shop but this too was a failure. Penniless again he joined the British Legion in 1835 under Sir George de Lacy Evans in Spain. The Carlist Risings were concentrated in the Basque provinces and many British volunteers died in the mountains. Again, Somerville distinguished himself; he was given several special commendations for his bravery.

He returned to England in 1837 and settled down to serious writing on social and economic reform. In this he found success and was asked to join a revolutionary movement in Wales. Instead of joining it he set himself against it and wrote against the use of violence in his pamphlet: *Warnings to the People on Street Warfare*. His newspaper articles against the Corn Laws came to the attention of the Anti-Corn Law League and Richard Cobden (1804-65) enlisted his help in collecting information throughout the country districts of England to assist the League.

He was now a well-known and respected author having published in London his *History of the British Legion and War in Spain* in 1839 and his *Public and Personal Affairs: An Enquiry* was published in London in 1839. He became a correspondent for the *Manchester Examiner* in 1844 and published his *Autobiography of a Working Man* in 1848. As a correspondent he was asked to enquire into the state of Ireland and the effect of the potato blight during 1845-6 and 1858 when 700,000 died of starvation and the population reduced from over 8 millions in 1841 to under 6.5 millions by 1851.

However, by 1858 the fraudulent practices of literary agents and publishers ruined him. His health suffered through overwork and anxiety; he tried to write his way out of debt with his *Financial Reform Catechism* (1849), *The Whistler at the Plough, Free Trade and the League* (1852), *Life of Roger Mowbray: a Tale* (1853) but still he remained in a state of dire poverty.

A few friends collected the fares to Canada for his wife and family and they arrived in Montreal in 1858. Sadly his wife took ill shortly after they arrived and she died soon after. He obtained work as a journalist and became editor of the *Canadian Illustrated News*. He published *The Conservative Science of Nations* which contained the first narrative of his life in Montreal (1860). After retiring, his funds gradually ran out. Obstinately, he refused help and on 17th June 1885, homeless, penniless and starved, he was found dead in a shed in York Street, Toronto.

His other publications were *Canada as a Battle-ground* (1862), *Living for a Purpose* (1865) and *A Narrative of the Fenian Invasion of Canada* (1866). He married the daughter of Francis Binks of Gretna Bridge in Yorkshire on 10th January 1841 and he was survived by his children who settled in Canada.

EBENEEZER and DAVID SYME

of North Berwick

The Syme brothers, Ebeneezer and David, of North Berwick were the sons of a schoolmaster and were educated in Dunbar. Ebeneezer was born in 1826 and David in 1827. They made their names in Australian journalism during the mid-1800s.

David worked as a proof reader in Glasgow. This was dull work for an active young man and his imagination was fired up while proof reading an account of the gold rush and the 'Forty-Niners' in California. He emigrated in 1851 to find that around 93,000 others had preceded him in the rush for riches and soon afterwards he crossed the Pacific Ocean to Australia where gold had been discovered at Ballarat, Victoria. His brother Ebeneezer joined him and they made sufficient capital from prospecting and contracting work to purchase the insolvent newspaper, *The Melbourne Age*.

Under their editorship *The Melbourne Age* gradually became the major and most influential newspaper in Australia. Its circulation at first was about 2000 copies per day and when Ebeneezer died in 1859 David made some changes; he cut its price by half and fearlessly took up issues such as land reform, protection against imports and self-government. He cut the price again in 1860 and the circulation increased to 15,000 copies per day in 1868 and after yet another price cut the daily circulation reached 120,000.

David Syme can justifiably be described as Australia's first press baron but he was a quiet and thoughtful man who made no attempt towards the familiar flamboyance of his Australian and American contemporaries. In fact he was almost a recluse without the selfishness of such a life; he gave generously to the poor and championed their plight. He fought for the rights of the working man and in fearlessly promulgating Liberal reforms his political influence was powerful. His newspaper led rather than followed public opinion. Today, The *Melbourne Age* still follows this philosophy.

The self-effacing David Syme, newspaper man, philosopher, Liberal, philanthropist and devoted family man died in 1908 surviving his brother by almost fifty years.

SIR JOHN ARTHUR THOMSON

a born teacher, 'the Prince of Lecturers' and eminent zoologist

The eminent zoologist and inspiring teacher, John Arthur Thomson was born in Salton, East Lothian on 8th July 1861 a son of the manse. He was appointed the Regius Professor of Natural History at Aberdeen, a post he held with distinction for thirty-one years. He published over thirty books and numerous zoological papers especially on Alcyonaria (the study of sea-pens, red coral and organ-pipe coral) to be knighted in 1930 for his enormous contribution to science.

His younger brother James and he developed their interest and love of nature through their father, the Rev Arthur Thomson of Saltoun, a keen field-botanist. James also enthused by his father followed his brother in becoming a professional zoologist. This love of science could almost have been inherited: his maternal grandfather, the Rev Dr David Landsborough of Salcoats was a naturalist who published works on Zoophytes and seaweeds and on the natural history of the Island of Arran. An uncle, also Rev David Landsborough of Ayrshire was also a keen naturalist.

Arthur had intended to follow in his father's footsteps to become a minister and after his early schooling in East Lothian he attended New College, Edinburgh to study theology. He gained his MA(Hons) and LLD degrees but, in 1881, he found himself attracted to the practical botany and zoology classes at the University of Edinburgh under the tutelage of the inspiring Professor Patrick Geddes (1854-1932) with whom he would become a lifelong friend and scientific collaborator.

Thomson struggled with his conscience over his abandonment of his studies in theology and Geddes lent a sympathetic ear giving the young man sound and helpful advice. Geddes introduced him to Professor Ernst Heckel with whom he studied at the University of Jena in Germany in 1882 but in a letter to Geddes from Jena in 1883 he wrote of his continuing doubts about making a profession in science and of his intention to return to his studies in Theology (86 p. 70).

However he continued his studies to gain his doctorate of Science and it was now clear that he was destined for a life of academia and research. He was appointed to a lectureship in Zoology and Botany in the School of Medicine at the University of Edinburgh. His research was devoted to the study of heredity and his *Evolution of Sex* published in 1889, in collaboration with Professor Patrick Geddes (then Professor of Botany at University College, Dundee), was a standard work in its day and ran to three editions by 1901. This collaboration with Geddes was to last until the death of Geddes in 1932. Approximately 300 of Thomson's letters to Geddes are kept in the National Library of Scotland. Thomson freely admitted that many of his works were 'extensions and applications of ideas, theories, or keen guesses thrown out to him by his teacher and colleague' (86 p.443)

In August 1886 he wrote to Patrick Geddes to congratulate him on his wedding and to announce his own betrothal on 1st August to Margaret Stewart, daughter of the the Rev. John Stewart of Pitlochry. They were married in 1889 and had three sons and one daughter. Margaret was his constant helper and constructive critic and their children, with enthusiastic encouragement from their mother, all followed in their father's footsteps in becoming professional scientists.

In 1905, when Patrick Geddes was working in the Riviera, Thomson helped Geddes's wife, Anna, who was struggling with the deficits of the Outlook Tower business in the Royal Mile Edinburgh by giving a lecture. She wrote to her husband praising his lecture: 'You will have to look to your laurels, for JAT [Thomson] is without doubt a very attractive lecturer to follow you' (86 p.214). In addition to his brilliance as a lecturer Thomson's literary skill enabled him to reach a wide public as exemplified in his *Outlines of Science.*

Thomson was a born teacher, he was 'The Prince of Lecturers, the master of the exquisite and telling phrase...' - R D Lockhart. 'I have heard him, too, raise the imagination of a large audience by his "Drama of Life"'. We felt as if we were present at great moments of evolution' - W Leslie Mackenzie (87 pps. 289-90). Many of the titles of his publications tell us of his desires not only to serve the needs of his students but, in addition, to popularise nature and science to as wide a reading public as possible: *Evolution of Sex*, 1889 (jointly Patrick Geddes); *The Study of Animal Life*, 1892; *Outlines of Zoology* (8th edition 1929); *The Natural History of the Year; The Science of Life; Progress of Science of the Nineteenth Century*, 1904; Herbert Spencer, 1906; Heredity, 1908; *The Bible of Nature*, 1909; *Darwinism and Human Life*, 1910; *The Biology of the Seasons*, 1911; *Evolution* (jointly with Patrick Geddes), 1911; *Introduction to Science*, 1911; *Sex* (jointly with Patrick Geddes), 1914; *The Wonder of Life*, 1914; *Secrets of Animal Life*, 1919; *The System of Animate Nature* (Gifford Lectures), 1920; Nature All the Year Round, 1921; The Control of Life, 1921; The Haunts of Life, 1922; What is Man?, 1923; The Biology of Birds, 1923; Science, Old and New, 1924; Science and Religion, 1925; Concerning Evolution, 1925; *The Gospel of Evolution*, 1925; *The New Natural History*, 1925-26; *Towards Health*, 1927; *Modern Science*, (jointly with Patrick Geddes) 1929; *Life: Outlines of General Biology*, (2 vols.) 1931; *The Outline of*

Natural History, 1932; *Scientific Riddles*, 1932. In addition, he published many scientific research papers on Alcyonarians.

Such was his international reputation he was invited by the Prime Minister, Lord Salisbury, in 1899 to accept the Chair of Natural History at Aberdeen University - a regius appointment. It was at this time that his house guest in Aberdeen was Patrick Geddes with whom he wrote what he described as 'what will likely be our last book together'. The publication, two years in writing, was the 750,000-word *Life: Outline of General Biology* 1931, 'a comprehensive treatise on biology.....covering the entire world of living organisms....a summary of the life experience of two eminent scientists and scholars....one shrewd gentle, kindly, humorous, with a real talent for literary expression and lucid exposition [Thomson] ; the other [Geddes] vigorous, incisive, systematic, satirical, who like the teachers of Greece, communicates more fully in his conversation....' (86 p.412).

Professor John Arthur Thomson was knighted in 1930 for his lifelong work in the field of natural history. The universities of Edinburgh and Aberdeen awarded him honorary Doctorates of Law and in America he was similarly honoured at the Universities of McGill and California. He died in 1933 at Limpfield in Surrey where his grave is next to that of the composer Frederick Delius (1862-1934)

NIGEL TRANTER of Aberlady

Scotland's most prolific author – history comes alive from his pen

Most mornings in East Lothian a lone figure was seen striding out over the wooden bridge at Aberlady. This was the start of a two- or three-hour hike over the sand dunes during which he stopped occasionally to reach into his jacket pocket, retrieve his notebook and jot down a few ideas for his next book. The figure was that of nonagenarian Nigel Tranter, Scotland's most prolific author, and the more often he stopped to write in his little notebook the faster he typed later in the evening.

He was a master of the historical novel having written in excess of one hundred of them. He rightfully claimed to be a story teller rather than a historian, although many an academic historian would be proud to have published his five volumes of *The Fortified Houses of Scotland*, a dedicated work which deals with 663 castles, or to have written his four volumes of *The Queen's Scotland*. The stories of his novels are of course based on historical fact but with a difference - he puts imaginary flesh on the actual bones and gives character and spirit to hundreds of historical figures. History came alive from the pen of Nigel Tranter.

Asked which phrase in Scottish history which affected him most in his writing, his answer was a fascinating story around five words: "These things we write merrily" which were uttered by John Knox, the pre-eminent Scottish reformer. The event was the assassination of David Beaton, Archbishop of St Andrews who was stabbed to death and hung by his heels from his bedroom window in St Andrews. Nigel Tranter's point was that had Beaton written "these things" they would most certainly not be written 'merrily' and we should have had a completely different account. Nigel Tranter's aim is thus to avoid a one-sided story of history, which, of course, is an aim of any credible historian.

His favourite sources are interesting - the four volumes of Patrick Fraser Tytler's *History of Scotland*, A.O. Anderson's *Early Sources of Scottish History* and the eleven volumes of *The Register of the Great Seal of Scotland* - to mention a few.

Nigel Tranter was born in Glasgow, a son of the church, on 23rd November 1909. His two grandfathers were ministers, his great-grandfather, William Tranter, was a talented inventor who patented the famous 'Tranter Pistols' with a double-trigger system in 1853. His great-grandmother, Frances Watt was the great-granddaughter of his great-great-great grandfather who was James Watt (1736-1819) of steam engine fame after whom the unit of power is named - the Watt.

It was while researching his book *The Patriot* that he came across the existence of the Tranter Pistols. He was writing about the incident of the insult to Andrew Fletcher of Saltoun, the "Patriot", who had been slapped across the face by Alderman Dare during the Monmouth Rising in 1688. Fletcher drew his pistol and shot Dare who had accused him of stealing his best horse; in fact he had only borrowed the horse. Nigel Tranter's insistence on accuracy led him to investigate whether or not it was possible in 1688 to draw a pistol and fire it. He was unsure as to whether the pistol would not firstly have to be primed and loaded. This took him to the National Museum in Chambers Street, Edinburgh where he met the museum's expert on firearms. He assumed that Nigel had arrived to ask about the Tranter Pistols. Nigel had never heard of them and so his visit to the museum not only confirmed that the double action pistol had been invented by 1688 and that Fletcher could indeed have drawn such a weapon and used it as he had described but he discovered the patents of his ancestor.

He remembers little of Glasgow because the family moved to Edinburgh when Nigel was four years of age. He was the youngest of the family of one step-brother and two step-sisters who were several years his senior. He grew up rather detached from them but his young life was a happy one. He recalled the musical evenings during which his parents, who were members of the Royal Choral Union, would encourage him to sing but music did not appeal to young Nigel Tranter, although he did sing a solo in the Usher Hall at a school concert. His schooling at George Heriot's School fostered an early love of Scottish castles. The school itself catches the imagination; it is a 17th century castellated building first used as a hospital for the troops of Oliver Cromwell in 1650 after the Battle of Dunbar. It was while at 'Heriots', at the age of thirteen, that he first started to write about Scottish Castles and his expertly illustrated schoolboy jotters are testimony to certain future success. However, he gained little or nothing from history lessons which were, surprisingly for Heriots, devoid of Scottish history.

He developed an early curiosity about Scottish castles; for him there was always an air of mystery about them and his youthful ambition was to become a restoring architect. But as often happens in life, early ambitions are thwarted by family circumstances. His father died when

Nigel was about to start his seven-year apprenticeship as an architect and lack of money forced him to give up his studies. Instead he had to earn a living and he entered the world of insurance. His uncle was a founder member of the Scottish National Insurance Association Ltd., and this was to become the source of his income for the next few years.

He never lost his love of Scottish castles, so much so, that by the age of twenty-two he had published his first book, *The Fortalices and Early Mansions of Southern Scotland, 1400-1650*. The meticulous research for this book took him around many historic sites as did his five volumes of The Fortified House in Scotland which undoubtedly set the scenes for many of his future novels. These five volumes covered 663 castles in every Parish of Scotland.

Nigel Tranter's four volumes of *The Queen's Scotland*, started in 1969, was an arduous task over several years. This was a companion to Arthur Mee's *King's England* but whereas Mee's work tended to reflect the proclivities and idiosyncrasies of English Parish ministers, Tranter's was a place-by-place accurate guide of everything ancient and modern in each Parish of Scotland. This huge task was undertaken as therapy for himself and his wife, May Jean Campbell Grieve, who accompanied and helped him following the tragic death of their only son Philip who was killed in a car accident on his way home from a climbing expedition on the 5165m Mount Ararat in Turkey. But this great work was sadly brought to an abrupt halt by the death of his wife in 1979 and although the first four volumes were published he never had the heart to finish it; memories were too precious.

His first novel, *Trespass*, published in 1937, was followed with several books about the lives and mysteries of the inhabitants of the castles he had written about in his schoolboy notebooks. As never before history was brought to life, not perhaps particularly pleasing to academic historians but unquestionably interesting and fascinating to his readers the world over. There are Nigel Tranter fan clubs in many countries; France, Germany, several in America and even a Japanese fan club. The summer months for Nigel Tranter were particularly busy with visits from admiring fans to his house at Aberlady - these are the pilgrimages of young writers and students of all ages. Busy though he was, Nigel Tranter gave unstintingly of his time by taking them on conducted tours of his beloved castles. Americans arrived by the bus load and begged him to accompany them on their tours, this he did with unbounded generosity. He was closely involved with the restoration of over sixty castles throughout Scotland; there was no better guide in the country. At the age of eighty-nine he was actively involved in the restoration of another five Scottish castles.

In 1946 Nigel Tranter decided that he could earn his living as a professional writer and the world of adults as well as children has benefited from such as: *Spaniards' Isle* (which was translated into Swedish in 1958), *Nestor the Monster* (which is about to be translated into Japanese and re-issued in Britain in audio tape form), *Birds of a Feather, Something Very Fishy, Tinker Tess* and its sequel *To The Rescue* - to mention a few of his fourteen children's novels. His adult novels include *The Bruce Trilogy* (1969-71) which has sold over 1 million copies each, *The Wallace* (1975), which was written to do justice to his hero of Scotland, Sir William Wallace, *Lord of the Isles* (1983), *Highness in Hiding* (1995) - to mention a sample of over 100 novels.

There is a temptation to think of Nigel Tranter as simply an author; this is erroneous. He is devoutly Scottish in his thinking, he believed firmly that we Scots ought to manage our own affairs, "we ought to be responsible for making our own decisions." He is convinced that the extraordinary character of Scots makes us a nation of leaders which explains our tendency to argue and to quarrel with each other, and the price is rule from London which he considered to be unnecessary and unwanted. "We Scots are different, not better, but long live the difference." He averred that "the Scottish Parliament is a good start".

He has given generously of his time to dozens of practical works of restoration and Scotland owes the restoration of over sixty ancient castles and houses to his indefatigable energy and determination not to lose our Scottish heritage. He was Vice-Convenor of the Scottish Covenant Association in 1951, chairman of the National Forth Road Bridge Committee in 1953, he was chairman of the St Andrews Society of East Lothian since 1966 and he was chairman of the East Lothian Liberal Association for fifteen years during which he met and befriended such well-known Liberals as Jo Grimmond (the late Lord Grimmond), Lord John Bannerman, Sir Russell Johnson and Sir David Steel. He was President and Honorary President of Scottish PEN from 1962 to 1966, Chairman of the Society of Authors of Scotland from 1966 to 1970, Chairman of the National Book League for Scotland from 1971 to 1973 and Vice-Chancellor of the Order of St Lazarus of Jerusalem from 1982 to 1988

His life was devoted to his writing which he explained: "when you earn your living from writing you have to have discipline and I must write about 1500 words a day. History is terribly important, it is not simply a dry subject, it can be told as exciting stories. This is what I try to do. My ambition is to stimulate people to know the history of their country." It was not surprising therefore that the British Broadcasting Corporation chose him as 'Scot of the Year' in 1989 when he celebrated his 80th birthday, that he was made an Honorary Freeman of Blackstone, Virginia, USA, that Strathclyde University honoured him with the award of a Doctorate and that Her Majesty, Queen Elizabeth, made him an Officer of the Order of the British Empire (OBE).

Nigel Tranter's success is obvious to any who browse the shelves of any bookshop. He has given a new and sustained impetus to Scottish history. His last book, marking his 90th birthday, was *Envoy Extraordinary* and he was half way through his next book when suddenly, on 9th January 2000 after a few days of suffering from the influenza of that winter, he was taken from us. He died peacefully at his new home in Gullane. Thousands at home and abroad mourned this terrible loss but we knew that we could not keep him with us, but as his biographer, Ray Bradfied, said, 'we thought Nigel would live forever'.

GEORGE, VIII MARQUIS of TWEEDDALE

The Tweeddale monument, which stands just opposite County Buildings in Court Street, Haddington, is unusual in that it is a marble portrait bust of the Marquis in a red sandstone votive temple formed by a crown top on pillars; it was modelled on the well-head at Pinkie (4 p.240). Its base is quite low but in perfect proportion standing only about five feet high.

Who then does this attractive monument commemorate? The inscription tells us just that:

Erected by Public Subscription
AD 1881
In Grateful Rembrance of
The Public Services in War and Peace of
George, VIIIth Marquis of Tweeddale FM,KT,GCB
Lord Lieutenant of Haddingtonshire
Born February 1st 1787
Died October 16th 1876

George Hay (Hay being the family name of the Marquis of Tweeddale) was born on 1st February 1787 at Bonnington and, at the age of seventeen, he acceded to the title of 8th Marquis of Tweeddale and the East Lothian estates at Yester. He was a powerfully built young man and he decided upon a military career, following a family tradition. In fact, he entered the army as an ensign (sub-lieutenant) only two months before his father's death in August 1804.

In 1806 he was sent to Sicily and by May 1807 he was given his own company. Soon afterwards he was sent to the Iberian Peninsula to serve in the Peninsular War (1808-1814) under Sir Arthur Wellesley (later Duke of Wellington) who landed at Mondego Bay on 1st August 1808 with 12,000 men to advance to Lisbon. Tweeddale was twice wounded, firstly at the British victory over the French of Busaco on 27th September 1810 and then at Vittoria on 21st June 1813. Immediately following the latter he was promoted to Lieutenant-Colonel and invalided home. However, as soon as he was fit again he rejoined his regiment in the American War (1812-15). He distinguished himself as a daring and fearless cavalryman but again he was wounded; this time at Niagara in 1813 where he was captured but only after a great struggle in which he refused to surrender. It was a miracle that he was not killed. His reflexes were needle sharp; he was a master swordsman and his bravery bordered on audacity. That he survived his incarceration was due not only to his robustness and his strong mental powers but to the humanity of his captors.

At the end of the American war he returned home to Yester and was made a Companion of the Most Honourable Order of the Bath (CB) for his valiant military service. Whilst he saw no further active service he remained on the employed list and during the rest of his life he was steadily promoted: Colonel, 27th May 1825; Major-General, 10th January 1837; Lieutenant-General, 9th November 1846; General, 20th June 1854; Field Marshall 29th May 1875. His honours included the Knighthood of the Most Ancient and the Most Noble Order of the Thistle (KT) in 1820. Queen Victoria knighted him in 1862 as Knight Commander of the Most Honourable Order of the Bath (KCB) and he was awarded the Knight Grand Cross of that Order (GCB) in 1867.

On 28th March 1816 he married Lady Susan Montagu, third daughter of the 5th Duke of Manchester. They had seven sons and six daughters. One of his daughters, Lady Elizabeth Hay, married the son of the Duke of Wellington in 1839. Gray and Jamieson (50 p.73) notes that the disproportionately large amount of money collected by the ladies of East Lothian towards the statue of the equestrian 'Iron Duke' (by Sir John Steell, 1852) in front of Register House in Edinburgh was due in no small measure to this relationship (£1153 out of £10,000).

Tweeddale was East Lothian's war hero and he was invited to lay the foundation stone for the new bridge over the Tyne at Briery Bank - the Waterloo Bridge. This duty he carried out amid masonic honours on the second anniversary of Wellington's great victory of Waterloo - 18th June 1817.

The Marquis was Lord Lieutenant of East Lothian from 1822 to 1842 and at Yester he maintained a strong interest in farming; he pioneered deep ploughing and tile-draining and spent considerable sums in farming experiments when he developed and invented several farm implements. A man of great energy he proved his expertise as a coachman when he drove the mail coach, non stop and without relief, from London to Haddington. He was vice president of the elite Agricultural Society of East Lothian whose membership consisted of fifty-five nobles and other gentry.

8th Marquis of Tweeddale by Sir Francis Grant (Courtesy of the Scottish National Portrait Gallery)

His interest in the affairs of the Royal Burgh of Haddington extended to the proposal to build a new Court House in what was then called King Street and renamed Court Street. He was appointed chairman of the committee to oversee its erection in 1833 after its foundation stone was laid by Sir John Gordon Sinclair of Stevenson 'in presence of the beauty and fashion of the neighbourhood' (5 p.229). The committee membership included: The Marquis of Tweeddale, Lord Lieutenant; Sir John Gordon Sinclair; Sir David Kinloch; David Anderson of St Germains; James Hamilton of Bangour; and Robert Riddell, Sheriff-Substitute.

He demitted the office of Lord Lieutenant in 1842 on taking up the Governor-Generalship of Madras in India where he was Commander-in-Chief of the armed forces; the latter command was given by special arrangement of the Duke of Wellington because of the poor state of the local army. The select membership of the East Lothian Agricultural Society (founded in 1819) gave their vice-president, the departing Marquis, a public dinner in his honour. It was held on 20th May 1842 in the Assembly Room of Haddington and over 150 'gentlemen' attended. It was presided over by Lord Elcho who, in extolling the virtues and accomplishments of the Marquis, referred to:

> "... his glorious career, his signal military talents that were afterwards developed in the Peninsular War, where the Marquis of Tweeddale had the good fortune to attract the attention of that illustrious commander (Wellington), who repeatedly placed him in offices of trust and responsibility, and by his heroism gained that distinguished memorable opportunity of expressing." (5.p.167).

The Marquis replied:

> "This going to India was no seeking of mine: I was commanded by my sovereign. I was asked by the East India Company, in these times of difficulty, to serve them in a civil capacity, and also in a military capacity; and sorry would I be to think that anyone bearing my name, when such a call was made upon him, would refuse the last drop of his blood in the service of his native country. My noble friend has alluded to the compliment paid me on a late occasion, as well as to my services under that great man (Wellington) whose career commenced in India. I, a humble imitator, go to follow in his steps..."

He returned home from India in 1848 and for the next twenty-six years he followed with intense interest his farming pursuits at Yester, his dedicated work and expertise being recognised in his presidency of the Agricultural and Highland Society. His eldest son, the Earl of Gifford, died in 1862 and his wife died on 5th March 1870. Only sixteen months after his promotion to the rank of Field Marshall, in 1876 at the age of eighty-nine years he suffered an accident from which he died on 10th October. He was succeeded by his second son Arthur.

The monument in Court Street therefore commemorates a great and brave soldier, a man of many accomplishments, not only military but in farming and the new science of meteorology and one who took great pride in his community as well as his colonelcy of the 30th Foot (1830), the 42nd Foot (1862) and of the Lifeguards (1863).

JOHN VERT

his generosity helped build the Vert Hospital, Haddington

The name John Vert is commemorated in Haddington with the Vert Memorial Hospital. It is the red sandstone building on the A1 at the corner of Aberlady Road and was built from the red sandstone obtained from the recently demolished Palladian mansion house of Amisfield. The Vert Memorial Hospital and its 1950s maternity extension, having been closed for several years, has been redesigned internally to form private flats and renamed Vert Court.

This cottage hospital was the dreamchild of a far-seeing local doctor, Dr Henry Robarts (1879-1951) *qv*; he was the prime-mover of the plan and chief advisor to the committee appointed to oversee the fund-raising and construction under the chairmanship of Lady Hersey Baird of Lennoxlove. The principal benefactor was John Vert who, having amassed his fortune in America, gifted the sum of £7000 (over £250,000 today) for the erection of a cottage hospital in 1927. As building progressed it soon became apparent that although local subscription equalled Vert's generosity there would be insufficient funds for its completion and Vert unhesitatingly provided the outstanding amount of a further £3000 (£110,000 today).

John Vert was born in Haddington in 1852. His father, Francis Vert (1821-1888), an auctioneer, was elected Provost of Haddington from 1866 to 1869 and during his Provostship he campaigned successfully for the removal of road tolls. This involved a change in legislation and previous attempts by the Town Council objecting to additional tollbars in 1792 had failed. For his long and devoted service to the Town Council he was presented with a magnificent piece of silver plate which his son John took with him to America after the death of his father.

John Vert married Jessie S.S. McLean of Kirriemuir and the young couple emigrated to America about 1875 where he worked hard in the estate agency business in the town of Pendleton in Oregon. He built a successful and highly lucrative business for himself and towards the end of his life he decided to make a tangible gift to the town of his birth, Haddington. He gifted a substantial proportion of the money to build the cottage hospital and in addition he presented to the Town Council his father's silver plate and a valuable 18th century clock. He returned to Haddington for the opening ceremony of the hospital in 1929 and was accorded the Freedom of the Royal Burgh. In Kirriemuir he contributed the funds required to build a cottage for the local nurse in memory of his wife and her parents.

He died in 1934 at the age of eighty-two at his home in America.

JAMES VETCH FRS

a soldier, surveyor and military engineer

Vetch Park in Haddington is named after the land-owning Vetch family of Haddington. A glance at John Wood's 1819 Survey Plan of Haddington and Nungate shows that Robert Vetch owned land in the north-west part of the town and in the vicinity of Vetch Park. His property at Hawthornbank including Hawthornbank House, which became Caponflat House, was the home of the Vetch family. The land between Aberlady Road and Hospital Road was sold by Miss Vetch to the Town Council for the housing developments at Caponflat, Hopetoun Drive, Baird Terrace and Davidson Terrace in Haddington.

A later relative, Henry Vetch (1857-1936), fifth son of Lieutenant-Colonel Vetch, re-purchased the property in 1916 and gifted part of the land on which the Vert Hospital in Haddington was built. (ref. John Vert p386)

Young James Vetch, the subject of this story, spent his early years at Caponflat House. He became a military engineer of distinction. As a surveyor and engineer he served under the Duke of Wellington during the Peninsular War (1808-14). He became known for his extremely hard and competent work at home and abroad and was elected to Membership of the Royal Society in recognition of his geographical, historical and engineering publications.

James Vetch was born in Haddington on 13th May 1789, the third son of Robert Vetch of Caponflat. He was educated in Haddington, and soon after leaving school he joined the army. He served under the great Glasgow general Sir John Moore during the Peninsular War (1808-14).

At the end of the Napoleonic War in 1815 he was invited to carry out the first full survey of the Orkney and Shetland Islands; he then triangulated the Western Isles of Scotland, again a first. In 1824 he was offered and accepted the post of manager of a silver mine in Mexico. He returned twelve years later to become resident engineer of the Birmingham to Gloucester Railway Company. A man of considerable vision, he proposed the building of a ship canal to link the Mediterranean Sea with the Red Sea but his design was opposed by Lord Palmerston who considered it to be against British interests. However, in 1855 the great French engineer, Vicompte de Ferdinand Lesseps, included Vetch's proposals in his own report to the French Government. At that time Lesseps was at the height of his fame having completed the design and construction of the Suez Canal.

Vetch went on to design the sewage and drainage systems of Leeds. Prince Albert had exerted great influence over the government by his exhortations for improved sewage and drainage systems in London and at Windsor Castle. The Prince was disgusted by the foul smells and had described the Thames as 'Aqua Mortis'. Vetch was appointed to design and install the drainage system for Windsor Castle and for Southwark.

In 1846 Vetch was appointed by the Admiralty as consulting engineer to advise on harbours, rivers and railway bridges to ensure their safety. He was invited to take over the design work of a new pier at Port Natal (Durban), South Africa and to deepen the entrance to the harbour in 1851. The work was already underway by another engineer, John Milne, but the Cape Governor, no doubt bowing to conditional financing from the British Government, decided, unwisely as it turned out, to commission the services of the British Admiralty's hydrographer, Captain James Vetch, who promptly submitted his design of two converging breakwaters for a protected entrance to the harbour. Theoretically, his design was sound enough but he had never set foot in Natal and was unaware of the ferocity of the breakers of the Indian Ocean. His scheme was estimated at £165,000 and during a storm his timber structures fell to pieces. Part of 'Vetch's Pier', as it is known locally, can still be seen today. Milne's scheme was reinstated and proved successful.

James Vetch retired in 1863 having published several learned papers including: *Account of the Island of Foula* (1821), *Monuments and relics of the ancient inhabitants of New Spain* (1836), *Political Geography Nomenclature of Australia* (1836), *On the Structural Arrangements most favourable to the health of Towns* (1842), *Havens of Safety* (1844). He published reports on the harbours of Ramsgate, Tyne, Isle of Man, Holyhead, Portpatrick, and of South Africa - Table Bay and Port Natal (Durban).

Such was his reputation and his highly valued expertise he was elected to membership of many learned societies and to the highest academic honour in Britain - his election as a Fellow of the Royal Society (FRS). Before his death he received his award of the Military General Service Medal (1793-1814) with two bars, the medal having been authorised in 1847 and issued to living survivors. He died in London on 7th December 1869 and was buried at Highgate Cemetery.

WILLIAM WATERSTON of Spott

The long-established firm of stationery and sealing wax manufacturers, George Waterston & Son Limited of Edinburgh, was founded by an East Lothian schoolmaster in 1752. He was William Waterston born in the village of Spott about a mile south of Dunbar where his father, John Watherston (original spelling) was, for fifty years, gardener to Lord Alexander Hay. It was he who planted the lovely avenue of trees leading to Spott House.

William Waterston (he dropped the h in Watherston), born in 1729 and educated at the village school, had a thorough grounding in reading, writing, arithmetic and an appreciation of natural philosophy. He was a bright pupil and became firstly a pupil teacher then a fully fledged teacher at about the age of twenty. However, teaching proved not to be a vocation for young William Waterston, the excitement of the big City of Edinburgh attracted him.

At the age of twenty-two Waterston sought employment, not as an apprentice, because he considered himself competent in clerical and accounting work, but as an assistant to James Lorimer a manufacturer of torches and flambeau and of sealing wax and paste wafers (which were necessary before the invention of gummed envelopes). Flambeaux were the 3-foot torches of low flame carried by the 'link boys' who ran ahead of sedan chairs to guide their way through the dark streets and closes of Edinburgh. This was not exactly Waterson's main aim in life but he learned quickly and gained a salutory lesson about the ruthlessness of business when Lorimer found himself imprisoned in the Tolbooth for debt.

Waterston, now out of work, decided to set up in business for himself - a courageous decision considering the consequences of the financial disaster he had just experienced. He leased a workshop in the Cowgate at an annual rent of thirty shillings (£1.50) having doubtless bought much of Lorimer's equipment from his creditors. At that time the houses of the Lawnmarket reached down to the Cowgate (Victoria Street did not exist until 1837), the living quarters overlooking the Lawnmarket, the business or manufactory in the centre of the building and the livestock at the Cowgate end. By a stroke of good luck Waterston's first order for sixty-six flambeaux priced at £6 was from the Duke of Hamilton, the Hereditary Keeper of Holyrood House. Undoubtedly, this prestigious order augured well for the future. He had been fortunate too in gaining the expertise of a rather secretive figure known only as 'Chase' and thought to be a fugitive from debt who had previously taken refuge in the 'Sanctuary' in Abbey Strand at the foot of the Royal Mile. Chase knew the secret formula and the methodology for making sealing wax and such was the excellence of Waterston's product he was awarded two silver medals for his exhibits at the Industrial Exhibition of the Edinburgh Society for the Promotion of Arts and Manufacturers.

By now the name Waterston had become known and his order book quickly expanded as is illustrated from his 1763 ledger with 169 customers. Confident of success William Waterston travelled to Glasgow, Dundee, Perth, Greenock and as far as Liverpool to sell his products. These were arduous journeys by coach over rough terrain with the constant danger of attacks by highwaymen. The business expanded and a move in 1764 to larger premises was necessary. The first Edinburgh Directory of 1773 shows his business in Edinburgh's Royal Mile, in Dunbar's Close just east of Bank Street.

Little has been recorded of William Waterston's social activities except for his membership of the Edinburgh Musical Society in which he played the violin. His first wife, Theodosia Jackson, the daughter of an Edinburgh lawyer, died in 1775; they had no children. During his travels to Perth he met Catherine Sandeman, the daughter of a prominent Perth family in the linen trade and wine shipping business. In fact, her uncle, David Sandeman, with the Provost of Perth were taken hostage by the Jacobite army in 1745 for their refusal to pay Prince Charles's levy. After his release he, a strong supporter of the British Linen Company was the first to supply 10,000 yards of linen from his factory and he became the first agent of the British Linen Bank Ltd., newly formed from the British Linen Company. Catherine's brother, David, was a founder of the Commercial Bank of Scotland and her other brother, George, founded the Wine Shipping House of Sandemans of London and Oporto in Portugal. William Waterson was a popular visitor to the Sandeman family and he, through their recommendation, became a Burgess of the city.

In spite of the twenty-six year difference in their ages they fell in love and married in 1776. The happy couple lived at Dunbar Close and their first son, William, was born in 1777. The following year their second son, George was born and in 1780 their third boy, John, arrived. That year William Waterston became violently ill and died almost without warning aged only fifty-one.

His wife, Catherine, was a young lady of strength and capability and in spite of incredible difficulties she carried on the business. Her strength of character and determination must have been formidable; with three babies and the unexpected loss of a key craftsman she carried on with help from a sympathetic customer, Alexander Kincaid, the King's Printer, and her cousin Robert Sandeman. She was an excellent business woman. The business prospered and she moved its premises and announced the new opening by means of an advertisement in 1782 in the Caledonian Mercury:

'Mrs Waterston, Wax Chandler, in Galloway's Close, has now opened a shop on the North Side of the Lawnmarket, opposite to the head of Forrester's Wynd, Edinburgh, where for the convenience of the public, may be had a complete assortment of the different kinds of Sealing wax, Wafers, and other Articles in the Wax-Chandlery way, which of late have been greatly improved.'

After eight years she moved the business to St John's Hill where she established her workshop and home. Her second husband, Robert Ferrier, was a minister and so in love that he resigned his ministry of the Church of Scotland to join his future wife's religion, the Glassites [or Sandemanians from Robert Sandeman (1718-81) who was disciple of the founder John Glas (1695-1773)]. They married in 1786 and although Ferrier was not a good businessman he did his best to encourage his wife's success. He died in 1795 and she made her fifteen year-old son, George Waterston, a partner.

Six generations of the Waterston family have expanded and modernised this company of high quality stationery (they print banknotes and cheques for the Bank of Scotland) and sealing wax; its quarter millennium is approaching (2002) and undoubtedly will be cause for celebration.

THE EARLDOM OF WEMYSS

The Wemyss family originated at Wemyss in Fife where an important branch of it still holds Wemyss Castle. Their connection with East Lothian began in the early eighteenth century, but before then, indeed between 1215 and 1231, there are charters by John son of Michael of lands at Penshiel, near the present Whiteadder Reservoir in Lammermuir, to the monks of the Isle of May, to the Church of Melrose etc.

However, the present and much more important connection could be said to begin in 1720 when the 5th Earl of Wemyss married in secret, Janet, the only daughter of the rich and notorious gambler, Colonel Charteris *qv* who held lands in East Lothian, Midlothian and elsewhere including those which came to be called Amisfield (previously Newmills), east of Haddington and named after the original Charteris lands near Dumfries. These lands passed to the colonel's grandson, Francis, who became the 7th Earl of Wemyss.

The story of the Wemyss earldom starts with the **Sir John Wemyss** who was born c1586 and created a Baronet of Nova Scotia (3rd October 1626), Lord Wemyss of Elcho (23rd April 1628) and **Earl of Wemyss** on 25th June 1633; the last during the visit of Charles I to Scotland when he was crowned and ordered that Edinburgh be known as the capital of Scotland.

Of course, the Wemyss family has a much longer lineage; the earliest was Michael of Wemyss and Methil who was born c1165 (92 p.2979). A later Sir Michael Wemyss (born c1231) supported John Balliol in his claim to the throne of Scotland in 1291 and yet another Sir Michael, who was knighted in 1316, was captured at Halidon Hill when the Scots suffered a defeat by the English in 1333. Several generations later Sir John Wemyss of Wemyss fought at the Battles of Pinkie (1547) and Langside (1568) for Mary Queen of Scots; he was the great-grandfather of Sir John Wemyss, the 1st Earl of Wemyss.

Fearful of a return to Episcopalianism and royal authority over the Church, the 1st Earl was one of many signatories of the National Covenant on 28th September 1638 which was a serious reaction against Archbishop Laud's 'creeping Catholicism' and the Prayer Book (1637) which was insisted upon by Charles I and which caused a riot within St Giles Cathedral when Jenny Geddes was said to have thrown her stool in protest at Dean Hannay when he read from the Service Book for the first and last time.

On 15th September 1609 the future 1st Earl had married Jean, daughter of Patrick, 6th Lord Gray. They had six children of which only their son David survived. The 1st Earl died on 22nd November 1649.

David Wemyss, the **2nd Earl of Wemyss**, known as the 'Great Earl', was born on 6th September 1610. He became Master of Wemyss in 1628 and took the courtesy title of Lord Elcho when his father was created Earl of Wemyss in 1633. He succeeded to the Earldom in 1649 and married three times. By his first wife, Ann (married 4th February 1626/7) who was the eldest daughter of 2nd Lord Balfour of Burleigh, he had eleven children but the eighth and last surviving son David died unmarried in 1671. His daughter, Jean, survived and married twice: the Earls of Angus and of Sutherland. The 2nd Earl's second wife (married 26th April 1650) was Lady Eleanor Fleming, daughter of the 2nd Earl of Wigtoun; they had no children. By his third marriage to Margaret (13th January 1652/3), daughter of the 6th Earl of Rothes and widow of Lord Balgonie and the 2nd Earl of Buccleuch, he had two sons and a daughter: one son who died in childhood and the other who lived till age fifteen and one surviving daughter, Margaret.

The 2nd Earl was a Covenanter and as Colonel of the Fifeshire Foot in the Scots army he helped to defeat the Royalists after a minor skirmish at Newburn (1640) and occupied Newcastle. However he suffered defeats by the Royalists commanded by the Marquis of Montrose at Tippermuir (1644) against Montrose himself, Alford (1645) and Kilsyth (1645). During the Interregnum (1649-60) the 2nd Earl was Sheriff of Fife.

He greatly developed the coal in his estates in Fife and he built Methil harbour in preparation for the transport of coal and other goods. He sunk several pits, one of which was called the 'Happy Mine'. These pits were owned by the Wemyss family until nationalisation of the coal industry in 1947. From his salt pans alone his weekly profit was 4,000 merks (18 p.177).

The 2nd Earl's last surviving son died in 1671 and the titles and estates were passed by a regrant of his peerage, honours and lands (23rd August 1672) to his younger daughter, Lady Margaret, and by this special arrangement with the Crown she became the Countess of Wemyss in her own right. She was the daughter of the Earl's third wife Margaret. Her elder sister, Jean, Countess of Sutherland, objected strongly but unavailingly. The 2nd Earl died in June 1679.

Margaret, Countess of Wemyss, is counted as the **3rd Earl of Wemyss**. She was twenty years old when she succeeded her father. She was born on 1st January 1658/9 and married her third cousin twice removed, Sir James Wemyss, who was created Lord Burntisland for life in 1671. He died in 1682 and his title became extinct. They had one son, David, and two daughters: Anne and Margaret as well as another son and daughter both of whom died young. The countess's second husband was George MacKenzie, Lord Tarbert. They married in 1700 and in 1703 he was created Earl of Cromartie; they had no children. The countess died on 11th March 1705 and her son, David, by her first marriage, succeeded her.

The **4th Earl of Wemyss, David Wemyss**, was baptised on 29th April 1678 being styled Lord Elcho. In 1703 he became an Ensign of the Company of Archers, Lieutenant-General in 1713 and Captain-General in 1715 of the renamed (1704) Royal Company of Archers. He was honoured with the Fellowship of the College of Physicians of Edinburgh in 1705 which was the year of his mother's death and his succession as the 4th Earl. He was appointed Lord High Admiral of Scotland but this office was abolished after the Union in 1707, of which he was a strong supporter having been one of the Scottish Commissioners for the Union. He was now appointed Vice Admiral of Scotland, a Privy Councillor and a was representative peer until 1710.

His first wife (married 13th August 1697) was Lady Anne Douglas, only daughter of the 1st Duke of Queensberry and sister of the Hon. William Douglas, 1st Earl of March, who died of accidental burns on 3rd February 1700 only two and a half years after her marriage. She had two sons, the second and only survivor, James, succeeded to the Wemyss titles and estates. The Earl's second wife, Mary, was the daughter of Sir John Robinson of Farmingwood, Northamptonshire. She died in 1712 after three years of marriage. His third marriage, in 1716, to Elizabeth, daughter of 1st/10th Lord Sinclair gave them two daughters, Elizabeth and Margaret. His elder son, David, Lord Elcho, died in 1715 aged seventeen. The 4th Earl took no part in the Jacobite rising of 1715 and died on 15th March 1720.

The **5th Earl, James Wemyss**, was born on 30th August 1699. In 1714 he became a member of the Royal Company of Archers, Brigadier in 1724, Lieutenant-General in 1726 and Captain-General in 1743. He inherited the earldom and estates in 1720 and married secretly, Janet, the very rich heiress and only daughter of the notorious Colonel Francis Charteris of Amisfield, Haddington who gave Amisfield its name. The 5th Earl's concerns over money were as a result of the spendthrift ways of himself and the countess; they separated in 1732. His eldest son supported the '45 Rising. The Earl, although sympathetic to the Jacobite cause, had little interest in politics, but he went to France to see the Foreign Secretary there which was part of the Jacobite intrigue. His estates, in the absence of his first son, became the property of his third son, James, while the second son, Francis, who had to change his name and arms to those of Charteris, inherited the colonel's properties. The 5th Earl died on 21st March 1756.

David Wemyss, the titular 6th Earl of Wemyss, although attainted in Britain was known as Earl of Wemyss on the continent and being attainted in 1746 his claim to the title was forfeited. As the eldest son he became known as 'Lord Elcho of the '45'.

He was born on 21st August 1721 and educated at Winchester and the military school at Angers in France following which (1740) he visited the Old Pretender in Rome who made him a Colonel of Dragoons. He was a member of the Royal Company of Archers (1742) and his ardent support of the Jacobite cause was aided by his younger brother, Francis Charteris Wemyss, who advanced him 1500 guineas for the Jacobite cause. On his return to Scotland David Wemyss collaborated with John Murray of Broughton (who was to become Prince Charles Edward's secretary during the '45 and to betray the Jacobites after his capture at the Battle of Culloden). David joined Prince Charles Edward to become a member of his Council. He was present at the Battle of Prestonpans (21st September 1745) and gave distinguished service in command of the 1st Troop of Horse Guards during the advance through England and the retreat to the Highlands.

After the defeat at Culloden he escaped to France never to return to Scotland. In later years Lord Elcho's nephew, Sir James Stewart Denham, described his uncle's dissatisfaction at Culloden when the Chevalier rode off the field with Elcho's words ringing in his ears, "There you go for a d....d cowardly Italian" (97 p.190)

In France, Lord Elcho became a captain of the Regiment of FitzJames and a Colonel of the Royal Scots from 1756 to 1763. He was awarded the *Ordre pour le Merite* by Louis XV. He married the daughter of Baron d'Uxhull in France and died in Paris on 29th April 1787.

Francis Wemyss Charteris, 7th Earl of Wemyss succeeded his brother David in 1787 but he too was not officially recognised as Earl of Wemyss because of the attainder of his brother. He used the title de jure meaning 'as of right', after his brother's death in 1787 and counts as the 7th Earl. He was born on 21st October 1723 and his wealth increased considerably when he inherited his maternal grandfather's estate including Amisfield. On 13th September 1745, at Preston Hall, he married Catherine, 6th daughter of Alexander, 2nd Duke of Gordon. The story is told of the bridal party's arrival at Haddingtom when warning was given that the Jacobites were advancing upon Sir John Cope's army which was standing down in that town. It was a false alarm which doubtless amused the bride and groom (50 p.57). 'Lady Kitty's Garden and Doocot' in Haddington takes its name from his wife Catherine.

Francis Charteris bought the Elcho estate from his father in 1750 for £8500 (the old nunnery, Elcho Castle near the River Tay, four miles from Perth). In 1771 he obtained a private Act of Parliament enabling him to keep the Charteris name and estates even if he became Earl of Wemyss and March, evading a part of the colonel's will.

In 1755 the 7th Earl built the magnificent Palladian Amisfield mansion by Issac Ware (demolished in 1923/4). He had bought the Gosford estate with its old house in 1781 (2.5 miles from Longniddry) and commissioned Robert Adam in 1790 to design a new house. [This house has passed through many vicissitudes, being left uninhabited for nearly a century, during which time the wings were demolished. Then in 1890 it was restored and new wings were built by the 10th Earl. There followed the fire in 1940 and the removal of the north wing roof in 1948. It remains the present day Wemyss connection with East Lothian, being occupied by the present Earl of Wemyss].

'The Property of the Earl of Wemyss and March' shown on *John Wood's 1819 Plan of Haddington and Nungate* is the land on the east side of Haddington on the east side of the Tyne, encompassing the Nungate and land southwards. In addition the Wemyss family hold estates in Peeblesshire and Selkirkshire including Neidpath Castle.

Francis Wemyss Charteris died at Gosford on 24th August 1808 six months after the death of his only son, also **Francis Wemyss Charteris**, who was born on 31st January 1748/9 in Edinburgh. He was a Member of the Royal Company of Archers (11th December 1786) and was known as Lord Elcho after 1787. He was elected MP for Haddingtonshire in three Parliaments (1780-87). On 18th July 1771 he married Susan, 2nd daughter of Anthony Tracy-Keck and Susan, daughter of the 4th Duke of Hamilton. It was through this marriage that the Stanway estates in Gloucestershire were eventually inherited by the Wemyss family. Following a long and painful illness at Amisfield he died aged fifty-eight on 20th January 1808. His ageing father was undoubtedly affected by his son's protracted illness and died six months afterwards. The estates and titles now passed to his grandson.

The **8th Earl of Wemyss, Francis Charteris** (grandson of Francis Charteris (1723-1808)), was born on 15th April 1772 and educated at Eton from the age of eight until he was fifteen years old. In 1793, when France declared war on Britain, he became ADC to his great uncle, Lord Adam Gordon, who was commander of the army in Scotland.

When his father died in January 1808 he became Lord Elcho and a few months later, on the death of his paternal grandfather (24th August 1808) he became Earl of Wemyss, although it was not until the 'reversal' of 1826 when three peerages were restored (the plea for restoration having been made by Sir Walter Scott to George IV) that he became officially recognised as the 8th Earl.

On the death of a distant cousin he became heir to considerable estates in Peebleshire, including Neidpath Castle the trees of which were cut down by this distant cousin, the 4th Duke of Queensberry (known as 'Old Q'), to impoverish the estate before it descended to the heir of entail [the Earl of Wemyss] (33 p.763).

Francis Charteris was the surviving male heir of his great-great grandmother, Lady Anne Douglas, the only daughter of the 1st Duke of Queensberry who married the 4th Earl of Wemyss. He thus became Earl of March, Viscount Peebles, Lord Douglas of Neidpath, Lyne and Munard. As Earl of Wemyss and March from 1810 he took the name Francis Wemyss-Charteris-Douglas. He was Lord Lieutenant of the County of Peebles from 1821 until his death. On 31st May 1794 he married Margaret, 4th daughter of Walter Campbell of Shawfield, who died at Gosford in 1850. He died there on 28th June 1853 aged eighty-one years

The **9th Earl of Wemyss, Francis Wemyss-Charteris-Douglas**, was born on 14th August 1796. He matriculated for Christ Church, Oxford in 1812. He became a Member of the Royal Company of Archers in 1824 in which he was given the rank of Lieutenant-General in 1842. He was Grand Master Mason of Scotland from 1827 to 1830 and Lord Lieutenant of Peeblesshire from 1853 to 1880. He was a trustee of the Scottish National Portrait Gallery from 1856 to 1866.

On 22nd August 1817 he married Louisa, 4th daughter of Richard Bingham, 2nd Earl of Lucan. She died at Gosford on 16th April 1882; her effigy in marble is in Aberlady Church. The 9th Earl died eight months later on 1st January 1883 aged eighty-seven. They were buried at Seton Collegiate Kirk.

The **10th Earl of Wemyss, Francis Richard Wemyss-Charteris-Douglas GCVO, DL, BA** was born in Edinburgh on 4th August 1818. He was educated at Edinburgh Academy and Eton (1832-35) and matriculated for Christ Church, Oxford where he gained his BA degree and was a friend of John Ruskin (1819-1900), the writer and art critic.

He was a member of the Royal Company of Archers (1838), Conservative MP for East Gloucestershire (1841-6) and for Haddingtonshire from 1847 until 1883 when he succeeded to the Earldom on the death of his father and took his seat in the House of Lords. In April 1848 the 10th Earl purchased the anchorage in Aberlady for £375 (50 p. 87). Martine in his *Reminiscences* (59 p.10) referring to the parish church in Aberlady describes it as 'formerly an ugly, ungainly structure, by the liberal generosity of the Earl of Wemyss, in renovating and almost rebuilding it, has perhaps not its equal in the county, or elsewhere'.

As an MP he was a strong Conservative at first but his disenchantment with the Conservatives led him towards Liberalism and latterly he described himself as a Liberal/Conservative. He was the power behind the Act of Parliament of 1859 which created the General Medical Council and a few other useful Acts, but his main interest was in military matters. He was appointed the Scotch Lord of the Treasury from 1853 to 1855 under Lord Aberdeen's coalition ministry of 1852-55 during which he was acutely aware of the government's total neglect of the army and navy at the start of the Crimean War in March 1854; his brother Walter was killed at Balaklava in 1854. Because of this the Earl strongly promoted the Rifle Volunteer movement from its beginning in 1859 when he was instrumental in the creation of the London-Scottish Regiment becoming its Commanding Officer. By 1860 the Haddington contingent, commanded by Captain Roughhead of Haddington, consisted of almost 300 volunteers and took part in the review of Scottish Rifle Volunteers in the Queen's Park at Holyrood in Edinburgh on 7th August by Queen Victoria. Grant's *Old and New Edinburgh* states: 'the whole force was commanded by Major General Alastair Macdonald; and perhaps none were more applauded in the march past than the London Scottish, led by Lord Elcho'. (13 Vol.II p.322)

He was the first chairman of the National Rifle Association to which he presented the Elcho Challenge Shield awarded annually. In 1879 he relinquished command of the London-Scottish Regiment remaining Honorary Colonel till 1900. He became ADC to Queen Victoria (1881-1901) to Edward VII (1901-1910) and to George V (1910-1914). For his services to the Crown he was created a Knight Grand Cross of the Royal Victorian Order (GCVO).

He never lost interest in military matters and in 1907 he strongly opposed the army reforms of Viscount Haldane (1856-1928) who amalgamated yeomen and volunteers to form a Territorial force of fourteen divisions and fourteen cavalry brigades in addition to many other reforms.

The 10th Earl's interest in art was undoubtedly influenced through his friendship from his student days with John Ruskin, the champion of Turner and art critic of the day. The earl was a discerning collector with an eye for a bargain; he painted in pastel and practised sculpture as a leisure activity.

His marriage to his first wife, Anne Frederica, 2nd daughter of Thomas William Anson, 1st Earl of Lichfield gave them six sons and three daughters: (1) Francis (1844-1870), (2) Arthur (1846-47), (3) Alfred Walter (1847-1873), a lieutenant of the 71st Foot who, while serving under Sir Garnet Wolseley in the Ashanti War, became seriously ill of dysentery and fever and died at sea on his way home, (4) Hugo Richard who became the 11th Earl of Wemyss, (5) Alan Dudley (1860-1901) and (6) Sir Evan Edward KC (1864-1940). The two surviving sons were Hugo Richard who succeeded to the titles and estates, and Sir Evan Edward who was a lieutenant in the Coldstream Guards, a Staff Captain, a barrister (1891) and bencher (1924) of the Inner Temple. His published works include: *Affairs of Scotland 1744-46) and William Augustus, Duke of Cumberland.*

The 10th Earl's second wife whom he married on 2nd December 1900 was Grace, 3rd daughter of Major John Blackburn and niece of Baron Blackburn of Killearn; she died on 30th June 1946.

The 10th Earl's death in 1914 was widely mourned. His obituary in *The Times* of 1st July 1914 described him, "a lone individualist, protesting vigorously against every kind of social legislation that debarred men from making use of what they liked of their liberty."

The **11th Earl of Wemyss, Hugo Richard Charteris**, was born on 25th August 1857 and was educated at Harrow (1871-74). He matriculated at Oxford (Balliol 1876). When his father took his place in the House of Lords in 1883, Hugo was elected Conservative MP for Haddingtonshire. On 9th August 1883 he married Mary Constance, 1st daughter of Hon. Percy Wyndham who was Conservative MP for West Cumberland for twenty-five years. They lived at the Wemyss estate at Stanway in Gloucestershire and had four sons: (1) Hugo Francis, Lord Elcho, born 28th December 1884, a captain of the Gloucestershire Hussars who was killed in action during the Great War on 23rd April 1916; (2) Guy Laurence born 23rd May 1886 and educated at Eton and Trinity College, Cambridge. He became a captain in the Scots Guards and won the 4th Class Order of St Sava of Serbia, he died in 1967; (3) Colin Charteris born 1st June 1889 and died on 27th December 1892; (4) Ivo Alan born on 6th October 1896 and as a 2nd lieutenant of the 1st Battalion Grenadier Guards was killed in action on 17th October 1915. Lady Wemyss's *A Family Record* (1932) gives an insight of their family life, especially the lives of two of her sons who were killed during the 1914-18 War.

The 11th Earl was MP for Ipswich from 1886 until 1895 and a member of London County Council from 1904 until 1910. He succeeded his father as the 11th Earl in 1914. After the first year of the 1914-18 War losses were so devastating that a recruitment drive was necessary (there was no conscription at this stage) and the Earl of Wemyss addressed a public meeting in Haddington to try to overcome what he referred to as, 'the orgy of pessimism' (50 p.79). After the war he was

Lord Lieutenant of East Lothian and honorary colonel of the 7th Volunteer battalion of the Royal Scots. His wife died on 29th April 1937 and he died less than three months later on 12th July and was buried at Aberlady.

Their eldest son, Hugo Francis, Lord Elcho (1884-1916) married Lady Violet Manners, a daughter of the 8th Duke of Rutland. They had two sons: (1) Francis David Charteris, the 12th and present Earl of Wemyss, and (2) Martin, Lord Charteris of Amisfield, (1913-1999).

The **12th Earl of Wemyss and March, Francis David Charteris KT, LLD, DUniv, JP** is the present and longest holder of the Earldom having succeeded to the earldom in 1937. He was born on 19th January 1912 and educated at Eton and Oxford (Balliol) where he took his BA degree in 1933. His honours and titles include the Knighthood of the Most Ancient and Most Noble Order of the Thistle (KT), Viscount Peebles, Lord Elcho and Methil and Baron Douglas of Neidpath, Lyne and Munard and Baron Wemyss in Fife and honorary Doctorates of the universities of St Andrews and Edinburgh.

He entered the Colonial Service to become an Assistant District Commissioner in Basutoland from 1937 to 1944 before which he was a lieutenant of the Lovat Scouts but became a Major with the Basuto troops in the Pioneer Corps in the Middle East (1942-44).

He was less interested in politics than his predecessors but his record of public service is enormous. He returned to Scotland in 1943. With the East Lothian Antiquarian and Field Naturalists' Society he was instrumental in saving Haddington House from demolition. His presidencies and chairmanships give an indication of the breadth of his interests - The Royal Scottish Geographical Society, The National Trust for Scotland (of which he was elected Chairman of Council in 1946), The Thistle Foundation for Severely Disabled Scottish Ex-servicemen, The National Bible Society of Scotland, The Friends of St Mary's in Haddington, The Royal Commission on Ancient and Historical Monuments for Scotland and the Scottish Committee of The Marie Curie Memorial Foundation. He was three times Lord High Commissioner to the General Assembly of the Church of Scotland. He was a director of Scottish Television (1964), Lord Lieutenant of East Lothian (from 1967 to 1986), Lord Clerk Register of Scotland and Keeper of Her Majesty's Signet, Ensign in the Royal Company of Archers (The Queen's Bodyguard for Scotland).

On 24th February 1940 he married Mavis Lynette Gordon Murray BA, elder daughter of the late Edwin Edward Murray of Hermanus, Cape Province. Lady Wemyss died in 1988. They had two sons: Iain David, Lord Elcho, who was born on 20th June 1945 and died tragically aged nine on 3rd April 1954 as a result of a car accident; James Donald, born in 1948, is the present heir and was given the courtesy title of Lord Neidpath after his elder brother's death. He was educated at Eton and Oxford where he graduated BA (1969), MA (1974) and PhD (1975). He is an acknowledged historian; his publications include *The Singapore Naval Base and the defence of Britain's Eastern Empire 1919-14*.

He married the Hon. Catherine Ingrid Guinness, elder daughter of the Hon Johnathon Guinness. They were divorced in 1988 and he married Amanda, youngest daughter of Basil Fielding in 1995. They reside at Stanway House in Gloucestershire with his son, grandson of the present Earl, the Hon Francis Richard Charteris born in 1984.

The 12th Earl of Wemyss married Canadian born Shelagh Thrift or Kennedy BA in Aberlady Church on 29th April 1995. They met in 1980 through their shared interest in conservation and the arts when Lord Wemyss was President of the National Trust for Scotland. She was especially involved first with the Trust's development at Gladstone's Land, the 16th century town house in the Royal Mile, Edinburgh and later with the Georgian House, No.7 Charlotte Square, Edinburgh.

On 6th July 2000, aged 88, Lord Wemyss was presented to HM the Queen when she opened the new headquarters of the National Trust for Scotland, Wemyss House in Charlotte Square, Edinburgh, named after the Earl in recognition of his enduring service spanning fifty-four years for the Trust of which he was Chairman of its Governing Council from 1946 to 1969. He was President until 1991 and is currently the President Emeritus.

The Earldom of Wemyss Family Tree (male line)

Michael of Wemyss and Methil (c1165-c1214)

son: Sir John Wemyss of Wemyss and Methil (c1202-c1263)

married: Amabilla, daughter of Sir John Anesley

sons: Sir Michael Wemyss of Wemyss and Methil (c1231-c1320)

married: heiress of Sir David Lochore of Lochore

son: Sir David Wemyss of Wemyss (c1270- 1332)

married: (i) c1290, Annabella Sinclair
(ii) c1304, Marjory, daughter of Walter Ramsay

sons: (1) Sir Michael Wemyss of Wemyss (knighted c1316, died c1342)
(2) Sir John Wemyss of Leuchars (died c1392)

son: Sir John Wemyss of Leuchars, Kilcaldrum, Reres and Methil

son: David Wemyss of Methil and Wemyss (died c1430)

son: John Wemyss of Wemyss (c1425-?)

son: Sir John Wemyss of Wemyss, Strathardle, Inchmartin, Elcho and Dron etc (died 1508)

son: Sir David Wemyss of Wemyss (died c1542)

son: David Wemyss of Wemyss

sons (i) Sir John Wemyss of Wemyss (died c1571/2)
(ii) James of Caskieberran (died c1608)

son: David Wemyss of Wemyss (died 1596)

sons: (1) Sir John (died c.1622)
(2) Sir James of Bogie
(3) Andrew of Newton
(4) Patrick of Rumgay
(5) David of Fingash
(6) Henry of Foodie

5 daughters: Margaret, Jean, Cecelia, Elizabeth and Isobel

sons: **Sir John 1st Earl of Wemyss** (1586-1649)

married: Jean, daughter of Patrick 6th Lord Grey

son: **David, 2nd Earl of Wemyss** (1610-1679)

married (i) 1626/7, Ann, eldest daughter of 2nd Lord Balfour of Burleigh
(ii) 1650, Lady Eleanor Fleming, daughter of 2nd Earl of Wigtoun
(iii) 1652/3, Margaret, widow of 2nd Earl of Buccleuch

11 children (8th and last surviving son died 1671)

2 sons (died young)
daughter: **Lady Margaret Wemyss (3rd Earl of Wemyss)** (1658/9-1705)

married: (i) Sir James Wemyss, Lord Burntisland (died 1682)
(ii) George Mackenzie, 1st Earl of Cromartie

son: **David, 4th Earl of Wemyss** (1678-1720)
daughters: Anne (1675-1702)
Margaret

married: (i) Lady Anne Douglas, only daughter of 1st Duke of Queensberry
(ii) Mary, daughter of Sir John Robinson
(iii) Elizabeth, daughter of 1st/10th Lord Sinclair

sons: David, Lord Elcho (died 1715)
James, 5th Earl of Wemyss (1699-1756)
daughters: Elizabeth and Margaret

married: Janet only daughter of Col. Francis Charteris

sons: (1) **David ('Lord Elcho of the '45') 6th Earl of Wemyss** (1721-1787)
(2) **Francis Charteris, 7th Earl of Wemyss** (1723-1808)
(3) James

married 1745, Lady Catherine Gordon, 6th daughter of the 2nd Duke of Gordon

son: Francis (1749-1808) - predeceased his father
daughter: Frances (married 1799 Rev. W Trail)

married Susan, 2nd daughter of Anthony Tracy-Keck

son: **Francis, 8th Earl of Wemyss** (1772-1853)
daughters: Henrietta, Susan, Katherine, Augusta

married Margaret, 4th daughter of Walter Campbell of Shawfield

sons: **Francis, 9th Earl of Wemyss** (1796-1883)

daughters: Eleanor, Charlotte, Louisa, Harriet, Jane, Caroline

married: Lady Louisa, 4th daughter of Richard Bingham, 2nd Earl of Lucan

sons: (1) **Francis Richard, 10th Earl of Wemyss** (1818-1914)
(2) Richard Charteris DL (1822-74)
(3) Walter (killed in action, Balaklava 1854)
(4) Frederick William (1833-87)
daughter: Louisa

married: Lady Anne Frederica, daughter of Thomas William Anson, 1st Earl of Lichfield

sons: (1) Francis (1844-70)
(2) Arthur (1846-47)
(3) Alfred Walter (1847-73)

(4) **Hugo Richard, 11th Earl of Wemyss** (1857-1937)
(5) Alan Dudley (1860-1901)
(6) Sir Evan Edward KC (1864-1940)
daughters: Evelyn, Lilian, Hilda

married: 1833, Mary Constance, daughter of Hon. Percy Scawen Wyndham

sons: (1) Hugo Francis, Lord Elcho (1884-1916)
(2) Guy Laurence (1886-1967)
(3) Colin Charteris (1889-1892)
(4) Ivo Alan (1896-1915)
daughters: Cynthia, Mary, Irene

married: Lady Violet Catharine Manners, daughter of 8th Duke of Rutland

sons: (1) **Francis David, 12th Earl of Wemyss** (1912-)
(2) Martin Michael, Lord Charteris of Amisfield (1913-99)

married: (i) 1940, Mavis Lynette Gordon Murray (died 1988)
(ii) 1995, Shelagh Thrift or Kennedy

sons: (1) Ian David, Lord Elcho (died 1954)
(2) James Donald, Lord Douglas of Neidpath (1948-)
daughters: Elizabeth Mary, Lady Elizabeth Bemson (1941-)
Caroline (b &d 1946)

married: (i) 1983 (div. 1988), Hon Catherine Ingrid Guinness, daughter of 3rd Baron Moyne
(ii) 1995, Amanda Clare, youngest daughter of Basil Feilding

son: Hon Francis Richard Charteris (1984-)
daughter: Mary Olivia (1987-)

(Sources: Guidance from 12th Earl of Wemyss and *Burke's Peerage and Knightage*)

LADY CATHERINE CHARTERIS WEMYSS

after whom Lady Kitty's Doocot and Garden of Haddington is named

Lady Kitty's Doocot and Garden is immediately opposite the southern end of the Nungate Bridge. It dates from 1771 when Lady Catherine ("Kitty") Charteris Wemyss, the wife of Francis Charteris, 7th Earl of Wemyss, petitioned the Town Council to have the gateway of St Mary's Parish Church moved eastwards so that the wall surrounding her 'Garden' could be built. It was probably about this time that the old buildings were demolished and removed, the site having been used for archery, bowling and executions centuries before.

On the Sands nearby the Battle of the Sands in 1548 took place during the 'Siege of Haddington' when the English occupied Haddington against the French who had arrived from Edinburgh to assist the Scots to regain their town. English bullets were said to have ricocheted off the walls of St Catherine's Chapel the grounds of which became **Lady Kitty's Garden**.

Archery was practised on the Sands during the reign of Mary Queen of Scots (r.1561-1567) and this was said to have been the site of the first bowling green in Scotland in 1657 when the Burgh Treasurer was authorised to 'purchase bowls and to engage a greenkeeper' (50 p.124).

Lady 'Kitty' took over ownership of the Sands, when she claimed payment of debts incurred by Lewis Gordon Esq., an English road surveyor (59 p.156). At the north end of Lady Kitty's Garden there was a house in what was then known as Friars Croft; it was probably built by Alexander Maitland (of Haddington House). In 1920 Lady Kitty's Garden was acquired by the Parish Council as an extension to the church grounds.

Lady 'Kitty' was the 6th daughter of Alexander, the 2nd Duke of Gordon (1678-1728) an ardent Jacobite who commanded reinforcements for the 'Old Pretender' in the 'rising' of 1715. Her mother was Henrietta, daughter of the Earl of Peterborough and Monmouth and Catherine was born c.1720 at Edinburgh.

On 13th September 1745, three days before the 'Young Pretender' entered Edinburgh, she married Francis Wemyss, second son of the 5th Earl of Wemyss and Janet, the only daughter of the infamous Colonel Francis Charteris who gave Amisfield its name. The wedding took place at the enlarged old house of Preston Hall (6 km ESE of Dalkeith, by William Adam in 1738) (30 p. 395) and was attended by the groom's elder brother, David, on his way to join Prince Charles Edward.

After the wedding ceremony the young couple were driven to Haddington when the wedding party received an urgent message that the Jacobites were about to attack. This could well have been true but was, in fact, a practical joke at the expense of Sir John Cope who immediately called out his men in readiness. He covered his embarrassment by thanking his men for their speedy reaction to his command. (50 p.57)

They were an exceedingly rich young couple. As the favoured grandson, Francis Wemyss Charteris had inherited his maternal grandfather's (the infamous Colonel Charteris's *qv*) fortune including the estates of Amisfield in 1731/2. With her husband, Lady Kitty must have spent many happy hours in the planning of their new mansion house, Amisfield, which was designed for them by Isaac Ware in 1755. During the planning stage she gave birth to her only son, Francis Wemyss Charteris on 31st January 1748. The new Amisfield House, became the magnificent red sandstone mansion of Grecian grandeur, the finest example of the Palladian school in the country (30 p.76) (sadly, it was demolished in 1923/4).

To the delight of Lady Catherine, Francis bought the Elcho estate in 1750 from his father, the 5th Earl, for the sum of £8,500. It consisted of the old nunnery and Elcho Castle overlooking the River Tay, 4 miles from Perth. The old Earl had amassed huge debts due to the spendthrift ways of himself and his wife Janet (daughter of the infamous colonel) and his son's expenditure in support of the '45 Rising.

A happy event for the family was the marriage of their son, also Francis Charteris Wemyss, on 18th July 1771 to Susan, 2nd daughter of Anthony Tracy-Keck and Susan, daughter of the 4th Duke of Hamilton. They gave the Earl and Countess, Lady 'Kitty', five grandchildren: Francis, born on 15th April 1772 who succeeded to the earldom as 8th Earl on the death of his grandfather in 1808; Henrietta Charlotte (born 3rd February 1773, died 30th January 1838); Susan (died 17th August 1816); Katherine (died 8th October 1863); Augusta (died 28th July 1840).

In 1780 and in 1784 her husband was elected MP for the Haddington Burgh in the Tory Government of William Pitt the Younger and some of their time had to be spent in London. In 1781 Francis bought the old Gosford House and estate and again Lady Kitty took a great interest in the planning of their new house which was designed by the famous Scottish architect Robert Adam (1790). Sadly, she did not live to see its completion. She died suddenly on 21st January 1786 (her husband died 22 years later in 1808, aged 85 years).

ANDREW "JOCK" WEMYSS MC

War hero, rugby internationalist and broadcaster

Andrew 'Jock' Wemyss, a founder member of Haddington Rugby Club, was the first of Haddington's Scottish internationalists. In his day he was arguably the best known figure in rugby in the UK. He lived for the game and became match secretary of Haddington Rugby Club in 1911. He founded another well-known rugby club - the Co-optomists in the Railway Hotel of Haddington. He was a hero on the field who, in spite of losing an eye during the 1914-18 war, played at international level and became a well-loved broadcaster and journalist of the game.

Andrew (Jock) Wemyss (Courtesy of Haddington Rugby Football Club)

Jock Wemyss, as he was popularly known, was born on 22nd May 1893 in Galashiels. He was a small boy when he arrived in Haddington, his father, John Strachan Wemyss, having been appointed manager of the Haddington Co-operative Store in Market Street. With his wife, Isabella Simpson Weir, also of Galashiels, the family set up home in Lodge Street. They had three children - Andrew or 'Jock' and twin sisters Isabella and Janet who became well-known and popular singers in Haddington - this was a talented family.

Young Jock attended the Knox Memorial Institute and was a contemporary of Sir William Gillies *q.v.* and the scholarly Porteous brothers, Professors Alexander and Norman Porteous *q.v.* Jock Wemyss's forte was sport and Professor Norman Porteous (102 years of age at the time of writing) remembers him as 'a big strapping lad who never opened a gate; he simply leapt over it.'

Jock was to become a Scottish international rugby player, a prop forward of renown and a BBC sports commentator and journalist. His first article for the press about rugby landed him a reprimand from the

Scottish Rugby Union; in those days it was forbidden to publish while still playing but this was to be the fore-runner of a successful career in sports journalism.

After leaving school he gained employment in banking, firstly at Haddington and later at Morningside in Edinburgh, and he followed his interest in sport by founding and playing for Haddington Rugby Club. In a letter dated 7th November 1954 to F D Burnet, the Club Secretary and nephew of the first Club Captain, Jock Wemyss described the circumstances:

> *To the best of my recollection Frank, 'Ander' Hutchison (eldest of the brothers, Walter Romanel, 'Toby' Stevenson and myself founded the club squatting one night on Dodds' window [now the Fish and Chip shop in Market Street]. I can't be sure of the year.*

In fact, the club was founded on 16th February 1911 at a meeting held in Haddington. F D Burnet was elected Club Captain, W Romanel Vice-Captain and Jock Wemyss match secretary. Matches were played at Neilson Park and the Railway Hotel (of which Walter Romanel's mother was Proprietrix) was used as a meeting place and changing rooms. Jock Wemyss 'was a glutton for practice, especially kicking, he and the others spent many evenings in the Neilson Park' (98 p.3). He played centre and forward and at that early stage he 'saw to it as often as he could that a piece got into the paper (the Courier). As well as playing for Haddington he played for Galashiels Rugby Club, Edinburgh Wanderers and the Co-optimists. In 1914 he was selected for Scotland - his first international game was against Wales on 7th February 1914; Scotland lost 5:14. That season he was capped again against Ireland; another loss - the score was Scotland 0: Ireland 6.

He joined the army at the outbreak of World War I in 1914 and was commissioned in the Royal Scots. In France, near the end of the war, he was amazed and pleasantly surprised to meet his old school contemporary Norman Porteous of his Knox Institute days. Sadly, Jock Wemyss lost an eye when a grenade exploded in front of him. He was awarded the Military Cross for his bravery under fire and the Italians honoured him with their Italian Silver Medal. Norman Porteous and he met again in Ireland during one of the rebellions there; he recalled the spectacle: "he was a formidable figure, complete with eye patch, atop an armoured vehicle - the rebels of Mullingar (west of Dublin) seemed to dissipate before him as he was driven through." He attained the rank of Major in the Royal Scots.

After the war he played for Edinburgh Wanderers and was capped for Scotland on five more occasions between 1920 and 1922:
Scotland v France (Scotland won 5:0) 1st January 1920
Scotland v England (Scotland lost 13 to 4) - 20th March 1920
Scotland v France (draw 3:3) - 2nd January 1922
Scotland v Wales (draw 9:9) - 4th February 1922
Scotland v Ireland (Scotland won 6 to 3) - 25th February 1922

He was selected for the Barbarians with which he maintained close contact becoming a committee member and record-keeper for the club. His knowledge of the game and its players was encyclopaedic. Bill McLaren, the famous rugby commentator and journalist, recalled an amusing incident in his book *Talking of Rugby* - during one of Jock's many games for the Barbarians, he was admonished by the referee for a minor infringement. The referee was seen to emphasise his point by poking Jock on the chest and Jock, drawing himself up to his full six foot two inches, looked hard at the referee and was heard to say, "Sir, will you kindly remove your digit from my person!" (56)

Jock Wemyss wrote the history of the Barbarians and was the natural choice of the BBC to give the main commentaries on international games on radio. He was sports correspondent for the *Scottish Daily Express* and having made his career in journalism he was in constant demand as an after-dinner speaker. He never lost touch with his boyhood home of Haddington and was the guest speaker at the 50th and 60th anniversary dinners of the Haddington Rugby Club.

Bill McLaren, in his book *Talking of Rugby* recalls, with enormous affection, his days as a junior reporter when Jock Wemyss regaled him with wonderful stories of the old days of rugby. This paved the way for the youthful McLaren in broadcasting in a most generous way by introducing his young protégé to most of the leading figures of the day. In his book McLaren described the reaction of Jock Wemyss at the end of a poor spell for Scottish rugby during the early 1950s. The match was Scotland versus Wales in 1955. Scotland was a mere single point ahead with a few minutes left; the tension was at breaking point. Suddenly, Scotland's scrum-half scored a magnificent try to secure victory at last. Bill McLaren handed the microphone to Jock who, with a tear in his eye, said hesitatingly, "Well, I can hardly speak. It has been such a long journey but at last we have come out of that long, dark tunnel into the sunshine once more." (56)

The great-hearted Jock Wemyss retired in 1969 and his sudden death in Edinburgh on 21st January 1974, at the age of eighty, was mourned by his wife Aileen Melville and rugby enthusiasts all over Britain.

WILLIAM I (The Lion) KING OF SCOTS

at the Royal Palace of Haddington

The Royal Palace of Haddington was the residence of two Scottish kings: William the Lion (r.1165-1214) and his son Alexander II (r.1214-1249) *qv*. The evidence for this is in the not always reliable fourteenth-century chronicle of John of Fordun. However, the Town Council of Haddington decided to erect a plaque on the north-facing wall of the County Buildings in Court Street (previously named King Street) in commemoration of this long-since demolished historic building and its two kings of Scotland; the plaque is inscribed:

> This is the site of
> THE ROYAL PALACE
> occupied by KING WILLIAM I,
> styled WILLIAM the LION,
> and here his son,
> ALEXANDER II of SCOTLAND
> was born, 24th August 1198.

What other evidence is there? Jamieson in his *A Short History of Haddington* (50) explains that the site chosen for the County Building in 1833 - among some 'nondescript structures....was a fragment of arched Norman masonry, which, ...was all that remained of the palace of the early Scottish kings' (50 p.139). James Miller (1792-1865) *qv*, author of the *Lamp of Lothian* who was living in Haddington in 1833, witnessed the demolition and described a vault and part of an arched passage. A drawing by Adam Neill, reproduced in the East Lothian Register of 1834, indicated a design of twelfth century style.

William I was born a son of the House of Canmore in 1143. His father was Prince Henry, the son of David I, and his mother was Ada, daughter of the earl of Varenne. Prince Henry died in 1152 and the kingdom was inherited by William's eldest brother, Malcolm IV, when his grandfather David I died in 1153. William inherited the 'kingdom of Scotland' from his brother who had no children and who died in 1165. Whilst his brother's reign was short (twelve years) William's was long (forty-nine years); in fact it was to be the longest reign until that of James VI (r.1567-1603-1626). William's elder brother was a mere twelve years old when he succeeded his grandfather. Malcolm had lost territories to Henry II of England which his grandfather had gained previously through marriage. This undoubtedly irked William who still held the title of Earl of Northumberland when he became king and he decided to invade England in 1174.

William was known among his contemporaries as Guillaume de Varenne' from his mother's birthplace in France. He was 'rather Frenchman [ie Norman] both in race and in manners, language and culture' (60 p.14). He was a warlike king and he adopted a single lion in red on a yellow background as his emblem which became his arms and led to his name: William the Lion. He took part in jousting tournaments in France and was easily recognised from the distinctive single red lion on a yellow background of his arms.

Although his kingdom was that of Scotland he had to contend with old revolts and William was the first king to tackle the rebels of the north. Nearer home he granted Hugh de Gifford the baronial lands of Yester and a homestead with land to the monks of Melrose (59 p.260).

William's army besieged Alnwick but the English under the cover of thick fog surprised the Scots and in the ensuing battle William had his horse killed from under him. He was quickly captured and taken to France to be imprisoned in the castle of Falaise in Brittany. He was given his freedom on condition he signed the Treaty of Falaise of 1174 in which he had to 'accept Henry II as feudal overlord of Scotland and to subject the Scottish Church to the English' (60 p.27). As a further condition of his release William had to agree the delivery to Henry, his son and his heirs, the castles of Jedburgh, Maidens (Edinburgh), and Stirling and to 'deliver up to the lord king his brother David as hostage, and Earl Duncan, and Earl Waldeve [and several others]' (60 pps.28-29). His imprisonment had lasted just under a year and after his return home he had to yield to English domination for the next fifteen years, that is, until Henry died in 1189.

William did not marry until he was forty-three years old in 1186, but he had several illegitimate children before then. His queen, Ermengarde, was nominated by Henry II in exchange for the return of Edinburgh Castle. They had almost given up hope of having a son to succeed to the Scottish throne and after twelve years of marriage they were greatly relieved when their baby, a healthy boy, Alexander, was born in the King's Palace at Haddington on 24th August 1198. Alexander was three years old when a General Council of Nobles confirmed him as Heir Designate at Musselburgh.

William was plagued with various rebellions but he succeeded in uniting the kingdom; in fact he brought together nobles, prelates and landowners in a 'parliament' (the first of its kind) so that he could adjudicate over their complaints and learn of other grievances. But of their loyalty he was certain as he had granted conquered lands and power to Norman knights who relied on his patronage.

Henry's son, Richard Coeur-de-Lion, was more interested in his crusades to the Holy Land and by the 'Quitclaim of Canterbury' in 1189 he 'sold back to William, for 10,000 merks, the rights his father had acquired by the Treaty of Falaise' (60 p.29). His castles of Roxburgh and Berwick were restored [Edinburgh having been restored earlier] and the lands which he had in England were also returned. William had now regained the freedom of Scotland from English domination and by the time he died in 1214 his son, Alexander II *qv* the heir to the throne, became the ruler of a united and free Scotland [except for remote and rebellious Argyle which Alexander put down in 1222].

ROBERT WILSON of Dunbar

the inventor of the ship's propeller

This underrated inventor was the son of a fisherman of Dunbar. Born in a fisherman's cottage in 1803, he had little schooling but his father fed his son, Robert, on an intellectual diet of thoughtful answers to his innumerable questions. The answers came to an abrupt halt when his father was drowned at sea in 1810.

Young Robert loved playing about in the water of Dunbar harbour and he became quite an expert sculler; he could propel his boat using one oar in a screw action with consummate ease. This led him to the idea of making a propeller to be rotated at the stern of a boat. His curiosity to know how things worked was never ending - the first pre-requisite of an engineer is this insatiable curiosity. He left school aged about twelve and after a few years he left Dunbar to become an apprentice joiner in Edinburgh.

The idea of a propeller continued to puzzle him and his flair for engineering was evident when he produced a working model in 1827 at the age of 24. This was the age of sail; there was stiff opposition to the idea of steam propulsion which was so far confined to wooden paddle-wheelers. However, his model propeller caught the attention of James Hunter who demonstrated it to the 10th Earl of Lauderdale, Admiral Anthony Maitland, who in turn promised to bring the idea to the attention of the Admiralty.

In 1828 the Highland Society agreed that this invention was feasible and granted Wilson £10 on condition that he produced a working model. He did so with enthusiasm and such was its success the Royal Scottish Society of Arts awarded him their silver medal in 1834. The Society introduced Wilson's propeller to the Admiralty and although a committee of officials discussed it they dismissed the idea with almost discourteous neglect. It is interesting to note however that these same officials adopted a similar invention of Sir Francis Pettit Smith in 1840.

Undeterred Robert Wilson, having spent several years in Edinburgh as an engineer, travelled to Manchester in 1838 to work with Edinburgh born James Nasmyth (1808-90) who had started his Bridgewater Foundry in 1836. Wilson was made the manager of the foundry at Patricroft and perfected the self-acting motion of Nasmyth's new invention of the steam-hammer in 1839. It was used for the first time at the Low Moor Ironworks near Bradford where Wilson was now the engineer and he added the 'circular balanced valve' to the hammer which was in continuous use there from August 1843 to 1853. The hammer was also used to forge a huge wrought iron paddle shaft.

In 1856 Nasmyth retired and Wilson left Low Moor to become managing partner of the firm now called Nasmyth, Wilson & Company. Wilson then constructed the great double-acting hammer for the Woolwich Royal Arsenal which was patented in 1861. In 1860 he published a pamphlet entitled *The Screw-Propeller: Who invented it?* Whether or not this regenerated the interest of the Navy is unknown but in 1862 the War Department made a grant of £500 to Wilson for the use of his double-action screw-propeller to be applied to the fish torpedo. This very underrated inventor had at last attained the recognition he richly deserved. When John Rennie *qv* was involved in the construction of the *Dwarf*, a Royal Naval vessel, he used one of Wilson's screw propellers.

Between the years 1842 and 1880 he took out twenty-four patents for valves, pistons, and hydraulic and other machinery. In 1856 his first patent for an hydraulic press was taken out jointly with Nasmyth and Wilson added many improvements to this successful machine. In recognition of his work he was elected a Fellow of the Royal Society of Edinburgh (FRSE) in 1873 and was a Member of the Royal Scottish Society of Arts.

He died at Matlock in Derbyshire on 28th July 1882 being surived by his second wife and four sons and four daughters. He was buried at St Catherine's, Barton-on-Well, not far from his home Ellismere House, Patricroft.

REV. JOHN WITHERSPOON

of Gifford and Princeton, U.S.A.

Opposite Yester Parish Church of Gifford on the old manse wall there are two bronze plaques commemorating two famous sons of East Lothian - Rev. John Witherspoon and Professor John Mackintosh MP *qv*. This is the story of the former .

The Church is often visited by American visitors anxious to pay their respects to John Witherspoon, the only Scot to sign the American Declaration of Independence (1776), the first Moderator of the Presbyterian Church of America and President (Principal) of Princeton College. He was described as the father of the Presbyterian Church of America and such was his influence and eloquence during the Continental Congress of 1776 he convinced those who hesitated to support the signing of the Declaration of Independence. Historian, author and MP Horace Walpole blamed the revolt entirely on Witherspoon saying: "Our cousin America has run off with a Presbyterian parson." He was of course, referring to John Witherspoon of Gifford. Undoubtedly, Witherspoon was regarded as a traitor having joined the American revolutionaries against British interests.

John Witherspoon was born on 5th February 1723 in Gifford in the Parish of Yester. Gifford, like Inverary in the west of Scotland, was purpose built to replace the old village of Bothans. The village of Gifford seemed complete when its Parish Church was built in 1710. Its minister, from 1720, was the Rev. James Witherspoon father of John Witherspoon. The Witherspoons were descended from a long line of Calvinist dominies and even claimed maternal descent to John Knox (although this was never validated). John was educated at Haddington Grammar School which, in his day, was one of the schools provided by the heritors (landowners) as required by an Act of the Scottish Parliament of 1696.

He enjoyed some relaxation from the hard regime of the study of Latin and Greek when he was permitted to take part in play-acting. One of their plays was that of Allan Ramsay *The Gentle Shepherd* (Ramsay's statue is just above the Floral Clock in West Princes Street Gardens in Edinburgh). There would have been considerable doubt about this activity in the Witherspoon household; play-acting was not work and in any case was considered to inflame the populace. At the age of 13 years he matriculated at the University of Edinburgh and gained his MA degree three years later in 1739. This was roughly equivalent to a secondary school education, although most lectures were delivered in Latin. Being destined for the ministry, he took a further degree in divinity in 1743.

On 6th September 1743 he was licenced to preach by the Haddington Presbytery and he was called to Beith in Ayrshire in January 1745. He was a real 'fire and brimstone' preacher, a puritan Calvinist who described the new intellectualism of the 'golden age' as spiritual vaccilation. *The Essays Moral, Political and Literary* of David Hume (1711-1776), the great philosopher and historian, had been published in 1741 and did not impress this uncompromising young preacher. Hume's scepticism and implied atheism almost led to his expulsion from the Church and Witherspoon referred to him as 'a wicked sceptic sage'.

In September 1748 John Witherspoon married Elizabeth Montgomery; they had ten children, five of whom died in infancy. In 1757 he was called to Paisley where he remained until 1768, and during this ministry he became the leader of the Popular Party which advocated purity of Church doctrine. He pointed accusingly at the Moderator of the General Assembly of the Church of Scotland because, to Witherspoon, the Church was weakening by giving credence to doubtful humanism in science and literature. The Rev. John Home *qv* of Athelstaneford had written his tragedy *Douglas*, it had been performed in Edinburgh with great acclaim in 1756. Witherspoon was furiously angry. He declared the drama, and play- acting in general to be unlawful because it 'agitates the passions too violently'. He campaigned to have Home expelled from his ministry and described him as 'a stage-playing priest'. John Home resigned from his ministry in 1757, such was the offence to the Edinburgh Presbytery. Witherspoon extended his fearless attacks by his unrelenting criticism against the philosopher/judge Henry Home, Lord Kames, referring to him as 'an impious judge' for his learned works: *Essays on Morality* (1751) and his *Introduction to the Art of Thinking* (1761). It is anachronistic to consider him a religious bigot. In his day ministers of the church felt that they had to defend stoutly their faith in God and Jesus Christ. Witherspoon's faith was unwavering, uncompromising and so strong that he could brook no doubts, arguments or scepticism; the new enlightened philosophies struck at the very depth of his faith, they were anathema to him.

At this time the Popular party lived up to its name in its defence of the people in "the right of personal conscience" and their right to choose their own ministers. In 1759 John Witherspoon delivered his last sermon of doom and gloom as Moderator of Glasgow and Ayr, and he castigated the ministry as 'weak-kneed, decadent and intellectually dishonest' in *The Trial of Religious Truths by its Moral Influence*. His exceptional, if not extreme, piety and leadership were recognised by the University of St Andrews when, in 1764, he was made an honorary Doctor of Divinity.

The Witherspoon family emigrated to America in August 1768. He had taken two years to make this decision having been offered the presidency (principalship) of the College of New Jersey (now Princeton University) in 1766. The delay was in deference to his wife's wishes but he had been persuaded by Benjamin Rush (1745-1813), an alumni of the College and a student of medicine in Edinburgh, that the college presidency was effectively the bishop of "all our American Churches". There was a split in the church in America which Witherspoon, with characteristic zeal, was to heal, this, without any sacrifice in his devotion to the College. To it he brought the Scottish commonsense philosophy of Thomas Reid (1710-96) and quickly dispensed with the phenomenalism of George Berkeley (1685-1753) then popular with his tutors. In addition he changed the teaching method and introduced history and rhetoric whilst encouraging mathematics and science. Through his charismatic energy he replenished the somewhat impoverished funds of the college and he coerced the trustees into many purchases of books and scientific equipment.

The threat of revolution took him into politics. This necessitated frequent absence from the college and he put his son-in-law in charge. Sadly the college was damaged during the upheaval and students left. At first Witherspoon's political activities were modest; he served on many committees and by 1775 he was chairman of his county delegation. In 1776 he was a delegate to the Continental Congress and he urged action for the *Declaration*. His writings were acclaimed in Britain and America. His service in Congress, although intermittent, lasted until 1782 and his committee membership exceeded over one hundred committees. His influence extended over a wide range - the Board of War, the foreign affairs of the new government, the Articles of Confederation, instructions of peace commissioners, the over-supply of paper money - in his *Essay on Money* he wrote, "no business can be done, some say, because money is scarce...It may be said, with more truth, money is scarce, because little business is done."

Towards the end of his life he devoted more time to rebuilding the college which had suffered badly during the revolution and never fully recovered during his time. In 1783 the State Legislature called upon his services and from 1785, for the next four years, he worked on the organisation of the Presbyterian Church nationally. He was Moderator of its first General Assembly in 1789. A difficult time was ahead: he was nearing the end of his life and sadly his wife died, he lost his sight, his personal resources were diminished and the College itself was in straightened financial circumstances but he astounded the College community by marrying a twenty-four year-old widow, Ann Dill on 30th May 1791. They had two daughters one of whom died in infancy. His new found happiness was short-lived, he died on 15th November 1792 at 'Tusculum'. He was buried in the Presidents' Lot at his beloved Princeton College and so passed a fearless man of unswerving convictions who never wavered in the face of tremendous pressure to do so. He had worked himself to death for his maker, his college, for his adopted country and for the spiritual well-being of his fellow man.

In addition to the commemorative plaque at Gifford Edinburgh University have decided to honour him in a similar way in the year 2000.

WILLIAM WALKER WOOD MBE

the champion of champion bowlers

Willie Wood is a household name of sportsmanship not only throughout East Lothian but nationally and internationally. He is of course the champion of champion bowlers, the only sportsman world wide who can claim to have won medals in each of the world's five continents: Australasia, Asia, Africa, America and Europe. He has won the club championship of his local bowling club at Gifford a total of twenty-one times and has represented the county of East Lothian every year since he was old enough to qualify; he has been capped for Scotland on no fewer than 104 times since he was first nominated in 1966. This is bound to be a record which will remain unbeaten and it does not even count the number of times he has represented Scotland at the Commonwealth Games and the World Championships.

Courtesy of William Wood

William Walker Wood MBE was born on 26th April 1938 at the Vert Hospital in Haddington. His mother was Jennie, nee Bisset, of Garvald and his father, William Edward Wood, gave his son the middle name of Walker for the good reason that he admired and supported the Heart of Midlothian Football Club of which the legendary "Tommy" Walker was a star player and known for his exceptional courtesy on the field.

Willie's schooldays were spent at Gifford Primary School followed by the Knox Academy in Haddington, but academic study was unattractive to him and he gladly left school aged fifteen firstly to work with his father and subsequently to become an apprentice motor mechanic with Young's Garage in Gifford then at Rose's Garage in Haddington.

His father and his two grandfathers were fine bowlers; in fact his father was Scottish Singles Champion in 1967. Almost all conversation in the Wood houshold was centred on bowling and it was natural that Willie should begin playing at about the age of twelve. At that time the minimum age to be allowed to enter the Club championship was eighteen and Willie won his first championship medal in 1956 at that age. He had already won many junior competitions and his game was so consistent he was now selected to play for East Lothian.

He was conscripted for National Service in 1956 and during three years of military service, mostly in Germany, he never rolled a ball. Life as a Craftsman in the Royal Electrical and Mechanical Engineers was good to Willie Wood. As a trained motor mechanic he was a member of a small group of the 'light-aid detachment' the duties of which required the group to carry out emergency repair work at short notice; this meant that they were exempt from the usual round of guard duties and interminable drills. It was during his service in Germany that the disastrous plane crash occurred in which many Manchester United football players were tragically killed in Munich. His regiment thoughtfully organised buses to take soldiers to the charity match which was played in August 1967 between Hamburg SV and the sorely diminished team of Manchester United, all players wearing black armbands. The income from this game was used to help the bereaved families. He recalled with sadness his visit to the Nazi concentration camp of Belsen which was situated within a mile of his army camp. He took photographs showing huge mounds of earth in which bodies had been hurriedly buried before the arrival of the advancing allied army.

On his return home to Scotland in 1960 he was immediately welcomed back to his bowling club and won the championship once again. In fact, he has held the championship intermittently ever since and has similarly represented East Lothian every year from 1960. His club nominated him in 1966 for a place in the Scottish team. His selection was successful and he has represented his country ever since - a total of 104 caps in thirty-four years of consistent bowling. Asked to explain how he has been able to maintain his form for so long (he is now in his 63rd year at the time of writing), his answer was that he has never smoked and his intake of alcoholic refreshment is minimal. He is a man of slight build and therefore agile - he explained:

"you have to get down low to be a successful bowler, but there is a great deal more to it than that: a keen eye and the ability to mark your spot on the green so that your line is deadly accurate".

He can gaurantee to place a bowl to within a foot of the jack at every roll of the bowl on a good rink. Practice is essential; he plays bowls every night of every week and occasionally on his own in order to perfect his action which has had to be adjusted over the years to allow for his imperceptibly advancing years.

He explained that "bowls is rather like chess or snooker, you have to think ahead and try to anticipate your opponent's next shot." He stopped for a moment and said, "Davie Bryant is the best player that ever lived", then he added wryly, "I have beaten him a few times though." He continued by explaining that, "David Bryant, many times a world champion, is not only highly skilled in his play but he is a scholar of bowls who gives great thought to the game; his is an intellectual approach, bowls are his life, he talks of nothing else." Willie Wood had the honour of playing against him many times and in 1973, playing in South Africa he beat him for the first time in a major final overseas. Such was Bryant's sportsmanship he seemed delighted for Willie's success and even more delighted with his astonishing skill. The two champion bowlers met again the following year in New Zealand at the Commonwealth Games in Christchurch where Willie won the bronze medal and David Bryant won the gold medal for his overall scores. They met again on Bryant's home ground at Worthing in the Woolwich Masters final on two occasions where Bryant knew every blade of grass and every nuance of the green and won on these occasions. They have probably competed against each other a dozen times and in singles play the honours are about even, but still Willie insists that "Davie Bryant is the world's best."

William Wood MBE at Ayr 1998, International Series. (Courtesy of Mrs D Nicholson, Bridge of Earn)

In 1964 Willie Wood met his future wife, Morag Turnbull, the daughter of an Edinburgh chartered accountant, at a local dance in Garvald where her parents had a country cottage. They married at the Kirkgate Church in Leith on 12th August 1967 and had a daughter, Sylvia and a son Colin, neither of whom played bowls but were keen supporters of their father. Today, Willie's and Morag's delight is their three year-old granddaughter, Lily Abigail Henderson.

Willie was deservedly honoured in 1993 with the award of the MBE (Member of the Most Excellent Order of the British Empire) which was presented to him at Buckingham Palace by HM Queen Elizabeth. He was introduced to the Queen and Prince Philip in Kuala Lumpur in Malaysia and appeared with Her Majesty on the same television production in 1998; in fact, over the years he has had the honour of meeting and chatting with several members of the royal family.
List of medals and trophies:

Gifford Bowling Club Champion ...21 times, 1966-2000
Winner of all competitions in the East Lothian Bowling Association
Runner-up. Scottish Singles, 1970 and 1998
South African Games singles, gold medal, 1973
Commonwealth Games singles bronze medal, 1974
Commonwealth Games pairs silver medal, 1978
Winner Scottish fours, 1980
World Championship Fours silver medal, 1980
Commonwealth Games singles gold medal, 1982
Winner Australian Jack High singles, 1983 (first British player to win)
Runner-up World Championship singles, 1984 and 1988
Winner Hong Kong Classic Pairs, 1985 and 1986
World Championship Triples silver medal, 1988
Commonwealth Games fours gold medal, 1990
Winner Scottish Woolwich Masters, 1990 and 1998
Winner World Championship Fours Gold medal, 1992
World Championship Team gold medal, 1992
World Championship Triples bronze medal, 1992
Winner Scottish Players Association, singles, 1995
World Championship Triples gold medal, 1996
World Championship Team gold medal, 1996
World Triples bronze medal, 2000
World Fours bronze medal, 2000

At the time of writing he had just returned from the World Championships 2000 in South Africa where he won bronze medals in the fours and the triples. The Scottish team were well in the lead in the overall team event when the Australians team protested that the organising committee had misread the rules. Their protest was upheld and Scotland's players had to be content with another bronze medal. However, Willie Wood has the distinction of being the oldest ever medal winner in the World Championships.

There seems little else that he could win or records that he could break but he savours a long-cherished ambition: to emulate his father in winning the Scottish Championships. Willie has reached the final play-offs many times and although he is a past World Champion and Commonwealth Champion he would be more than delighted to win the Scottish Championship gold medal.

References:

1. *The Holy Bible* with notes and Observations by The Rev. John Brown - Memoir of the Rev. John Brown.
2. *Itinerating Libraries and their Founder*, by Samuel Brown. Printed by William Blackwood & Sons, Edinburgh, 1856.
3. *East Lothian Biographies*, by Gray and Jamieson. 4th Vol. Transactions of the East Lothian Antiquarian and Field Naturalists' Society.
4. *Reminiscences of the Royal Burgh of Haddington*, by John Martine. Pub. John Menzies, Edinburgh and Glasgow. 1883.
5. *The Lamp of Lothian*, by James Miller. Pub. William Sinclair, Haddington. 1900.
6. The Journal of the University of Leeds - *The Gryphon*, May 1938
7. *Yorkshire Post* of 10th June 1940 - Obituary of Sir James Baillie.
8. *Leeds Mercury* of 10th June 1940 - Obituary of Sir James Baillie.
9. *Introduction to Sir James Baillie, Reflections on Life and Religion* published by George Allen and Unwin, 1952
10. *Scottish Kings* by Gordon Donaldson. Pub. Book Club Associates.
11. *The Complete Peerage of England, Scotland, Ireland and Great Britain*, by G.E.C. Pub. St Catherine's Press, 1912.
12. *Most Famous of Men - John Cockburn* by TC Barry. *East Lothian Life* (Issue 6.) Editor: Pauline Jaffray. Pub PJ Design, Dunbar.
13. *Old and New Edinburgh* Vols. I, II & III by James Grant. Pub. Cassell & Co. Ltd.
14. *Glencoe* by John Prebble. Pub. Penguin Books.
15. *The North Berwick Story* by Walter M Ferrier. Pub. Royal Burgh of North Berwick Community Council.
16. *Traditions of Edinburgh*, by Robert Chambers LL.D. Pub. W&R Chambers Ltd.
17. *Scottish Art 1460-1990* by Duncan McMillan. Pub. Mainstream
18. *Scotland, A New History*, by Michael Lynch. Pub. Century Ltd.
19. *Who's Who in Scotland*, Pub. Carrick Publishing, Ayr.
20. *East Lothian Studies*, by David Louden and Rev. William Whitfield, Pub. John Hutchison 1891.
21. *Historic South Edinburgh* Vol.1 by Charles J Smith. Pub. Charles Skilton Ltd., Edinburgh & London
22. *Scotland's Work and Worth* by Charles W Thomson. Pub. Oliphant, Anderson & Ferrier, Edinburgh & London.
23. *The Place Names of Edinburgh* by Stuart Harris. Pub. Gordon Wright Publishing Ltd., Edinburgh 1996

24. *East Lothian Life*, Issue 2. p.11. Edited by Pauline Jaffray. Pub. PJ Design, Dunbar.
25. *Dictionary of National Biography*, Editors: Leslie Stephen and Sydney Lee. Pub. Smith Elder & Co. Ltd.
26. *A Small Country*, by Neill McCallum. Pub. James Thin, The Mercat Press
27. *The Darien Disaster* by John Prebble. Pub. Penguin Books.
28. *Street Biographies of the Royal Burgh of Haddington* by David Dick. Pub. Clerkington Publishing Co. 1997
29. *The Times* 23rd September 1990, Business Profile - Alistair Grant, by Gillian Bowditch
30. *The Buildings of Scotland, Lothian, except Edinburgh* by Colin McWilliam. Pub. Penguin Books. 1978.
31. Transactions of the East Lothian Antiquarian and Field Naturalists' Society, Fourth Volume.
32. *The Scottish Enlightenment* by David Daiches. Pub. The Saltire Society, 1986.
33. *Statistical History of Scotland*, 1853 by J.H. Dawson. Pub. W.H. Lizars, St James Square, London.
34. *George Harley FRS or The Life of a London Physician* by Mrs Alec Tweedie. Pub. The Scientific Press Ltd. 1899.
35. *A Biographical Dictionary of Eminent Scotsmen* by Robert Chambers. Pub. Blackie & Son, Glasgow. 1835.
36. *Most Famous of Men - George Hope* by TC Barry Pub. *East Lothian Life* Issue 5 p.9
37. *A Small Country* by Neil NcCallum. Pub. James Thin, The Mercat Press.
38. *100 Years of Golf 1857 to 1962, Ben Sayers North Berwick. Doreen Sayers's Scrap Book.* Publ. Stephenson Press, North Berwick. 1994
39. *Who was Who in the Royal Mile, Edinburgh*, by David Dick, 1997. Pub. Clerkington Publishing Co.,Ltd., Haddington.
40. *The Dictionary of British Artists 1880-1940*, compiled by J. Johnson and A. Greutzner. Pub. Antique Collectors' Club, 1976
41. *Pastoral Art in East Lothian* by Martin Forrest, Pub. East Lothian District Council.
42. Bourne Fine Art, Edinburgh & London
43. *Scottish Portrait* by Augustus Muir (1948), The Hoptoun Press, Edinburgh
44. *The Scottish School of Painting* by William Darling McKay 1906.
45. *Life of Colonel Gardiner*, by Rev Doddrige DD, 1748.
46. *Lives of the Engineers*, by Samuel Smiles, 1874

47. *The Autobiography of Samuel Smiles, LLD*. Ed. Thomas Mackay, Pub. John Murray, Albemarle Street, London, 1905.
48. *A Biographical Essay of Samuel Smiles* by Alison Smiles, 1956
49. *Engineering at Edinburgh University, A short History 1673 - 1983*, by Ronald M Birse.
50. *A Short History of Haddington* by W. Forbes Gray and James H. Jamieson, Pub. Spa Books Ltd.
51. *Collins Encyclopaedia of Scotland*, Edited by John Keay and Julia Keay, Pub. Harper Collins Publishers, London. 1994
52. *Who was Who, 1897-1916, 1916-28*. Pub. A & C Black, London
53. *Scotsman* - Obituary of Andrew "Jock" Wemyss 22nd January 1974
54. *East Lothian Courier* - Obituary of Andrew "Jock" Wemyss, 22nd January 1974.
55. *The History of Scottish Rugby* by Sandy Thorburn. Pub. Johnston and Bacon, London.
56. *Talking of Rugby, an Autobiography*, by Bill McLaren. Pub. Stanley Paul, London.
57. *Mary Queen of Scots* by Antonia Fraser. Pub. Weidenfield and Nicolson Ltd.
58. *East Lothian Homes - Winton House*, Pub. East Lothian Life, Issue 15.
59. *Reminiscences and Notices of the Parishes of the County of Haddingtonshire* by John Martine. Pub. East Lothian Council Library Service, 1999
60. *Scottish Historical Documents* by Gordon Donaldson. Pub. Neil Wilson Publishing.
61. *Story of a Nation SCOTLAND A Concise History* by P. Hume Brown. Pub. Lang Syne Publishers Ltd.
62. *Great Contemporaries* by The Right Hon. Winston S. Churchill. Pub. Readers Union Ltd & Thornton Butterworth Ltd
63. *The Autobiography of Samuel Smiles, LLD*. Ed. Thomas Mackay, Pub. John Murray, Albemarle Street, London, 1905
64. A Biographical Essay of Samuel Smiles by Alison Smiles, 1956
65. *Broadwood by Appointment* by David Wainwright. Pub. Quiller Press Ltd., London. 1982.
66. *Lays of the Scottish Cavaliers and other Poems* by William Edmonstoune Aytoun. Pub. RE King London.
67. *Dictionary of Scottish Art and Architecture* by Peter JM McEwan. Pub. Antiques Collectors' Club.

68. *Australian Dictionary of National Biography.* Vol. 3 A-C General Editor Douglas Pike. Pub. Melbourne University Press.
69. *Memorials of His Time*, by Lord Cockburn. Pub. Robert Grant & Son Ltd, Edinburgh, 1946.
70. *Genealogical Account of the Dalrymples of Stair Earls of Stair* by Honble. Hew Hamilton Dalrymple. Privately printed. 1909
71. *Lauder and Lauderdale* by A. Thomson FSA Scot. Pub. Craighead Bros, Galashiels.
72. *William Nicol FRSE C.1771-1851 Lecturer, Scientist and Collector* by A D Morrison Low. The Book of the Old Edinburgh Club, New Series Vol. 2 1992
73. *The Lives of the Kings and Queens of England*, Edited by Antonia Fraser. Pub. Macdonald Futura Publishers. 1980
74. *Present State of Husbandry in Scotland*, Extracted from Reports made to the Commissioners of the Annexed Estates, Vol.II, Edinburgh 1778
75. *Tranent and its Surroundings* by P McNeill, 1883. Reprint 1984 by Remploy Ltd, Leicester
76. Unpublished letters of Sir Hew Dalrymple, 2nd Baronet and Lady Dalrymple, Margaret [Sainthill], 21st July to 27th August 1747
77. Unpublished extract from the diary of Joseph Farington RA, 2nd August 1788.
78. *Ordering the Foundations* by David S. Ritchie Pub. Natural Science March 1966
79. *The Enlightenment*, Studies I, Edited by Michael Bartholomew, Denise Hall and Anthony Lentin. Pub. The Open University.
80. *Longitude* by Dava Sovell. Pub. Forth Estate Limited, 1998.
81. Wellington - The Years of the Sword by Elizabeth Longford. Pub. Word Books,m London.1971.
82. The Stuart Age, England 1603-1714 by Barry Coward. Pub. Longman, an imprint of Pearson Education, 1994
83. The History of Crieff by Alexander Porteous FSA Scot. Pub. Oliphant, Andrews and Ferrier, Edinburgh & London, 1912
84. John Knox and the Scottish Reformation by G Barnett Smith. Pub. The Religious Tract & Book Society of Scotland, Edinburgh, 1905.
85. *East Lothian Life*, Issue 17 *Robert Noble RSA (1857-1917)* by Roger Durman.
86. *The Worlds of Patrick Geddes, Biologist, Town Planner, Re educator, Peace-warrior* by Philip Boardman. Publ. Routledge Paul Ltd, London. 1978.

87. *The Fusion of 1860. A Record of the Centenary Celebrations and a History of the United University of Aberdeen 1860-1960*. Edited by W Douglas Simpson. Publ. Oliver and Boyd, Edinburgh.
88. BBC Radio 4 broadcast, *Making Radio Waves*, 15th May 2000.
89. *Grey River Argus*, New Zealand, Obituary of William Rae FIANZ, 4th February 1911.
90. *The Cyclopedia of New Zealand* Nelson, Malborough and Westland provincial Districts, Vol.5, 1906
91. *Industries of New Zealand*, Arthur Cleave Publishing Co.,New Zealand. 1898
92. *Burke's Peerage, Baronetage and Knightage*, 1998
93. *The Trial of Sir Archibald Gordon Kinloch of Gilmerton Bart*. Printed by C.Denovan for J Elder, Edinburgh. 1795
94. Unpublished Genealogical Account of the Family of Kinloch of Gilmerton, Haddingtonshire.
95. *The Place Names of Edinburgh their Origins and History* by Stuart Harris. Pub. Gordon Wright Publishing, Edinburgh. 1996
96. Princes and Peoples, France and the British Isles, 1620-1714. An Anthology of Primary Sources, Edited by Margaret Lucille Kekewich. Publ. Manchester University Press in association with the Open University, 1999.
97. *Scott on Himself*, Ed. David Hewitt. Publ. Scottish Academic Press. 1981
98. *The History of Haddington Rugby Football Club, 1911-1986* by FD Burnett and JE Jones. Publ. HRFC. 1986
99. *The Honours of Scotland, The Story of the Scottish Crown Jewels* by Charles J Burnett and Christopher J Tabraham. Publ. Historic Scotland

INDEX

THE AUTHOR:
DAVID DICK OBE

Although by profession David Dick is an Electrical Engineer, mathematician and educator he has been studying and writing biographical histories for the last fifteen years as well as studying history with the Open University. He has written and edited several books:
Capital Walks in Edinburgh - The New Town ISBN 1 897784 20 1 (1994)
Street Biographies of the Royal Burgh of Haddington ISBN 0 9530274 0 6 (1997)
Who was Who in the Royal Mile, Edinburgh ISBN 0 9530274 1 4 (1997)
Who was Who in Durban Street Names, ISBN 0 620 20034 0 (1998)
A Scottish Electrical Enlightenment, 100 Years of the Institution of Electrical Engineers, ISBN 0 9537790 09 (2000) Editor.

In addition, he has published many articles for magazines and newspapers such as: *East Lothian Life, Scottish Memories, The Scotsman, The Glasgow Herald, East Lothian Courier, The Natal Mercury* and several technical journals. He was Press Secretary for the Probus Club of Haddington (1992-94) and Secretary of Haddington's History Society and Editor (1992-96) of its Proceedings. He is a regular speaker to Rotary Clubs, Probus Clubs, Local History Societies etc.

He is a former (the first) Depute Principal of Napier College of Science & Technology (now Napier University of Edinburgh); former (the first) Principal of Stevenson College, Edinburgh; former Chairman of the Fire Services Examination Board (Scotland) and former Lay Inspector of Fire Services for Scotland. He has chaired and served on several committees of the former Scottish Technical Education Council and The Scottish Business Education Council. He was Chairman and Honorary Secretary of the Institution of Radio and Electronic Engineers and Honorary President of the former Edinburgh & District Spastics Association.

David Dick was awarded the OBE in 1982 for his services to the Scottish Fire Service and to Education in Scotland. He is a Diplomate of the Imperial College, London, a Fellow of the Institution of Electrical Engineers and a Chartered Engineer. He lives near Haddington, East Lothian and is married to Muriel (nee Buchanan) with five daughters and thirteen grandchildren.